Using Subject Headings for Online Retrieval

Library and Information Science

Consulting Editors: *Harold Borko and Elaine Svenonius*
Graduate School of Library and Information Science
University of California, Los Angeles

Harold Borko and Charles L. Bernier
Abstracting Concepts and Methods

F. W. Lancaster
Toward Paperless Information Systems

H. S. Heaps
Information Retrieval: Computational and Theoretical Aspects

Harold Borko and Charles L. Bernier
Indexing Concepts and Methods

Gerald Jahoda and Judith Schiek Braunagel
The Librarian and Reference Queries: A Systematic Approach

Charles H. Busha and Stephen P. Harter
Research Methods in Librarianship: Techniques and Interpretation

Diana M. Thomas, Ann T. Hinckley, and Elizabeth R. Eisenbach
The Effective Reference Librarian

G. Edward Evans
Management Techniques for Librarians, Second Edition

Jessica L. Milstead
Subject Access Systems: Alternatives in Design

Dagobert Soergel
Information Storage and Retrieval: A Systems Approach

Stephen P. Harter
Online Information Retrieval: Concepts, Principles, and Techniques

Timothy C. Craven
String Indexing

Lois Swan Jones and Sarah Scott Gibson
Art Libraries and Information Services

The list of books continues at the end of the volume.

Using Subject Headings for Online Retrieval

Theory, Practice, and Potential

Karen Markey Drabenstott
The University of Michigan
Ann Arbor, Michigan

Diane Vizine-Goetz
OCLC Online Computer Library Center, Inc.
Dublin, Ohio

Published under the auspices of
OCLC Online Computer Library Center, Inc.

Academic Press
A Division of Harcourt Brace & Company
San Diego New York Boston London Sydney Tokyo Toronto

This book is printed on acid-free paper. ♾

Academic Press, Inc.
A Division of Harcourt Brace & Company
525 B Street, Suite 1900, San Diego, California 92101-4495

United Kingdom Edition published by
Academic Press Limited
24–28 Oval Road, London NW1 7DX

Library of Congress Cataloging-in-Publication Data

Drabenstott, Karen Markey.
Using subject headings for online retrieval : theory, practice, and potential / Karen Markey Drabenstott, Diane Vizie-Goetz.
p. cm. -- (Library and information science)
"Published under the auspices of OCLC Online Computer Library Center, Inc."
Includes index.
ISBN 0-12-221570-2
1. Online bibliographic searching. 2. Subject headings. 3. Online catalogs--Subject access. I.. Vizine-Goetz, Diane. II. OCLC. III. Title. IV. Series: Library and information science (New York, N.Y.)
Z699.35.055D73 1994
025.3'132--dc20 93-42568
CIP
r94

PRINTED IN THE UNITED STATES OF AMERICA
94 95 96 97 98 99 BC 9 8 7 6 5 4 3 2 1

To Our Families

Contents

14

The Future of Subject Headings for Online Information Retrieval

Appendices

Appendix A

Appendix B

Appendix C

Appendix D

Preface

Subject analysis in online library catalogs is limited to the assignment of one or two subject headings per book. Most headings are actually an assemblage of several separate components. The sequence of components is not fixed because the meaning of subject headings is often dependent on the sequence of their individual components.

When searching online catalogs, system users are faced with a bewildering task. The cataloging records they hope to retrieve are assigned a limited number of subject headings. The sequence of subject heading components is difficult to predict. The subject searching approach featured in the online catalog has its own particular limitations and idiosyncrasies. The few online catalogs that offer more than one subject searching approach provide little, if any, guidance as to which approach is appropriate in view of the particular subject query entered. Furthermore, users express their subject queries in a variety of unpredictable forms, such as single words, phrases, questions, and even whole sentences.

The purpose of this book is to describe subject analysis and subject searching in online catalogs, to discuss their limitations on retrieval, and to demonstrate how such limitations can be overcome through system design and programming to enable systems to respond to user queries with the subject searching approach most likely to succeed.

The book begins with an introductory chapter on subject analysis. It describes the Library of Congress Subject Headings (LCSH) system and focuses on system characteristics such as vocabulary, structure, and syntax that impede retrieval.

Chapters 2 and 3 discuss the subject information stored in machine-readable files of authority records and bibliographic records. Chapter 4 investigates the relationships between records in these two files. The next five chapters address the subject queries users enter into online bibliographic systems. Chapter 5 surveys studies of user queries. Chapter 6 gives readers a broad picture of user queries and their closeness to authorized subject headings in the authority file. Chapters 7 through 10 focus on characteristics of user queries that are likely and those that are not likely to produce retrievals. For example, users are quite successful entering subject terms that match topical subject headings in the authority file; they are rarely successful retrieving bibliographic records when they enter queries that contain a topical element and a personal name element. We make suggestions about system responses to user queries that are intended to increase precision, encourage browsing, and thus produce more useful retrievals.

Chapters 11 and 12 detail system responses and the characteristics of user queries best suited to specific responses. A new approach—the exact approach—is described in Chapter 11. It handles user queries that are exact or almost exact matches of catalog headings and references. This approach summarizes in a single screen the many options available for the matched heading, for example, availability of related terms, scope notes, and subdivided forms. The exact approach can be implemented in existing online catalogs, but certain enhancements are required in both bibliographic and authority files to make this approach work more effectively. Chapter 12 discusses several subject searching approaches now available in operational systems and the characteristics of user queries best suited to these approaches.

Chapter 13 focuses on search trees, which are defined as a set of paths with branches or choices that enable online systems to carry out the subject search approach most likely to succeed. Search trees control system responses and determine appropriate subject searching approaches to user queries. Users do not explicitly choose a particular approach. Rather, systems respond with an approach based on the extent to which queries match the catalog's controlled vocabulary and produce retrievals. The benefit of incorporating search trees into online bibliographic systems is that it places on the system the responsibility of determining which approach produces the best results.

The concluding chapter, Chapter 14, is a think piece on the future of subject headings for online retrieval. The authors speculate about the viability of the LCSH system for online retrieval, discuss planned changes in the system, and hypothesize about changes that would make the system more responsive to end-user needs and behavior.

Each chapter begins with a brief introductory section that gives readers a broad picture of the scope, issues, and subject coverage of the chapter and concludes with Synthesis and Summary sections that pull together the various points made in the chapter, interprets them for readers, and summarizes important details.

The analyses presented in this book span multiple years of effort; therefore, some LC subject headings or references used in examples may no longer represent current forms. We chose not to amend these terms since the premises put forth in the book remain valid despite ongoing changes to the LCSH system.

We hope that this book becomes an indispensable tool for online system designers who are grappling with developing new systems or refining existing ones. Practitioners in institutions using or considering the installation of an online catalog can consult this book to generate system specifications and to evaluate vendor proposals. The book will appeal to researchers in library systems, information retrieval, and user behavior because its recommendations are based on the results of empirical studies of library practice and end-user behavior. This book also addresses the interests both of advanced students in library and information studies schools and of instructors in library automation, information retrieval, cataloging, indexing, and user behavior.

Using Subject Headings for Online Retrieval is truly unique. Although several books discuss subject searching capabilities and the problems of subject access, none specifically recommends which capability is best suited to the wide variety of subject queries users enter into online bibliographic systems.

This book demonstrates how the limitations of subject analysis and subject searching can be overcome through system design and programming to enable systems to respond to user queries with the subject searching approach most likely to succeed in providing relevant information. Despite our efforts to generate a new subject access design that does not require editorial review of existing subject access tools, we recognize that computers cannot solve all the problems of subject retrieval. Editorial changes that we suggest may be more difficult for the library and information science community to implement than automated changes because they require a concerted effort by the community to support the Library of Congress in making the revamping of LCSH a top priority.

As a new century approaches, the LCSH system will be called on to handle new forms of communication that are not represented on paper. If LCSH is not up to the task, it may be supplanted by an entirely new subject analysis tool. The data, analyses, and recommendations in this book are intended to motivate the library and information science community to think deeply about the future of LCSH and its potential as a subject access tool in online systems.

Acknowledgments

The OCLC and University of Michigan project team consisted of Karen Markey Drabenstott, Tony Ershadi, Martha O'Hara Conway, and Diane Vizine-Goetz.

In this book, we promulgate a new design for subject access to online catalogs. The new design was generated from the results of two major research efforts: an analysis of data files that libraries use to build their bibliographic and authority databases, and an extensive, empirical study of the subject terms entered into online systems by end users. The Council on Library Resources (CLR) supported these research efforts through grants to OCLC and the University of Michigan. We are especially grateful to Deanna Marcum, formerly vice president of CLR, who gave useful suggestions on drafts of research proposals that helped us secure the grants. Serving as project monitor, Deanna Marcum was always available to answer our inquiries, review project plans and progress, and participate in formal project reviews.

The past dozen years have been marked by considerable research in catalog use, online catalogs, and subject access conducted by OCLC's Office of Research thanks to the leadership, encouragement, and support of several administrations. Martin Dillon, formerly Director of the Office of Research, carried on this tradition by providing us with useful criticism, direction, and resources throughout the CLR-sponsored research project. Upon the termination of the CLR grant, he gave Karen Drabenstott an appointment at OCLC as Visiting Scholar which made it possible for her to devote several quiet months to the writing of this book in collaboration with coauthor Diane Vizine-Goetz.

There were many staff members at participating libraries who contributed to the success of the CLR-sponsored research project. University librarians David M. Stam at Syracuse University, Paul Willis at the University of Kentucky, and Gloria Werner at the University of California, Los Angeles, consented to our analysis of transaction logs of their respective libraries' online catalogs. John Wyman and Lee Radigan at Syracuse University, Jim Fayollat and Diane Bisom at UCLA, and Jimmy Thomas and Pat Stevens in OCLC's Local Systems Division for the University of Kentucky programmed their libraries' online catalogs to generate machine-readable tapes of user subject-searching activity, provided us with documentation on their respective catalogs' transaction log format, and answered our occasional inquiries about logs, system capabilities, and system use.

At the University of Michigan, Martha O'Hara Conway took the lead in categorizing assigned subject headings from a bibliographic file and user queries from the online catalogs of the three participating libraries. Martha spent many long, odd, and late hours finding just the right subject heading to describe a particularly puzzling user query; we acknowledge her dedication and diligence and thank her for a job well done. Bonnie A. Dede, Head, Special Formats at the University of Michigan libraries, gave freely of her time and advice answering our questions about erroneous and unauthorized headings. Also at Michigan, Barbara A. Griffis was always cheerful in answering questions about the project budget. Dawn Nugent tackled various clerical tasks so that Karen could keep focused on writing. Robert M. Warner, formerly Dean of the School of Information and Library Studies, was especially generous in giving advice, providing insight, or making resources available.

We wish to thank many individuals at OCLC who contributed to the success of the projects and helped prepare this book. Tony Ershadi provided creative and effective programming support for the automated analyses of LCSH-mr, machine comparisons of LCSH-mr with the sample bibliographic file, and analyses of transaction log data. Erik Jul and Kezia V. Sproat provided valuable editorial assistance. Graphics were originally provided by Kym Pocius and later refined and completed by John B. Sweet, who promptly and cheerfully made numerous revisions along the way. Bonnie Preece provided budget tracking and financial reports. And special thanks go to Becky Hawk, Carol Hickey, and Diane Morris for proofreading and support preparing the text.

Advice from our project consultants was encouraging and supportive throughout the project. We appreciate the efforts of Lois Mai Chan, Pauline A. Cochrane, and Carolyn O. Frost who reviewed draft interim and final reports and attended and assessed the project team's progress at a mid-project review. Other participants in the mid-project review guided our progress and offered helpful suggestions: Lucia Rather, Mary Kay D. Pietris, and Mary Lou Miller of the Library of Congress, and Deanna Marcum and Warren J. Haas of CLR.

Numerous colleagues provided critical enlightenment and were themselves sources of information, particularly Marcia J. Bates, Charles R. Hildreth, Francis Miksa, Edward T. O'Neill, and Amy J. Warner. We would also like to thank Allyson Carlyle, who supplied us with a preprint of her study and advised us on the use of her coding scheme.

1

Subject Analysis in Library Catalogs

1.1 Introduction

Over the last century, libraries and information centers have made substantial investments to build library catalogs and machine-readable cataloging databases that use Library of Congress Subject Headings (LCSH) as an indexing language. This process began nearly one hundred years ago, when the Library of Congress (LC) began distributing printed catalog cards to subscribers. These cards proved so popular that librarians asked LC to publish its cataloging rules. If all librarians followed the same rules when cataloging materials unique to their collections, local catalog cards and the printed cards purchased from LC would be consistent, and libraries would be easier to use.

In 1901, LC published its classification scheme, beginning with individual schedules for the E-F class. From 1903 through the 1930s, LC also published its cataloging rules on printed cards. In 1968, LC supplemented its printed catalog card program with a distribution program for its machine-readable cataloging (MARC) records (Avram 1968). The first subscribers to the distribution program were bibliographic services such as the not-for-profit OCLC Online Computer Library Center Research Libraries Group (RLG), and Western Library Network (WLN). These services built centralized, mainframe-based online cataloging systems in which MARC records from LC's distribution service served as the foundation for their development of online cataloging databases. Membership status in a bibliographic service gave libraries access to MARC records produced by LC (i.e., LC/MARC records) and capabilities for entering their own catalog records and for using the machine-readable catalog records entered by other member libraries.

In the mid-1980s, the conversion of LCSH to machine-readable form made it possible for LC to print the subject headings list more frequently and make a machine-readable version of the list available to subscribers. Starting with the eleventh edition in 1986, LCSH has been published annually. The machine-readable version is also available in electronic form on a cumulative master tape that can be updated weekly. Subscribers to the machine-readable LCSH (LCSH-mr) have been bibliographic services and libraries who have incorporated the file into their respective systems to facilitate authority control and information retrieval.

In this study, LCSH denotes the subject heading system that underlies the printed *LCSH.* Although LCSH was originally developed for LC's own collection, the availability of LC cataloging copy through the almost century-old printed card program and quarter of a century-old MARC record distribution has fostered wide adoption of the LCSH system by libraries and information centers in the United States. Widespread use of this system is evident among the eleven thousand OCLC member libraries. As of December 31, 1992, LC/MARC records constituted only 15% of the OCLC database; however, nearly 69% of the 25.8 million cataloging records in the OCLC database have subject headings based on the LCSH system.

As the indexing language of LC/MARC records, LCSH also functions as the subject retrieval language to the LC/MARC database. This language is used on a variety of systems. At LC, end users and staff use the MUMS and SCORPIO systems for information retrieval. Since the 1970s, the LC/MARC database has been available for online searching on several different commercial retrieval systems, including DIALOG, ORBIT, and WILSONLINE. Bibliographic services such as RLG and WLN have supported online searching of LC/MARC and member-contributed records for many years. In January 1990, OCLC introduced subject searching of the Online Union Catalog through its EPIC information retrieval system.

In the early 1980s, at least two factors made it possible for libraries to acquire stand-alone automated library systems: (1) computer equipment became increasingly more affordable; and (2) commercial firms made stand-alone library system software available (Hildreth 1987). The foundation for the databases of these stand-alone systems was the cataloging records libraries had created on centralized bibliographic systems in the late 1960s and the 1970s. Stand-alone systems first automated circulation, acquisitions, and cataloging because these three functions increased the efficiency of library operations. By the mid-1980s, dozens of public and academic libraries offered end users access to their cataloging databases through the online catalog subsystem of their stand-alone library systems.

The online catalog is the information retrieval component of automated library systems. Library patrons access the online catalog directly, that is, without the assistance of an intermediary such as a specially trained member of the library staff, to search and retrieve bibliographic information (Hildreth 1982, 235). Although automated systems had been deployed in libraries for fifteen years, the online catalog marked the first time that public users of libraries could interact directly with these systems to satisfy their information needs.

The earliest study of online catalog use reported problems end users were having with subject searching (Pritchard 1981). Studies were conducted throughout the 1980s to gain a greater understanding of end users' subject searching problems. Online catalog system designers responded by introducing improvements that could be achieved through computer programming. Today's online catalogs are easier to use than their earlier counterparts (Hildreth 1989, 10). They can also support keyword, Boolean-based searching, a subject searching approach that characterized few early online catalogs but was highly desired by many library practitioners and spokespersons (Hildreth 1989, 19).

Throughout the 1980s, online catalog research revealed inadequacies in libraries' bibliographic databases in terms of the amount of subject information they contain and the indexing language they enlist. Improvements to bibliographic databases have not been undertaken because they require substantial intellectual and/or clerical work by human intermediaries to enhance, amend, or change existing records.

When searching today's online catalogs, system users face a bewildering task. The cataloging records they hope to retrieve are assigned one or two subject headings. The forms of subject headings used in the LCSH system are unpredictable, making it difficult for end users to enter subject queries that match the subject headings used in the catalog to describe their topics of interest. The sequence of subject heading components is difficult to predict. The subject searching approach featured in the typical online catalog has its own particular limitations and idiosyncrasies. The few online catalogs that offer users more than one subject searching approach provide little guidance as to which one is appropriate for their particular subject query. To varying degrees, all these factors contribute to the difficulty of subject searching in online catalogs.

The purpose of this book is to demonstrate how the difficulty of subject searching in online catalogs can be overcome through system design and programming to enable systems to respond to user queries with the subject searching approach most likely to succeed. This book presents search trees to control systems responses and determine appropriate subject searching approaches to user queries. Users do not explicitly choose a particular approach. Rather, systems respond with an approach based on the extent to which queries match the catalog's controlled vocabulary and produce retrievals. The benefit of incorporating search trees into online catalogs is that it places the responsibility of determining which approach produces the best results on the system.

This book begins by describing subject analysis in online catalogs. A look at the role of LCSH as the indexing language of online library catalogs is in order because of its widespread use. We turn first to its early history, basic principles, and other factors that determined its development because they underlie its features and potential as the retrieval language of online catalogs.

1.2 Brief History of LCSH

Until the late 1800s, closed-shelf policies required patron requests for subject information to come directly to librarians. "The shelves, arranged in classified order, served librarians well, because librarians, having been educated by college curricula that typically stressed the classificatory nature of all knowledge, could respond to requests in terms of the classified categories of the shelf arrangement" (Miksa 1983, 158).

Librarianship as a profession was just becoming organized by the end of the century. "Among the various goals of the new profession, one of those most strongly stated was to bring cultural enlightenment to a general populace which was viewed as having little" (Miksa 1983, 83). Indicative of the library movement's cultural uplift objective are the adoption of open-shelf policies and the dictionary subject catalog (Miksa 1983, 158–159). Open shelves enabled a general populace to go directly to the bookshelves and browse books on their favorite subjects. When they wanted books on particular subjects, they consulted the dictionary catalog, which contained common subject names familiar to them, to find their exact location on the bookshelves. "In contrast, the classified catalogs appeared to cater to those users who were more highly educated, those, in other words, who often represented the upper classes" (Miksa 1983, 159).

In 1895, the *List of subject headings for use in dictionary catalogs*, based on various printed catalogs, was published. It was compiled by a committee of the American Library Association that included Charles Cutter, whose *Rules for a dictionary catalog* had been published almost two decades earlier. Before the publication of *List of subject headings for use in dictionary catalogs*, "alphabetical subject catalogs when made at all were based on headings borrowed from notable printed library catalogs or simply on catchwords taken from the titles of books" (Miksa 1983, 158). Thanks to the publication of *List of subject headings*, the dictionary catalog was "well on its way to becoming the predominant catalog form in American libraries" by the turn of the century (Chan 1986, 4).

Shortly after LC moved from the Capitol to its new building in 1897, it established a new classification system, adopted a dictionary catalog, and started distributing its printed catalog cards to subscribers. According to J. C. M. Hanson, the first chief of LC's Catalogue Division, LC's decision to adopt the dictionary form for the catalog was "a desire to be in a position to cooperate with the largest possible number of American libraries" (Hanson 1909, 387).

As LC's printed catalog cards came to be used more widely, many librarians asked LC to publish its cataloging tools so that they could catalog materials unique to their collection and ensure consistency between local cataloging copy and the printed catalog cards they purchased from LC. After five years of preparation, the subject headings list was published in 1914 under the title *Subject headings used in the dictionary catalogues of the Library of Congress*. The first seven editions and supplements were published under the same title; the title was shortened to *Library of Congress Subject Headings* (herein called LCSH) with the publication of the eighth edition in 1975. The most recent edition of LCSH is the fifteenth, published in spring 1992 in several formats: (1) printed book, (2) microfiche, (3) machine-readable form on magnetic tape, and (4) CD/ROM database.

Chan (1986, 5) credits the first two chiefs of the Catalogue Division, J. C. M. Hanson and Charles Martel, with providing the "initial guiding principles" for LCSH. Managing the Division from 1897 to 1910, Hanson borrowed and modified features from existing systems, including features from Cutter's *Rules* such as conventional subject names, analyses that began with books themselves, uniform subject headings, the elimination of synonyms, and cross-references to tie the subject heading system together (Miksa 1983, 233). Practices in the establishment of subject headings such as phrase headings and inverted forms of phrase headings that eventually led to inconsistencies in the forms of subject headings were first adopted during Hanson's tenure. Miksa attributes such practices to Hanson's vision as a pragmatist: "Hanson did not develop systems that were rationalized every step of the way on the basis of philosophical premises as Cutter had done; he approached the organization of knowledge as a pragmatic matter in which one organized the means of achieving practical results into a coherent operating mechanism" (Miksa 1983, 181).

In the introduction to the fourth edition of LCSH, Donald Judson Haykin, Chief of the Subject Catalog Division, commented on LC's pragmatic approach to subject heading establishment (Library of Congress 1943, iii):

> Whatever measure of logic and consistency has been achieved in the headings is due to the continuity of oral tradition which stems from J. M. C. [*sic*] Hanson, who was chief of the Catalog Division from 1897 to 1910, Charles Martel, Chief from 1912 to 1930, and their associates in the Catalog division, and the occasional written instructions issued by them. The failures in logic and consistency are, of course, due to the fact that headings were adopted as needed, and that many minds participated in the choice and establishment of headings.

Haykin's *Subject headings: A practical guide* (1951) was the first manual of LCSH principles and practice. Haykin's guide contains only passing references to Cutter (Chan 1986, 6), but Cutter's influence is present in Haykin's division of the topic into four principles: (1) the reader as the focus, (2) unity, (3) usage, and (4) specificity.

The long introduction to the eighth edition of LCSH contains an alphabetical list of most commonly used subdivisions along with scope notes governing their application (Library of Congress 1975). The omission of the list from the ninth edition provoked librarians to call for an updated list. LC responded by publishing it separately under the title *Library of Congress Subject Headings: Guide to subdivision practice* (Library of Congress 1981).

By the early 1980s, the annual production of unique machine-readable cataloging records by libraries in the United States exceeded that of LC on a scale of six to one (OCLC 1984, 10). Yet catalogers contributing records to the shared cataloging databases of bibliographic services were following statements on LCSH principles and practice that were thirty years old, that is, Haykin's 1951 *Subject headings*. *Guide to subdivision practice* (Library of Congress 1981) became rapidly outdated because it was not published on a regular basis. In the mid-1980s, LC responded to the library community's call for up-to-date subject cataloging tools. In 1984, LC published *Subject cataloging manual: Subject headings* (SCM:SH), a compilation of the Subject

Cataloging Division's internal memoranda on subject heading practice. Two new editions of SCM:SH were published in 1985 and 1990. The first edition of an index to the subdivisions listed in SCM:SH was published in 1989. In 1986, the library community could also turn to the second edition of Chan's book, *Library of Congress Subject Headings: Principles and application*, for the most comprehensive treatment of LCSH principles and practice to date.

Inconsistencies and irregularities in the LCSH system have been attributed to the lack of a subject cataloging code (Chan 1986, 13; Studwell 1985, 1987; Intner 1988). Since Cutter's *Rules*, the closest thing to a code has been Haykin's 1951 *Subject headings*. However, Haykin's work has been considered "more an account and exposition of Library of Congress practice, with occasional apologetics, than a code" (Chan 1986, 13).

In preparation for an invitational working meeting on subdivisions sponsored by LC in spring 1991, Chan summarized "both principles that underlie the structure of the Library of Congress subject headings system and the policies that govern the assignment of subject headings to LC MARC records" (Chan 1990, 1). Although LC has responded to its critics by supplying today's catalogers with copious publications on LCSH practice (Library of Congress 1990a, 1991; Chan 1990), such documentation is not sufficient for those calling for a subject cataloging code.

1.3 Basic Principles

In the absence of a statement published by LC on principles, scholars infer principles from practice and policy statements written by the chiefs of the Subject Cataloging Division (Chan 1986; Miksa 1983). They also use Cutter's *Rules for a dictionary catalog* (1904) to infer principles; however, no LCSH editions have ever cited Cutter, and Haykin's *Subject headings* gives only passing references to Cutter's *Rules* (Chan 1986, 6). Official recognition of Cutter's influence on LC's catalog finally came in 1972 from the chief of the Subject Cataloging Division (Angell 1972, 143):

> The final formulation of Cutter's objectives and rules was taking place at the same time that the Library of Congress was expanding and reorganizing the collections at the turn of the century. His work had a considerable influence on the founders of the Library of Congress catalog.

In the following sections, five LCSH principles are presented: (1) the user and usage, (2) uniform heading, (3) terminology, (4) specific and direct entry, and (5) specificity. Although these principles have a long history, some stretching back to the earliest beginnings of LCSH, they affect subject searchers of today's online catalogs. The discussion of each principle includes its implications for online catalog users.

1.3.1 The User and Usage

According to Cutter, the most important subject cataloging principle is consideration of the best interest of the catalog user. In the preface to the fourth edition of the *Rules*, Cutter states: "The convenience of the public is always to be set before the ease of the cataloger" (Cutter 1904, 6).

Haykin (1951, 7) echoes Cutter's sentiments about the user and calls this principle "the reader as a focus."

> The reader is the focus in all cataloging principles and practice. All other considerations, such as convenience and the desire to arrange entries in some logical order, are secondary to the basic rule that the heading, in wording and structure, should be that which the reader will seek in the catalog, if we know or can presume what the reader will look under.

Chan (1986, 18) acknowledges that the meaning of this principle about the user is "self-evident, but how to make it operational is not. The problem is delineating the user."

In naming subjects in the catalog, Cutter and Haykin have different approaches. Cutter (1904, 69) recommends usage of the public as the guiding principle. Haykin (1951, 8) recommends "common usage or, at any rate, the usage of the class of reader for whom the material on the subject within which the heading falls is intended." In contrast to Cutter's straightforward approach, Haykin's approach gives the cataloger the freedom of naming subjects in the catalog based on the audience addressed by the material itself.

Research has demonstrated that the catalog works pretty much as Cutter had intended. Bates (1977) showed that users knowledgeable in a particular subject were no more successful in retrieving citations from the catalog than users without such knowledge. The most successful users were those without subject expertise but with knowledge of the structure and content of the catalog.

LCSH has been criticized because of its awkward, archaic, biased, and sometimes offensive vocabulary. The perceived slowness and inaction on the part of the LC to change vocabulary and add new subjects for new topics and concepts have also been targets of critics (Clack 1978; Harris & Clack 1979; Berman 1984, 1987, 1988; Nelson 1986; Colman 1987).

In naming new subjects, catalogers face a more difficult task than their predecessors because of the diversity of today's catalog users. The decision to establish a new subject heading must be guided by the best interest of users, the usage of the class of reader for whom the material is intended, and avoidance of potentially offensive terminology.

Today's catalogers, however, have tools to aid in naming subjects that their predecessors could not have dreamed of. Before the advent of online catalogs, researchers and library practitioners had no accurate and systematic method of determining the subjects users had trouble finding in library catalogs. Today, we can examine an online catalog's transaction log to identify user queries that fail to produce retrievals and determine whether these queries should be represented in the controlled vocabulary as established headings or as *see* references.

When Cutter proposed his principle of the best interest of the user, he did not have a problem knowing users and usage because library users were a homogeneous group (Miksa 1983, 74). Although we have a much more diverse user population today than in Cutter's day, we also have much more sophisticated tools to ensure that the naming of new subjects is based on the terminology users enter into present-day online catalogs.

1.3.2 Uniform Heading

The principle of uniform heading is found in both descriptive and subject cataloging. In the former, one form of an author's name is used so that all works by the author are brought together under the one name. In the latter, the principle of uniform heading enlists one subject to represent material on a topic. For Cutter and other writers, uniform heading "was considered a remedy for the scattering that resulted from the earlier practice of catchword title entry, in which entry was made under a term used by the author of the work being cataloged" (Chan 1986, 20).

In naming new subjects, catalogers sometimes have to make a second decision about the entry element of the heading because LCSH is a single-entry system. Examples of subjects containing two or more elements that can serve as the entry element for the heading are:

- Libraries, Naval
  Naval Libraries
- Gas, Natural, in submerged lands
  Natural gas in submerged lands
  Submerged lands, Natural gas in

1.3.3 Terminology

Subject headings function both as the indexing language for library collections and as the retrieval language for users who want material on particular subjects. Ideally, the terminology of system users who are searching for material on a subject should be the same as the vocabulary used to index materials in the collection on this subject. In practice, the terminology is often very different. When differences can be predicted before retrieval, the catalog can give users direction in the form of *see* references to established subject headings. Cutter, Hanson, Haykin, and other writers provided guidelines for the creation of *see* references.

See references guide users from terms that are not used to established subject headings in the LCSH system. Since the publication of the eleventh edition of LCSH, *see* references have been given the designation "USE" references. Chan (1986, 94–101) identifies nine situations in which LCSH can be expected to provide *see* references.

Occasionally, LCSH dispatches a complex *see* reference to explain the several relationships that exist between the unused term and established subject headings that cannot be adequately expressed in one or more simple *see* references. An example is the complex *see* reference under the unused term "Defense budgets":

> USE subdivision "Appropriations and expenditures" under names of individual defense agencies, e.g., United States. Dept. of Defense--Appropriations and expenditures; and subdivision "Armed Forces--Appropriations and expenditures" under names of countries, e.g., "United States--Armed Forces--Appropriations and expenditures."

A complex *see* reference is more appropriate than a simple *see* reference because of the several relationships that exist between main headings naming defense agencies and countries and the subdivision "Appropriations and expenditures."

1.3.4 Specific and Direct Entry

Cutter's explanation of the rule of specific entry is: "Enter a work under its subject-heading, not under the heading of a class which includes the subject . . . Put Lady Cust's book on *The Cat* under 'Cat' not under 'Zoology' or 'Mammals,' or 'Domestic animals' " (1904, 66). In an alphabetico-classed catalog, the subject heading for Lady Cust's book could be "Zoology--Vertebrates--Mammals--Domestic animals--Cats." This heading is as specific as the heading "Cats" for the dictionary catalog. The difference is the entry element. In an alphabetico-classed catalog, users have to navigate through a series of increasingly narrower terms to reach the term that describes their topic of interest. In a dictionary catalog, users go directly to the heading that describes their topic of interest. Chan (1986, 29) clarifies the distinction between subject headings for alphabetico-classed and dictionary catalogs:

> The difference lies in the arrangement of the headings in the catalog resulting from different entry elements for the same heading. In the alphabetico-classed catalog, headings are arranged to a large extent according to their subject relationships. Each heading begins with the broadest term and contains a hierarchical chain of terms leading to the specific subject, an arrangement that results in grouping related subjects together. In the dictionary catalog, subject relationships are abandoned in favor of alphabetical arrangement for the sake of ready or direct access.

The decided advantage of the alphabetico-classed catalog for grouping related subjects together has tested the resistance of the keepers of the LCSH system. They have occasionally broken the rules of specific and direct entry and established subdivided subject headings that would be better suited for an alphabetico-classed catalog. Examples are subdivided subject headings on automobile motors:

- Automobiles--Motors--Control systems
- Automobiles--Motors--Cooling systems
- Automobiles--Motors--Crankshafts
- Automobiles--Motors--Cylinder blocks

To remain faithful to the principle of specific and direct entry, LC catalogers would have to establish subject headings in which the trailing subdivision would be the entry element. They would use qualification to give the new subject headings context, for example, "Crankshafts (Automobiles)" and "Control systems (Automobiles)."

LC's practice of creating inverted subject headings also violates the principle of specific and direct entry. Examples are inverted subject headings under "Insurance":

- Insurance, Accident
- Insurance, Agricultural
- Insurance, Athletic accident
- Insurance, Automobile
- Insurance, Aviation

The inverted element(s) in these subject headings should be placed before the original entry element, for example, "Accident insurance" and "Agricultural insurance." However, the alphabetical arrangement of the dictionary catalog would place the new subject headings created from alphabetico-classed strings and inverted headings in a different alphabetical arrangement that would not necessarily be close to related subjects. For example, "Aviation insurance" would be placed between the unrelated subjects "Aviaries" and "Aviation mechanics (Persons)" in what Cutter would have called "a most absurd proximity" (1904, 79).

Proliferation of subjects that break the rule of specific and direct entry has resulted in a "loss of consistency and predictability of the forms of headings" (Chan 1986, 31). They have also provided fodder for critics of the LCSH system in their raillery about the difficulty of determining forms of headings (Cochrane & Kirtland 1981, 15; Mischo 1982).

In an information retrieval environment, systems can be programmed to create additional entries for direct forms of inverted subject headings when no *see* reference exists for the direct form. Thus, inverted forms of subject headings do not pose much of a problem. Alphabetico-classed subjects are more difficult to handle because the trailing elements may be the ones sought by system users. Access to these elements may be possible only by rotating selected subdivisions into the leading element position for online display (Mischo 1981), or by offering keyword searching of subdivided headings.

Cutter incorporated the advantages of the alphabetico-classed catalog into the dictionary catalog through *see also* references. Cutter (1904, 79) instructs catalogers on the two types of relationships these references should express: "Make references from general subjects to their various subordinate subjects and also to coordinate and illustrative subjects." In modern indexing, relationships between general and subordinate subjects have come to be known as broader and narrower term relationships; relationships between "coordinate and illustrative subjects" have come to be known as related term relationships.

The fifth through the tenth editions of LCSH use the designation "sa" preceding narrower and related terms to indicate *see also* references and the designation "xx" to indicate broader and related terms. For example, the entry under "Helping behavior" in these early LCSH editions is:

Helping behavior
xx Altruism
Caring
Human behavior
Interpersonal relations
sa Altruism
Caring
Counseling
Encouragement
Psychotherapy

Beginning with the 1986 microfiche and eleventh printed edition of *LCSH*, LC converted the "sa" and "xx" symbols into new symbols indicating broader (BT), narrower (NT), and related term (RT) relationships because the former two symbols "were generally considered by users to be unintelligible" (Library of Congress 1988, x). In the eleventh edition of LCSH, the entry under "Helping behavior" looks like this:

Helping behavior
BT Human behavior
Interpersonal relations
RT Altruism
Caring
NT Counseling
Encouragement
Psychotherapy

Two of the four references designated by "xx" in early LCSH editions are enumerated among the references designated by "sa," that is, "Altruism" and "Caring." In more recent LCSH editions, these terms have become related terms and given the RT designation. Remaining terms are given the designations BT or NT depending on whether they were originally given "xx" or "sa" designations, respectively.

The introduction to the eleventh edition explains the use of the new codes in LCSH (Library of Congress 1988, xi):

> The code (BT) precedes a subject heading representing, according to current policy, the class of which the heading is a class member. The code NT precedes a subject heading

> representing, in most cases, a member of the class represented by the heading under which the NT appears. The codes BT and NT function as reciprocals. . . . The associative relationship, expressed by the code RT meaning related term, links two terms that are associated in some manner other than by hierarchy.

LC's adoption of standard thesaural codes came on the heels of considerable encouragement by the library community (Holley & Killheffer 1982, 132; American Library Association 1985; Council on Library Resources 1982; Cochrane 1984, 147). The library community also recognized the need to establish true hierarchical relationships between subject headings. LC's description of how the obsolete codes were automatically converted by computer to BT, RT, and NT codes acknowledges that the new codes are sometimes not accurate indicators of relationships between subject headings (Library of Congress 1986, 62):

> If a term appeared only in the listing of "xx" (refer from) tracings, it was coded "g" for broader term. If the term appeared both in the listing of "xx" and "sa" tracings, it was coded "n" for related term. Because no intellectual evaluation of the references was done and because a new policy on making cross references was introduced in 1985, these designations in many cases will be incorrect.

LC acknowledges that "these modernly coded terms will not conform to current rules for the making of related terms" and the need for "plans to engage in a systematic updating of references in the forthcoming years" (Pietris 1987b, 11). Dykstra (1988) and Petersen (1983) give suggestions as to how such an update could be undertaken.

Occasionally, LCSH employs a complex *see also* reference to explain the several relationships that exist between the established heading and several other established subject headings that cannot be adequately expressed in one or more simple *see also* references. An example is the complex *see also* reference under the authorized subject heading "Crime": "*See also* headings beginning with the word 'Criminal.'" Had simple *see also* references been used instead of the complex *see also* reference, there would have been dozens of the former references because of the many established subject headings printed in LCSH beginning with the word "Criminal." The complex *see also* reference conveys these many relationships by a simple instruction to catalog users.

1.3.5 Specificity

Chan (1986, 33–37) discusses specificity from three perspectives: (1) specificity in relation to the hierarchical structure of a particular indexing language; (2) specificity in relation to the document being indexed; and (3) specificity with regard to the depth of indexing. The first rationale focuses on specificity of terms in relation to other terms in the same indexing language. It can also address "the optimal level of specificity in a particular indexing language" (Chan 1986, 34). With respect to the latter, "specificity has been a growing concern because of increased specialization and the interdisciplinary approach to research" (Cochrane & Kirtland 1981, 15). To give an example, scholars and practitioners in the visual arts have abandoned LCSH because its specificity is inadequate for their needs and are constructing and maintaining their own controlled vocabularies to handle bibliographic, visual, and object-oriented data (Barnett & Petersen 1990; Parker 1987).

The second perspective on specificity addresses the assignment of the most specific subject heading available in the controlled vocabulary to a particular work. Miksa (1983, 53–54) clarifies Cutter's notion of specificity in this regard:

> For Cutter, identifying the specific subject of a work was not an exercise in making the most complete description possible of a work's aboutness, using language as the ultimate measuring device. Rather, it meant to locate a work at the narrowest point possible in an already established order of subjects independent of the work. Determining a work's specific subject did not refer to assigning a label to a book that uniquely characterized its subject totality by some measure of entirety, but rather referred to assigning the work to a label that was the most appropriate one available in a system of labels already extant.

Cutter's notion of specificity has led to the requirement that catalogers analyze the book at hand and assign it the most specific subject headings available in the controlled vocabulary. This requirement is passed indirectly onto catalog users during information retrieval because they must query the catalog using subject terms that are as specific as the topic they have in mind to find relevant library material. Research demonstrates the contrary, however: users enter subject terms that are broader than their topics of interest (Bates 1977; Markey & Demeyer 1986, 158).

In the third perspective, specificity is used to refer to depth of indexing, which is "the degree to which individual parts of a publication are represented in indexing" (Chan 1986, 374). LC follows a policy of summarization, in which subject headings are assigned to express the overall subject content of library material. This practice has resulted in an average of about 1.4 subject headings assigned per book (Atherton 1978; O'Neill & Aluri 1981; McClure 1976; Markey & Demeyer 1986, 301). A longitudinal study of cataloging records in LC's National Union Catalog (NUC) suggests that the average number of subject headings per NUC record steadily increased over a five-year period (Dwahan & Yerkey 1983, 220). Still, LC has been criticized for the low number of subject headings assigned to works and encouraged to adopt a policy of indexing in depth that includes indexing chapters of books (Atherton 1978; Holley 1983; Mandel & Herschman 1983; Simonds 1984; Hoffman & Magner 1985; Mandel 1985; Studwell 1990).

Since books are assigned only one or two subject headings, the number of subject access points per book is small. Computer programming can increase the number of subject access points by rotating the words and phrases following the comma in inverted headings into the entry-element position and by rotating subdivisions into the entry-element position. These additional access points would be added to alphabetical lists of assigned subject headings for online browsing. Indexing the individual words in subject heading and title fields also increases the number of subject access points. These additional subject access points would enable subject catalog users to retrieve bibliographic records in keyword, Boolean-based searching. An undesirable consequence of keyword searching is the system response to keyword searches composed of words occurring so frequently in subject headings that the large numbers of retrieved records discourage users from displaying them.

1.4 Topical Subject Headings

Subject catalogers in LC's Subject Cataloging Division are responsible for establishing topical subject headings. They also create subject authority records in which established headings for topical subjects reside in MARC fields tagged 150. When catalogers assign such headings to cataloging records, they reside in MARC fields tagged 650.

The introductions in recent editions of *LCSH* give categories of topical subject headings that are still not included in the printed list (Library of Congress 1990b, xvi–xvii). Examples are certain music headings, chemical headings, topical subject headings with the free-floating phrases "in art" and "in literature, and headings authorized by LCSH scope notes.

The sections that follow address topical subject headings. The discussion shows how the variety of forms used for such headings in the LCSH system affects retrieval in the online catalog environment.

1.4.1 Forms of Headings

Subject headings in the LCSH system employ natural and artificial forms of the English language. Subject headings expressed as single nouns, adjectival phrases, and prepositional phrases are natural forms; subject headings that are qualified, subdivided, and inverted are artificial forms of the English language (Chan 1986, 46).

A single noun is often sufficient to describe topical subjects. This form of heading is a natural form of the English language. Single noun headings may conjure up several different feelings, images, or concepts; however, they represent one object or concept. Chan includes adjectives and participles used as nouns in this category. Examples are:

- Calendars
- Gardening
- Handicapped
- Homelessness
- Odors
- State, The
- Werewolves

An adjectival modifier followed by a noun or noun phrase makes up an adjectival heading. All different kinds of adjectives occur in these headings, for example, common adjectives, proper adjectives, and possessive cases. Examples are:

- Boolean rings
- Children's gardens
- Exercise equipment industry
- Malmedy Massacre, 1944-1945
- Polarity therapy
- Welsh literature

Like single noun headings, adjectival phrase headings are expressed in natural language. Some express concepts, entities, or objects that are difficult to imagine without the adjectival qualifier, for example, "Broken homes," "Guerilla warfare," "Jet stream," and "Old age." Other adjectival headings express two topics and could be represented by two single noun headings. For example, "Handicapped children" could be expressed using two separate headings, "Handicapped" and "Children," and "Fishing villages" could become "Fishing" and "Villages." The availability of single headings for topics such as "Handicapped children" and "Fishing villages" ensures the precision of catalog searches for these topics. If catalogers have adhered to the rule of specific entry, works assigned these subject headings address these topics, whereas works assigned the separate headings do not address these topics. For example, a work assigned "Handicapped" and "Children" could be about the children of handicapped adults.

Effective subject searching approaches for adjectival phrase headings enable users to retrieve works assigned single subject headings. Keyword approaches that retrieve words from subject headings fields of cataloging records would retrieve records bearing the single heading, that is, "Handicapped children," that describes their topic of interest. Keyword approaches would also retrieve records bearing separate headings, for example, "Handicapped" and "Children," that are not relevant to their interests because, according to the rule of direct and specific entry, material on handicapped children would be assigned the specific subject heading describing this topic, that is, "Handicapped children."

Conjunctive phrase headings are composed of nouns and/or phrases that are combined using the conjunctions "and" or "or" or a trailing "etc." to express an additive feature or to represent relationships (Chan 1986, 52). Examples of conjunctive phrases are given along with the purpose of the conjunction in the heading.

Conjunctive phrase heading	*Purpose*
Art and revolutions	Relationship
Associations, institutions, etc.	Additive
Cabala and Christianity	Relationship
Hunting and fishing clubs	Additive
Recruiting and enlistment	Additive
Religion and state	Relationship

Speeches, addresses, etc.	Additive
Stunt men and women	Additive
Therapist and patient	Relationship
Volcanic ash, tuff, etc.	Additive

Conjunctions are used in almost opposite ways in these subject headings. When conjunctions serve an additive purpose, they allow the subject headings to be assigned to material on one or both topics. For example, the subject heading "Stunt men and women" can be assigned to a book on stunt men, stunt women, or stunt men and women. Separate headings would normally not be established in LCSH for "Stunt men" and "Stunt women," nor would there necessarily be *see* references under these terms. The relationship purpose actually limits the use of the subject heading to works in which the interrelationship of the two topics named are discussed. Separate headings would be established under each topic separately. *See* references would be made for transposed forms of these headings, for example, "State and religion," *see* "Religion and state."

The availability of single headings to assign to works about the interrelationship of two topics such as "Religion and state" and "Therapist and patient" ensures the precision of catalog searches for these two topics. If catalogers have adhered to the rule of specific and direct entry, works assigned these subject headings address these topics together, whereas works assigned the separate headings do not address the relationship of the two topics. Effective subject search approaches for conjunctive phrase headings of this type help users retrieve works assigned single subject headings. Keyword approaches that retrieve words from subject headings fields of cataloging records would not produce equally useful results because they would retrieve records containing the single heading "Cabala and Christianity" *and* the separate headings "Cabala" and "Christianity."

Prepositional phrase headings consist of two or more nouns and/or adjectival phrases, connected by one or more prepositions. Examples are given that include characteristics of other forms of headings, for example, "etc." and "and" from conjunctive phrase headings, and possessive cases from adjectival phrase headings.

- Busing for school integration
- Cataloging of special collections in libraries
- Discarding of books, periodicals, etc.
- Games for travelers
- Marriage with deceased wife's sister
- Trading with the enemy
- Transport of sick and wounded
- Women volunteers in social service

Prepositional phrase headings express two or more topics. For example, two topics are present in "Games for travelers," namely games and travelers, and three topics are present in "Busing for school integration," namely busing, schools, and integration. Although prepositional phrase headings are natural forms of the English language, other grammatical forms of the words in these subject headings can be used to express the same concept, for example, "Busing for integrating schools," "Games for traveling," and "Transporting the sick and wounded." Users could enter these new expressions as subject queries for these subjects, but they would not retrieve material assigned the authorized subject headings because the terminology of the two are not the same. Online systems would have to enlist keyword, Boolean-based searching capabilities with automatic truncation to retrieve cataloging records bearing these subject headings.

Qualified headings are not expressed in natural language forms; consequently, the subject queries users enter into online catalogs will seldom match these headings. Qualified headings are important in online browsing of alphabetical lists of subject headings because they help users (1) distinguish between homographs, for example, "Cold (Disease)" and "Cold (Temperature)"; (2) clarify meaning of a heading that might not be obvious otherwise, for example, "AIDS (Disease)," "Comment (The French word)," "Current noise (Electricity)," and "Splitting (Psychology)"; and (3) recognize a special application of a general concept, for example, "Bridges (Dentistry)," "Cookery (Filo dough)," and "Damage control (Warships)."

Inverted headings were introduced at the turn of the century during Hanson's tenure as chief of the Catalogue Division. Inverted headings "allowed Hanson to do what could only be partially achieved by his other methods—the very extensive yet selective incorporation of subject collocation into his otherwise conventional name and specific entry subject catalog" (Miksa 1983, 231). For example, inversion brings together over one hundred different subject headings beginning with the word "Insurance." If direct entry were used for these subject headings, they would be scattered throughout the catalog.

The problem with inverted headings is absence of specific guidelines or discernible patterns for inverting headings (Chan 1986, 55). Critics of LCSH have especially singled out LC's practice of establishing inverted headings as being inconsistent with the principle of specific and direct entry. Mischo (1982, 111) gives several examples of LCSH's inconsistency in this regard:

	School libraries
BUT	Libraries, College and university
	Libraries, Children's
BUT	Libraries, Black, *see* Blacks and literature
YET	Libraries and Afro-Americans
	Artificial fur
BUT	Leather, Artificial
	Wool, Artificial

Inverted headings are artificial forms of the English language. Inverted forms of headings are less of a problem in online catalogs than in traditional library catalogs. In manual catalogs, the entry elements of subject headings are static. In online catalogs programmed to disregard word order and punctuation, multiple or normalized entry elements may be constructed in attempts to match user queries with subject headings. For example, online systems would retrieve the subject heading "Insurance, Life" in response to the query "life insurance."

See references are made for the inverted form of adjectival phrase headings when "the adjective, or adjectival noun, serves primarily to modify or qualify" (Haykin 1951, 21). Such references would be accessible to online catalog users through an online catalog browsing capability that displays alphabetical lists of assigned subject headings to system users in response to their subject queries. When users select a *see* reference from an alphabetical list, systems respond with the established heading that is used for that *see* reference.

The great variety of forms of subject headings makes it difficult for users to predict the form of heading used for their topics of interest. For example, several forms could be used to express the topic "Black athletes":

Possible heading	*Form of heading in LCSH system*
Black athletes	adjectival phrase
Athletes, Black	inverted adjectival phrase
Blacks as athletes	prepositional phrase
Blacks; Athletes	two separate single nouns
Blacks in athletics	prepositional phrase

Of the five forms listed, LCSH uses "Athletes, Black" to express this topic. Determining the form used in the catalog to express this and many other topics is not an easy task because there are several ways to formulate topics in forms used by topical subject headings in the LCSH system.

1.4.2 Introduction to Subdivision Practice

Limited use of free-floating subdivision dates back to the second edition (1919) of *Subject headings used in the dictionary catalogues of the Library of Congress*, in which certain form subdivisions were used in cataloging but omitted from the alphabetical list. Pattern (or model) headings were introduced almost 25 years later in the fourth edition (1943).

Until 1974, subject catalogers at LC regularly established heading–subdivision combinations by submitting proposals for review, approval, and printing in *LCSH*. In 1974, it was decided that most heading–subdivision combinations would in the future be constructed according to rules instead of according to individual authorizations. The term "free-floating subdivision" was coined to designate subdivisions that could be appended to headings according to rules.

The long introduction to the eighth edition (1975) of LCSH includes a list of the most commonly used free-floating subdivisions and scope notes governing their application. The list was revised and published in 1981 under the title *Library of Congress Subject Headings: Guide to subdivision practice*. When the *Guide* became outdated, LC published *Subject cataloging manual: Subject headings* (SCM:SH). SCM:SH serves as the primary source for finding appropriate subdivisions and guidelines governing their application (Library of Congress 1990c). The publication, *Free-floating subdivisions: An alphabetical index* (Library of Congress 1990a), currently in its fourth edition, serves as an index to the subdivisions in SCM:SH.

Subdivisions are used extensively in the LCSH system. They serve one of two purposes, depending on institutional policy regarding subdivision: (1) to subarrange the library catalog when a substantial amount of material on a subject is in the collection or (2) to increase the specificity of subject headings. LC's policy with respect to subdivision is to serve the latter purpose (Chan 1986, 64).

The LCSH system employs four types of subdivisions: (1) topical, (2) form, (3) geographic, and (4) period. In machine-readable cataloging records, topical and form subdivisions are designated by the subfield code $x in subfields of subject heading fields, geographical subdivisions are designated by subfield code $z, and period subdivisions are designated by subfield code $y. In the printed *LCSH*, these subdivisions are indistinguishable because subdivision is represented by a double hyphen, for example, "Aged--Care." This book uses double hyphens unless the discussion warrants the use of subfield codes.

When subdivisions are added to topical subject headings, the result is almost always an artificial form of the English language, such as the subdivided subject headings "Arts and youth--Cross-cultural studies," "Foreign exchange--Accounting," and "Prisons--Michigan--Finance." In the online retrieval environment, the words in some user queries are likely to match the words in these subdivided subject headings; however, users cannot be expected to duplicate all the words in these subjects nor their order in the headings. To retrieve library material assigned these headings, keyword searches of subdivided subject headings are required.

Some subdivided headings retain their natural language form after subdivisions are added, for example, "Art--Forgeries," "Television--Antennas," and "Water--Purification." During retrieval, user queries are most likely to match the terminology of the latter subdivided headings; however, online systems must be programmed to disregard punctuation in their attempts to match user queries with subject headings.

A few subdivided headings are close to natural language forms, but they are grammatically incorrect as English language phrases, for example, "Agriculture--Research" instead of the grammatically correct "Agricultural research," "Mexico--History" instead of "Mexican history," and "Dogs--Training" instead of "Dog training." Manipulating user queries to match these subject headings requires truncation of words in both user queries and subject heading as well as disregard for punctuation and, sometimes, word order.

1.4.3 Topical Subdivision

The LCSH system allows for topical subdivision, but the developers of the system caution against the formulation of subdivided headings that resemble subject headings in an alphabetico-classed catalog. As a result, "topical subdivisions are most often used to bring out aspects or facets of the main subject, rather than to indicate its kinds or parts. Nonetheless, a small number of headings characteristic of the classed entries (i.e., hierarchically divided headings) have been introduced into the list" (Chan 1986, 66). Types of such entries are: (1) genus–species type subdivision (e.g., "Wages--Minimum wage,") and (2) part–thing type (e.g., "Automobiles--Motors--Cylinders").

Generally, topical subdivisions are derived from four sources: (1) subject headings printed in *LCSH,* (2) pattern headings printed in *LCSH,* (3) pattern lists in SCM:SH, and (4) free-floating lists in SCM:SH. Topical subdivisions printed in *LCSH* are limited for use with the subject headings in which they occur. Topical subdivisions enumerated on pattern lists are authorized for use with main headings that are governed by a particular pattern heading. Pattern headings are frequently occurring subject headings in the catalog that serve as models for subdivisions that can be used with other headings in the same subject category. For example, the subject heading "Football" is governed by "Soccer," the pattern heading for Sports, and thus, subdivisions used under "Soccer" in LCSH, or enumerated on the SCM: SH memorandum for Sports (H1188.5) are authorized for use with "Football."

Lists of free-floating subdivisions in SCM:SH are available for use under subject headings that describe classes of persons (H1100) and ethnic groups (H1103). SCM:SH also contains a list of general subdivisions (H1095) that are authorized for use under subject headings provided they meet the specifications given in the scope notes accompanying the subdivisions in this list. A few topical subdivisions are not enumerated in SCM:SH lists but they are authorized for use by the instructions in SCM:SH memoranda, for example, "States." In rare instances, topical subdivisions are authorized in an LCSH scope note, for example, scope notes under "Campaign literature" and "Literature, Comparative" (Drabenstott 1992).

1.4.4 Form Subdivision

Haykin defines form subdivision as "the extension of a subject heading based on the form or arrangement of the subject matter in the book. In other words, it represents what the book is, rather than what it is about, the subject matter being expressed by the main heading" (Haykin 1951, 27). Form subdivisions describe the physical or bibliographic makeup of library material, for example, "--Bibliography," "--Charts, diagrams, etc." "--Drawings," "--Encyclopedias," "--Forms," "--Maps," "--Prayer-books and devotions," and "--Telephone directories." Subdivisions that indicate authors' approaches to their subjects, for example, "--History," "--Juvenile literature," and "--Study and teaching," can also be considered form subdivisions, occasionally referred to as inner forms (Chan 1986, 78).

Form subdivisions share subfield code $x with topical subdivisions. Of the subdivisions coded $x, the majority are form (O'Neill & Aluri 1979, 78; Drabenstott 1992). The LC Subject Subdivisions Conference recommended introducing a separate subfield code for form subdivisions (Library of Congress 1992, 9).

Form subdivisions are derived from the same four sources in LCSH and SCM: SH as topical subdivisions. Form subdivisions printed in *LCSH* are limited for use with the subject headings in which they occur. Form subdivisions enumerated on pattern lists are authorized for use with main headings that are governed by a particular pattern heading. For example, the pattern heading for Wars, that is, World War, 1939–1945, authorizes the use of form subdivisions such as "--Autographs," "--Pamphlets," "--Registers of dead," and "--Treaties" under subject headings for wars, for example, "Crimean War, 1853–1856," and "Thirty Years' War, 1618–1648." Although these subdivisions are listed under other pattern headings, they are not enumerated in the general list (H1095) for use under subject headings generally.

Form subdivisions are enumerated on lists of free-floating subdivisions in SCM:SH for use under subject headings that describe classes of persons and ethnic groups. The SCM:SH list of general subdivisions (H1095) also includes form subdivisions and authorizes their use under subject headings, provided they meet the specifications given in the scope notes accompanying the subdivisions in this list.

1.4.5 Geographic Subdivision

In LCSH, the designation "May Subd Geog" authorizes the use of geographic subdivisions with the subject heading. This designation accompanies almost two-fifths of the topical subject headings in LCSH (Markey & Vizine-Goetz 1988, 85).

Chan (1986, 67) summarizes geographic subdivision practice in the LCSH system:

> When a heading is subdivided by a place within a country, the name of the relevant country with certain exceptions . . . is interposed between the subject heading and the name of any subordinate political, administrative, or geographical division. With the exception of Antarctic regions and the names of certain island groups, no geographical name higher than the level of a country is to be used as an interposing element, and none below the level of a city or town is used as a geographic subdivision. Furthermore, no geographic subdivision may contain more than two levels of geographic elements.

The placement of an intervening subdivision for the relevant country between the subject heading and the subordinate political division is called indirect subdivision. In direct subdivision, the intervening subdivision is placed after the subordinate political division in a qualifier or separate subfield, or it is left out altogether. Over the years, LC's policy on geographic subdivision has shifted between direct and indirect subdivision without entirely embracing either approach. LC reaffirmed its current policy of indirect subdivision in the recommendations of the LC Subject Subdivisions Conference (Library of Congress 1992, 10).

In an alphabetical arrangement of subject headings, indirect subdivision facilitates browsing because users do not have to know all the specific place names in a state or country to find library material on a subject. In the following list of subject headings on trees, the two subject headings naming places in Papua New Guinea file in proximity to one another. Thus, users would not have to know all the regions, cities, towns, and villages in a country to approach the subject from a geographic perspective.

Alphabetical list with indirect subdivision
Trees--Georgia--Macon
Trees--Germany--Marburg
Trees--Indiana--Marion
Trees--Madagascar
Trees--Maine
Trees--Papua New Guinea--Madang
Trees--Papua New Guinea--Manus Island
Trees--Philippines--Manila
Trees--Wisconsin--Madison

In the following alphabetical list, direct subdivision is used. The alphabetical list disperses the two subject headings naming specific places in Papua New Guinea and places them in proximity to subject headings naming specific places in distant countries. To obtain all material on trees in Papua New Guinea, users would have to be familiar with specific places in this country and/or browse the entire alphabetical list of subject headings under "Trees."

Alphabetical list with direct subdivision
Trees--Macon (Ga.)
Trees--Madagascar
Trees--Madang (Papua New Guinea)
Trees--Madison (Wisc.)
Trees--Maine
Trees--Manila (Philippines)
Trees--Manus Island (Papua New Guinea)
Trees--Marburg (Germany)
Trees--Marion (Indiana)

Subject catalogers in LC's Subject Cataloging Division are responsible for establishing headings to describe geographic areas or entities that are not jurisdictional units and recording the direct forms of these subject headings in subject authority records. These records are used to print new *LCSH* editions and are also accessible through online bibliographic services such as OCLC and WLN.

Descriptive catalogers in LC's Descriptive Cataloging Division are responsible for establishing headings to describe geographic entities for jurisdictional units. They also record the direct forms of these subject headings in name authority records. These records are accessible through online bibliographic services such as OCLC and WLN.

Geographic subdivisions are the most frequently-occurring type of subdivision added to topical subject headings (Drabenstott 1992). Furthermore, almost 94% of the geographic subdivisions occurring with topical subject headings can be verified through subject or name authority records (Drabenstott 1992); however, after verifying names, catalogers must convert direct forms of geographical names found in authority files into indirect forms by following instructions for indirect subdivision detailed in SCM:SH memoranda (H830-832). Catalogers are not limited to the place names in authority records. They can establish headings for place names that have not already been established in authority records by following instructions in Chapter 23 of the *Anglo-American cataloging rules* (American Library Association 1988) (hereafter, AACR2) and rules for indirect subdivision (SCM:SH, H830–832).

1.4.6 Period Subdivision

Period subdivision varies depending on a particular topic or place. Haykin gives the following direction regarding period subdivision: "The period subdivisions used should either correspond to generally recognized epochs in the history of the place or should represent spans of time frequently treated in books whether they possess historic unity or not" (Haykin 1951, 33).

Under "American literature," LCSH gives the following period subdivisions:

- American literature--Colonial period, ca. 1600-1775
- American literature--Revolutionary period, 1775-1783
- American literature--1783-1850
- American literature--19th century
- American literature--20th century

The period subdivisions established with the subject heading "American literature" can be used only under this subject. That is, they are not free floating under related subject headings such as "American diaries," "American drama," or "American fiction" that have some of the same subdivisions or no period subdivisions at all.

Period subdivisions are sprinkled throughout SCM:SH free-floating and pattern lists. These subdivisions are applied in three different ways. First, lists of free-floating period subdivisions are authorized under subject headings governed by a particular pattern heading. For example, pattern lists under Groups of Literary Authors (H1155.2) and Literatures (H1156) have separate lists of period subdivisions that are authorized for use with subject headings governed by these patterns. Second, period subdivisions are enumerated in SCM:SH free-floating and pattern lists and bound to the topical subdivision preceding them. For example, the period subdivision "--1500–1799" can be used only as the trailing subdivision in the topical–period subdivision combination "--Grammar--1500–1799" under subject headings for languages and groups of languages. Third, multiple subdivisions are used in pattern lists as a type of shorthand to show the many different types of period subdivisions authorized with subject headings governed by a particular pattern. These period subdivisions are usually bound to a particular topical subdivision. For example, the period subdivision in the phrase "--History--Revolution, 1775–1783, [War of 1812, etc.]" is a multiple subdivision and comes from the pattern heading for Military Services (H1159). This phrase authorizes the use of a topical–period subdivision combination in which the topical subdivision "--History" precedes a period subdivision describing American wars.

Period subdivisions are never truly given free-floating status in LCSH or SCM: SH. They come closest to free-floating status in the SCM:SH general list of free-floating subdivisions. Five topical–period subdivision combinations are given in which the topical subdivision "--History" is followed by individually numbered centuries beginning with the sixteenth century, for example, "--History--16th century," and "--History--17th century." The only restriction is that these topical–period subdivision combinations be used under corporate bodies and topical headings.

Topical subject headings printed in *LCSH* sometimes express chronological aspects of a subject. Examples are the inverted adjectival phrase headings "Art, Renaissance," "Drawing, Abstract," "Painting, Gothic," and "Sculpture, Classical." Even though these subject headings convey period characteristics of subjects, they are not tagged differently from other topical subject headings in authority or cataloging records.

1.4.7 Precoordination and Synthesis

Documents are written on single subjects, aspects of subjects, or two or more subjects treated in relation to each other (Chan 1986, 37). Normally, LCSH is adequate for providing subject headings to represent single subjects. When documents treat subjects at a deeper level than allowed by LCSH, the subject heading system is not adequate. Two or more terms must be used to achieve the specificity required of aspects of subjects or of two or more subjects treated in relationship to each other, (Chan 1986, 37).

In dealing with a complex subject for which no single heading exists, it is sometimes difficult to predict LC's approach to representing this subject in its controlled vocabulary. Will LC express the complex subject in a single subject heading? What form will the subject heading take? If two or more subject headings are used, what form will these subject headings take?

Precoordination, the representation of a complex subject by means of combining separate elements of the subject in indexing terms, is a feature of the LCSH system. Synthesis, the device used to express complex subjects by combining terms in a heading, takes several forms in the LCSH system (Chan 1986, 39–40):

- Adjectival phrases
- Conjunctive phrase headings
- Prepositional phrase headings
- Qualified headings

- Subdivided headings
- Combinations of the above

LCSH has no fixed rules concerning which form to choose to express relationships between subjects. It also has no fixed rules about the citation order in which terms or subdivisions are combined in subject headings. This lack of rules increases the difficulty of cataloging documents and makes information retrieval much more difficult because online catalog users cannot predict the form of subject headings for expressing two or more subjects. For example, the topic "drug use among athletes" can be expressed using the following different forms of topical subject headings:

Possible headings	*Forms used in the LCSH system*
Athletes and drugs	Conjunctive phrase
Athletes' drug use	Adjectival phrase
Athletes--Drug use	Single noun with a topical subdivision
Athletes; Drugs	Two separate single nouns
Drug use in athletics	Prepositional phrase
Drug use in sports	Prepositional phrase

Of the six forms listed above, LCSH uses "Athletes--Drug use" to express this topic. Online systems can be programmed to disregard minor differences between subject headings such as stopwords, word order, and punctuation. It is much more difficult for them to effect a match between a user query expressed as a prepositional phrase such as "drug use in athletics" to retrieve cataloging records given the subdivided heading "Athletes--Drug use" for this subject because of the different grammatical forms used for the "Athletes" facet of the query; however, online system programming that includes stemming algorithms can retrieve subject headings despite differences in grammatical forms. Even more difficult is for systems to handle the user query "drug use in sports." The word in the "Athletes" facet of this query, that is, "sports," is not a grammatical form of "athletes" which is used in the relevant subject heading for this topic, that is, "Athletes--Drug use;" consequently, stemming will not produce retrievals. This example demonstrates how the lack of a predictable order and of consistency among similar headings in the LCSH system limits retrieval effectiveness in the information retrieval environment of the online catalog.

1.5 Names in Subject Headings

The sections that follow address the three types of names typically assigned as subject headings, that is, personal, corporate, and geographic names. The sources of these headings in LC's subject and name authority files are discussed. The forms used to express name headings are highlighted because of the important role that the form of headings plays in online retrieval.

1.5.1 Personal Names

LC's policy of enlisting descriptive catalogers to establish headings for personal names is to ensure consistency in the form of such names used as author and subject entries. The few personal names printed in *LCSH* are included because they are pattern headings or they are needed to display cross-references or subdivisions. Machine-readable subject authority records are available for these few personal names; however, LC advises catalogers to consult LC's name authority file to assign the correct form of personal name in subject headings. Catalogers unable to find name authority records for the individuals that are subjects of books can formulate headings using the rules in Chapter 22 of AACR2.

Descriptive catalogers at LC are responsible for establishing headings and name authority records for certain categories of ambiguous headings: (1) named biblical characters, (2) clans, (3) houses of counts, dukes, earls, (4) dynasties, (5) families, (6) houses (families), and (7) royal houses. Subject headings for mythological, legendary, and fictitious characters and gods and goddesses are established by LC subject catalogers. They are printed in *LCSH* and given subject authority records in LCSH-mr.

Personal names of most contemporary individuals are straightforward, consisting of elements for given name, middle name or initial, and family name. These elements are inverted in name headings. This inversion makes surnames the entry elements in name headings to facilitate alphabetical browsing. Dates in name headings help to distinguish between similar names. Examples of name headings are:

- Faulkner, William, 1897–1962
- Iacocca, Lee A.
- Mead, Margaret, 1901–1978
- Oates, Joyce Carol, 1938–
- Reagan, Ronald

The names of some contemporary and historical individuals are not as simple as the ones listed above because they involve initials, titles, descriptive phrases, foreign language articles and prepositions, numeration, qualifiers, and unknown birth or/ and death dates. Elements such as given names and family names may not be readily apparent in the examples below:

- Aristotle
- Black Elk
- Gogh, Vincent van, 1835–1890
- John Paul, II, Pope, 1920–
- Lawrence, D.H. (David Herbert), 1885–1930
- Polo, Marco, 1254–1323?
- Nicholas, II, Emperor of Russia, 1868–1918
- Ruth (Biblical character)
- Sebastian, Saint
- Tecumseh, Shawnee Chief, 1768–1813

- Teresa, Mother, 1910–
- X, Malcolm, 1925–1965

These subject headings name notable individuals that are likely to be of interest to library catalog users. Users might have difficulties expressing these names in subject queries because the rules catalogers follow to determine the correct entry element sometimes result in the creation of headings with unexpected entry elements, for example, "Gogh" instead of "van Gogh," "Sebastian" instead of "Saint Sebastian," and "John Paul" instead of "Pope John Paul." Users might be unsure how to enter names such as "Black Elk" and "Aristotle" into online catalogs that require inversion of personal names.

All but period subdivisions are used with personal name headings. One free-floating list of topical and form subdivisions is available for use under names of persons (H1110). A pattern list of topical and form subdivisions is available for use under Individual Literary Authors (H1155.4). Geographic subdivision is usually authorized by appearance of the "May Subd Geog" designation under topical and form subdivisions in these two lists. An example is the topical subdivision "--Journeys (May Subd Geog)" that authorizes geographical subdivision in the assigned subject heading "Polo, Marco, 1254–1323?--Journeys--China."

1.5.2 Corporate Names

LC descriptive catalogers are also responsible for establishing headings and creating name authority records for corporate names. The authority records for the corporate names they establish are added to the Name Authority File, but catalogers can use records in this file for author or subject entries. The few corporate names printed in *LCSH* are included there for the same reasons as personal names: they are pattern headings or they are needed to display cross references or subdivisions. Machine-readable authority records for corporate name subject headings printed in *LCSH* are also available in LCSH-mr. Catalogers unable to find authority records for corporate names in LCSH-mr or the Library of Congress Name Authority File (LCNAF) can formulate headings using the rules in Chapter 24 of AACR2 to use as the subject entries of library material.

Corporate names include public and private organizations, institutions, government agencies, churches, projects, expeditions, fairs, and religious denominations. Subject entries for corporate names can include qualifiers, subordinate units, and locations and dates of meetings.

- Attica Prison
- Buffalo Bills (Football club)
- Grateful Dead (Musical group)
- International Conference on AIDS (4th : 1988 : Stockholm, Sweden)
- Syracuse University
- University of Michigan. School of Business Administration

All four types of subdivisions can be used with corporate name headings. One free-floating list of topical and form subdivisions is available for use under corporate bodies generally (H1105). Topical and form subdivisions enumerated in pattern lists for Legislative Bodies (H1155), Military Services (H1159), Individual Educational Institutions (H1151), and Christian Denominations (H1187) can be used in corporate-name headings describing such organizations or entities. Geographic subdivision is authorized by appearance of the "May Subd Geog" designation under topical and form subdivisions in SCM:SH lists. Several topical–period subdivision combinations are available in the general free-floating list (H1095) that begin with "$x History" and include an abbreviated century name, for example, "18th century" or "19th century."

1.5.3 Place Names

Responsibility for establishing headings for place names is divided between LC's Subject Cataloging and Descriptive Cataloging Divisions. The former division establishes headings to describe geographic areas or nonjurisdictional entities. These types of places include ancient cities, bridges, canals, estates, forests, highways, mines, parks, playgrounds, plazas, refugee camps, streets, tunnels, and waterways. Direct forms of these places are recorded in established heading fields of subject authority records. These records are used to print new *LCSH* editions and are accessible through online bibliographic services such as OCLC and WLN.

Descriptive catalogers establish headings to describe geographic entities for jurisdictional units. Such entities are counties, countries, dioceses, provinces, states, and territories. The direct form of established headings for names of such places is recorded in name authority records. These records are accessible through online bibliographic services such as OCLC and WLN.

Qualifiers are used to identify place names more clearly or to differentiate between places with the same name. In the direct forms of place names encoded in authority records, qualifiers are placed in parentheses after the place name. If two qualifiers are needed, they are placed in parentheses and separated by spaces and a colon. If no authority records exist for place names, catalogers can create headings for such names by following Chapter 23 of AACR2 (American Library Association 1988), SCM:SH memoranda (H405, H690–810), and Chan (1986, 128–150). Examples of subject headings for place names are:

- Buffalo (N.Y.)
- Erie, Lake
- Grand Island (N.Y. : Island)
- Hormuz, Strait of
- New York (State)
- Niagara Falls (N.Y. and Ont.)
- Ontario

All four types of subdivisions can be used with subject headings for place names; however, SCM:SH lists for free-floating and pattern subdivisions limit the use of period and geographic subdivisions. One free-floating list of topical and form subdivisions is available for use under names of places (H1140). Topical and form subdivisions enumerated in pattern lists for Colonies (H1149.5), Military Services (H1159), and Wars (H1200) can be used in geographic-name headings describing such topics. The few period subdivisions in these lists are either bound to the topical subdivision preceding them, or they allow catalogers to enter a relevant date after the initial word or phrase, or they are multiple subdivisions that show the many different types of period subdivisions authorized with subject headings governed by a particular pattern. Geographic subdivision is authorized by appearance of the "May Subd Geog" designation under topical and form subdivisions in these two lists. Very few (.5%) geographic names printed in *LCSH* are accompanied by the "May Subd Geog" designation (Markey & Vizine-Goetz 1988, 88). Examples are "Alpine regions," "Cumberland Road," "Interstate 69," and "Mars (Planet)--Geology."

1.5.4 Synthesis in Name Headings

The citation order in which terms are combined in personal name, corporate name, and place name headings is somewhat easier to predict than the order in topical subject headings. Subject headings for the names of most contemporary individuals are straightforward, consisting of an inverted element for family name, followed by elements for given name and middle name or initial. Direct forms of corporate names are entered into subject headings unless they are subordinate units of larger bodies, in which case the larger body becomes the entry element in the subject heading. The use of generic terms or names of places as qualifiers is sometimes prescribed by AACR2 and LC's descriptive cataloging policies. Direct forms of place names are entered into subject headings; qualifiers are usually added to subject headings when the place named is anything but a name of a country.

If more than one subdivision is used in subject headings for personal and corporate names, citation order is relatively predictable. Common subdivision combinations are topical–period or topical–geographic combinations; if used, form subdivisions would be the trailing subdivisions in most combinations.

Citation order is not as predictable in subject headings for place names. Topical, period, and form subdivisions are used widely. Some combinations of main headings for place names and topical subdivisions could also be expressed as combinations of topical subject headings and geographical subdivisions. For example, of the following possibilities, "Edmonton (Alta.)--Shopping malls" or "Shopping malls--Alberta--Edmonton," the latter is the authorized subject heading in the LCSH system. However, the following subject headings are also authorized: "Edmonton (Alta.)--Public lands," "Parks--Alberta--Edmonton," "Edmonton (Alta.)--Industries," and "Petroleum chemicals industry--Alberta--Edmonton." Predicting whether the entry element is the place name or topic in these subject headings is not easy. If online systems require users to know the correct order of subject heading elements, online catalog users are going to have problems retrieving material on topics that include geographic elements.

1.6 Maintaining LCSH as a Controlled Vocabulary

The considerable investment libraries have made in terms of applying subject headings based on the LCSH systems in millions of cataloging records suggests that libraries need to make the most of their investment in LCSH by improving subject retrieval in their automated systems. The following sections describe how LC maintains the LCSH system and how libraries that use LCSH can add new subject headings and references to the system.

1.6.1 Literary Warrant

Two basic approaches are used to build controlled vocabularies. In one approach, the controlled vocabulary covers the universe of knowledge. All subjects, regardless of their specificity or generality, have their place in the system. In the second approach, the collection itself is used as the basis for developing the system. Subjects are established only for those topics covered by the collection. This approach is called literary warrant.

Literary warrant governs the LCSH system. This policy is stated in the earliest editions of the list: "The list covers subjects in all branches of knowledge so far as the cataloguing of the corresponding classes of books in the Library of Congress progressed" (Library of Congress 1928, iii).

LC's policy of literary warrant directly affects users at LC as well as at the many libraries that use and apply subject headings in the LCSH system. When users query the catalog with a subject that is not represented in it, they will neither retrieve cataloging records nor receive direction about the subject terms they need to use to retrieve library material on a related subject. If LCSH described the universe of knowledge, then users could at least obtain guidance about the latter. However, the system "was not conceived at the outset as, nor has it ever been intended to be, a comprehensive system covering the universe of knowledge" (Chan 1986, 10).

The policy of literary warrant also affects the many libraries that use the LCSH system because they have collections covering subjects that are not represented by subjects in the LCSH system. When subjects are not available to adequately express their collection, libraries have several possible courses of action. They can wait for LC to establish the subject, formulate a local subject heading to assign to the material, or assign a subject heading from the LCSH system that is broader than the subject of the material.

Numerous critics of the LCSH system have assailed LC for its inability to incorporate new subjects into the system on a timely basis (Cochrane & Kirtland 1981, 21–222; Mischo 1982; Berman 1984, 1987, 1988; Nelson 1986). LC has responded by encouraging the library community to submit proposals for new subject headings and *see* references for inclusion in LCSH through the Cooperative Subject Cataloging Project (CSCP 1991). Libraries participating in a pilot project to add subject headings to bibliographic records for works of fiction may find themselves submitting proposals for new subject headings and *see* references (OCLC 1991a). LC has not applied subject headings to fiction in the past; consequently, enhancement of the controlled vocabulary for fiction may be needed. LC's willingness to develop LCSH for fiction would be a departure from the policy of literary warrant in which the establishment of new subject headings is closely connected to the LC collection.

1.6.2 Thesaurus Construction and Maintenance

Topical subject headings in LCSH are a controlled vocabulary; only terms authorized as subject headings can be assigned to cataloging records. Activity directed toward developing, maintaining, and updating a controlled vocabulary is called thesaurus construction and maintenance. Such activity is pursued at LC through an editorial group composed of staff members from the Office of Subject Cataloging Policy. This group and interested observers meet weekly to consider proposals on the following changes: additions, alterations, or cancellations of headings, heading–subdivision combinations, cross-references, and free-floating subdivisions (Chan 1986, 153). It also reviews proposals on new headings that require deliberations on "terminology (wording, form [phrase or subdivision], language, entry element), conformity to existing patterns and broad policies of the system, compatibility with descriptive headings (if applicable), cross references, and notes" (Chan 1986, 153).

Until recently, proposals for changes and new headings emanated exclusively from catalogers at LC. The Vocabulary Improvement Project (Cochrane 1983) and SAC Subcommittee on New Subject Headings were pilot projects that demonstrated to LC that librarians could propose *see* references and new subject headings using the same procedures that LC librarians followed. Today, librarians are encouraged to submit new subject headings and *see* references by following the guidelines in SCM: SH (H200-202) and taking part in cooperative projects like CSCP.

1.6.3 Impact of Automation

A batch system was developed and implemented between 1969 and 1972 to help LC produce new printed editions of *LCSH*. This system was developed shortly after LC began creating and distributing LC/MARC records in 1968; thus, it was one of the oldest automation efforts in LC.

Mary K. D. Pietris (1987a, 13), Chief of LC's Office of Subject Cataloging Policy, described the advantages of LC's new online system that was implemented in steps from 1985 to 1986:

> First, it is easier to change authority records than before. Second, our products are much more up-to-date than before because they are spin-offs from the on-line database. Third, the library now can offer the tape distribution service of subject authority records. Fourth, subject authorities can be searched on-line at LC.

Today, LCSH-mr contains over 181,000 subject authority records and 320,000 cross-references (Library of Congress 1990b, vii). Between 7000 and 10,000 new subject headings are added to LCSH yearly. LC catalogers consult subject headings in the online subject authority file in the creation of approximately 245,000 LC/MARC records per year. A link between subject authority records and cataloging records in the online system would facilitate cataloging; however, LC has no plans to link these two record files (Chan 1986, 165).

1.6.4 The Library Community's Commitment to LCSH

Since 1968, LC has produced 3.4 million cataloging records and distributed these records in the form of a cumulative master tape and weekly update tapes to subscribers. Bibliographic services such as the not-for-profit OCLC Online Computer Library Center, Research Libraries Group (RLG), and Western Library Network (WLN) built centralized, mainframe-based systems for online cataloging to give member libraries access to MARC records produced by LC (i.e., LC/MARC records) and capabilities to enter their own cataloging or use the machine-readable cataloging records entered by other member libraries.

Libraries' investment in the LCSH system can be counted in terms of the number of cataloging records that bear subject headings based on the LCSH system and the number of unique subject headings that have been constructed through the rules and guidelines of the LCSH system. Of the OCLC database of nearly 26 million cataloging records, 15% are LC/MARC records and 85% are member-contributed machine-readable cataloging records. Over 95% of the LC/MARC records and 68% of the member-contributed records contain topical and geographic subject headings based on the LCSH system (O'Neill & Aluri 1979, 5). The number of unique topical subject headings in the OCLC database is estimated to be 4 million. Many of these subject headings have been constructed using rules and guidelines for free-floating subdivision, subdivision based on pattern headings, and geographic subdivision.

The annual production of machine-readable cataloging records by OCLC member libraries is over twenty-three million records (OCLC 1991b, 3). Not only do libraries add these machine-readable cataloging records to the OCLC database and to the databases of other bibliographic services, they add them to the online catalog database of their integrated library systems. When libraries first create their online catalog database, they are using cataloging records that have been created over a long period of time. Over time, changes in the cataloging code, new policies in descriptive and subject cataloging, and new editions of LCSH have made older cataloging records inconsistent with later ones and rendered access points obsolete. Libraries enlist database services of library automation vendors to improve the quality of older cataloging records, update the name and subject access points in their cataloging records, and create name and subject authority files for their online catalog (Miller 1984). These vendors enlist authority records in LCSH-mr and NAF to update access points and to generate cross-references in local authority records. To keep pace with cataloging policy changes and changes in the controlled vocabulary, vendors also offer customer libraries several approaches to updating their cataloging databases and authority files (Drabenstott 1991, 4–5).

The subject headings in libraries' cataloging records are based on the LCSH system. They serve as both the indexing language and retrieval language in online catalogs. Title fields of cataloging records also contribute subject terms that can be used during information retrieval. Whether or not title fields are used for retrieval depends on the design of the online catalog and the library staff decisions regarding profiling of the system.

The failure of machine-readable cataloging records to provide adequate subject access to library materials was demonstrated in the landmark Subject Access Project (Atherton 1978). As a result, the library community has encouraged LC to adopt a policy of indexing in depth that includes indexing chapters of books. Although only a few libraries regularly enhance their cataloging records (Posey & Erdmann 1986; Byrne 1986), enhancement of cataloging records for improved subject access continues to be an active area of research (Dillon & Wenzel, 1990; Van Orden 1990).

We acknowledge research efforts to enhance subject access and support the development of databases with enhanced cataloging records. Our focus in this book is to improve subject retrieval in online systems in which subject access is limited to title and subject heading fields of cataloging records. LC and thousands of libraries in North America have produced millions of cataloging records bearing a limited amount of subject information. Subject indexes in online catalogs in libraries throughout the continent are constructed from title and subject heading fields of cataloging records and they contribute only ten unique subject terms per record (Markey & Calhoun 1987). Although the number of subject headings has increased over the years, this field only contributes an average of 1.4 subject headings per record to the subject indexes of online catalogs. Libraries have made considerable investments in terms of cataloging record production, subject heading assignment using the LCSH system, and staff training in LC subject cataloging policies and procedures. Our recommendations for improving subject retrieval will help libraries maximize the return on their investments in these areas.

1.7 Plan of this Book

In this introductory chapter, we have looked at subject analysis using the LCSH system and focused on system features such as basic principles, terminology, and synthesis that affect subject retrieval. The remainder of this book will describe subject analysis and subject searching in online catalogs, discuss their limitations on retrieval, and demonstrate how such limitations can be overcome through system design and programming to enable systems to respond to user queries with the subject searching approach most likely to succeed.

Chapters 2 to 4 highlight the characteristics of the machine-readable data files that libraries use to build the databases in their automated library systems. Chapter 2 describes the machine-readable file of subject authority records. Chapter 3 focuses on machine-readable records for bibliographic data. Chapter 4 investigates the relationships between records in subject authority and bibliographic files.

Chapters 5 to 10 address the subject queries that users enter into online bibliographic systems. Chapter 5 surveys studies of user queries. Chapter 6 gives readers a broad picture of user queries and their closeness to authorized subject headings in the authority file. In Chapters 7, 8, 9, and 10, we target characteristics of user queries that are likely and not likely to produce retrievals. In these four chapters, suggestions are made about system responses to user queries that are intended to increase precision, encourage browsing, and produce more useful retrievals.

Chapters 11 and 12 detail system responses and the characteristics of user queries best suited to specific responses. A new approach—the exact approach—is described in Chapter 11. It handles user queries that are exact or almost exact matches of catalog headings and references. This approach summarizes in a single screen the many options available with respect to the matched heading, for example, availability of related terms, scope notes, and subdivided forms. The exact approach can be implemented in existing online catalogs, but certain enhancements are required in both bibliographic and authority files to make this approach work more effectively. Chapter 12 discusses several subject searching approaches now available in operational systems and the characteristics of user queries best suited to these approaches.

Chapter 13 focuses on search trees, defined as a set of paths with branches or choices that enable online systems to carry out the subject search approach most likely to succeed. Search trees control system responses and determine appropriate subject searching approaches to user queries. Users do not explicitly choose a particular approach. Rather, systems respond with an approach based on the extent to which queries match the catalog's controlled vocabulary and produce retrievals. The benefit of incorporating search trees into online bibliographic systems is to place the responsibility of determining which approach produces the best results on the system.

The concluding Chapter 14 speculates about the future of subject headings for online retrieval. We consider the viability of the LCSH system for online retrieval, discuss planned changes in the system, and hypothesize about changes that are necessary to make this system more responsive to end user needs and behavior.

References

American Library Association. Subject Analysis Committee. (1985). *Format of LCSH: Report of survey.* (Photocopy of original.)

Angell, Richard S. (1972). *Library of Congress Subject Headings—review and forecast.* In Hans Wellisch & Thomas D. Wilson (eds.), *Subject retrieval in the seventies: New directions; Proceedings of an international symposium* (pp. 143-162). Westport, CT: Greenwood.

Atherton, Pauline A. (1978). *BOOKS are for use: Final report of the Subject Access Project to the Council on Library Resources.* Syracuse, NY: School of Information Studies. ERIC ED 156131.

Avram, Henriette D. (1968). *The MARC Pilot Project: Final report on a project sponsored by the Council on Library Resources.* Washington, DC: Library of Congress.

Barnett, Patricia J., & Petersen, Toni. (1990). Extending MARC to accommodate faceted thesauri: The AAT model. In Toni Petersen & Pat Molholt (Eds.), *Beyond the book: Extending MARC for subject access* (pp. 7–23). Boston: G.K. Hall.

Bates, Marcia J. (1977). Factors affecting subject catalog search success. *Journal of the American Society for Information Science 28,* 3 (May), 161–169.

Berman, Sanford. (1984). Out of the kitchen—but not into the catalog. *Technical Services Quarterly, 2,* 1/2 (Fall/Winter), 167–171.

Berman, Sanford. (1987). The terrible truth about teenlit cataloguing. *Top of the News, 43,* 3 (Spring), 311–320.

Berman, Sanford. (1988). Not funny any more. *Library Journal, 113,* (June 1), 80.

Byrne, Alex. (1986). Life wasn't meant to be whimsical: Painless subject augmentation. *Australasian College Libraries, 4,* 2 (June), 83–90.

Chan, Lois Mai. (1986). *Library of Congress Subject Headings: Principles and application* (2nd ed.). Littleton, CO: Libraries Unlimited.

Chan, Lous Mai. (1990). *Library of Congress Subject Headings: Principles of structure and policies for application.* Washington, DC: Library of Congress.

Clack, Doris Hargrett. (1978). The adequacy of Library of Congress Subject Headings for Black literature. *Library Resources & Technical Services, 22,* 2 (Spring), 137–144.

Cochrane, Pauline A. (1983). *LCSH entry vocabulary project: Final report to the Council on Library Resources and to the Library of Congress.* ERIC ED 233746.

Cochrane, Pauline A. (1984). Modern subject access in the online age. *American Libraries, 15,* (March), 145–150.

Cochrane, Pauline A., & Kirtland, Monika. (1981). *Critical views of LCSH—the Library of Congress Subject Headings: A bibliographic and bibliometric essay.* Syracuse, NY: ERIC/Information Resources Clearinghouse.

Colman, Gould P. (1987). Documenting agriculture and rural life. *The Midwestern Archivist, 12,* 1, 20–27.

Council on Library Resource. (1982). *Subject access: report of a meeting sponsored by the Council on Library Resources, Dublin, Ohio, June 7–9, 1982.* Keith W. Russell (Ed.). Washington, DC: Council on Library Resources.

CSCP. (1991). *(CSCP) Cooperative Subject Cataloging Projects: Summary of records processed through September 1991.* 4 pp. (Photocopy.)

Cutter, Charles A. (1904). *Rules for a dictionary catalog* (4th ed.). Washington, DC: U.S. Government Printing Office.

Dillon, Martin, & Wenzel, Patrick. (1990). Retrieval effectiveness of enhanced bibliographic records. *Library Hi Tech, 8,* 3, 43–46.

Drabenstott, Karen M. (1991). Introduction. In Karen M. Drabenstott (Ed.), *Subject authorities in the online environment: Papers from a conference program held in San Francisco, June 29, 1987* (pp. 1–8). Chicago: American Library Association.

Dwahan, S. H., & Yerkey, A. Neil. (1983). Trends in subject assignment in cataloging records during 1974–1978. *Information Processing and Management, 19*, 4, 213–222.

Dykstra, Mary. (1988). Can subject headings be saved? *Library Journal, 113*, 15 (September 15), 55–58.

Hanson, J. C. M. (1909). The subject catalogs of the Library of Congress. *Bulletin of the American Library Association, 3* (July 1), 385–386.

Harris, Jessica L., & Clack, Doris Hargrett (1979). Treatment of people and peoples in subject analysis. *Library Resources & Technical Services, 23*, 4 (Fall), 374–390.

Haykin, Donald Judson. (1951). *Subject headings: A practical guide.* Washington, DC: U.S. Government Printing Office.

Hildreth, Charles R. (1982). *Online public access catalogs: The user interface.* Dublin, OH: OCLC.

Hildreth, Charles R. (1987). Library networking in North America in the 1980s. Part 1: The dreams, the realities. *The Electronic Library*, 5 4 (August), 222–228.

Hildreth, Charles R. (1989). General introduction; OPAC research: Laying the groundwork for future OPAC design. In Charles R. Hildreth (Ed.), *The Online catalogue: Developments and directions* (pp. 1–24). London: The Library Association.

Hoffman, Herbert H., & Magner, Jeruel L. (1985). Future outlook: Better retrieval through analytical catalogs. *Journal of Academic Librarianship, 11*, 3 (July), 151–153.

Holley, Robert P. (1983). Constraints of the 3 × 5 card. *Cataloging & Classification Quarterly, 4*, 1 (Fall), 29–35.

Holley, Robert P., & Killheffer, Robert E. (1982). Is there an answer to the subject access crisis? *Cataloging & Classification Quarterly, 1* (2/3), 125–133.

Inter, Sheila S. (1988). ASCR: The American subject cataloging rules (Part 1). *Technicalities, 8* (July), 5–7.

Library of Congress. (1928). *Subject headings used in the dictionary catalogues of the Library of Congress* (3rd ed.). Washington, DC: Library of Congress.

Library of Congress. (1943). *Subject headings used in the dictionary catalogs of the Library of Congress* (4th ed.). Washington, DC: Library of Congress.

Library of Congress. (1975). *Library of Congress Subject Headings: Guide to subdivision practice.* Washington, DC: Library of Congress.

Library of Congress. (1984). *Subject cataloging manual: Subject headings* (1st ed.). Washington, DC: Library of Congress.

Library of Congress. (1986). "Cross-reference structure in the LC automated subject authority file. *Cataloging Service Bulletin, 33*, 62.

Library of Congress. (1988). *Library of Congress Subject Headings* (11th ed.). Washington, DC: Library of Congress.

Library of Congress. (1989). *Free-floating subdivisions: An alaphabetical index.* Washington, DC: Library of Congress.

Library of Congress. (1990a). *Free-floating subdivisions: An alphabetical index* (2nd ed.). Washington, DC: Library of Congress.

Library of Congress. (1990b). *Library of Congress Subject Headings* (13th ed.). Washington, DC: Library of Congress.

Library of Congress. (1990c). *Subject cataloging manual: Subject headings* (3d ed.). Washington, DC: Library of Congress.

Library of Congress. (1991). *Library of Congress Subject Headings* (14th ed.). Washington, DC: Library of Congress.

Library of Congress. (1992). *The future of subdivisions in the Library of Congress subject headings system: Report from the Subject Subdivisions Conference.* Martha O'Hara Conway (Ed.). Washington, DC: Library of Congress.

McClure, Charles R. (1976). Subject and added entries as access to information. *Journal of Academic Librarianship, 2* (March), 9–14.

Mandel, Carol A. (1985). Enriching the library catalog record for subject access. *Library Resources & Technical Services, 29*, 1 (January–March), 5–15.

Mandel, Carol A., & Herschman, Judith. (1983). Online subject access: Enhancing the library catalog. *Journal of Academic Librarianship, 9*, 3 (July), 148–155.

Markey, Karen, & Calhoun, Karen. (1987). Unique words contributed by MARC records with summary and/or contents notes. In Ching-Chih Chen (Ed.), *ASIS '87, proceedings of the 50th ASIS annual meeting* (pp. 153–162). Medford, NJ: Learned Information.

Markey, Karen, & Demeyer, Anh N. (1986). *Dewey Decimal Classification Online Project: Evaluation of a library schedule and index integrated into the subject searching capabilities of an online catalog.* Dublin, OH: OCLC. OCLC Research Report series OCLC/OPR/RR-86/1.

Markey, Karen, & Vizine-Goetz, Diane. (1988). *Characteristics of subject authority records in the machine-readable Library of Congress Subject Headings.* Dublin, OH: OCLC. OCLC Research Report series OCLC/OPR/RR-88/2.

Miksa, Francis L. (1983). *The subject in the dictionary catalog from Cutter to the present.* Chicago: American Library Association.

Miller, Dan. (1984). Authority control in the retrospective conversion process. *Information Technology & Libraries, 3*, 3 (September), 286–292.

Mischo, William H. (1981). *A subject retrieval function for the online union catalog.* Columbus, OH: OCLC. OCLC Technical Report series OCLC/DD/TR-81/4.

Mischo, William H. (1982). Library of Congress Subject Headings: A review of the problems, and prospects for improved subject access. *Cataloging & Classification Quarterly, 1* (2/3), 105–124.

Nelson, Milo. (1986). Catalogers as librarians. *Wilson Library Bulletin, 61*, 2 (October), 4.

OCLC. (1984). *OCLC annual report, 1983/84.* Dublin, OH: OCLC.

OCLC. (1991a). Libraries begin adding subject headings to fiction records in project sponsored by Library of Congress and OCLC." OCLC press release, December 6.

OCLC. (1991b). *OCLC annual report, 1990/91.* Dublin, OH: OCLC.

O'Neill, Edward T., & Aluri, Rao. (1981). Library of Congress subject heading patterns in OCLC monographic records. *Resources & Technical Services, 25*, 1 (January/March), 63–67, 70–80.

O'Neill, Edward T., & Aluri, Rao. (1979). *Subject heading patterns in OCLC monographic records.* Columbus, OH: Ohio College Library Center. OCLC Research Report series OCLC/RDD/RR-79/1.

Parker, Elisabeth Betz. (1987). *LC thesaurus for graphic materials: Topical terms for subject access.* Washington, DC: Library of Congress.

Petersen, Toni. (1983). The AAT: A model for the restructuring of LCSH. *Journal of Academic Librarianship,* 9, 4 (September), 207–210.

Pietris, Mary K. D. (1987a). Keynote address: Characteristics of LC Subject Headings that should be taken into account when designing on-line catalogues. *Cataloguing Australia, 13*, 3 (September), 70–80.

Pietris, Mary K. D. (1987b). Library of Congress Subject Headings: Past imperfect, future indicative. *Cataloguing Australia, 13,* 3 (September), 8–19.

Posey, Edwin D., & Erdmann, Charlotte A. (1986). An online UNIX-based engineering library catalog: Purdue University Engineering Library. *Science and Technology Libraries, 6*, 4, 31–43.

Pritchard, Sarah M. (1981). *SCORPIO: A study of public users of the Library of Congress information system.* Washington, DC: Library of Congress. ED 198801.

Simonds, Michael J. (1984). Database limitations and online catalogs. *Library Journal, 109*, 3 (February 15), 329–330.

Studwell, William E. (1985). Why not an 'AACR' for subject headings? *Cataloging & Classification Quarterly, 6*, 1 (Fall), 3–9.

Studwell, William E. (1987). Academic libraries and a subject heading code. *Journal of Academic Librarianship, 12* (January), 372.

Studwell, William E. (1990). Subject suggestion 6: Some concerns relating to quantity of subjects. *Cataloging & Classification Quarterly, 10*, 4, 99–104.

Van Orden, Richard. (1990). Content-enriched access to electronic information: Summaries of selected research. *Library Hi Tech, 8*, 3, 27–32.

2

Subject Authority Records in the Machine-Readable LCSH

2.1

Introduction

The printed version of *Library of Congress Subject Headings* is an alphabetical arrangement of authorized subject headings and *see* references to authorized subject headings. Both types of terms are left justified, but the former are set in bold typeface. Entries for authorized subject headings vary in length and complexity. The data elements of some entries consist of only the authorized subject heading set in bold typeface. Other entries include a lengthy scope note, several classification numbers, and dozens of related terms.

The printed page contains many visual cues—spacing, typography, indention, and layout—to help catalog users distinguish between individual entries and between data elements of individual entries printed in *LCSH*. Computer systems also need cues to make individual entries and elements of entries in the machine-readable LCSH (LCSH-mr) decipherable. These computer systems cannot use visual cues from the printed page because they cannot see, read, understand, and interpret these cues in the same way that human beings can. Visual cues must be formalized into a standardized set of symbols that computer systems can be programmed to recognize and interpret. When such symbols are applied to individual entries for subject headings, they enable computer systems to distinguish between individual entries and between their data elements. This standard set of symbols makes up the format, the formal mechanism for representing data in machine-readable form so that computer systems can be programmed to recognize and interpret the data.

A format is "like a compartmentalized container, designed to fit the data in such a way that each data element is recognizable and can be separately recalled, correlated, sorted, printed, etc." (Hagler & Simmons 1982, 109). The format used for subject headings in the LCSH system is the *USMARC Format for Authority Data* (Library of Congress 1987). (USMARC is an acronym for United States Machine-Readable Cataloging.)

USMARC is an exchange format for authority data. An exchange format is also known as a communications or interchange format. Exchange formats facilitate the exchange of records between computer systems. Systems staff program computers to receive authority data in the USMARC format. Systems staff also program computers to pick and choose among the data elements of subject authority records and store desired elements in a local processing format. (The adjectives local, in-house, and internal are used interchangeably here to refer to a local processing format.) If institutions exchange records between computer systems, systems staff must first write computer programs to convert records from the local processing format back into the exchange format. Since USMARC is a recognized standard, many library systems are already programmed to convert records from a local processing format to the USMARC format.

LC distributes name and subject authority records to subscribers in the form of a cumulative master tape of USMARC format authority records and weekly tape subscription service. Subject authority records for topical subject headings (MARC tag 150) are created and distributed exclusively by LC because subject catalogers in LC's Subject Cataloging Division are solely responsible for creating subject headings. LC's subject catalogers also establish subject headings to describe geographic areas or nonjurisdictional entities (MARC tag 151). These types of places include ancient cities, bridges, canals, estates, forests, and highways. Subject authority records for these places are included in LC's distribution service for subject authority records.

Name authority records for persons, corporate bodies, uniform titles, and jurisdictional geographic names (MARC tags 100, 110, 130, and 151, respectively) are distributed separately from subject authority records by LC. Creation of these records is done jointly by descriptive catalogers in LC's Descriptive Cataloging Division and by catalogers at libraries participating in the National Coordinated Cataloging Operations (NCCO).

The authorized headings in name authority records can be used as name and/or subject access points depending on the subject content of the item in hand. For example, the subject heading "600 Twain, Mark $d 1835-1910" would be assigned to a book on the life and times of Mark Twain. MARC tag 600 designates subject headings for personal names. Works written by Mark Twain, for example, *Huckleberry Finn, The Prince and the Pauper,* would contain a main-entry or added-entry heading tagged 100 or 700 to designate Mark Twain as the principal or joint author of these works. LC establishes only one authority record per subject or name in the subject or name authority file to eliminate duplication of effort, reduce maintenance of two separate records, and conform to the principle of uniform heading. There are exceptions. The few names of persons, corporate bodies, jurisdictions, meetings and conferences, and uniform titles that have records established in both subject and name authority files display special subdivisions, unique references, or specific instructions, or serve as pattern headings (Chan 1986, 116; Library of Congress 1990a, xvi). In this book, LCNAF denotes the machine-readable records in the Library of Congress Name Authority File.

Incorporated in online cataloging and catalog systems, machine-readable subject authority records are a tool for catalogers and catalog maintenance staff to ensure that the subject access points used in these systems are authorized subject headings. Subject authority work refers to the process of checking subject headings used in a library catalog or database against an authority file to verify that the form of entry matches the form in use in the catalog or database and that linking references are made for headings requiring them (Clack 1990, 207). Stand-alone automated library systems and modules of integrated library systems are now available to support authority work (Taylor, Maxwell, & Frost 1985; Baer & Johnson 1988; Johnston 1989, 1990).

Machine-readable subject authority records are also a tool to help end users and reference staff during subject retrieval because of the linking references made to subject headings during authority work. References guide users from synonymous terms that are not used to established subject headings (*see* references). They also suggest subjects that have a hierarchical relationship (i.e., broader or narrower terms) to the subject heading at hand. These references and other pertinent information about authorized subject headings help users determine whether they are on the right track with respect to the subject heading they are consulting. Such data occur in subject authority records with varying degrees of frequency.

This chapter describes the structure, codes, and data elements used in the USMARC format for authority data to represent the machine-readable file of subject authority records that is the LC Subject Headings (LCSH-mr). Although LCSH-mr is an important component of authority work, our emphasis is on the potential of LCSH-mr as an end user's tool for subject retrieval. Our focus is on improving subject searching.

The brief history of the USMARC format for authority data below is followed by a description of the structure, codes, and data elements used in the USMARC format for authority data. A statistical analysis of a recently produced cumulative master tape of LCSH-mr records will reveal the depth of the reference structure in LCSH-mr records and the extent to which LCSH-mr records provide references and informational data elements to guide users to other subject headings for their topics of interest that are more appropriate than the original subject headings they consulted.

2.2

Brief History of the USMARC Format for Authority Data

A detailed account of the 25-year history of USMARC formats is beyond our scope here. More comprehensive histories are given in several texts and articles (Avram 1975; Long 1984; Crawford 1989; Rather & Wiggins 1989; Gredley &

Hopkinson 1990). Below is a strictly selective overview of the development of a USMARC format for authorities.

Development of a format for representing cataloging data in machine-readable form can be traced to the 1963 King Report entitled *Automation and the Library of Congress* in which cataloging, authority file maintenance, and information retrieval were among the functions recommended for automation (King *et al.* 1963, 40–42). A private contractor, Inforonics, was supported by the Council on Library Resources (CLR) to study the conversion of LC's printed catalog cards into machine-readable form (Buckland 1965). Representatives from LC, universities, research agencies, government agencies, and private industry discussed the report of the Inforonics study at the First Conference on Machine-Readable Copy held at LC in January 1965. In response to the encouragement of conference participants, LC delegated a team of staff members headed by Henriette Avram to draft a machine-readable cataloging format. Between March and June 1965, the team drew up a preliminary draft format under the title *A proposed format for a standardized machine-readable catalog record* and solicited comments from LC, libraries with ongoing automation projects, and major library interest groups (Avram 1968, 3).

At the Second Conference on Machine-Readable Copy in November 1965, participants accepted the preliminary draft format as the basis for machine-readable records and urged LC to develop an experimental magnetic tape distribution service for such records. LC made a proposal to CLR requesting support for a conversion project, initial tape distribution service, and conferences with project participants. In December 1965, the Council responded with support of the MARC (Machine-Readable Cataloging) Pilot Project. The first test tapes sent to sixteen project participants in October and November 1966 contained both bibliographic records and cross-reference records in the MARC I format. "It soon became evident that although the cross-reference information was valuable, it was not as useful as had been anticipated because the cross-reference records were not linked to the associated catalog records" (Avram 1968, 5). Promising further investigation of cross-reference records, LC ceased production of cross-reference records in April 1967.

In March 1967, LC began a formal evaluation of the MARC I format. Drawing on its own experiences and those of project participants, LC designed the MARC II format and solicited reviews from the library community. LC formally published the specifications of the USMARC II format in January 1968 (Avram, Knapp, & Rather 1968) and began distribution of bibliographic records for English-language monographs in the USMARC II format through the MARC Distribution Service (later renamed Cataloging Distribution Service).

In 1970, LC established the MARC Development Office to develop, implement, and promote MARC-based formats, systems, and records. The American Library Association (ALA) gave the Committee on Representation in Machine-Readable Form of Bibliographic Information, an interdivisional ALA committee now known as MARBI, the responsibility of working together with LC on MARC format changes.

The preliminary version of the authorities format was first issued under the title *Authorities: A MARC format* (Library of Congress 1976). When LC began distributing name authority records in 1978 to subscribing institutions, it had already distributed over one million USMARC bibliographic records for monographs in English and other roman-alphabet languages. In 1977, LC initiated the Name Authority Cooperative (NACO) "to build an authority file in machine-readable form of the size and quality that was needed to support its bibliographic database" (Clack 1990, 18). NACO's objective was "to share the burden of producing authority data, believed to be one of the most expensive operations in bibliographic record creation" (Gredley & Hopkinson 1990, 84). NACO began with an agreement between LC and the U.S. Government Printing Office (USGPO) for USGPO-produced name authority data to be included among LC-distributed name authority records.

After a decade of NACO activity, about three dozen libraries were submitting name authority records to LC in certain categories of name headings. Two NACO participants were entering authority records directly into LC's online system. The remaining institutions had search-only access to the LCNAF through their respective bibliographic services or used manual tools such as the National Union Catalog and Name Authorities on microfilm. By the time libraries' authority work reached LC through the U.S. Postal Services, new headings might have already been established by other libraries or LC itself.

The first application of the Linked Systems Project (LSP) is direct transmission of name authority records from participating libraries through their respective bibliographic services to LC (McCallum 1985; Fenly & Wiggins 1988). Most NACO participants have been transmitting name authority records to LC through direct computer-to-computer links between RLIN (Research Libraries Information System) and LC's online system since 1985 and between OCLC and LC's online system since 1987. LSP has reduced the time required to establish a new name authority record from "months to days or hours" (Schuitema 1988, 92). "Since authority work is the most costly and labor-intensive aspect of the cataloging function, LSP has great potential for revolutionizing authority control in libraries" (Clack 1990, 29).

Although the authorities format is designed to represent in one record authority and informational data pertaining to a particular name or subject heading, cumulative master tapes are produced separately for name and subject authority records. After the preliminary edition of the authorities format was published, a cumulative master tape of an estimated 110,000 subject authority records that corresponded to subject headings in the eighth edition of the printed *LCSH* was made available to selected libraries and institutions. Institutions that mounted the tape on their online systems had to devise ways to keep the file up to date because LC offered no updating service (Rood 1991, 32).

In 1981, the authorities format was redesigned and published as the first edition to facilitate early LSP implementations (Library of Congress 1981). Changes to the first edition of the authorities format were subsequently issued as Updates No. 1 (June 1983) and No. 2 (June 1986). Although a new cumulative master tape of LC subject headings was made available to selected institutions in 1983, few mounted this file on their systems because LC still offered no tape updating service (Rood 1991, 34; Ludy 1985). Finally, in spring 1986, LC issued a cumulative master tape corresponding to the tenth edition of the printed *LCSH* and weekly tape subscription service. Shortly afterward, OCLC and RLIN mounted the machine-readable LCSH on their respective online systems. Although subject headings are not linked to the bibliographic file in either system, the online subject authority file gives library staff access to LCSH-mr records for new headings shortly after they are established, thus saving staff from time-consuming manual searches in LC's printed updates.

In 1987, LC published the *USMARC format for authority data: Including guidelines for content designation.* This publication incorporated changes to the first edition that were issued as Update No. 1 (1983) and Update No. 2 (1986) and other format changes approved in 1987. The fourth and most recent update to the *USMARC format for authority data* was issued in 1991. It reflects the results of a general review of content designation terminology, provides expanded guidelines for the application of content designators, and incorporates national-level requirements that had been published separately.

LC's first CD/ROM product, *CDMARC Subjects*, was issued in 1988. *CDMARC Subjects* allows keyword searches of LCSH-mr records and is used by subscribing libraries to perform authority work. Quarterly subscriptions to *CDMARC Subjects* are available.

In 1989, the USMARC format for authority data was augmented to accommodate classification authority data. When the library community voiced adverse reaction to the augmentation, LC created a new USMARC format for classification data that is separate from the USMARC format for authority data (Library of Congress 1991).

The future of subject authorities is evident in the recommendations of the LC Subject Subdivisions Conference (Library of Congress 1992, 7). Conference participants called for the development of a "National Authority File" in which libraries could contribute authority records for subdivided topical subject headings that do not require formal editorial review. The submission of name authority records through LSP could serve as a model for the exchange of subject authority data (Schuitema 1988). The library community could submit proposals for new subject headings and *see* references directly to LC using electronic transmission capabilities of online systems. The ability to transmit proposals electronically should encourage libraries to contribute new subject headings and increase their stake in the LCSH system, especially the future of its vocabulary.

2.3 USMARC Format for Authorities

Underlying the construction of USMARC format records are three basic elements: (1) record structure, (2) content designation, and (3) record content. Record structure involves the use of codes to identify the individual units of information in records. Examples are the three-digit tags used by USMARC formats to identify units of particular kinds of data: 150 is the three-digit tag for authorized headings for topical subjects and 680 is the three-digit tag for scope notes. Content designation involves the definition of codes used in a particular USMARC format. Record content is governed by standards, codes, and cataloging tools outside the USMARC format such as the *Anglo-American Cataloguing Rules* (AACR), *Art & Architecture Thesaurus* (AAT), and *Dewey Decimal Classification.* For example, USMARC formats for bibliographic data allow for subject terms based on the AAT to be specifically coded and represented in fields of bibliographic records; however, a cataloger is responsible for ensuring that the subject headings entered into these fields conform to AAT guidelines for heading formulation.

2.3.1 ISO 2709

USMARC records conform to an international standard adopted in 1973 by the International Standards Organization known as the ISO 2709 for the exchange of machine-readable bibliographic data. ISO 2709 is a format structure that divides the format into three distinct areas: (1) record leader (also known as a record label), (2) directory, and (3) data fields (also known as data elements or bibliographic fields). Figure 2.1 shows the pattern of these three distinct areas in USMARC records. We now turn to a discussion of these three areas with an emphasis on the USMARC format for authorities.

2.3.2 Leader in the USMARC Format for Authorities

The record leader is fixed in length at 24 character positions (00–23). It conveys information about the record itself, (e.g., the length of the record), codes to help relate this record to other records, (e.g., the status of the authorized heading as a new, corrected, or deleted heading), and codes to instruct the computer program where within the record to find certain specific kinds of data (e.g., the starting position of the first data field). Most leader data are provided automatically by the computer program when the record is created.

Leader	Directory	Data fields

Figure 2.1
USMARC format structure

Two character positions in the leader of authority records are interesting to note. Character position 6 for Type of Record is set to "z" for authority records. LC assigns a single alphabetic character "c," "d," or "n" in character position 5 of the record to designate whether the record is corrected or revised, deleted, or new, respectively.

2.3.3 Directory in the USMARC Format for Authorities

The directory facilitates computer processing of data fields in machine-readable records. It comprises a number of separate units. Each unit gives the identity, length, and location within the complete record of each data field following the directory. Data field identity is denoted by a three-digit tag. Length of the data field is given in a four-digit number. Location of the data field in the complete record is given in a five-digit number. The number of individual units corresponds to the number of data fields following the directory. Figure 2.2 shows the number of characters in the leader and units in the directory. The directory contains sample data for a variable data field given MARC tag 150 (authorized heading for topical subjects). This field is only fourteen characters long and starts on the 98th character of the record.

A field separator comes at the end of the entire directory. Since it is the first field separator to occur in the record, it conveniently introduces the location of data fields. Except for three-digit field tags, a computer program automatically compiles the directory when records are created.

2.3.4 Variable Control Fields in the USMARC Format for Authorities

Data in variable control fields are expressed in codes. The codes in variable control fields convey one or many pieces of information. For example, the control number field of subject authority records (MARC tag 001) simply tells the number, while the 008 control field of subject authority records (also known as the MARC

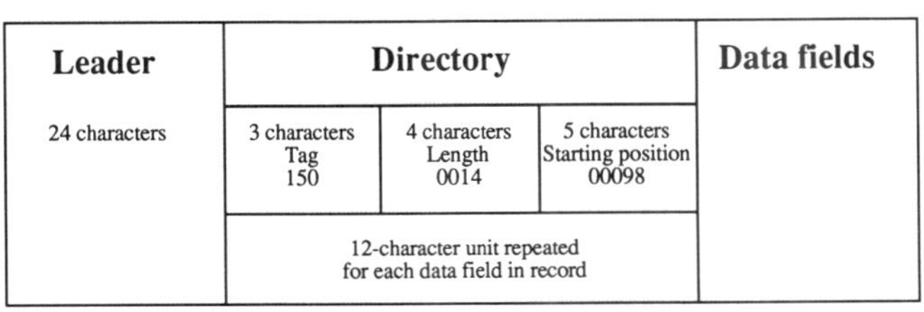

Figure 2.2
Directory in USMARC format records.

fixed field) contains 23 different fixed-length data elements. If a USMARC record were displayed in the exchange format, a user would have to consult the documentation for the MARC format for authority data to distinguish between fixed field elements because these 23 codes are added onto one another forming an undifferentiated, alphanumeric string of 40 characters. USMARC formats reserve nine data fields 000 to 009 for variable control fields. Specific variable control fields in the USMARC format for authorities are discussed below.

2.3.5 Variable Data Fields in the USMARC Format for Authorities

Data in variable data fields are expressed in text. Frequently, variable data fields are subdivided into subfields to allow for the representation of several data elements within a single field. Subfields within a field are identified through the use of subfield codes, which consist of a single letter or number immediately preceded by a delimiter sign. (A double dagger looks most like the delimiter sign. A dollar sign [$] is often used in place of the double dagger to represent the delimiter sign, because the double dagger cannot be displayed on many computer screens or printed with some word processing software.)

Subfield $a is the default for the first subfield occurring in a field of USMARC records; consequently, subfield $a does not have to be explicitly coded in USMARC records because subfield $a is always expected to be the first subfield in a field. If a subfield other than subfield $a occurs first in a field, this subfield is explicitly coded. Both the directory and each field end with a field terminator character.

Beginning each variable data field are two indicator positions. Indicators are used for several reasons: "(1) to provide additional information about a field, (2) to facilitate specific methods of data manipulation, and (3) to show relationships between one field and another" (Hagler & Simmons 1982, 136). Indicator positions are set from 0 to 9 or left blank, depending on the cataloger's response to instructions given for setting indicators in the *USMARC format for authority data* (Library of Congress 1987).

In USMARC formats, data fields numbered from 010 to 999 are reserved for variable data fields; however, many fields within this range have not yet been defined. Variable data fields used most frequently in LCSH-mr records are discussed below. A record terminator marks the end of the record, and thus is always the last character of a USMARC record.

2.3.6 USMARC Subject Authority Record in Exchange Format

When LC exports USMARC records on tape, records are formatted in the exchange format. Individual data elements are difficult to distinguish from one another because they are concatenated together into a single undifferentiated string of

```
Symbol:                      Meaning:
Pound sign (#)               Deliberately coded space
Dollar sign ($)              Subfield delimiter
Greater than symbol (>)      End-of-field delimiter
At sign (@)                  End-of-record delimiter

Numbers along the top (e.g., 0, 10, etc.) and at the left of figure
(e.g., 0, 50, 100, etc.) indicate character position


                 1         2         3         4
       0         0         0         0         0

  0    00705nz###2200193n##45000010012000000005001700012OO
 50    80041000290530019000701500024000894500025001134500
100    02500138450002300163450002200186550002200208550002
150    4002305500018002545500016002726800224002 88>sh 8502
200    8977>19930106084508.1>871218in#anannaabn##########
250    #a#ana######>00$aHG6046$bHG6051>#0$aCommodity exch
300    anges>#0$aCommodities exchange>#0$aExchanges, Comm
350    odity>#0$aExchanges, Produce>#0$aProduce exchanges
400    >#0$aFutures market$wg>#0$aCommercial products>#0$
450    aProduce trade>#0$aSpeculation>00$iHere are entere
500    d general works on commodity exchanges. Works on e
550    xchanges dealing in a single commodity or class of
600     commodities are entered under the specific commod
650    ity industry, e.g.,$aCotton trade; Grain trade;$ie
700    tc.>@
```

Figure 2.3
Authority record for "Commodity exchanges" in USMARC exchange format.

characters. Figure 2.3 shows a subject authority record for "Commodity exchanges" in the USMARC exchange format and numbers rows and columns to help readers differentiate the individual components of the record from one another.

2.3.7 USMARC Subject Authority Record in Processing Format

When the subject authority record for "Commodity exchanges" is added to the OCLC Online System, the record is converted from the USMARC exchange format into the OCLC Authority Record Internal Processing Format (ARIPF). This format facilitates record processing because it eliminates data that are not used by OCLC applications software programs.

Computer programs that display USMARC subject authority records omit most data elements from the leader. They extract MARC tags from the directory and place them immediately preceding variable data fields. Since the computer program rearranges data elements, the original location data from the directory are now meaningless, so they are eliminated from USMARC records when they are converted to ARIPF format. Data elements from the 008 control field and a few leader elements are placed in fixed fields and preceded by display constants that are abbreviated labels

```
ARN:    2023617              Rec stat:     c
Entered:     19871218        Replaced:     1990021
Type:      z          Enc lvl:      n       Source:                Lang:
Roman:                Upd status:  a        Mod rec:               Name use: b
Govt agn:             Ref status:  a        Subj:        a         Subj use: a
Series:    n          Auth status: a        Geo subd:  i           Ser use:  b
Ser num:   n          Auth/ref:     a       Name:        n         Rules:    n
   1  010         sh 85028977 ¶
   2  040         DLC $c DLC $d DLC ¶
   3  053         HG6046 $b HG6051 ¶
   4  150   0     Commodity exchanges ¶
   5  450   0     Commodities exchange ¶
   6  450   0     Exchanges, Commodity ¶
   7  450   0     Exchanges, Produce ¶
   8  450   0     Produce exchanges ¶
   9  550   0     Futures market $w g ¶
  10  550   0     Commercial products ¶
  11  550   0     Marketing ¶
  12  550   0     Produce trade ¶
  13  550   0     Speculation ¶
  14  680         $i Here are entered general works on commodity
exchanges. Works  on exchanges dealing in a single commodity or
class of commodities are entered  under the specific commodity
industry, e.g. $a Cotton trade; Grain trade; $i  etc. ¶
```

Figure 2.4
Display of "Commodity exchanges" in the OCLC Subject Authority File.

preceding fixed-field data elements. Figure 2.4 shows a display of the subject authority record for the "Commodity exchanges" in the OCLC subject authority file.

The display of the subject authority record in Figure 2.4 probably looks foreign to an observer untrained in the meaning of fixed-field display constants, MARC tags, and authority data. However, users of the OCLC subject authority file are library catalogers who become familiar with USMARC record structure, content designation—that is, the meaning of codes used to identify elements of authority records—and record content, through daily use of subject authority records on

```
Commodity exchanges
     POSSIBLE BROWSING NUMBER(S):  HG6046-HG6051   (SEARCH WITH SPS/
     Here are entered general works on commodity exchanges.  Work o
          exchanges  dealing  in  a  single  commodity  or  class  o
          commodities  are  entered  under  the  specific  commodit
          industry, e.g., Cotton trade; Grain trade; etc.
     SEARCH ALSO UNDER:
          Arbitrage (11 TITLES)
          Commercial products (65 TITLES)
          Floor traders (Finance) (2 TITLES)
          Marketing (771 TITLES)
          Produce trade (46 TITLES)
          Speculation (198 TITLES)
```

Figure 2.5
LCS display of "Commodity exchanges."

OCLC and other online systems. They can also consult USMARC and OCLC documentation to decipher new elements or infrequently used elements.

The Library Control System (LCS) online catalog of The Ohio State University Libraries displays subject authority data to system users. Figure 2.5 shows the LCS display of the subject authority record for "Commodity exchanges." Fixed-field elements are totally eliminated from the display. The only data elements included in the display are those that guide the searcher to related subject headings used in the catalog that may be more appropriate terms to express the subjects that users consult and shelf locations that may contain additional material on the searcher's topic of interest. LCS also replaces MARC tags with terminology to help searchers interpret how to use displayed data elements.

2.4 Variable Control Fields in the USMARC Format for Authorities

Data in variable control fields are expressed as codes. These fields contain one or several pieces of information. When several pieces are encoded in one variable control field, each piece is a fixed-length data element that is identifiable by its character position(s) in the control field.

Of the three variable control fields defined in the MARC format for authority data, fields 001 and 008 are used most frequently in subject authority records and thus deserve to be described further.

2.4.1 001 or 010: Library of Congress Control Number

When LC catalogers create a new subject authority record, an LC Control Number is automatically generated by LC's online system. In records distributed by LC's Cataloging Distribution Service, LC control numbers are given in control field 001 and/or variable data field 010. Organizations using USMARC records for authority data typically move the LC control number from field 001 to field 010 and use field 001 for their own control numbers (Library of Congress 1987, 010-1). Online systems that offer searching of LCSH-mr records typically index LC control numbers to enable users to retrieve one particular subject authority record.

2.4.2 008: Control Field

The 008 control field contains 23 different fixed-length data elements that are represented in 40 character positions. A few need explanation because they contain codes that signify whether or not the subject heading in the authorized heading field of the authority record (i.e., MARC tags 1xx) can or cannot be assigned to a bibliographic record.

008, Position 6: Direct/Indirect Geographic Subdivision Code

A single character code indicates whether the subject heading in the authorized heading field can be subdivided geographically. The position can be coded in three different ways. When a heading cannot be subdivided geographically, the position is left blank. Indirect subdivision is represented by an "i." Code "d" specifies direct geographic subdivision. Since the LCSH system does not use direct geographic subdivision, code "d" is not used in LCSH-mr records. Code "n" is used in conjunction with codes in position 9 and 15 of the 008 control field to designate that the subject heading in the authorized heading field cannot be assigned to bibliographic records.

Almost three quarters of LCSH-mr records contain a fill character in the Direct/Indirect Geographic Subdivision Code (Markey & Vizine-Goetz 1988, 10). The fill character is used in a field when the authority format specifies a code to be used, but the creator of the record did not attempt to supply a value. Fill characters are used in LCSH-mr records of subdivided subject headings that can be subdivided geographically. Programmers have devised techniques to "intelligently 'interpret' fill characters, i.e., determine whether indirect geographic subdivision applies to the subject heading in the authority heading field" (Markey & Vizine-Goetz 1988, 11).

008, Position 9: Kind of Record Code

A single character code indicates whether the subject heading in the authorized heading field can be assigned to bibliographic records. In subject authority records, LC uses the codes "a" to designate an authorized subject heading and "b" to designate a heading that cannot be assigned to bibliographic records. Records coded "b" also contain a complex *see* reference (MARC tag 260) to guide users to authorized subject headings.

008, Position 11: Subject Heading System/Thesaurus Code

A single-character alphabetic code identifies the subject heading system or thesaurus used to formulate the subject heading in the authorized heading field. Subject authority records bearing the code "a" are LC subject headings. Code "n" indicates that the subject heading in the authorized heading field cannot be assigned to a bibliographic record.

008, Position 15: Heading Use Code—Subject Added Entry

A single-character alphabetic code indicates whether the subject heading in the authorized heading field can be assigned to bibliographic records. The codes "a" and "b" are used to designate an authorized subject heading and a subject heading that cannot be assigned to bibliographic records, respectively.

2.5 Variable Data Fields in the USMARC Format for Authorities

Variable data fields differ from variable control fields in that they contain text. They are also as long or as short as required by their contents. Variable control fields discussed in this chapter are used most frequently in subject authority records. More information about variable data fields is given in the *USMARC format for authority data* (Library of Congress 1987) and textbooks (Byrne 1991; Crawford 1989).

2.5.1 1xx: Authorized Heading Fields

Each authority record has *one* authorized heading field (also known as established heading field). The three-digit MARC tag assigned to the authorized heading designates whether it is a personal name (100), corporate name (110), meeting or conference name (111), uniform title (130), topical subject (150), or geographic name (151). Although this field is called the authorized heading field, the codes in positions 9 and 15 of the 008 control field designate whether the subject heading in the authorized heading field of subject authority records (MARC tag 150) is an authorized heading or reference.

150: Topical Subject Headings

Four subfields are typically used for topical subject headings in the LCSH system. Main headings are given in a single subfield $a. Topical, period, and geographic subdivisions are given in repeatable subfields $x, $y, and $z, respectively. Occasionally, topical subject headings have two or more topical subdivisions. Two geographic subdivisions are common in topical subject headings because of indirect subdivision.

151: Geographic Name Headings

Three categories of subject headings for geographic names are printed in *LCSH* and distributed on LCSH-mr subscription tapes: (1) nonjurisdictional headings, (2) headings included for the purpose of displaying special subdivisions, unique references, specific instructions, and (3) pattern headings. Headings in the latter two categories often contain topical (subfield $x) and period (subfield $y) subdivisions. Main headings are given in a single subfield $a. Geographic subdivisions (subfield $z) in geographic headings are unusual because few geographic headings can be subdivided geographically.

100, 110, 111, 130: Authorized Headings for Personal, Corporate, Meeting Names, and Uniform Titles, Respectively

These four types of headings are name or title headings and can be used as main or added entries in bibliographic records (i.e., MARC tags 1xx and 7xx). They can also be used as subject headings in bibliographic records (i.e., MARC tag 6xx). Main headings are given in a single subfield $a. These headings are only included in LCSH when they are pattern headings, or special subdivisions, unique references, or specific instructions need to be displayed. Thus, topical, period, and geographic subdivisions are typically printed with these headings in *LCSH.* Authority records for most of these headings are maintained in the Library of Congress Name Authority File (LCNAF).

Subdivisions used to complete the name portion of personal name headings are:

- $b Numeration
- $c Titles and other words associated with the name
- $d Dates associated with the name
- $q Fuller form of name

Subfield $b is used for the subordinate unit of the body named in the main heading (subfield $a) portion of corporate name headings.

2.5.2 Tracings and Reference Fields

Variable data fields trace terms and names not used as subject headings to authorized subject headings. They also trace terms and names used as subject headings to other authorized subject headings and express a broader or related term relationship between the two headings in a separate subfield. Tracing fields lead directly from one heading to a single other heading. Tracing fields are repeatable fields in LCSH-mr records.

Reference note fields contain explanatory text and the headings referred to that are required when relationships exist between the heading in the authorized heading field (MARC tags 1xx) and other authorized subject headings that cannot be adequately conveyed by one or more simple cross-references generated from tracing fields. Reference note fields lead from one term or name not used as subject headings to one or several authorized headings or subdivisions. They also lead from terms and names used as subject headings to one or several other authorized headings or subdivisions.

4xx: *See from* Tracings

See from tracings are terms and names not used as subject headings that refer to authorized subject headings. *See from* tracings are made for personal names (MARC tag 400), corporate names (MARC tag 410), meeting names (MARC tag 411), uniform titles (MARC tag 430), subject terms (MARC tag 450), and geographic names (MARC tag 451). Although *see from* tracings are sometimes subdivided, the topical, period, and/or geographic subdivisions that occur with them are valid only when appended to an authorized subject heading.

5xx: *See also from* tracings

See also from tracing fields trace terms and names used as subject headings to other authorized subject headings. *See also from* tracings are made for personal names (MARC tag 500), corporate names (MARC tag 510), meeting names (MARC tag 511), uniform titles (MARC tag 530), subject terms (MARC tag 550), and geographic names (MARC tag 551). The same subdivisions used with authorized headings are used with *see also from* tracings.

The presence of a code "g" in subfield $w of *see also from* tracing fields indicates that a broader term relationship exists between the tracing and authorized heading. When this code is missing, a related term relationship exists between the tracing and authorized heading. The *USMARC format for authority data* authorizes the use of code "h" in subfield $w in *see also from* tracing fields to designate narrower terms; however, LC does not explicitly code narrower terms with code "h." Libraries generate narrower terms from the reciprocals of *see also from* tracings bearing codes "g" in subfield $w using a computer program. For example, the subject authority record for "Commodity exchanges" shown in Figure 2.4 contains five *see also from* tracings (MARC tag 550). Code "g" in subfield $w of MARC field 550 accompanies one of the five, "Futures market." This coding designates that a broader term relationship exists between the tracing "Futures market" and the subject heading "Commodity exchanges" in the authorized heading field. A computer program would add "Commodity exchanges" as a narrower term to the subject authority record in which "Futures market" is given in the authorized heading field.

The *USMARC format for authority data* does not define a separate field for narrower terms. Libraries can add narrower terms in a MARC field tagged 550 with subfield $w coded "h." They can also place narrower terms in a local data field that has not been defined for use in USMARC formats.

If tracings and references are to be used for searching a bibliographic file, the computer program must also determine whether they are used in the bibliographic file. Otherwise, local authority records will refer searchers to terms that are not posted in the bibliographic file, that is, blind references.

260: Complex *See* Reference

This field contains explanatory text and the headings referred to that are required when relationships exist between an unused subject term in the authorized heading field (MARC tags 1xx) and authorized subject headings that cannot be adequately conveyed by one or more simple *see* references generated from *see from* tracing fields (MARC tags 4xx). Explanatory text and instructions are given in subfield $i and authorized subject headings are given in subfield $a. When LCSH-mr records contain complex *see* reference notes, code b is given in position 9 of the 008 variable control field to indicate that the subject in the authorized heading field (MARC tags 1xx) does not contain an authorized subject heading.

360: Complex *See Also* Reference

This field contains explanatory text and the headings referred to that are required when relationships exist between the authorized subject heading in the authorized heading field (MARC tags 1xx) and authorized subject headings that cannot be adequately conveyed by one or more simple *see also* references generated from *see also from* tracing fields (MARC tags 5xx). Explanatory text and instructions are given in subfield $i and authorized subject headings are given in subfield $a.

2.5.3 Remaining Variable Data Fields

040: Cataloging Source Fields

This field contains the National Union Catalog (NUC) symbol of the organization(s) that created the original record, assigned USMARC content designation, and transcribed the record into machine-readable form, or modified an existing machine-readable record. LC is responsible for LCSH-mr records, and, thus, this field gives LC's NUC symbol.

053: LC Classification Number

This field contains a single LC classification number or a range of numbers associated with the subject heading in the authorized heading field. Three subfields can be used in this field: (1) subfield $a for a single number or beginning number of a range, (2) subfield $b for the end number of a range, and (3) subfield $c containing a term or phrase that describes the subject of the classification number. Each classification number or range is specified in a separate 053 field.

670, 675: Source Data Fields

Source data fields contain a citation to reference sources for information about the heading being established. Source data found fields (MARC tag 670) give a citation to reference sources for information about the heading being established. If there are more than one source data found fields in an LCSH-mr record, the source data found field listed first contains the citation for the work for which the heading is being established. Two subfields are used in this field: subfield $a contains the citation to the source and subfield $b contains a parenthetical statement of the information found in the source.

Source data not found fields (MARC tag 675) refer to a source consulted by a cataloger in which no information was given about the heading being established. A single field may contain multiple citations to consulted sources. Each source citation is given in a separate subfield $a.

680: Scope Note

Scope notes "limit the scope of a heading as used in the catalog, thereby helping readers to determine to what extent it covers the material they seek, and making it possible for catalogers to maintain consistency in assigning the heading to new works being cataloged" (Library of Congress 1990b, H400-1). Scope notes use subfield $a for subject headings and subfield $i for instructions.

681: Subject Example Tracing Note

This field "documents the use of the 1xx subject heading or subdivision term in an established heading record or a subdivision record as an example or reference in 260 complex *see* reference, 360 complex *see also* reference, and/or 680 scope note fields of another authorized heading or reference record" (Library of Congress 1987, 681-1). The headings traced in this field are listed after the designation "e.g." in complex *see* and *see also* references (MARC tags 260 and 360), respectively, and in most scope notes (MARC tag 680).

2.6 Variable Data Fields Used in the Machine-Readable LCSH

2.6.1 Introduction

Having looked at the structure and content designation of USMARC records for authority data, we now consider what information is typically supplied in a subject authority record in LCSH-mr. This section answers questions about the extent to which subject authority records provide scope notes, *see from* tracings, related terms, and other useful information about authorized subject headings. In an information retrieval environment, such information is helpful to subject searchers because it enables them to find additional subject headings to express their topics of interest and tells them whether the subject heading they are consulting fits their purposes.

Statistics on LCSH-mr records were obtained by analyzing a cumulative master tape containing 160,706 subject authority records created or modified through July 6, 1987. This version of LCSH-mr almost corresponds to the eleventh edition of the printed *LCSH*, which contains headings and references established by LC through August 1987.

Understanding the cross-reference structure of LCSH-mr (because a concern of this book is integrating LCSH-mr) is a necessary step in integrating LCSH-mr and its term relationships into online systems. Computer programs were written and implemented to generate *see also* references from *see also from* tracings, that is, terms coded 5xx, and to add these references to LCSH-mr records. The following designations are used for *see also* references in subsequent discussions of LCSH-mr records:

- Local tag 900: *See also* references for personal names
- Local tag 910: *See also* references for corporate names

- Local tag 911: *See also* references for conference and meeting corporate names
- Local tag 930: *See also* references for uniform titles
- Local tag 950: *See also* references for topical subjects
- Local tag 951: *See also* references for geographic names

See also references consist of narrower terms (i.e., references generated from tracings in MARC fields tagged 5xx with code "g" in subfield $w), and related terms (i.e., references generated from tracings in MARC fields tagged 5xx with no subfield $w present).

Figure 2.6 shows the percentages of the six different types of authorized subject headings in LCSH-mr. Most (80.4%) LCSH-mr records contain topical subject headings. Geographic names account for 12.0% of LCSH-mr records. The four remaining types of authorized subject headings for names and titles total to less than 8% of LCSH-mr records. These headings are only included in LCSH when they are pattern headings, or when special subdivisions, unique references, or specific instructions need to be displayed. A closer look at the composition of LCSH-mr records for topical subject headings and geographical names will be helpful.

2.6.2 Subject Heading Records

Table 2.1 presents statistics on the use of variable data fields in LCSH-mr records for topical subject headings. The first column enumerates the number of records bearing the individually tagged fields listed on the fourth column; the second column lists the percentages of records that contain one or more fields of this type, and the third column cites occurrences of the particular field divided by the total number of subject heading records. This table excludes statistics for 831 subject heading records bearing complex *see* references (MARC tag 260) because the sub-

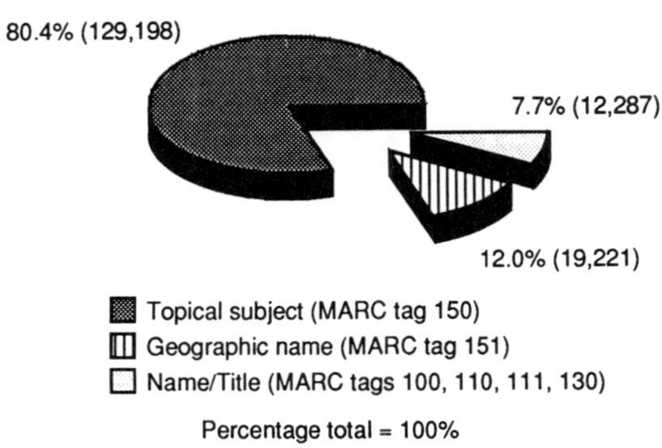

Figure 2.6
Types of authorized subject headings.

Table 2.1
Variable Data Fields in Topical Subject Heading Records

Number	Records (%)	Occur./ records	Tag	Variable data field
128,367	100.0	1.00	001	Control number
128,367	100.0	1.00	040	Cataloging source
62,587	43.0	0.49	053	LC classification number
128,367	100.0	1.00	150	Authorized heading for topical subjects
3,034	2.4	0.02	360	Complex *see also* reference
545	0.2	0.00	400–430	*See from* tracing for names
96,980	42.5	0.76	450	*See from* tracing for topical subjects
277	0.2	0.00	451	*See from* tracing for geographic names
585	0.4	0.00	500–530	*See also from* tracing for names
139,355	61.2	1.09	550	*See also from* tracing for topical subjects
2,903	1.8	0.02	551	*See also from* tracing for geographic names
10,676	4.4	0.08	670	Source data found note
1,306	1.0	0.01	675	Source data not found note
3,309	2.4	0.03	680	Subject scope note
5,161	4.0	0.04	681	Subject example tracing note
2,008	0.9	0.02	900–930	*See also* reference for names
139,233	29.7	1.09	950	*See also* reference for topical subjects
10,056	2.6	0.08	951	*See also* reference for geographic names

ject terms in the authorized subject heading field of these records are not used as subject headings.

An average of 6.73 variable data fields per LCSH-mr record for topical subjects is obtained by adding the third column of Table 2.1. Seven variable data fields contribute most of the fields to topical subject heading records: (1) LC control number (1.00) (MARC tag 001), (2) cataloging source (1.00) (MARC tag 040), (3) authorized heading (1.00) (MARC tag 150), (4) *see from* tracing for topical subjects (0.76) (MARC tag 450), (5) *see also from* tracing for topical subjects (1.09) (MARC tag 550), (6) *see also* reference for topical subjects (1.09) (local tag 950), and (7) LC classification number (0.49) (MARC tag 053). A subject heading fitting this profile is "Hydrological forecasting":

001 sh85063452
040 DLC
053 GB845
150 Hydrological forecasting
450 Hydrology $x Forecasting
550 Earth sciences $x Forecasting
950 Flood forecasting

Topical subject heading records average about one *see also* reference per record. However, not all topical subject heading records contain cross-references because percentages in the second column of Table 2.1 fall well short of 100.0% for cross-reference fields. Even though a total of 139,233 *see also* references occur in 128,367 LCSH-mr records for topical subjects, these references are found in only 29.7% of subject heading records. Thus, over 70% of LCSH-mr records contain no *see also* references. *See from* tracings and *see also from* tracings for topical subjects (MARC tags 451 and 551) occur in 42.5 and 61.2% of subject heading records, respectively. Subject heading records that contain tracings usually contain many tracing fields.

Less than 5% of LCSH-mr records for topical subject headings contain any of the remaining variable data fields for notes and references. Scope notes are found in only 2.4% of subject heading records. Cross-references other than those for topical subjects (i.e., MARC tags x50) rarely occur among the 128,367 topical subject heading records. Complex *see also* references are scarce, occurring in only 2.4% of subject heading records. Source data notes are also rare.

2.6.3 Geographic Name Records

Table 2.2 presents statistics on the use of variable data fields in LCSH-mr records for geographic name headings. The first column enumerates the number of records bearing the individually tagged fields listed on the fourth column; the second column lists the percentages of records that contain one or more fields of this type, and the third cites occurrences of the particular field divided by the total number of subject heading records. This table excludes statistics for three geographic name records bearing complex *see* references (MARC tag 260) because the places named in the authorized subject heading field of these records are not valid for use as subject headings.

An average of 5.0 variable data fields per LCSH-mr record for topical subject headings is obtained by adding the third column of Table 2.2. The five variable data fields contributing most of the fields to topical subject heading records are: (1) LC control number (1.00) (MARC tag 001), (2) cataloging source (1.00) (MARC tag

Table 2.2
Variable Data Fields in Geographic Name Records

Number	Records (%)	Occur./ records	Tag	Variable data field
19,218	100.0	1.00	001	Control number
19,218	100.0	1.00	040	Cataloging source
2,102	10.3	0.11	053	LC classification number
19,218	100.0	1.00	151	Authorized heading for geographic names
22	0.1	0.00	360	Complex *see also* reference
321	0.2	0.00	400–430	*See from* tracing for names
666	2.3	0.04	450	*See from* tracing for topical subjects
9,043	24.5	0.47	451	*See from* tracing for geographic names
20	0.1	0.00	500–530	*See also from* tracing for names
10,085	38.5	0.53	550	*See also from* tracing for topical subjects
2,532	12.4	0.13	551	*See also from* tracing for geographic names
6,204	12.9	0.32	670	Source data found note
1,415	7.4	0.07	675	Source data not found note
196	1.0	0.01	680	Subject scope note
292	1.5	0.02	681	Subject example tracing note
301	0.2	0.02	900–930	*See also* reference for names
2,894	5.9	0.15	950	*See also* reference for topical subjects
2,514	4.6	0.13	951	*See also* reference for geographic names

040), (3) authorized heading for geographic names (1.00) (MARC tag 151), (4) *see from* tracing for geographic names (0.47) (MARC tag 450), and (5) *see also from* tracing for topical subjects (0.53) (MARC tag 550). These five fields are a typical profile of many geographic name records. Two examples fitting this profile are shown in which authorized geographic names are accompanied by one *see from tracing* for an alternative form of the authorized name and one *see also from* tracing for a topical subject heading that describes the place as a geographic feature and thus is designated as a broader term in subfield $w.

001	sh 85073972	001	sh 85073824
040	DLC $c DLC	040	DLC $c DLC
151	Laguna Madre (Tex.)	151	Lachine Canal (Quebec)
451	Madre, Laguna (Tex.)	451	Canal de Lachine (Quebec)
550	Estuaries $z Texas $w g	550	Canals $z Quebec (Province) $w g

Cross-reference fields are not very prevalent in geographic name records. About one quarter (24.5%) of geographic name records contain *see from* tracings. Almost two of every five records (38.5%) contain *see also from* tracings for topical subjects. Percentages of *see also* references are quite low (i.e., below 6.0%).

Note fields occur infrequently in geographic name records. About 10% contain LC classification numbers; source data found and not found notes occur in 12.9 and 7.4% of geographic name records, respectively. Scope notes and complex *see also* references are also scarce.

2.6.4 Cross-Reference Structure

The availability of cross-references in alphabetical subject catalogs mitigates the adverse effects of the principles of uniform heading, specific and direct entry, and alphabetical arrangement. Cross-references carry the burden of guiding users to relevant material on their topics of interest.

Cross-reference fields in LCSH-mr records are examined in this section. MARC tags identify cross-references for complex references (MARC tags 260 and 360), and *see from* and *see also from* tracings (MARC tags 4xx and 5xx). Coding in subfield $w of *see also from* tracing fields designates some *see also from* tracings as broader terms and other tracings as related terms. Computer programs are required to interpret coding in subfield $w of *see also from* tracing fields and to generate narrower terms from the reciprocals of *see also from* tracings.

2.6.4.1 Complex *See* References

All but six of the 837 complex *see* references occurring in LCSH-mr records are given in subject heading records (MARC tag 150). Subject heading records with complex *see* reference fields average just four fields: (1) LC control number (MARC tag 001), (2) cataloging source (MARC tag 040), (3) authorized heading field for subjects (MARC tag 150), and (4) complex *see* reference (MARC tag 260). Although complex *see* references are repeatable fields in the USMARC format for authorities, no record contains more than one occurrence of these fields. Scope notes and source data found fields occur in these records but only rarely.

Complex *see* references are composed of subfields for instructions (i.e., subfield $i), and for subject headings referred to in instructions (i.e., subfield $a). Subfields for subject headings (subfield $a) refer searchers to one or more of five types of references: (1) subdivisions, (2) unsubdivided subject headings that begin with a certain word or phrase, (3) examples of unsubdivided subject headings, (4) examples of subdivided subject headings, and (5) subdivided subject headings that are examples of the subdivision(s) referred to elsewhere in the reference. The imperative "see" is implied preceding the instructions and references in the examples of the five types of complex *see* references that follow:

1. Term in the authorized heading field:
   150 Enlistment
   Complex *see* reference to subdivision(s):
   260 $i subdivision $a Recruiting, enlistment, etc. $i under names of individual military services
2. Term in the authorized heading field:
   150 British–Dutch War . . .
   Complex *see* reference to unsubdivided subject headings beginning with a certain word or phrase:
   260 $i subject headings beginning with the words $a Anglo-Dutch War
3. Term in the authorized heading field:
   150 Ecclesiastical rites and ceremonies
   Complex *see* reference to example(s) of unsubdivided subject headings:
   260 $i particular rites and ceremonies, e.g., $a Funeral rites and ceremonies; Lord's Supper
4. Term in the authorized heading field:
   150 Precolumbian art
   Complex *see* reference to example(s) of subdivided subject headings:
   260 Indians--Art; Indians of Mexico--Art; Indians of Central America--Art; $i and similar headings
5. Term in the authorized heading field:
   150 Instrumental settings
   Complex *see* reference to subdivided subject headings that are examples of the subdivision(s) referred to elsewhere in the reference:
   260 $i subdivision $a Instrumental settings $i under headings for vocal music, e.g., $a Folk-songs--Instrumental settings; Operas--Instrumental settings; Spirituals (Songs)--Instrumental settings

Subject example tracing notes (MARC tag 681) for authorized subject headings contain tracings from subject headings referred to in complex *see* references when subject headings are preceded by "e.g." in these references. Thus, subject headings preceded by the "e.g." in Examples 3 and 5 above would be traced in subject heading records. Subject headings referred to in complex *see* references in Examples 1, 2, and 4 above are not necessarily traced in other LCSH-mr records. References are not traced when they are made to subject headings beginning with certain words or phrases because there are no authority records under which to put such tracings (Example 2). In Example 4, the "e.g." designation does not precede example subject headings, thus, they are not traced in authority records. Complex *see* references are also not traced when references are made to subdivisions because LCSH-mr does not contain authority records for subdivisions (Examples 1 and 5).

When deciding whether to display complex *see* references to catalog users, library and systems staff need to consider two issues: (1) adding a display constant such as "see" or "search under" before references to make them understandable, and (2) ensuring that the subject headings traced in these references are used in the catalog. With respect to the first issue, the phrase "*See* names of exploring expeditions" under the subject term "Polar expeditions" would probably make more sense to a catalog user than this phrase without display constant, that is, "names of exploring expeditions." Handling the second issue is much more complex. An estimated 1500 references to subject headings and subdivisions are given in the complex *see* references of about 800 subject authority records (Markey & Vizine-Goetz 1989, 41). Online systems must have capabilities to enable library staff to find authority records with complex *see* references, search for the subject headings and subdivisions in these references, and replace blind references in these references with used references in the catalog. Review of the headings traced in complex *see* references is an ongoing process because the catalog's authority and bibliographic files are constantly changing due to new records, deleted records, and changes to records.

2.6.4.2 Complex *See Also* References

Complex *see also* references are not common, occurring in only 2.4% of subject heading records (Table 2.1) and 0.1% of geographic name records (Table 2.2). Over 98% of the complex *see also* references occurring in LCSH-mr records come from subject authority records (MARC tag 150). What is most interesting about subject authority records with complex *see also* references is how large these records are in terms of variable data fields. They average about eighteen variable data fields for: (1) one LC control number (MARC tag 001), (2) one cataloging source (MARC tag 040), (3) one LC classification number (MARC tag 053), (4) one authorized heading field for subjects (MARC tag 150), (5) one complex *see also* reference (MARC tag 360), (6) about two *see from* tracings for subjects (MARC tag 450), (7) between two and three *see also from* tracings for subjects (MARC tag 550), and (8) almost nine *see also* references for subjects (local tag 950). Subject heading records with complex *see also* references that come close to fitting this profile are "Brakes," "Drugs--Administration," "Naval History," "Pathology, Cellular," and "Terms and phrases."

Complex *see also* references bear subfields for subject headings (subfield $a) that refer searchers to one or more of four types of references: (1) subdivisions, (2) unsubdivided subject headings that begin with a certain word or phrase, (3) subdivided subject headings that are examples of the subdivisions(s) referred to elsewhere in the reference, and (4) unsubdivided subject headings in which a certain word or phrase is usually embedded in parentheses. A few complex *see also* references remain that guide searchers to examples of unsubdivided subject headings, but LC is now converting these examples to simple *see also from* tracings in LCSH-mr records. The imperative "see" is implied preceding the instructions and references in the examples of the four types of complex *see also* references that follow:

1. Authorized subject heading:
   150 Armored troops
   Complex *see also* reference to subdivision(s):
   360 $i subdivision $a Armored troops $i under individual military services; and subdivision $a Armed Forces--Armored troops $i under names of countries
2. Authorized subject heading:
   150 Chemistry
   Complex *see also* reference to unsubdivided subject headings beginning with a certain word or phrase:
   360 $i subject headings beginning with the word $a Chemical
3. Authorized subject heading:
   150 Hormone therapy
   Complex *see also* reference to subdivided subject headings that are examples of the subdivisions referred to elsewhere in the reference:
   360 $i subdivision $a Therapeutic use $i under specific hormones and groups of hormones, e.g., $a Estrogen--Therapeutic use; Steroid hormones--Therapeutic use
4. Authorized subject heading:
   150 Islam
   Complex *see also* reference to a certain word or phrase in unsubdivided subject heading(s):
   360 $i special headings with $a Islam $i added in parentheses, e.g., $a Angels (Islam); $i and subdivision $a Islam $i under special topics, e.g., $a Mysticism--Islam; $i also headings beginning with the words $a Islamic $i and $a Muslim

Subject example tracing notes (MARC tag 681) for authorized subject headings contain tracings from subject headings referred to in complex *see also* references when subject headings are preceded by "e.g." in these references. Thus, subject headings preceded by the "e.g." in Examples 3 and 4 would be traced in subject heading records. References are not traced when they are made to subject headings beginning with certain words or phrases because there are no authority records under which to put such tracings (Examples 2 and 4). Complex *see also* references are also not traced when references are made to subdivisions because LCSH-mr does not contain authority records for subdivisions (Examples 1, 3, and 4).

Displaying complex *see also* references to catalog users requires library and systems staff to resolve the same issues they have to address in working with complex *see* references, that is, using display constants with such references and deblinding cross-references. Complex *see also* references occur with greater frequency than complex *see* references. Over 7000 references to subject headings and subdivisions are given in the complex *see also* references of almost 3000 subject authority records (Markey & Vizine-Goetz 1989, 44). Thus, replacing unused headings and subdivisions in these records with terms used in the library's database will require a more substantial work effort than that required by complex *see* references.

2.6.4.3 Broader and Narrower Terms

See also from tracing fields (MARC tags 5xx) contain two types of term relationships: related and broader terms. The latter relationship is designated by the presence of code "g" in subfield $w of these fields. The number of related and broader terms in LCSH-mr is listed in Table 2.3, which also gives the percentages of *see also from* tracing fields that are related or broader terms and the occurrences of each field per LCSH-mr record.

Except for personal name *see also from* tracings, most *see also from* tracings in LCSH-mr records are broader terms. Broader terms for topical subjects are the most common type, and broader terms for geographic names are the next most common type. Of related terms, those for topical subjects are the most common type, followed by related terms for personal names.

Statistics on broader and related terms are given for all LCSH-mr records because they give a complete picture of the reference structure. If statistics are restricted to a certain type of established heading field in the LCSH-mr file, the reference structure would not be complete because subject headings in the established heading field of subject authority records have relationships with headings that are not of the same type. An example of a subject authority record bearing references of a different type than the subject heading in the established heading field is the record for "Niagara River (N.Y. and Ont.)":

151 Niagara River (N.Y. and Ont.)
550 Rivers $z New York (State) $w g
550 Rivers $z Ontario $w g

The subject heading in the established heading field is a geographic subject heading (MARC tag 151). The two *see also from* tracings are topical subject headings

Table 2.3
Related and Broader *See Also from* Tracings

Tag	Occur. of broader terms	(%) of Refs.	Occur./ Records	Occur. of related terms	(%) of Refs.	Occur. record	Total no. of refs.
500	349	15.7	.00	1,876	84.3	.01	2,225
510	394	96.3	.00	15	3.7	.00	409
511	0	0.0	.00	0	0.0	.00	0
530	139	93.3	.00	10	6.7	.00	149
550	134,452	88.9	.84	16,800	11.1	.10	151,252
551	5,596	97.5	.04	142	2.5	.00	5,738
Total	140,930	88.2	.88	18,843	11.8	.12	159,773

(MARC tag 550). The presence of code "g" in subfield $w in both *see also from* tracing fields indicates that a broader term relationship exists between the subject heading in the established heading field and the two *see also from* tracings.

Narrower terms can be generated from the reciprocals of *see also from* tracings bearing code "g" in subfield $w. From every broader term can be generated a narrower term in the authority record of the listed broader term. Consider the two *see also from* tracings in the geographic name record for "Niagara River (N.Y. and Ont.)":

151 Niagara River (N.Y. and Ont.)
550 Rivers $z New York (State) $w g
550 Rivers $z Ontario $w g

Both *see also from* tracings for "Rivers" are coded as broader terms. Thus, the heading "Niagara River (N.Y. and Ont.)" may be added as a narrower term to the topical subject authority records for these two "Rivers" headings. (The local tag 951 is used in the examples below to designate a narrower term for geographic names.)

1. 150 Rivers $z New York (State)
   951 Niagara River (N.Y. and Ont.)
2. 150 Rivers $z Ontario
   951 Niagara River (N.Y. and Ont.)

Table 2.4 gives the number of *see also* references generated from *see also from* tracing fields of LCSH-mr records and divides these references into related and narrower terms. It gives the percentages of *see also* references coded as related or narrower terms and cites the occurrences of related and narrower terms in LCSH-mr records.

Related terms in *see also* reference fields (tags 9xx) are the same terms as the related terms in *see also from* tracing fields (MARC tags 5xx). Thus, occurrences of related terms in individually tagged MARC fields for *see also from* tracings (center

Table 2.4
Related and Narrower *See Also* References

Tag	Occur. of narrower terms	(%) of Refs.	Occur./ Records	Occur. of related terms	(%) of Refs.	Occur. record	Total no. of refs.
900	642	25.5	.00	1,876	74.5	.01	2,518
910	1,653	99.1	.01	15	0.9	.00	1,668
911	33	100.0	.00	0	0.0	.00	33
930	251	96.2	.00	10	3.8	.00	261
950	125,905	88.2	.79	16,800	11.8	.10	142,705
951	12,446	98.9	.08	142	1.1	.00	12,588
Total	140,930	88.2	.88	18,843	11.8	.12	159,773

column of Table 2.3) and in individually tagged local fields for *see also* references (center column of Table 2.4) are the same.

Occurrences of narrower terms in individually tagged local fields for *see also* references (far left-hand column of Table 2.4) are different from occurrences of broader terms in individually tagged MARC fields for *see also from* tracings (far left-hand column of Table 2.3). Differences are due to subject headings in established heading fields of subject authority records that have relationships with headings that are not of the same type. The subject heading "Niagara River (N.Y. and Ont.)" was discussed earlier in this chapter as an example of a geographic subject heading (MARC tag 151) that had two broader terms of a different type, that is, broader terms for topical subjects (MARC tag 550). Table 2.4 gives a lower number of narrower terms for topical subjects than the number of broader-term references in Table 2.3. It also gives higher numbers of narrower terms for all other types of subject headings (i.e., uniform titles and personal, corporate, meeting, and geographic names) than the number of broader-term references in Table 2.3. Narrower terms for topical subjects are the most frequently occurring type of narrower-term reference. In fact, the number of narrower terms for topical subjects (tag 950) is at least ten times greater than the number of narrower terms for all other types of subject headings.

When libraries augment LCSH-mr records with narrower terms, they would generate narrower terms only for those headings posted in their bibliographic file. Generating narrower terms from *all* broader terms in LCSH-mr records would occasionally result in the creation of blind references. Such references would lead catalog users to subject headings that are not used in the catalog.

2.6.4.4 Orphan Headings

Several definitions of orphan headings are possible. One definition of an orphan heading is a subject heading that has no parents, that is, no broader terms. A second definition is a subject heading that has no parents and no children, that is, no broader terms and no narrower terms.

The third and fourth definitions address the ability of LCSH to guide the searcher to any other established subject heading(s) or shelf locations(s). In the third definition, authority records bearing one or more fields for established headings (MARC tags 1xx) and zero or one or more *see from* tracings (MARC tag 4xx), source data notes (MARC tags 670 or 675), and subject example tracing note (MARC tag 681) do not direct searchers to other subject headings or shelf locations. The fourth definition is the same as the third definition but it includes authority records bearing LC classification number fields (MARC tag 053) because these fields do not guide searchers to shelf locations in libraries using the Dewey Decimal Classification (DDC).

Briefly, the four definitions of orphan headings are subject headings that do not have: (1) parents (i.e., no broader terms), (2) parents and children (i.e., no broader or narrower terms), (3) fields that refer to other subject headings or shelf locations,

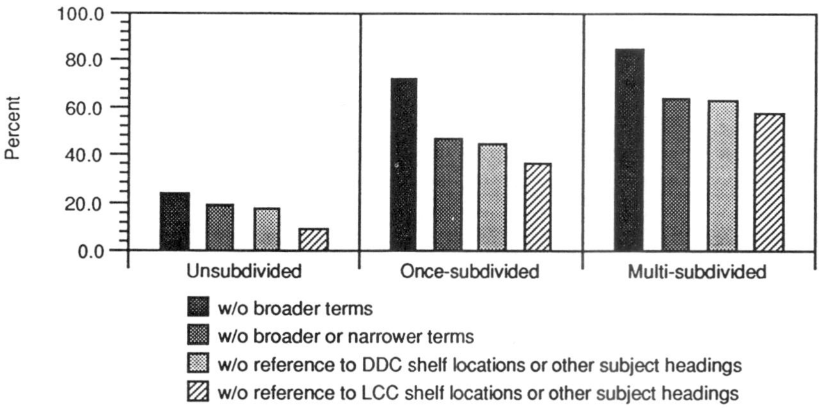

Figure 2.7
Percentages of orphan headings for topical subjects (MARC tag 150).

or (4) fields that refer to other subject headings. Figure 2.7 shows percentages of orphan headings for unsubdivided subject headings, once-subdivided subject headings, and subject headings subdivided by two or more subdivisions. Figure 2.8 shows percentages of orphan headings for geographic names depending on the extent to which the names are subdivided.

Figures 2.7 and 2.8 show that percentages of orphan headings increase as the length of headings increases. Percentages of orphan headings are lowest for unsubdivided headings and highest for headings with two or more subdivisions.

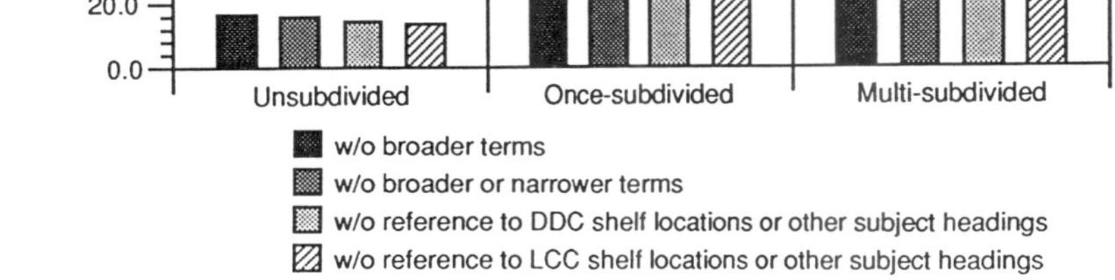

Figure 2.8
Percentages of orphan headings for geographic names (MARC tag 151).

Findings about orphan headings tell us that the subject authority records for few subdivided headings are going to contain references and notes. However, references and notes under the unsubdivided form of the subdivided heading also pertain to subdivided headings. In the printed *LCSH*, references and notes are easy to find because they are printed immediately before subdivided headings. In an information retrieval environment, references and notes are not apparent because they are contained in different authority records than the heading consulted. Online systems must be programmed to help users find and use this information in their ongoing search.

2.6.4.5 *See from* Tracings

See from tracings are terms and names not used as subject headings that refer to authorized subject headings. Figure 2.9 shows the percentages of topical subject headings and geographic names of various lengths that have no *see from* tracings.

About 50% of unsubdivided topical subject headings and geographic names contain no *see from* tracings. Percentages for subdivided headings are much higher. *See from* tracings are particularly scarce for subdivided geographic names. Findings about subdivided *see from* tracings are not unexpected because subdivided headings express complex subjects in which *see from* tracings are given once, usually in the authority record for the unsubdivided form of the subject heading.

2.6.5 LC Classification Numbers

LC classification numbers are not truly cross-references in that they do not direct users to other subject headings. In libraries arranged by LC classification, these

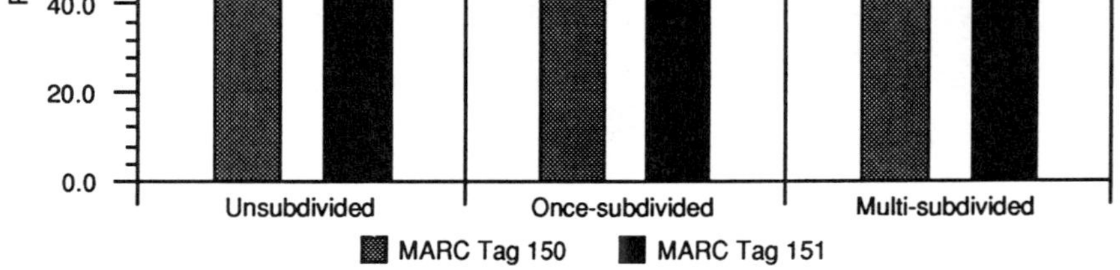

Figure 2.9
Records without *see from* tracings.

numbers do, however, direct users to shelf locations where material on subjects is found. The number and percentages of LC classification numbers in subject heading and geographic name records appear in Table 2.5.

LC classification numbers do not occur in 57.0% of subject heading records and 89.7% of geographic name records. When they do occur in LCSH-mr records, there are from one to ten LC classification numbers per record. However, most of the time only one class number occurs, that is, in about 90% of subject heading records and 95% of geographic name records.

Figure 2.10 shows the 21 broad classes of the LC Classification (LCC) combined into three categories: (1) science and technology, (2) language, literature, and the arts, and (3) social sciences. About half of LCC numbers fall into the science and technology category. Remaining LCC numbers are split between the two other categories. The largest single contributors of LC classification numbers are the Q, M, and T classes for Science (26.4%), Music (10.6%), and Technology (9.7%).

Previous card and online catalog studies have demonstrated that patrons often find a few items on their topics, jot down their call numbers, then search the bookshelves to find the exact items and similar material located nearby (Markey 1984; Willard & Teece 1983; Prabha, Rice, & Cameron 1988). Searchers looking for known items also enlist this strategy (Hancock 1987). Displays of local subject authority records should include LC classification numbers to direct catalog users to one or more shelf locations where there is library material on their topics of interest. The problem with these numbers is that they may not be current because LC's Subject Cataloging Division has not maintained the integrity of this information: "If the subject heading was established in 1921 and never revised, then the class number listed with it in the Subject Authority File has not been revised, even though a better number may have been found to arrange the subject in a classified sequence" (Cochrane & Markey 1985, 100). To rectify this problem, LC has an ongoing project to review and update LC classification numbers (Pietris 1987, 16).

Table 2.5
Occurrences of LC Classification Number Fields

	Number of occurrences			
	0	1	2	3–10
Subject heading records (MARC tag 150)				
No. records	73,143	49,401	4673	1150
(%)	57.0	38.5	3.6	0.9
(%) > 1	N/A	89.5	8.5	2.0
Geographic name records (MARC tag 151)				
No. Records	17,240	1,884	76	6
(%)	89.7	9.8	0.4	0.1
(%) > 1	N/A	95.3	3.8	0.9

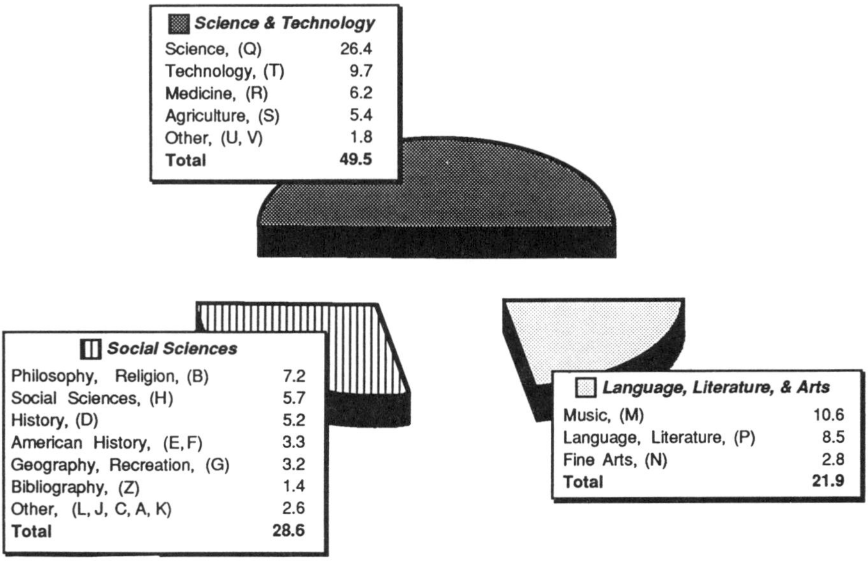

Figure 2.10
Broad categories of LCC numbers.

Some online catalog system designers have chosen to display LC classification numbers in local subject authority records. For example, the LCS online catalog at The Ohio State University Libraries displays LC classification numbers in local subject authority records and accompanies them with a brief message informing users how to search for these numbers in the catalog (see Figure 2.5) (Logan 1987).

Classification numbers in retrieved records can be used to help catalog searchers find additional bibliographic records. Operational systems enlist an approach in which they employ a classification number found in a single record judged relevant by the catalog user (Walker & De Vere 1990, 29; Markey 1990; Hildreth 1991). Experimental and prototype systems enlist an approach in which systems suggest classification numbers based on their frequency in retrieved records (Walker & De Vere 1990, 79; Vizine-Goetz 1990). These two approaches are likely to guide users to additional relevant material on their topics of interest because system-suggested classification numbers are based on assignment of classification numbers to records in the bibliographic database, not on the classification numbers suggested in LC-produced subject authority records.

2.6.6 Scope Notes

Scope notes explain the scope of a heading as used in the catalog, thereby helping users to determine whether the subject heading is appropriate for finding material on the topics they seek. Occasionally, scope notes suggest other headings that may be more appropriate for expressing users' topics of interest.

Scope notes are not common, occurring in only 2.4% of subject heading records (Table 2.1) and 1.0% of geographic name records (Table 2.2). Over 90% of the scope notes occurring in LCSH-mr records come from records for topical subjects (MARC tag 150). What is most interesting about topical subject heading records with scope notes is how large these records are in terms of variable data fields. These records average about fourteen variable data fields for: (1) one control number (MARC tag 001), (2) one cataloging source (MARC tag 040), (3) one LC classification number (MARC tag 053), (4) one authorized heading field for subjects (MARC tag 150), (5) about two *see from* tracings for subjects (MARC tag 450), (6) two *see also from* tracings for subjects (MARC tag 550), (7) one scope note, and (8) almost five *see also* references for subjects (local tag 950). Scope notes are repeatable fields in authority records. Although over 95% of records bearing scope notes contain one such note, there are LCSH-mr records with as many as eight scope notes.

Scope notes bear subfields for subject headings (subfield $a) that refer searchers to one or more of five types of references: (1) subdivisions, (2) unsubdivided subject headings, (3) unsubdivided subject headings that serve as examples (including additional entries that are unsubdivided), (4) subdivided subject headings, and (5) subdivided subject headings that serve as examples (including additional entries that are subdivided). Examples from LCSH-mr of each of these five types of subject headings in scope notes follow:

1. Established subject heading:
   150 Consular law
   Scope note referring to a subdivision(s):
   680 $i here are entered works on the legal status of foreign consults and the legal aspects of consular service in general. Works on the law governing the consular service of an individual country are entered under the name of that country with the subdivision $a Diplomatic and consular service.
2. Established subject heading:
   150 Home labor
   Scope note with an unsubdivided subject heading(s):
   680 $i Here are entered works on persons in urban areas producing goods at home for an outside employer. Works on industries carried on by persons and their families in rural areas producing goods at home for an outside employer are entered under $a Cottage industries. $i Works on self-employed persons producing and marketing goods or services in their homes are entered under $a Home-based businesses.
3. Established subject heading:
   150 Chaplains

Scope note with an unsubdivided subject heading(s) that serves as an example:
680 $i For works limited to a specific type of chaplain, the heading is qualified by the functional adjective, e.g., $a Chaplains, Hospital; Chaplains, Military.

4. Established subject heading:
150 Equality before the law
Scope note with a subdivided subject heading(s):
680 $i Works on the doctrine of equal protection of the law are entered under the heading $a Equality before the law--United States. $i Works on the doctrine of due process of law are entered under the heading $a Due process of law.
5. Established subject heading:
150 Deep-sea temperature
Scope note with a subdivided subject heading(s) that serves as an example:
680 $i Subdivided by locality, e.g., $a Deep-sea temperature--Pacific.

Unsubdivided and subdivided subject headings referred to in scope notes are usually traced in a subject example tracing note (MARC tag 681) in the LCSH-mr records for these subject headings. For example, the topical subject heading "Equality before the law" in scope note type 4 refers to two topical subject headings, namely "Equality before the law--United States" and "Due process of law." The authority records of both headings referred to have the following subject example tracing note (MARC tag 681) referring back to the scope note in the subject authority record for "Equality before the law": "$i Note under $a Equality before the law." The only references that are not traced in the five types of scope notes are references to subdivisions (type 1).

Displaying scope notes to catalog users requires library and systems staff to resolve the same issue about deblinding references in the local catalog as they have to address in working with complex *see* and *see also* references. Scope notes occur with greater frequency than complex *see* references. Over 3500 references to subject headings and subdivisions are given in the scope notes of about 2000 subject heading records (Markey & Vizine-Goetz 1989, 48). Thus, replacing unused headings and subdivisions in these records with terms used in the library's database will require a substantial work effort.

2.7

Synthesis and Summary

USMARC records for authority data can be traced back to the earliest days of USMARC format development when the first test tapes sent to MARC Pilot Project participants in 1966 contained both bibliographic and cross-reference records. The preliminary version of the USMARC format for authority data was published in 1976. LC began a distribution service for name authority records in 1978. Until LC initiated a distribution service for subject authority records in 1986, institutions were reluctant to mount subject authority records in their online systems because they had to devise their own ways of keeping the file up to date. Online system designers responded to the availability of a current subjects file by developing subject authority capabilities in their systems to enable library staff to perform subject authority work and public catalog users to use the notes and references in subject authority records in their subject searches.

Most (80.4%) LCSH-mr records contain topical subject headings. These records are not long, averaging only 6.73 variable data fields per record. Three of these fields contain "housekeeping" data, that is, control number, cataloging source, and the authorized subject heading itself. Three of the four remaining fields are given to simple cross-reference fields for topical subjects, one for each type, that is, *see from* tracing, *see also* reference, and *see also from* tracing. One field is given to an LC classification number. This profile describes a few subject heading records, but it is not representative of the vast majority of these records because subject heading records that contain cross-reference fields usually contain many such fields. Records with many cross-references are also likely to have fields for scope notes or complex *see also* references.

Online system designers must be prepared to incorporate capabilities that facilitate browsing and selection from long lists of references. For example, graphical interfaces enlist capabilities such as pop-up windows, scrolling bars, and buttons in various shapes (e.g., arrows, pointing hands) that are manipulated by a mouse or other pointing and clicking device to encourage browsing and selection from long lists or reading of lengthy texts. MARC tags and subfield coding must also be replaced in displays of subject heading records with informative labels. Pop-up windows could be used to give instructions on the use of the data elements in these records.

Geographic name headings are 12.0% of LCSH-mr records. These records are even shorter than subject heading records, consisting of only 5.0 variable data fields per record. Three of these fields contain "housekeeping" data, that is, control number, cataloging source, and the authorized subject heading itself. The two remaining fields are simple cross-references for a *see from* tracing for geographic names and a *see also from* tracing for topical subjects. This profile of variable fields is indicative of many geographic name records. Findings about orphan headings are similar to findings about subject heading records, that is, most unsubdivided geographic names are connected to the cross-reference structure, and the majority of subdivided geographic name headings are orphan headings.

Library systems staff are selective of the data they process from LCSH-mr into the local subject authority records of their automated library systems. Only headings and references posted in the bibliographic file are going to be added to the database.

Consequently, fewer references are going to be connected with authorized headings than would be connected if all possible references were made regardless of postings in a bibliographic file.

The question of whether to keep LC classification numbers in subject authority records is not easy to answer. Although these numbers are assigned to 43.0% of authority records for topical subject headings, they have not been updated throughout the years. Consequently, they may not be indicative of the LC class numbers assigned by libraries to material on a subject. In several existing online catalogs, the solution to this problem is to design subject searching capabilities that prompt system users to enlist the classification numbers assigned to retrieved bibliographic records to find additional material on a subject.

Scope notes and complex *see* and *see also* references sometimes trace subject headings and subdivisions not used in a library's bibliographic file. Systems staff could undertake a project to deblind references in scope note and complex *see* and *see also* reference fields of LCSH-mr records. It may be a significant effort because estimates of the references in each type of field are in the thousands. Furthermore, online systems must have capabilities to search for subject headings and subdivisions in these fields and replace them with used terms. Library staff have to periodically review the references in these three fields because the catalog's authority and bibliographic files are constantly changing due to new records, deleted records, and changes to records. A library's decision about selecting data in LCSH-mr may be driven by the time, personnel, and computer resources required to make the LCSH-mr file of subject authority records indicative of the subject headings used in the library's bibliographic file.

Findings about orphan headings tell us that the subject authority records for few subdivided headings are going to contain references and notes. References and notes printed under the unsubdivided form of the subdivided heading also pertain to the subdivided heading; however, they are not as apparent in online systems as in the printed *LCSH* because they are contained in different authority records than the heading consulted. How can online systems help users to find and use this information in their ongoing search?

Systems would have to prompt users to browse and select from a list of narrower terms for the unsubdivided form of heading, then add the subdivisions to the selected terms in searches for the selected narrower terms. Let's say the user is interested in library material assigned the subject heading "Handicraft--Exhibitions--Judging." Unable to find enough material on this topic, the user responds to a browsing list of narrower terms under the unsubdivided subject heading "Handicrafts" by selecting "Craft festivals," "Hobbies," and "Textile crafts." The system could then search for these subject headings used with both subdivisions "--Exhibitions" and "--Judging." The problem with this strategy is that subdivisions are not assigned on an entirely free-floating basis; consequently, the subdivisions printed with one subject heading are not necessarily authorized for use with other subject headings. In our example, only the subdivision "--Exhibitions" comes from the general free-floating list, and, thus, could be used with the three other subject headings, that is, "Craft festivals," "Hobbies," and "Textile crafts," selected by the user. To improve the potential of this strategy for retrieving bibliographic records, systems could employ keyword searching of all subject-rich fields of bibliographic records for the words in subject headings and subdivisions. In our example, systems would retrieve bibliographic records bearing the words "craft," "festivals," "exhibitions," and "judging"; or "hobbies," "exhibitions," and "judging"; or "textile," "crafts," "exhibitions," and "judging."

Findings about *see from* tracings are not encouraging. Almost 50% of unsubdivided headings for topical subjects and geographic names contain no *see from* tracings. Percentages of subdivided headings without *see from* tracings are even higher. Over half of the authorized subject headings in LCSH cannot be found by entry vocabulary other than the authorized headings themselves. Later chapters recognize the value of *see from* tracings for expressing topics in the terms searchers use in their subject queries and for guiding searchers to subject headings used in the catalog to express their topics of interest.

LC accepts and reviews proposals for new *see from* tracings from the library community. Most proposals are submitted by libraries participating in the Cooperative Subject Cataloging Projects (CSCP 1991). If LC accepts their proposals, new tracings are included in changes to LC-distributed subject authority records. Future development of electronic transmission of authority data could include automatic submission of *see from* tracings to LC for review and subsequent distribution. This would especially speed up the process of establishing new *see from* tracings. It would also increase libraries' stake in the LCSH system because they are participating in its enhancement and improvement.

References

Avram, Henriette D. (1968). *The MARC pilot project: Final report on a project sponsored by the Council on Library Resources, Inc.* Washington, DC: Library of Congress.

Avram, Henriette D. (1975). *MARC: Its history and implications.* Washington, DC: Library of Congress.

Avram, Henriette D., Knapp, John F., & Rather, Lucia J. (1968). *The MARC II format: A communications format for bibliographic data.* Washington, DC: Library of Congress.

Baer, Nadine L., & Johnson, Karl E. (1988). The state of authority. *Information Technology and Libraries, 7*, 2 (June), 139–153.

Buckland, Lawrence F. (1965). *The recording of Library of Congress bibliographical data in machine form: A report prepared for the Council on Library Resources.* Washington, DC: Council on Library Resources.

Byrne, Deborah J. (1991). *MARC manual: Understanding and using MARC records.* Englewood, CO: Libraries Unlimited.

Chan, Lois Mai. (1986). *Library of Congress subject headings: Principles and application* (2nd ed.). Littleton, CO: Libraries Unlimited.

Clack, Doris Hargrett. (1990). *Authority control: Principles, applications, and instructions.* Chicago: American Library Association.

Cochrane, Pauline A., & Markey, Karen. (1985). Preparing for the use of classification in online cataloging systems and in online catalogs. *Information Technology and Libraries, 4*, 2 (June), 91–111.

Crawford, Walt. (1989). *MARC for library use: Understanding integrated USMARC formats.* (2nd ed.). Boston: G.K. Hall.

CSCP. (1991). *(CSCP) Cooperative Subject Cataloging Projects: Summary of records processed through September 1991.* 4 pp. (Photocopy.)

Fenly, Judith G., & Wiggins, Beacher. (1988). *The Linked Systems Project: A networking tool for libraries.* Dublin, Ohio: OCLC.

Gredley, Ellen, & Hopkinson, Alan. 1990. *Exchanging bibliographic data: MARC and other international formats.* Ottawa: Canadian Library Association.

Hagler, Ronald, and Simmons, Peter. (1982). *The bibliographic record and information technology.* Chicago: American Library Association.

Hancock, Micheline. (1987). Subject searching behaviour at the library catalogue and at the shelves: Implications for online interactive catalogues. *Journal of Documentation, 43*, 4 (December), 303–321.

Hildreth, Charles R. (1991). End users and structured searching of online catalogues: Recent research findings. In Robert Fugmann (Ed.), *Tools for knowledge organization and the human interface: Proceedings, 1st International ISKO-Conference, Darmstadt, 14–17 August 1990* (pp. 1–19). Frankfurt: Indeks Verlag.

Johnston, Sarah Hager. (1989). Current offerings in automated authority control: A survey of vendors. *Information Technology and Libraries, 8*, 3 (September), 236–264.

Johnston, Sarah Hager. (1990). Desperately seeking authority control : Automated systems are not providing it. *Library Journal, 115*, 16 (October 1), 43–46.

King, Gilbert W., Edmundson, Harold P., Flood, Merrill M., Kochen, Manfred, Libby, Richard L., Swanson, Don R., & Wylly, Alexander. (1963). *Automation and the Library of Congress: A survey sponsored by the Council on Library Resources, Inc.* Washington, DC: Library of Congress.

Library of Congress. (1976). *Authorities: A MARC format.* (Preliminary ed.). Washington, DC: Library of Congress.

Library of Congress. (1981). *Authorities: A MARC format.* Washington, DC: Library of Congress.

Library of Congress. (1987). *USMARC format for authority data including guidelines for content designation.* Washington, DC: Library of Congress.

Library of Congress. (1990a). *Library of Congress Subject Headings* (13th ed.). Washington, DC: Library of Congress.

Library of Congress. (1990b). *Subject cataloging manual: Subject headings.* Washington, DC: Library of Congress.

Library of Congress. (1991). *USMARC format for classification data.* Washington, DC: Library of Congress.

Library of Congress. (1992). *The future of subdivisions in the Library of Congress subject headings system: Report from the Subject Subdivisions Conference*, Martha O'Hara Conway (Ed.). Washington, DC: Library of Congress.

Logan, Susan J. (1987). The Ohio State University's Library Control System: From circulation to subject access and authority control. *Library Trends, 35*, 4 (Spring), 539–554.

Long, Anthony. (1984). UKMARC and US/MARC: A brief history and comparison. *Journal of Documentation, 40* (March), 1–12.

Ludy, Lorene E. (1985). The OSU Libraries' use of the Library of Congress subject authorities file. *Information Technology and Libraries, 4*, 2 (June), 155–160.

McCallum, Sally H. (1985). The Linked Systems Project, part 1: Authorities implementation. *Library Hi Tech, 3*, 2, 61–70.

Markey, Karen. (1984). *Subject searching in library catalogs: Before and after the introduction of online catalogs.* Dublin, Ohio: OCLC.

Markey, Karen. (1990). Keyword searching in an online catalog enhanced with the Dewey Decimal Classification. In Betty G. Bengtson & Janet Swan Hill (Eds.), *Classification of library materials: Current and future potential for providing access* (pp. 99–125). New York: Neal-Schuman.

Markey, Karen, & Vizine-Goetz, Diane. (1989). Untraced references in the machine-readable *Library of Congress Subject Headings. Library Resources & Technical Services, 33*, 1 (January), 37–53.

Markey, Karen, & Vizine-Goetz, Diane, (1988). *Characteristics of subject authority records in the machine-readable Library of Congress Subject Headings.* Dublin, OH: OCLC. OCLC Research Report series OCLC/OR/RR-88/2.

Pietris, Mary K.D. (1987). Keynote address: Library of Congress subject headings: Past imperfect, future indicative. *Cataloguing Australia, 13*, 3 (September), 8–19.

Prabha, Chandra, Rice, Duane, & Cameron, David. (1988). *Nonfiction book use by academic library users.* Dublin, Ohio: OCLC. OCLC Research Report OCLC/OPR/RR-88/1.

Rather, Lucia J., & Wiggins, Beacher. (1989). MARC: Mother Avram's remarkable contribution. *American Libraries, 20*, 9 (October), 855–857, 859–861.

Rood, Joanna. (1991). Practical considerations in dealing with LCSH-mr. In Karen M. Drabenstott (Ed.), *Subject authorities in the online environment: Papers from a conference program held in San Francisco, June 29, 1987* (pp. 31–40). Chicago: American Library Association.

Schuitema, Joan E. (1988). Cataloging activities using LSP: Authority records. In Judith G. Fenly & Beacher Wiggins (Eds.), *The Linked Systems Project: Networking tool for libraries* (pp. 91–95). Dublin, OH: OCLC.

Taylor, Arlene G., Maxwell, Margaret F., & Frost, Carolyn O. (1985). Network and vendor authority systems. *Library Resources & Technical Services, 29*, 2 (April-June), 195–205.

Vizine-Goetz, Diane. (1990). Cataloging productivity tools. In *Annual review of OCLC research* (pp. 6–8). Dublin, Ohio: OCLC.

Walker, Stephen, & DeVere, Rachel. (1990). *Improving subject retrieval in online catalogues. 2. Relevance feedback and query expansion.* London: British Library. British Library Research Paper 72.

Willard, Patricia, & Teece, Viva. (1983). The browser and the library. *Public Library Quarterly, 4*, 1 (Spring), 55–63.

3

Subject Information in Bibliographic Records

3.1 Introduction

The principal sources of *subject information* for accessing library collections are the fields and subfields of machine-readable cataloging records for bibliographic data. Bibliographic records consist of "an arrangement of bibliographic data elements concerning a single document and considered relevant for the purpose of the listing in question" (Hagler & Simmons 1982, 91). The USMARC format that governs the content and arrangement of data elements in bibliographic records is the *USMARC format for bibliographic data* (Library of Congress 1988b).

This chapter continues the history of USMARC formats with an emphasis on formats for bibliographic data. It reviews USMARC format structure as it pertains to records for bibliographic data. The discussion of variable fields in the USMARC format for bibliographic data begins with an ordered listing of the primary USMARC fields for books with a brief explanation of their function. It focuses on subject-rich fields of bibliographic records, particularly title and subject heading fields, the different types of online catalog subject indexes built from these data, and the subject searching approaches they support. Additionally, this chapter discusses the extent to which bibliographic records contain subject information.

3.2 Brief History of the USMARC Format for Bibliographic Data

The earliest history of the USMARC format for bibliographic data is closely linked with that of the USMARC format for authority data (see also Chapter 2, section 2.2). Figure 3.1 shows the major events and benchmarks in the 25-year evolution of USMARC formats for bibliographic and authority data.

3.3 USMARC Format for Bibliographic Data

For the purposes of this chapter, the history of USMARC formats begins in 1966 when the development of a USMARC format for authorities was set aside in favor of development of the USMARC format for bibliographic data. Between November 1966 and June 1967, LC supplied twenty-one libraries with test tapes of machine-readable cataloging records for English-language monographs in the MARC I (preliminary) format. These libraries gave encouraging reports of their experimental utilization of these records and participated in the review of the MARC I format (Avram 1968). Changes to the format eventually led to the release of the specifications for the USMARC II format in January 1968 titled *The MARC II format: A communications format for bibliographic data* (Avram, Knapp, & Rather 1968). In March of the following year, LC initiated a weekly tape distribution service for USMARC format records for bibliographic data through its MARC Distribution Service. At first, coverage was limited to English-language monographs with United States imprints. It was extended to serials, maps, and films in the early 1970s, shortly after the publication of USMARC formats for these types of materials. Three years after the inception of the MARC Distribution Service, subscribing institutions numbered 54; however, an estimated one thousand institutions were using LC's USMARC data indirectly through the production and secondary distribution of offline and online products generated by these data (Library of Congress 1972). The structure of USMARC II was adopted as a national standard (ANSI Z39.2) in 1971 and as an international standard (ISO 2709) in 1973.

Many libraries use the capabilities of bibliographic services such as OCLC and RLIN to access and edit USMARC records for bibliographic data. These systems also have capabilities to allow catalogers at member institutions to enter their own cataloging directly into the union catalog when no records exist for the item in hand. When OCLC member libraries enter records into the Online Union Catalog (OLUC) or use records entered by LC and other OCLC member libraries, their online transactions are recorded and stored on magnetic tape. These tapes, called archive tapes or subscription tapes, are acquired by libraries or groups of libraries. Initially, bibliographic records on archive tapes serve as the foundation for the development of a library's bibliographic database in a stand-alone automated library system. Libraries enter new cataloging into the union catalog of the bibliographic service and subscribe to archive tapes containing this cataloging to load into their automated systems.

At some libraries, the cataloging scenario is reversed. That is, they download records from the bibliographic service's database into their own database or create new records locally. Periodically, they send archive tapes of USMARC-format bibliographic records for newly cataloged materials to the bibliographic service to update their holdings in the union catalog. USMARC formats for bibliographic data

DATE	EVENT TYPE*	EVENT
1963	G	King report recommends automation of technical services.
1964	G	Inforonics' study of card catalog conversion published.
1965	G	(JAN.) 1st Conference on Machine-Readable Copy (M-RC) held to discuss Inforonics' study.
	G	(MAR.–JUN.) LC team drafts preliminary draft format.
	G	(NOV.) 2nd Conference on M-RC held to review draft format.
	G	(DEC.) CLR supports MARC Pilot Projects.
1966	G	(FEB.) LC chooses MARC Pilot Project contractors and library participants.
	G	(OCT.) First test tapes of bibliographic and cross-reference records sent to MARC Pilot Project participants for experimentation.
	G	(NOV.) Weekly distribution of records in preliminary format initiated.
1967	G	(MAR.) LC staff begin evaluation of preliminary format.
	B	(APR.) LC-produced test tapes sent to participants limited to bibliographic records.
1968	B	(JAN.) USMARC II format published.
	G	(JUN.) MARC Pilot Project final report published describing USMARC I and II formats and participants' experimentation with preliminary-format records.
	G	(JUN.) LC's weekly distribution of preliminary-format records ceases.
	B	(JUN.) LC and ALA sponsor workshop series to introduce library community to USMARC II format.
1969	B	(MAR.) LC's MARC Distribution Service begins weekly distribution of USMARC II records for English-language monographs.
1970	B	LC publishes serials and maps formats.
	G	LC establishes MARC Development Office to promote USMARC formats.
1971	G	ANSI adopts USMARC structure as a national standard (Z39.2).
	B	LC publishes films format.
1972	B	MARC Distribution Service includes films cataloging.
	G	LC reports on survey of USMARC subscribers.
1973	G	ISO adopts USMARC structure as an international standard (2709).
	B	LC publishes draft format for music and original manuscripts format.
	B	MARC Distribution Service includes serials and maps cataloging.
	B	ALA's interdivisional MARBI committee begins working with LC on USMARC format development and refinement.
1974	B	CONSER Project undertaken by LC, OCLC, and libraries to develop serials database.
1975		

Figure 3.1
USMARC format chronology.

1976	A	LC publishes preliminary authorities format entitled *Authorities: A MARC Format.*
1977	A	LC initiates NACO Project to develop name authority database.
1978	A	MARC Distribution Service includes name authority records.
1979		
1980	B	*MARC Formats for Bibliographic Data* generates interest in format integration.
	A	CLR funds the Linked Systems Project for exchange of name authority records.
1981	B	Weisbrod study recommends format integration as a top priority.
	B	LC publishes machine-readable data files format.
	A	First edition of the authorites format published.
1982	G	MARBI approves *The USMARC Formats: Underlying Principles.*
1983	B	Manuscripts format revised and changed to archival and manuscripts format.
	A	LC publishes update No. 1 to authorities format.
1984	B	MARC Distribution Service includes scores and sound recordings.
1985	B	Films format revised and changed to Visual Materials format.
	A	RLG and RLG-member libraries first to receive name authority records from LC via LSP.
1986	A	LC publishes update No. 2 to authorities format.
	A	CDS begins weekly distribution of USMARC II records for subject authority data.
1987	B	MARBI discusses objectives of paper on format integration.
	A	OCLC and OCLC-member libraries receive name authority records from LC via LSP.
	A	*USMARC Format for Authority Data* is published and incorporates changes issued as Updates No. 1 (1983) and No. 2 (1986).
1988	A	CDS publishes first CD/ROM product — CDMARC Subjects.
	B	MARBI accepts *USMARC Formats: Proposed Changes* based on reaction to 1987 format integration objectives.
	A	LC proposes changes to USMARC format for authority data to accomodate classification data.
1989		
1990	A	MARBI accepts preliminary version of a separate USMARC format for classification data.
1991	A	LC-sponsored conference on LCSH subdivision system recommends establishing a national authority file for subdivided subject headings.
	A	Update No. 4 to the *USMARC Format for Authority Data* issued.

*Event types: G, general; B, bibliographic format; A, authority format.

facilitate sharing and exchange of bibliographic records between institutions because their respective online systems are already programmed to receive and export bibliographic records in USMARC formats.

Eight different formats are now available: (1) monographs, (2) serials, (3) maps, (4) sound recordings, (5) scores, (6) archives and manuscripts, (7) visual materials, and (8) machine-readable data files. Although the formats have been developed according to the same principles, the inconsistencies that exist between formats for different materials require the use of separate computer programs or program modules for processing records from different formats. While the separate formats were proliferating in the early 1970s, the notion of MARC format integration appeared as a solution to the problem of separate formats (Library of Congress 1988a):

> Format integration is the validation of data elements for all forms of material, thus removing restrictions on data elements that currently make them valid only for specific forms of material. The result is a single bibliographic format that contains data elements that can be used to describe many forms of material.

Format integration is a current development with respect to USMARC formats for bibliographic data. LC and committees of the American Library Association have already engaged in several efforts to ensure acceptance of format integration by the library community and prepare it for the changes to come.

3.3.1 USMARC Format Structure

USMARC records for bibliographic data conform to the same national and international standards as records for authority data. The format structure of bibliographic records divides the format into three distinct areas: (1) record leader, (2) directory, and (3) data fields. The pattern of these three distinct areas is the same as that for authority data because these records conform to the same standard (see Figure 2.1).

Like authority records, the record leader for bibliographic records is fixed in length at 24 character positions (00–23). It conveys information about the record itself, codes to help relate this record to other records, and codes to instruct the computer program where to find certain kinds of data within records. Most leader data are provided automatically by the computer program when the record is created.

Two character positions in the leader of bibliographic records are interesting to note. Record status is given in position 5 of bibliographic records. A single alphabetical character conveys to the computer program whether the record should be handled as a new ("n"), changed ("c"), deleted ("d"), and upgraded ("p") record. Bibliographic records enlist a single character "a" to "r" in character position 6 for Type of Record. For example, books and monographs are given the alphabetical character "a."

The directory in USMARC records for bibliographic data is structured the same as the directory in USMARC records for authority data. The directory is comprised of separate units giving the identity, length, and location of each data field. Data field identity is denoted by a three-digit MARC field tag. Length of the data field is given in a four-digit number. Location of the data field in the complete record is given in a five-digit number. The number of individual units corresponds to the number of data fields following the directory. Figure 2.2 shows the number of characters in the leader and individual units of the directory in USMARC format records.

A field separator comes at the end of the entire directory. Since it is the first field separator to occur in the record, it conveniently introduces the location of data fields. Except for three-digit MARC field tags, a computer program automatically compiles the directory when records are created.

Data in variable control fields are expressed in codes. The codes in variable control fields convey one or many pieces of information. An example of the former is the control number field (MARC tag 001) of bibliographic records that contains the number assigned by the organization creating, using, or distributing the record. An example of the latter is the 008 control field of bibliographic records (also known as the MARC fixed field), which contains 19 different fixed-length data elements. USMARC formats reserve nine data fields 000 to 009 for variable control fields. Specific variable control fields in the USMARC format for books are discussed below.

Data in variable data fields are expressed in text. Most often, variable data fields are subdivided into subfields to allow for the representation of several data elements within a single field. Subfields within a field are identified through the use of subfield codes. Variable data fields in the USMARC format for bibliographic data also contain two indicator positions stored at the beginning of each field. Indicator positions are set from 0 to 9 or left blank depending on the cataloger's response to instructions given for setting indicators in the various USMARC formats for bibliographic data.

USMARC formats can use data fields numbered from 010 to 999 for variable data fields; however, many fields within this range have not yet been defined. Variable data fields used most frequently in bibliographic records are discussed later in the chapter. A record terminator is always the last character of USMARC records.

3.3.2 USMARC Bibliographic Record in Exchange Format

When LC exports USMARC records on tape, records are formatted in the exchange format. Individual data elements are difficult to distinguish from one another because they are concatenated into a single, undifferentiated string of characters. Figure 3.2 shows a bibliographic record for Francis Davis's book *In the Moment* in USMARC exchange format, and with numbers added to rows and columns to help readers differentiate the individual components of the record.

```
Symbol:                       Meaning:
Pound sign (#)                Deliberately coded space
Dollar sign ($)               Subfield delimiter
Greater than symbol (>)       End-of-field delimiter
At sign (@)                   End-of-record delimiter

Numbers along the top (e.g., 0, 10, etc.) and at the left of figure
(e.g., 0, 50, 100, etc.) indicate character positions

                    1         2         3         4
          0         0         0         0         0

  0       00618nam##2200204#a#4504001000800000000500170000800
 50       80041000250200015000660430012000810500022000930820
100       02100115100002000136245005800156260004800214300002
150       60026250000330028850000200032165000360034165000350
200       0377>86-8437>19930508081044.0>860401s1986####nyu##
250       ##########001#0#eng##>00$a0195040902>00$an-us--->00
300       $aML3508$b.D38 1986>00$a785.42/092/2$219>1#$aDavis
350       , Francis.>10$aIn the moment :$b jazz in the 1980s
400        /$cFrancis Davis.>##$aNew York :$bOxford Universi
450       ty Press,$c1986.>##$axiv, 258 p. ;$c22 cm.>##$aPre
500       viously published essays.>##$aIncludes index.>#0$a
550       Jazz$y1981-1990$zUnited States.>#0$aJazz musicians
600       $zUnited States.>@
```

Figure 3.2
Bibliographic record for *In the Moment* in USMARC exchange format.

3.3.3 USMARC Bibliographic Record in Internal Format

When the bibliographic record for *In the Moment* is added to the OCLC Online System, the record is converted from the USMARC exchange format into an OCLC internal processing format for bibliographic data. This format facilitates record processing because it eliminates data that are not used by OCLC applications software programs.

Computer programs that display USMARC bibliographic records omit most data elements from the leader. They extract MARC tags from the directory and place them immediately preceding variable data fields. Since the computer program rearranges data elements, the original location data from the directory are now meaningless, so they are eliminated from USMARC records when they are converted to an internal processing format. Data elements from the 008 control field and a few leader elements are placed in fixed fields and preceded by display constants. Figure 3.3 shows a display of the bibliographic record for *In the Moment* in the OCLC Online Union Catalog.

3.3.4 USMARC Bibliographic Record Display in Online Catalogs

The display of the bibliographic record in Figure 3.3 probably looks foreign to an observer untrained in the meaning of fixed-field display constants, MARC tags,

```
OCLC:  13455737              Rec stat:    c
Entered:    19860401         Replaced:    19911202         Used:    19920902
Type: a         Bib lvl: m         Source:                 Lang:  eng
Repr:           Enc lvl:           Conf pub: 0             Ctry:  nyu
Indx: 1         Mod rec:           Govt pub:               Cont:
Desc: a         Int lvl:           Festschr: 0             Illus:
                F/B:     0         Dat tp:   s             Dates: 1986,

  1  010       86-8437/MN/r90 ¶
  2  040       DLC $c DLC $d UKM ¶
  3  015       GB87-50287 ¶
  4  019       17224679 ¶
  5  020       0195040902 ¶
  6  043       n-us--- ¶
  7  050 00    ML3508 $b .D38 1986 ¶
  8  082 00    785.42/092/2 $2 19 ¶
  9  090       $b ¶
 10  049       OCLC ¶
 11  100 1     Davis, Francis. ¶
 12  245 10    In the moment : $b jazz in the 1980s / $c Francis Davis. ¶
 13  260       New York : $b Oxford University Press, $c 1986. ¶
 14  300       xiv, 258 p. ; $c 22 cm. ¶
 15  500       Previously published essays. ¶
 16  500       Includes index. ¶
 17  650  0    Jazz $y 1981-1990 $x History and criticism. ¶
 18  650  0    Jazz musicians $z United States. ¶
 19  653       United States $a Jazz $a Musicians ¶
```

Figure 3.3
OCLC Online Union Catalog Display of *In the Moment.*

and bibliographic data. However, users of the OCLC Online Union Catalog are library catalogers who become familiar with USMARC record structure, content designation, and record content through daily use of OCLC and other online systems. They can also consult USMARC and OCLC documentation to decipher new elements or infrequently used elements.

Of the many approaches online catalogs employ to display bibliographic records, two popular approaches are a card catalog format and a labeled format. The LCS online catalog enlists the former approach (Figure 3.4). The labeled bibliographic record comes from the online catalog of the University of Kansas (Figure 3.5). At the present time, there is no standard for labeling individual data elements of bibliographic records. Both online catalogs eliminate fixed-field elements from online displays of bibliographic records. The only variable data elements included in

```
ML3508D381986
Davis, Francis.
  In the moment : jazz in the 1980s /  Francis Davis.  New York :
Oxford University Press, 1986.  xiv, 258 p. ; 22 cm.
  Previously published essays.  Includes index.
SUB: 1. Jazz  2. Jazz musiciains--United States
LC CARD #: 86-8437  TITLE #: 3892836  OCLC #: 13455737  &2q870528
```

Figure 3.4
LCS display of *In the Moment.*

```
=== FULL RECORD DISPLAY ================= Screen 1 of 1 =====

        AUTHOR:  Davis, Francis.
         TITLE:  In the moment : jazz in the 1980s / Francis
                 Davis.
     PUBLISHER:  New York : Oxford University Press, 1986.
      SUBJECTS:  1)  Jazz.
                 2)  Jazz musicians--United States.
   DESCRIPTION:  xiv, 258 p. ; 22 cm.
         NOTES:  Previously published essays.
                 Includes index.


========================================= Screen 1 of 1 =====
   CALL NUMBER:  ML 3508 .D38 1986
      LOCATION:  Music Library
CURRENT STATUS:  not checked out
=============================================================
```

Figure 3.5
Online catalog display of *In the Moment* at University of Kansas.

displays are those that identify the item, enable a searcher to locate it on the bookshelf, and convey the item's subject matter. The display of bibliographic records in online catalogs has generated considerable interest and controversy. A discussion of bibliographic record displays is beyond the scope of this book, but readers are encouraged to explore this area (Borgman 1986; Janosky, Smith, & Hildreth 1986; Crawford 1987, 1989; Matthews 1987; Shaw 1991; Yee 1991).

3.4 Subject Indexes and Subject Information in Variable Data Fields

The subject content of written communication is conveyed through variable control fields and variable data fields of USMARC format records for bibliographic data. An ordered listing of the primary USMARC fields for books with an explanation of their function is followed by discussion of those fields containing subject information. Individual fields are discussed only inasmuch as they are suited to the various subject indexes in online catalogs. Readers can consult the specifications for individual formats and recently published textbooks (Byrne 1991; Crawford 1989) for definitions, descriptions, and examples of other data elements.

Table 3.1 is an ordered listing of variable fields in the USMARC format for books. Subject information is conveyed primarily by title and subject heading fields; however, a few note fields and certain subfields of main entry, added entry, and variant forms of entry fields also contain subject information. Subject information is also coded in classification number fields in the 01x–09x range; however, a discussion of classification data is beyond the scope of this book.

Table 3.1
Variable Fields of the USMARC Format for Books

Tags	Description	Function
01x–09x	Numbers and codes	Standard numbers, classification and call numbers, codes, and other data elements pertaining to the original item.
1xx	Main entry	The entity (i.e., name of a person, corporate body, or meeting) given primary responsibility for creating the work. A uniform title can also be used as a main-entry heading.
24x	Titles	Titles transcribed from the title page of the item or composed by the cataloging agency.
260	Publication	Information relating to the publication, printing, distribution, issue, release, or production of the work.
300	Physical description	Physical description of the item including extent and dimensions.
4xx 800–830	Series statement	A collective title applying to a group of separate items.
5xx	Notes	General and specialized notes about the item.
6xx	Subject terms	Terms describing the subject content of the item.
700–740	Name and title added entries	Other names and titles associated with the item besides the one in the main entry field.
87x	Variant forms of entry	Variant forms of entry for headings in main entry (100–130), series (4xx, 800–830), and added entry (700–730) fields.

Our discussion of variable data fields centers on title and subject heading fields and the subject indexes of online catalogs into which data from these fields are processed. The subject searching capabilities these indexes support are given in only a general way. Details about specific searching capabilities and user queries best suited for them are addressed in Chapters 11, 12, and 13.

3.4.1 Alphabetical Indexes for Browsing

Subject headings assigned to subject heading fields of bibliographic records (MARC tags 6xx) can be extracted from such fields and placed in an alphabetical list or index. In response to the subject queries users enter, online catalogs respond with a display of the subject heading index consisting of assigned subject headings in the alphabetical neighborhood of subject queries. Users browse the subject heading index to find a subject heading that expresses their topics of interest. Their selection of subject headings from the subject heading index results in the retrieval of bibliographic records assigned the selected subject headings. From the display of retrieved bibliographic records, users make note of information that will enable them to find the original items that interest them on the library's bookshelves.

Browsing alphabetical lists of indexed subject headings is a two-step approach to subject searching. The first step involves a user action, that is, entry of a subject query, to which online systems respond with an intermediary display of indexed subject headings. The second step involves a user action connected with manipulation of displayed subject headings, and selection of listed subject headings, to which systems respond by creating sets of retrieved bibliographic records.

The two-step browsing approach helps users overcome some of the difficulties of predicting the forms used by the controlled vocabulary to express their topics of interest. When user queries are different forms of the controlled vocabulary terms used in the library catalog, users find these forms by browsing lists of indexed subject headings because indexed terms are in close alphabetical proximity to their subject queries. Browsing is also an effective approach to subject searching when user queries match the initial terms in subject headings. It is particularly effective when users enter subject queries that match a subject heading and their interests lie in a more specific aspect of the matched subject that is expressed in a subdivision.

Table 3.2 lists fields and subfields of USMARC format records for books from which subject headings can be extracted for an alphabetical subject heading index for online browsing. Subject heading fields are limited to those in which the second indicator in the subject heading field is set to zero to indicate a subject heading based on the LCSH system. (In the genre heading field [USMARC tag 655], this indicator is set to 7 and subfield $2 contains code "lcsh" identifying LCSH as the source of the genre term.) Excluding subject headings from other systems ensures that the terms in alphabetical lists are consistent with one another in terms of their structure and syntax.

Table 3.2 divides selected subfields into two columns: (1) subfields for browsing and (2) subfields for user prompting. In response to the subject queries users enter into online catalogs, systems display subject headings in alphabetical order consisting of the former subfields. Users browse alphabetical lists to find subject headings expressing their topics of interest. For example, subject headings for personal names are composed of subfields for the name, qualification of name, and numeration, titles, and dates associated with the name. Online catalogs do not include MARC tags and subfield codes in alphabetical browsing lists:

- Churchill, Winston, Sir, 1874–1965.
- Haydn, Joseph, 1732–1809.
- Lawrence, D. H. (David Herbert), 1885–1930.
- Shakespeare, William, 1564–1616.

Subject headings for topical subjects consist only of the topical subject element:

- Air pilots
- Children
- Mathematics
- Sociopathic personality
- Women

When users select a listed subject heading, the system can prompt users to continue the search in several ways: (1) display related terms, (2) display bibliographic

Table 3.2
Fields and Subfields for Alphabetical Browsing

Tag	Field description	Subfields for browsing	Subfields for user prompting
Browsing for personal names			
600	Personal name	a /name	k /form subheading
		q /qualification of name	t /title of work
		b /numeration	m/medium of performance
		c /titles	r /key
		d /dates	x /topical subdivision
			y /period subdivision
			z /geographic subdivision
Browsing for subjects generally			
610	Corporate name	a /name of corporate body	k /form subheading
		b /subordinate unit	t /title of work
		n /number of part or section of work	m/medium of performance
			r /key
		d /date of meeting, treaty signing	x /topical subdivision
			y /period subdivision
		c /place of meeting	z /geographic subdivision
611	Meeting name	a /name of meeting	k /form subheading
		n /number of part or section of work	t /title of work
			x /topical subdivision
		d /date of meeting	y /period subdivision
		c /place of meeting	z /geographic subdivision
630	Uniform title	a /uniform title	t /title of work
		p /name of part or section of work	l /language
			k /form subheading
		s /version	m/medium of performance
		d /date of treaty signing	r /key
			x /topical subdivision
			y /period subdivision
			z /geographic subdivision
650	Topical subject	a /main heading, topical subject element	x /topical subdivision
			y /period subdivision
			z /geographic subdivision
651	Geographic name	a /main heading, geographic name element	x /topical subdivision
			y /period subdivision
			z /geographic subdivision
655	Genre heading	a /main heading, genre element	x /topical subdivision
			y /period subdivision
			z /geographic subdivision

records assigned the selected heading, or (3) provide more specific information about the selected heading in the form of subject subdivisions. The far right-hand column of Table 3.2 lists subfields that would be displayed to users who respond to the latter system prompt. This approach is especially helpful to users browsing in an alphabetical list who select a subject heading that is assigned to hundreds of bibliographic records. Furthermore, subdivided forms of the selected heading may be assigned to more bibliographic records, resulting in thousands of retrievals. For example, there are likely to be many retrievals for the topical subject headings "Children," "Mathematics," and "Women" in the above list. To make the display of subdivided subject headings more manageable, systems can prompt users to limit the display by selecting a subfield type that interests them. Subfields appropriate for user prompting are listed on the far right column of Table 3.2.

Table 3.2 is divided into two browsing lists: (1) lists of personal names, and (2) lists of subjects generally. The former consists of subject headings from personal name subject heading fields only (MARC tag 600). The latter includes subject headings from corporate name, meeting name, uniform title, topical subject, geographic name, and genre heading fields (MARC tags 610, 611, 630, 650, 651, and 655, respectively). Online systems would respond to the user's entry of a subject query with an alphabetical list of subject headings for personal names or for subjects generally based on the user's initial selection of a subject search for personal names or for subjects. A separate subject searching option for personal names is recommended because the order of elements in subject headings for personal names is much more rigid than the order of elements in other types of subject headings. The availability of a separate subject searching option for personal names helps filter out subject queries for personal names, which require special handling to compensate for the rigid order of personal name data elements. (Chapter 10 discusses subject queries and subject headings for personal names in greater detail.)

3.4.2 Fields and Subfields Contributing to Keyword-in-Heading Indexes

In response to the subject terms users enter into online catalogs, systems can respond with lists of subject headings containing words in user queries. This approach to subject searching is called the keyword-in-heading search approach. The searchable index that supports keyword-in-heading searches is composed of words from single subject heading fields of bibliographic records.

Keyword-in-heading approaches are also two-step approaches to subject searching: first, the user enters a subject query, and systems respond with a display of indexed subject headings that contain words in the query; second, the user browses up and down in the displayed list, and systems respond by creating sets of retrieved bibliographic records.

Two-step browsing approaches connected with keyword searching help users over some of the difficulties of predicting the forms used by the controlled vocabulary. Systems retrieve subject headings containing the same words as user queries, and possibly others in addition. Furthermore, the words in retrieved subject headings may not be in the same order as the words in user queries. Browsing is a particularly effective approach to subject searching when systems respond with subject headings that express the user query and the user's interest lies in a more specific aspect of the subject that is expressed in a subdivision.

This section discusses three different keyword-in-heading searches: (1) keyword-in-main-heading searches of topical subject headings, (2) keyword-in-subdivided-heading searches of subject headings for personal names, and (3) keyword-in-subdivided-heading searches of subjects generally.

The keyword-in-main-heading approach is limited to a searchable index of the words in the main heading or topical subject element of topical subject headings (MARC tag 650, subfield $a). This approach would be available to online catalog users who are performing a search for subjects generally; that is, it would not be available to users who perform a subject search for personal names. The result of keyword-in-main-heading searches is a list of topical subject headings bearing the words in user queries. For example, the result of a keyword-in-main-heading search for the subject query "jazz music" is a list of topical subject headings containing both words "jazz" and "music" in the unsubdivided form of the topical subject heading:

Double-bass and piano **music** (**Jazz**)
Guitar **music** (**Jazz**)
Jazz music
Monologues with **music** (**Jazz** ensemble with chamber orchestra)
Piano **music** (**Jazz**)
Saxophone **music** (**Jazz**)

To retrieve these six subject headings, online systems would perform a keyword search for the terms "jazz" and "music" in a searchable index of words from the topical subject element (main heading) of topical subject headings. Systems would retrieve two temporary sets of lists of subject headings. One set would contain the word "jazz" and the other set would contain the word "music." The system would then combine the temporary sets in an implicit Boolean "AND" operation to find subject headings common to both sets. The result would be a list of retrieved subject headings bearing both words "jazz" and "music" in the main heading subfield of topical subject headings. The list would be presented to users with options to display related terms, subdivided forms of the selected heading, or bibliographic records assigned to the selected heading.

Subdivided approaches would work similarly to the main heading approach except that the words in user queries could occur in the main heading subfield or in subfields following it. The keyword-in-subdivided-heading approach for personal names would be limited to a searchable index of the words in subject headings for personal names (i.e., MARC tag 600). Subfields contributing to the searchable index for this approach are listed in both subfield columns in Table 3.2. Online systems would invoke the keyword-in-subdivided-heading approach for personal names when users choose to search for personal names as subjects. The result of such an approach is a list of subject headings for personal names bearing the words in user queries. For example, the result of a keyword-in-subdivided-heading search for the personal-name subject query "lincoln assassination" is a list of subdivided subject headings containing both words "lincoln" and "assassination" in subdivided subject headings for personal names:

Lincoln, Abraham, 1809–1865--**Assassination** attempt, 1861
Lincoln, Abraham, 1809–1865--**Assassination** attempts
Lincoln, Abraham, 1809–1865--**Assassination**, 1865

The searchable index of the keyword-in-subdivided-heading approach for subjects generally would be composed of words in subject heading fields for corporate names, meetings, uniform titles, topical subjects, and geographic names (i.e., USMARC tags 610, 611, 630, 650, and 651, respectively). Subfields contributing to the searchable index for this approach are listed in both subfield columns in Table 3.2. Systems would invoke the keyword-in-subdivided-heading approach for subjects generally when users choose them, resulting in a list of subject headings bearing the words in user queries. Such a search for the subject query "business france," for example, would result in a list of topical subject headings containing both words "business" and "france" in the subdivided subject headings:

Big **business--France**
Master of **business** administration--**France**
Women in **business--France**

3.4.3 Fields and Subfields Contributing to Title Keyword Indexes

Titles often convey the subject matter of written communication. Examples of informative titles are *A History of Western Philosophy*, *Divorced Dads*, and *How To Write Songs That Sell.* Occasionally, titles are not indicative of an item's subject matter: *What Do You Say after You Say Hello?*, *The Big One*, and *Shining Trumpets*.

The USMARC format for books has many fields and subfields that convey title information (Table 3.3). Words from these fields would contribute to a title keyword index that is separate from other searchable keyword indexes of the online catalog. Title information resides in title statement, title added entry fields, and title subheadings of main and added entries for names and subjects. Subfields for named parts and sections of works (subfields $n and $p), form subheadings (subfield $k), and places of meetings (subfield $c) are included because they contain terms that users might enter in subject searches. Searchers of music information may enter terms included in subfields for medium of performance and key (i.e., subfields $m and $r, respectively). Examples of tagged subfields bearing title information are:

- 111 **Garden Seed Industry Conference** $n (**2nd** : $d 1963 : $c **Chicago, Illinois**)

Table 3.3
Fields and Subfields Conveying Title Information

Tag	Field description	Subfield(s)	Subfield description
Title statement			
130	Uniform title	atnpksdmr	Title(s); number, name of part or section; form subheading; version; date of treaty signing; medium; key
214	Augmented title	a	Augmented title
240	Uniform title	anpksmr	Title; number, name of part or section; form subheading; version; medium; key
242	Translation of title	anpb	(Same as 245)
243	Uniform title, collective	anpksmr	(Same as 240)
245	Title	anpb	Title; number, name of part or section; subtitle
Title added entries			
730	Uniform title	atnpkmrsd	Title(s); number, name of part or section; form subheading; medium; key; version; date of treaty signing
740	Title traced differently	anp	Title; number, name of part or section
Title subheadings in main and added entries for names			
111	Meeting name	ancktp	Meeting name; number of part or section; place of meeting; form subheading; title; name of part or section
700	Personal name	tknpmrs	Title; form subheading; name, number of part or section; medium; key; version
710	Corporate name	tpmrs	Title; name of part or section; medium; key; version
711	Meeting name	ancktp	(Same as 111)
Title subheadings in subject added entries			
600	Personal name	tknpmrs	(Same as 700)
610	Corporate name	tpmrs	(Same as 710)
611	Meeting name	ancktp	(Same as 711)
630	Uniform title	atnpkmrsd	(Same as 130)

- 111 **Expo '67** $c (**Montreal, Quebec**)
- 130 **Treaty of Utrecht** $d (**1713**)
- 130 **New York Herald Tribune** $s **European edition**
- 600 Schubert, Franz, $d 1797-1828. $t **Symphonies**, $n D. 759, $r **B minor**
- 700 Brahms, Johannes, $d 1833-1897. $t **Trios**, $m **Piano, strings**, $n no. 3, op. 101.
- 730 **Talmud** $l English $k **Selections**

Table 3.3 is a comprehensive listing of fields and subfields bearing title information. A more conservative listing would restrict the selection of subfields from title statements, uniform titles, and meeting names to subfields $a and $b and from name and subject added entries to subfield $t.

In an online catalog with title keyword searches, users would retrieve bibliographic records bearing these fields in response to queries such as "b minor symphonies," "montreal expo," "garden seed industry," and "trios for piano and strings."

Title keyword searching is a one-step approach to subject searching. The single user action of entering a subject query induces systems to respond by creating a set of retrieved bibliographic records. One-step approaches have the advantage of being quick and direct: users do not have to browse and select from an intermediary list of subject headings to create a set of retrieved bibliographic records. The disadvantage of one-step approaches is that they do not present users with suggestions for alternate terminology. Users would benefit from such feedback when their queries retrieve bibliographic records that are not relevant to the topics they are seeking and when their queries fail entirely.

3.4.4 Fields and Subfields Contributing to the Basic Keyword Index

The basic keyword index contains words from all subject-rich fields of bibliographic records. This includes words from subject heading fields (Table 3.2) that are used in browsing and keyword-in-heading searches and title (Table 3.3) fields. Keyword searches of the basic keyword index are also one-step approaches to subject searching. The single user action of entering a subject query induces systems to respond by creating a set of bibliographic records. For example, the result of a keyword search of the basic index for the subject query "homeless people" is a set of bibliographic records in which the word "homeless" comes from the subject heading "Homeless persons" and the word "people" comes from the title field. Keyword searches of the basic keyword index would be available to online catalog users who are performing a search for personal names or for subjects generally. Table 3.4 lists additional subject-rich fields and subfields of bibliographic records that are not listed in Tables 3.2 and 3.3. An online catalog's basic keyword index would contain words from fields and subfields listed in all columns of Tables 3.2, 3.3, and 3.4.

Variable data fields for corporate names, subjects, notes, and series convey subject content and should be added to the basic keyword index. Physical characteristics and bibliographic characteristics are subject information conveyed by codes in the 008 control field that should be converted to their English-language equivalents, then added to the basic index.

Subfields from corporate name headings should be selected for the basic index because these headings function similarly to subject headings in that they are assigned to bibliographic records representing works dealing with the corporate body itself (*Anglo-American Cataloguing Rules* 1988, 313). Examples of written communication assigned these headings are catalogs, inventories, directories, annual reports, financial reports, and conference proceedings.

Subject heading fields for uncontrolled subjects and faceted topical subjects are included in the list of fields contributing to the basic keyword index. The subject

Table 3.4
Additional Fields and Subfields for a Basic Keyword Index

Tag	Field description	Subfield(s)	Subfield description
Main-entry heading			
110	Corporate name	abncktp	Corporate body name; subordinate unit; number of part or section; place; form subheading; title; name of part or section
Subject added entries			
653	Uncontrolled subject	a	Subject term
654	Faceted topical subject	ab	Focus term; term other than focus term
Notes			
505	Contents note	a	Formatted contents note
520	Summary, annotation	a	Summary, annotation
Series			
440	Series statement	ap	Title; name of subseries, part, or section
490	Series statement, not traced	a	Series statement
800	Series added entry, personal name/title	t	Title of series
810	Series added entry, personal name/title	t	Title of series
811	Series added entry, meeting name/title	ancktp	Meeting name; number of part or section; place; form subheading; title of series; name of part or section
830	Series added	atnpkmrs	Titles; number, name of part or section; form subheading; medium; key, version
Physical characteristics			
008	Illustration code	Positions 18–21	Illustration terms
755	Physical characteristics	axyz	Access term; topical, period, geographic subdivision
Bibliographic characteristics			
008	Nature of contents	Positions 24–27	Nature of contents terms
008	Biography	Position 34	Type of biography term
008	Target audience	Position 22	Target audience term
008	Festschrift	Position 30	Festschrift term
008	Fiction	Position 33	Fiction term

terms from these fields are taken from subject heading lists and thesauri other than LCSH. Fields for these terms were not listed among the fields selected for browsing and keyword-in-heading indexes (Tables 3.2 and 3.3, respectively) because the structure and syntax of subject terms from these fields may be inconsistent with that of subject headings from the LCSH system. Inconsistencies in this regard would be apparent to users browsing alphabetical lists of subject headings and lists of subject headings retrieved as a result of keyword-in-heading search approaches. When subject terms from uncontrolled subjects and faceted topical subjects contribute words to the basic keyword index, the structure and syntax of subject headings is not evident to users who are searching across different fields in keyword searches of the basic index.

If a significant segment of a library's database is assigned subject headings from a system other than LCSH, serious consideration should be given to placing records with these headings in a database that is separate from the database of records assigned headings from the LCSH system. Our recommendations regarding subject searching capabilities for online catalogs are based on studies of the LCSH system and queries entered into online systems with bibliographic databases assigned LCSH. These capabilities could be extended to other subject heading systems; however, the authors have not yet undertaken the research necessary for making generalizations to other subject heading systems.

Words from series fields could be added to the basic keyword index of online catalogs. However, these words often express a topic or concept that is broader than the subject addressed by a book in a series. For example, the subject queries "literary criticism" and "history of literature" would retrieve all books from the series entitled "Dover Books on Literature, Literary History, Criticism." Examples of titles from the series are *A Life of William Shakespeare*, *Twentieth Century Stage Decoration*, and *Tolstoy*. The individual books in the series are about much more specific topics than the original queries and the title of the series that are responsible for producing retrievals.

Codes in the 008 control field of bibliographic records convey information about the physical and bibliographic characteristics of the item. Online systems can be programmed to convert these codes to full English-language terms. Terms could then be added to a note field preceded by a display constant explaining the term to users. The full terms and term variants, for example, plural, singular, adjectival forms, could also be added to the basic keyword index of online catalogs.

Of the nineteen pieces of information encoded in the 008 control field, six data elements convey subject information.

008, Positions 18–21: Illustration Code

Up to four single characters can be assigned to a bibliographic record to indicate the illustration terms used in the variable field for physical description (i.e., MARC tag 300, subfield $b). A choice of fifteen codes representing the following illustration terms is given. If this field is left blank, the item in hand has no illustrations.

a = diagrams	i = coats of arms
b = maps	j = genealogical tables
c = portraits	k = forms
d = charts	l = samples
e = plans	m = phonodiscs, phonowire, etc.
f = plates	o = photographs
g = music	p = illuminations
h = facsimiles	

Terms used in the physical description field (i.e., MARC tag 300, subfield $b) have varied over the years and several different abbreviations have been used. Thus, it would be much more difficult to identify and write out in full the terms in the variable field than to replace the codes used in the 008 fixed field with the terms they stand for. The full terms could be added to a note field preceded by a display constant such as "Contains" or "Includes." For example, a bibliographic record with the physical description "300 $b ill., ports., charts" would have the illustration codes "acd," which could be replaced with a note field "Includes diagrams, portraits, and charts." These terms could also be added to the basic keyword index of online catalogs.

008, Positions 24–27: Nature of Contents

Up to four single characters can be assigned to a bibliographic record to specify certain types of material used frequently for reference purposes. This information may also be repeated in the title, subject heading, or note fields of bibliographic records. A choice of several codes representing the following types of materials is given. If more than four codes apply to an item, the four most significant codes are selected and recorded in alphabetical order. If no codes are applicable, all positions contain blanks.

a = abstracts/summaries	l = legislation
b = bibliographies	n = literature surveys
c = catalogs	o = reviews
d = dictionaries	p = programmed texts
e = encyclopedias	q = filmographies
f = handbooks	r = directories
g = legal articles	s = statistics
i = indexes (other than its own index)	t = technical reports
	v = legal cases, case notes
k = discographies	w = law reports, digests

Codes could be replaced with the full, written-out term in plural or singular form. Terms would be added to a note field preceded by a display constant such as "Contents includes." For example, the codes "abi" in a bibliographic record would be replaced with the note field: "Contents includes abstracts/summaries, bibliography, and index." The plural and singular forms of these terms could also be added to the basic keyword index of online catalogs. This would enable a user to enter queries such as "indexes on psychology" and "psychology index" and retrieve material assigned the subject heading "Psychology" and nature of contents terms "index" and "indexes."

008, Position 34: Biography

Catalogers choose one alphabetical character from the following list of four characters to indicate that the item in hand is a biography: (1) a = individual autobiography, (2) b = individual biography, (3) c = collective biography or autobiography, and (4) d = contains biographical information. When the item in hand has no biographical information, catalogers leave this position blank.

Whenever users display bibliographic records containing one of the four codes, the display would include a note field saying "Contains biographical information" (for codes b, c, or d) or "Contains autobiographical information" (for code a). Terms relevant to the item, that is, biographies, biography, autobiography, autobiographies, and so on, could also be added to records for information retrieval.

008, Position 22: Target Audience

Only one character, "j," has been defined for the target audience position. This character is assigned to juvenile materials, that is, materials intended for use by children and young people through age 15 or ninth grade. Displays of bibliographic records could contain an explanatory note such as "Intended for use by children and young people through age 15 or 9th grade." The terms "juvenile material" or "children's material" could also be added to records for information retrieval.

008, Position 30: Festschrift

Catalogers set position 30 of the 008 control field to 0 or 1 depending on whether the item in hand is a festschrift. Displays of bibliographic records could include the term "festschrift" when the position is set to 1. The singular and plural forms of the term could also be added to keyword indexes for information retrieval to enable users to retrieve records in response to subject queries like "festschriften in information science" or "medieval art festschriften."

008, Position 33: Fiction

Catalogers set position 33 of the 008 control field to 0 or 1 depending on whether the item in hand is fiction. Displays of bibliographic records could include the term "Fiction" when the position is set to 1 and this term could also be added to keyword indexes for information retrieval.

3.5

Sparseness of Subject Terms in Bibliographic Records

The many subject-rich fields and subfields of bibliographic records listed in Tables 3.2, 3.3, and 3.4 are quite deceiving because they make it appear that bibliographic records are bursting with subject information. Unfortunately, this is not the case. Of the many subject-rich fields that contribute words to the basic keyword index, only fields for titles and subject headings occur in most bibliographic records.

To demonstrate the infrequency with which subject-rich fields occur, we are using field and subfield statistics generated in a March 1990 scan of 1% of the books format records in the OCLC database. Although the statistics are unpublished, they were generated using the same software for previously published statistics (Hickey 1981). Extracted from the statistics and listed in Table 3.5 is a dozen of the most frequently occurring subject-rich subfields in bibliographic records for monographs from the OCLC database.

The most frequently occurring subject-rich subfield is the topical subject element of topical subject headings (MARC tag 650, subfield $a). More topical subject elements (191,434) occur than bibliographic records in the sample (172,972); however, topical subject elements of topical subject headings occur in 62.5% of the bibliographic records in the sample. Thus, some records have several topical subject headings and some records have none. The second most frequently occurring subfield is the title proper (MARC tag 245, subfield $a). Every bibliographic record in the sample has one such subfield. A subfield for other title information (MARC tag 245, subfield $b) occurs in 38.4% of sample records. Other frequently occurring subfields for subject headings are topical subdivisions (MARC tags 650 and 651, subfield $x) and geographic subdivisions (MARC tag 650, subfield $z). Remaining frequently occurring subfields are found in fields for series (MARC tag 490), corporate names (MARC tag 110), and title added entries (MARC tag 740). Occurrences of the most frequently-occurring subject-rich subfields per bibliographic records range from 0.081 to 1.107. Over two dozen subject-rich fields are not listed in Table 3.5. These fields would occur less frequently than the last-listed subfield in Table 3.5, that is, less than 0.081.

Fields that hold the most promise for subject terms, that is, note fields for tables of contents and annotations, are not even listed in Table 3.5. The percentages of OCLC books records containing these fields are 0.3% and 1.0%, respectively.

Table 3.5
Frequently Occurring Subject-Rich Subfields in 172,972 Bibliographic Records

Tag/subfield name			Number	Records (%)	Occur./record
650	$a	Topical subject element	191,434	62.5	1.107
245	$a	Title proper	172,972	100.0	1.000
650	$x	Topical subdivision	85,343	N/A[a]	0.493
650	$z	Geographic subdivision	74,729	N/A	0.432
245	$b	Other title information	66,509	38.4	0.385
651	$x	Topical subdivision	34,134	N/A	0.220
651	$a	Geographic name element	34,497	N/A	0.199
490	$a	Series statement	31,372	N/A	0.181
600	$a	Personal name element	20,166	9.6	0.117
740	$a	Title added entry	19,648	N/A	0.114
110	$a	Name of corporate body	19,486	11.3	0.113
110	$b	Subordinate unit	14,062	8.1	0.081

[a]N/A, Not available in study statistics.

The average number of subject headings per bibliographic record is about 1.4 (Atherton 1978; Hickey 1981, 8; Markey & Demeyer 1986, 301; McClure 1976; O'Neill & Aluri 1981). The low number of subject headings per record is due to LC's policy of summarization, in which subject headings are assigned to express the overall subject content of library material (see also Chapter 1, Section 1.3.5).

Another measure of the subject information in subject-rich fields of bibliographic records is the number of unique words contributed by these fields. In a previous study, researchers divided subject-rich fields into five categories to determine how many unique subject terms each category contributed to bibliographic records (Markey & Calhoun 1987). The five categories were: (1) subject heading fields (MARC tags 6xx), (2) title fields (MARC tags 130, 24x, 730, 740), (3) note fields (MARC tags 505 and 520), (4) series fields (MARC tags 4xx and 830), and (5) sponsor fields (MARC tags 111 and 711). The contents of these five categories of subject-rich fields were analyzed to determine the average number of unique words contributed *successively* by subject-rich fields. The analysis required the calculation of the number of words per field. These words were then compared to one another, and duplicate words per field were discarded. The analysis continued with the calculation of the number of unique words contributed successively by each of the five subject-rich field categories. Figure 3.6 shows the result for a combined database of about 40,000 records from three research libraries and one public library.

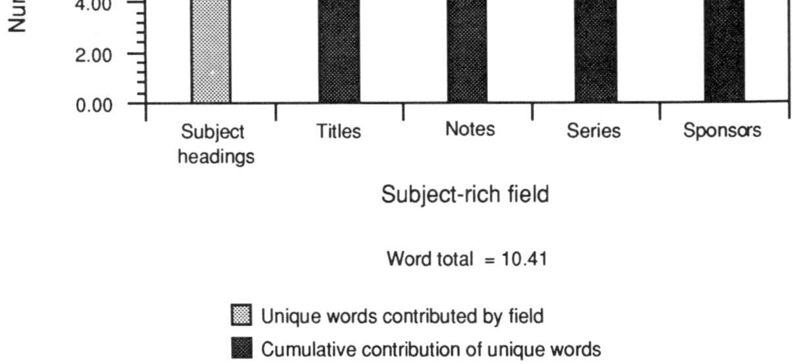

Figure 3.6
Unique words in subject-rich fields of bibliographic records.

Subject heading fields contribute about four unique words per bibliographic record. Even though title fields are second in the analysis, they contribute almost five unique words, that is, nearly one word more than subject heading fields that come first in the analysis. Fields for notes, series, and sponsors contribute less than one unique word per bibliographic record. When bibliographic records from the four libraries are analyzed individually, bibliographic records created by LC contribute the most unique words (14.2). Furthermore, subject heading fields in LC bibliographic records contribute more unique words (6.2) than title fields (5.1). If title fields come first in the analysis, the contributions of these fields are reversed, that is, title fields contribute about six words and subject heading fields contribute about five words per record.

Although the number of fields contributing to subject indexes for searching and browsing is quite large, these fields actually contribute few unique words and subject headings. Subject-rich fields of bibliographic records can be expected to contribute between ten and fifteen unique subject terms per record to keyword indexes and about six unique words to title keyword indexes. Subject heading fields contribute between one and two subject headings to the alphabetical subject heading index for browsing. The small contribution of subject-rich fields to subject indexes for searching and browsing presents a challenge to systems staff to design online systems with subject searching capabilities that maximize catalog users' chances of matching their subject queries with the words and phrases indexed in the catalog.

3.6 Synthesis and Summary

USMARC format integration scheduled for implementation in the mid 1990s should make the tasks of systems staff much easier because they will no longer have to write separate programs to handle bibliographic records from different formats. A review of the format structure for bibliographic data shows that it is the same as that for authority records because USMARC records for bibliographic data conform to the same national and international standards as records for authority data. USMARC content designation and record content for bibliographic data are different from those for authority data because the records from these two formats serve different functions in the catalog.

The discussion of data fields in this chapter centers on the fields and subfields of bibliographic records fields that convey subject content, the subject indexes of online catalogs into which data from these fields is processed, and the subject searching approaches each index supports.

Four indexes are presented: (1) alphabetical subject heading indexes, (2) keyword-in-heading indexes, (3) a title keyword index, and (4) a basic keyword index. Alphabetical subject heading indexes consist of the subject headings assigned to subject heading fields (MARC tags 6xx) of bibliographic records (Table 3.2). Subject heading fields are limited to those containing subject headings based on the LCSH system to ensure that the terms in alphabetical lists are consistent with one another in terms of their structure and syntax. Alphabetical subject indexes support a two-step approach to subject searching: (1) the user action of entering a subject query induces systems to respond with a display of indexed subject headings in alphabetical proximity to the query, and (2) the user action of selecting a listed subject heading induces systems to create a set of retrieved bibliographic records for display.

Keyword-in-heading indexes support keyword-in-main-heading and keyword-in-subdivided-heading search approaches. The index for the former approach consists of words from the main heading (i.e., subfield $a) of topical subject headings (MARC tag 650) (Table 3.2, far right-hand column). The index for the latter approach consists of words from the entire subject heading string, that is, main heading and subdivisions (MARC tags 6xx) (Table 3.2, middle and right-hand columns). The result of keyword-in-main-heading searches is a list of topical subject headings bearing the words in user queries. The subdivided approach works similarly to the main heading approach except that the words in user queries can occur in the main heading subfield or in subfields following it.

Keyword-in-heading indexes also support the two-step approach to subject searching. Two-step approaches feature an intermediary display of subject headings indexed in the online catalog that are in alphabetical proximity to user queries (alphabetical approach) or contain the words in user queries (keyword-in-heading approaches). Subject heading displays may contain subject headings relevant to the topics users seek that are different grammatical forms than those used in user queries. They may also contain words in addition to those in user queries. Intermediary displays of subject headings give users feedback about the subject terminology used in the library catalog. If listed subject headings express the topics users are seeking, they are likely to retrieve bibliographic records relevant to user needs because library catalogers are guided by the principle of specific and direct entry in the assignment of subject headings from the LCSH system.

Title information resides in title statement and title added entry fields and in main and added entries for names and subjects. Words from these fields are processed into a title keyword index. In an online catalog that features title keyword searches, users would retrieve bibliographic records bearing their query words in these selected title fields. Title keyword indexes support a one-step approach to subject searching in which the user action of entering a subject query results in the system's retrieval of bibliographic records bearing user query words in title fields of retrieved records.

The basic keyword index is the most comprehensive of the three indexes because it contains words from all subject-rich fields and subfields of bibliographic records (Tables 3.2-3.4). Subject heading (Table 3.2) and title fields (Table 3.3) contribute the most words to the basic keyword index. Subfields from several additional fields also convey subject content, for example, main entry fields for corporate names (MARC tag 110), title subheadings in main and added entry fields for name headings

(MARC tags 1xx, 7xx, and 87x, subfield $t), title added entries (MARC tags 730 and 740), and series statement fields (MARC tags 440 and 490); however, many of the subject-rich subfields in these fields occur so infrequently in bibliographic records that they contribute few words to the basic keyword index. Fields that hold the most promise for subject terms, that is, note fields for tables of contents and annotations (MARC tags 505 and 520), also occur infrequently in bibliographic records. Codes in several positions of the 008 control fields that convey subject information can be converted to their English-language equivalents, added to bibliographic records for display, and added to the basic keyword index for information retrieval.

Over three dozen data fields contribute words to the basic keyword index; however, only ten to fifteen unique words are contributed to the basic index per individual bibliographic record (Figure 3.6). Most of these words come from title and subject heading fields because these are the only subject-rich fields that occur with much frequency in bibliographic records.

The basic keyword index supports a one-step approach to subject searching. One-step approaches are quick and direct in that a single user action, that is, entry of a subject query, induces systems to produce a set of retrieved bibliographic records. One-step approaches have the disadvantage of being unable to suggest alternate terminology to users whose queries fail to retrieve relevant bibliographic records or fail entirely to retrieve bibliographic records. Furthermore, one-step approaches are supported by subject indexes consisting of words from subject headings fields and other subject-rich fields of bibliographic records. The principle of specific and direct entry pertains only to the assignment of terms to the former fields. Thus, the potential of retrieving relevant records based on retrievals from fields other than subject heading fields is tenuous in comparison to the potential of retrieving relevant records based on retrievals from subject heading fields.

The meager amount of subject information residing in fields of bibliographic records makes it imperative that online catalogs be equipped with subject searching capabilities that maximize users' chances of matching their subject terms with those in the catalog. This book will make recommendations in this regard. At this time, it is premature to make such recommendations. This book now turns to a study and analysis of the subject queries users enter into online catalogs. A thorough understanding of user terminology is necessary to determine which subject searching capabilities are best suited to their queries. The discussion of USMARC fields containing subject information in this chapter is intended to familiarize readers with this format's content to prepare for the study of user queries and subject searching capabilities in subsequent chapters.

References

Anglo-American Cataloguing Rules. (1988). 2nd ed., rev. Chicago: American Library Association.

Atherton, Pauline A. (1978). *Books are for use: Final report of the Subject Access Project to the Council on Library Resources.* Syracuse, NY: School of Information Studies. ERIC ED 156 131.

Avram, Henriette. (1968). *The MARC Pilot Project; Final report on a project sponsored by the Council on Library Resources, Inc.* Washington, DC: Library of Congress.

Avram, Henriette D., Knapp, John F., & Rather, Lucia J. (1968). *The MARC II format: A communications format for bibliographic data.* Washington, DC: Library of Congress.

Borgman, Christine L. (1986). Why are online catalogs hard to use? Lessons learned from information-retrieval studies. *Journal of the American Society for Information Science, 37*, 6 (November), 387–400.

Byrne, Deborah J. (1991). *MARC manual: Understanding and using MARC records.* Englewood, CO: Libraries Unlimited.

Crawford, Walt. (1987). Testing bibliographic displays for online catalogs. *Information Technology and Libraries, 6*, 1 (March), 20–33.

Crawford, Walt. (1989). *MARC for library use: Understanding integrated USMARC* (2nd ed.). Boston: G.K. Hall.

Crawford, Walt, Stovel, Lennie, & Bales, Kathleen. (1986). *Bibliographic displays in the online catalog.* White Plains, NY: Knowledge Industry Publications.

Hagler, Ronald, & Simmons, Peter. (1982). *The bibliographic record and information technology.* Chicago: American Library Association.

Hickey, Thomas. (1981). *Field, subfield, and indicator statistics in OCLC bibliographic records.* Dublin, Ohio: OCLC. OCLC Research Report OCLC/OPR/RR-81/1.

Janosky, Beverly, Smith, Philip J., & Hildreth, Charles R. (1986). Online library catalog systems: An analysis of user errors. *International Journal of Man-Machine Studies, 25*, 5, 573–592.

Library of Congress. (1972). *MARC user survey.* Washington, DC: Library of Congress.

Library of Congress. (1988a). *Format integration and its effect on the USMARC bibliographic format.* Washington, DC: Library of Congress.

Library of Congress. (1988b). *USMARC format for bibliographic data.* Washington, DC: Library of Congress.

Markey, Karen, & Calhoun, Karen. (1987). Unique words contributed by MARC records with summary and/or contents notes. In Ching-chih Chen (Ed.), *ASIS '87, Proceedings of the 50th ASIS annual meeting* (pp. 153–162). Medford, NJ: Learned Information.

Markey, Karen, & Demeyer, Anh. (1986). *Dewey Decimal Classification Online Project: Evaluation of a library schedule and index integrated into the subject searching capabilities of an online catalog.* Dublin, Ohio: OCLC. OCLC Research Report OCLC/OPR/86/1.

Matthews, Joseph R. (1987). Suggested guidelines for screen layouts and design of online catalogs. *Library Trends, 35*, 4 (Spring), 555–570.

McClure, Charles R. (1976). Subject and added entries as access to information. *Journal of Academic Librarianship, 2* (March), 9–14.

O'Neill, Edward T., & Aluri, Rao. (1981). Library of Congress subject heading patterns in OCLC monographic records. *Resources & Technical Services, 25*, 1 (January/March), 63–67, 70–80.

Shaw, Debora. (1991). The human-computer interface for information-retrieval. In Martha E. Williams (Ed.), *Annual review of information science and technology* (pp. 155–195). Amsterdam: Elsevier.

Yee, Martha M. (1991). System design and cataloging meet the user: User interfaces to online public-access catalogs. *Journal of the American Society for Information Science, 42*, 2 (March), 78–98.

4

Subject Heading Compatibility between LCSH-mr and Bibliographic Files

4.1 Introduction

The LCSH-mr file of subject authority records is a source file of subject terms that are authorized for use as access points in bibliographic files. LCSH-mr contains authority records for topical subjects, uniform titles, and personal, corporate, meeting, and geographic names (see Figure 2.6); however, it is primarily a source file for topical subject headings. Headings for names and uniform titles are only included in LCSH-mr when they are pattern headings, or when special subdivisions, unique references, or specific instructions are given.

This chapter takes a closer look at the assigned subject headings contained in a sample bibliographic file to determine the extent to which corresponding records for these headings appear in LCSH-mr. The sample of assigned subject headings was taken from a file of unique subject headings found in the OCLC Online Union Catalog through October, 1988. A one-percent systematic random sample was drawn from the unique headings file by extracting every 100th heading, yielding a sample of 34,279 topical subject headings (MARC tag 650).

The principal beneficiaries of subject authority records are subject catalogers and online catalog users. Catalogers need to know that the subject heading is authorized for use in the catalog. Online users find the information in the subject authority record helpful in determining the appropriateness of the subject heading for their topics of interest. This information, conveyed through cross-references, general references, classification numbers, scope notes, and simple and general *see* references, can direct users to subject headings authorized for topics they are seeking. General references and scope notes also give catalog users information about the subjects they seek. Additionally, the subject authority record may include suggestions for terms that may be more relevant to the online user's topics of interest. Users browsing broader, narrower, and related terms under subject headings may find terms used in the catalog that express topics of interest more precisely than the term they first consulted. Classification numbers reveal specific bookshelf locations that users may find fruitful for browsing. Thus, the availability of a subject authority record for an assigned subject heading is a boon to catalog searchers because the references and notes in these records can help catalog users decide whether they are on the right track and can suggest other terms authorized for use in the catalog.

4.2 Why Assigned Headings Are Not in LCSH-mr

A working knowledge of subject heading practice and application reveals reasons why assigned subject headings from bibliographic databases do not appear in LCSH-mr. Catalogers can add the following types of subdivisions to form authorized subdivided headings (Pietris 1987, 78): (1) free-floating subdivisions, (2) free-floating subdivisions controlled by pattern/model headings, (3) multiple subdivisions, either specifically listed or authorized in a scope note, or (4) geographic subdivisions. Additional causes for the creation of authorized main (i.e., unsubdivided) headings are listed below (Pietris 1987, 78–79):

- Catalogers use the following free-floating phrases to construct main headings as needed without creating subject authority records:
  [topic or place] in literature
  [topic or place] in art
- Unprinted music headings
- Before 1976, catalogers assigned headings that were not printed in *LCSH*; examples are chemical compounds, names of families, gods, archeological sites, structures, and biological names

Erroneous and unauthorized subject headings also occur in bibliographic records, and these headings do not match the subject headings in established heading fields of subject authority records. Erroneous subject headings are those containing one or more errors that can be corrected without requiring a human intermediary to refer to the bibliographic record, original item, and/or LCSH to correct the error: examples are the incorrect tagging and addition errors in the assigned subject headings "651 British" and "650 Geriatric nurssing," respectively. Unauthorized subject headings contain one or more problems that cannot be resolved without a human intermediary, who must refer to the bibliographic record, the original item, and/or LCSH to resolve the problem: examples are the made-up and obsolete subject headings "650 Cataloging of toys" and "650 Electronic data processing in research."

Two previous studies have reported on erroneous and unauthorized subject headings in bibliographic files. Lantz, O'Neill, and Vizine-Goetz (1984) found that an estimated 22% of subfields from a sample of assigned subject headings and geographical names contain erroneous or unauthorized headings. Most errors were attributed to incorrect capitalization, punctuation, or spacing; a distant second category of errors was incorrect MARC tags or subfield codes. Researchers at The University of Michigan extracted and analyzed a sample of subject headings and geographic names from catalog cards in the university library's shelflist. Forty-four percent of the assigned subject headings in the shelflist were exact matches of headings in the tenth edition of LCSH (Frost & Dede 1988, 292–293). Most exact matches were unsubdivided subject headings (90.1%) and unsubdivided geographic names (40.5%). Nonmatches were attributed to errors such as *see* references, spelling, punctuation, and capitalization, and to unauthorized headings such as obsolete headings, incorrectly formulated headings, and missing words in headings.

In 1984, systems staff at The Ohio State University Libraries incorporated subject headings, references, and notes from LCSH-mr into the LCS online catalog. This version of LCSH-mr corresponds to the ninth edition of LCSH and printed supplements from 1979 to 1981. One-third of the authorized subject headings (MARC tag 150) in LCSH-mr were exact matches of one-tenth of the unique assigned headings (MARC tag 650) in the LCS online catalog (Ludy 1985, 159). Staff verified an additional 10% of unique assigned headings bearing main headings matching LCSH-mr and one of seventeen common subdivisions. They found an additional 0.25% of unique assigned headings that matched *see* references in LCSH-mr and automatically replaced all but 3% of them with authorized subject headings. The remainder required a human intermediary to review and make decisions about changes, for several reasons, including instances when *see* references referred to more than one established heading.

Percentages of exact matches are much higher in The University of Michigan study than in The Ohio State University study because they are based on assigned heading occurrences in shelflist records. That is, headings occurring several times are counted for each occurrence. Percentages in the Ohio State study are based on matches of unique assigned subject headings in bibliographic records. Percentages of exact matches given later in this chapter are also based on matches of unique assigned subject headings, thus, these could be compared to the Ohio State results.

4.3 A Compatibility Study of Machine-Readable Subject Heading Files

4.3.1 Subject Heading Files Used in the Study

The LCSH-mr used in the compatibility study described in this chapter is the same cumulative master tape that was used to report on what information is typically supplied in a subject authority record in LCSH-mr (see Chapter 2, Section 2.6.1). The tape contained 160,706 subject authority records created or modified through July 6, 1987. It corresponded closely to the eleventh edition of the printed *LCSH*, and it contained headings and references established by LC through August 1987. To verify subject headings, tags, free-floating phrases, and subdivisions, the investigators consulted the eleventh edition of the printed *LCSH* (Library of Congress 1988) and the revised edition of the *Subject cataloging manual: Subject headings* (SCM:SH) (Library of Congress 1987).

4.3.2 Matching Procedure

The technique for matching LCSH-mr and assigned subject headings was first to attempt to find an exact match between the two classes of headings. When no exact match was found, various combinations of assigned subject headings were generated and then matched to LCSH-mr headings. The combinations consisted of the a-subfield and a series of combinations of subdivisions. Subdivisions were systematically removed from the assigned heading until one or more matches of an LCSH-mr heading was found. For example, the subdivided assigned subject heading "Fisheries--Economic aspects--Statistics" generated the following combinations:

Subdivision combination	*Combinations generated*
a-subfield--1st subdivision--2nd subdivision	Fisheries--Economic aspects--Statistics
a-subfield--1st subdivision	Fisheries--Economic aspects
a-subfield--2nd subdivision	Fisheries--Statistics
a-subfield	Fisheries

The matching procedure began with the original heading and then proceeded to combinations with four or fewer subdivisions until one or more matches of combinations of a particular length (i.e., number of subdivisions) were made, or all combinations had been attempted. All combinations of a particular length were tried because more than one LCSH-mr heading often matched the combinations generated. In the above example, the assigned subject heading "Fisheries--Economic aspects--Statistics" does not match an LCSH-mr heading, but two combinations, "Fisheries--Economic aspects" and "Fisheries--Statistics," match two LCSH-mr headings. Statistics on exact matches and the number of assigned subject headings matching LCSH-mr after subdivision removal are given below.

4.3.3 Lengths of Subject Headings

Numbers and percentages of assigned subject headings from the 1% sample of unique assigned headings (MARC tag 650) and from LCSH-mr (MARC tag 150) are listed in Table 4.1 according to their length.

Most (70.4%) LCSH-mr are unsubdivided; most (86.3%) assigned subject headings are subdivided. The length of exactly 50% of assigned subject headings exceeds one subdivision. Only 3.7% of LCSH-mr exceed one subdivision.

Table 4.1
Lengths of LCSH-mr and Assigned Subject Headings

Length of headings	No./% LCSH-mr	No./% Bibl. Records
a only	90,471 (70.4)	4,706 (13.7)
a + 1	33,246 (25.9)	12,431 (36.3)
a + 2	4,423 (3.5)	12,911 (37.7)
a + 3	224 (0.2)	3,782 (11.0)
a + 4	3 (0.0)	411 (1.2)
a + 5	N/A	35 (0.1)
a + 6	N/A	3 (0.0)
Total	128,367 (100.0)	34,279 (100.0)

If the assigned subject headings were compared to LCSH-mr and every heading exactly matched LCSH-mr, the percentage of exact matches would not be above 43.3%. The lower percentages in each row for subject headings bearing four or fewer subdivisions are summed to obtain this total. The compatibility study demonstrates that the percentage of exact matches is much lower due to the addition of the free-floating subdivisions and subdivisions based on a pattern, and due to unprinted, erroneous, and unauthorized headings.

4.3.4 Exact Matches of LCSH-mr

Numbers and percentages of assigned subject headings that are exact matches of LCSH-mr are listed in columns 3 and 4 of Table 4.2.

Table 4.2
Matching Assigned Subject Headings with LCSH-mr

Length of assigned headings (650)	Total	No./% exact match	No./% matching after sbdvns. removed	No./% failing to match
a only	4,706	1,836 (5.4)	NA	2,870 (8.4)
a + 1	12,431	467 (1.4)	9,866 (28.8)	2,098 (6.1)
a + 2	12,911	38 (0.1)	11,972 (34.9)	901 (2.6)
a + 3	3,782	12 (0.0)	3,626 (10.6)	144 (0.4)
a + 4	411	0 (0.0)	395 (1.1)	16 (0.1)
a + 5	35	NA	32 (0.1)	3 (0.0)
a + 6	3	NA	3 (0.0)	0 (0.0)
Total	34,279	2,353 (6.9)	25,894 (75.5)	6,032 (17.6)

Of the 6.9% of headings that are exact matches, the largest number (1836) are unsubdivided headings. This number only accounts for 5.4% of subject headings in the sample. The percentage (6.9%) of assigned subject headings that are exact matches of LCSH-mr is comparable to the ten percent of assigned subject headings in The Ohio State University Library study's database that exactly match LCSH-mr (Ludy 1985, 159). Percentages from the two studies suggest that seven to ten of every one hundred assigned subject headings are exact matches of LCSH-mr; thus, they are directly connected to subject authority records that have potentially useful information, such as cross-references, scope notes, and LC classification numbers for subject searching and browsing.

When one or more subdivisions are removed from subject headings from a bibliographic file, 75.5% of subdivided, assigned subject headings (Table 4.2) match one or more authorized headings in the LCSH-mr file of subject authority records. Section 4.3.5 below describes the subdivision removal process and the extent to which subject headings submitted to such a process match more than one subject heading in the established heading field of subject authority records.

Even after subdivisions are removed from subdivided headings, a total of 17.6% of assigned subject headings fail to match headings in the subject authority file. The largest percentage (8.4%) of nonmatching headings is for unsubdivided headings. An 8.0% random sample of nonmatching subject headings was examined manually to determine the reasons why they fail to match LCSH-mr headings. Subsequent sections attribute nonmatches to categories of subject headings not printed in *LCSH*, erroneous headings, and unauthorized headings.

4.3.5 Systematic Removal of Subdivisions

Systematic removal of subdivisions increases substantially the numbers and percentages of matches between the two vocabularies, especially for subdivided headings. Most of the subdivisions removed through this process are free-floating subdivisions or subdivisions that are based on a pattern, subdivisions that were omitted from the printed *LCSH* to keep the printed list from becoming too bulky and voluminous to be useful to catalogers or catalog users.

Overall, the removal of one or more subdivisions from assigned subject headings results in an additional 75.5% of subject headings that correspond to subject headings in the subject authority file (Table 4.2, columns 5 and 6). The largest number and percentage of matches effected from subdivision removal come from twice-subdivided assigned subject headings (11,972 or 34.9%).

Table 4.3 summarizes the numbers of assigned subject headings for exact matches and for matches effected through subdivision removal. Columns give the numbers of matched subject authority records. Rows give the length of the matched authorized heading in subject authority records.

Table 4.3
Matches of LCSH-mr through Subdivision Removal

Length of assigned subject hdgs. with sbdvn. removal (650, total)	Number of matched subject authority records (LCSH-mr)						
	1	2	3	4	5	6	Total
a subfield only	22,880	N/A	N/A	N/A	N/A	N/A	22,880
a + 1	4,929	225	10	0	0	0	5,164
a + 2	185	3	0	0	0	0	188
a + 3	15	0	0	0	0	0	15
a + 4	0	0	0	0	0	0	0
Total	28,009	228	10	0	0	0	28,247

Most assigned subject headings match one unsubdivided authorized heading in subject authority records. A total of 17,142 assigned subject headings contain two or more subdivisions (column 2 of Table 4.2). Less than 1.4% (238 of 17,142) of assigned subject headings bearing two or more subdivisions match more than one subdivided authorized heading in such records. Subdivision removal effects matches of the subject headings in established heading fields of subject authority records for over three-fourths of assigned headings.

The discussion of orphan headings (Chapter 2) demonstrates that most of the cross-references and other useful information in subject authority records are connected with the unsubdivided form of topical subject headings (see Figure 2.7). This connection suggests that even if subdivided assigned subject headings match subdivided LCSH-mr headings, the subject authority record(s) for the subdivided heading is not likely to have useful information to help the user improve the subject search. Such information is more likely to be found in the subject authority record for the unsubdivided form of heading. This finding underlines the need for online systems to help users find and use the information in subject authority records for the unsubdivided form of the subdivided subject heading they consult in library catalogs.

4.4

Subject Headings Failing to Match Authority File Headings

When exact matches and matches effected through subdivision removal are extracted from the sample of assigned subject headings, 17.6% of assigned subject headings remain. The following sections describe the analysis of an 8.0% random sample of the remaining headings to determine the reasons why they fail to match

LCSH-mr headings. These sections attribute nonmatches to categories of subject headings not printed in *LCSH*, erroneous subject headings, and unauthorized subject headings.

4.4.1 Subject Headings Not Printed in *LCSH*

Unprinted (or nonprint) headings are used as subject entries but do not appear in the printed *LCSH* (Chan 1986, 172). Descriptions of the five categories of unprinted headings listed in Table 4.4 for the sample of nonmatching assigned subject headings are:

a. Music headings. Printed editions of *LCSH* give catalogers instructions about formulating music headings that are not printed in the alphabetical list (Library of Congress 1988, xvii–xviii).

b. Biological names in Latin. Prior to 1976, several categories of headings, including biological names, were unprinted headings in *LCSH*. Since 1976, such headings are printed in *LCSH* when LC catalogers assign them (Library of Congress 1988, xvii).

c. Free-floating phrases. Catalogers add the free-floating phrases "in art" or "in literature" to assigned subject headings by following memorandum H362 in SCM:SH (Library of Congress 1987).

d. Authorized by LCSH references. Catalogers formulate selected headings by following general references, notes, and examples in LCSH. Such data may be candidates for inclusion in future editions of SCM:SH.

e. Authorized heading added to LCSH-mr. Some headings were assigned to Online Union Catalog (OLUC) records and found in the most current

Table 4.4
Unprinted Assigned Subject Headings[a]

Unprinted category	Length of assigned heading: Total	a only	a + 1
a. Music headings	9 (1.9)	5 (3.5)	4 (3.8)
b. Biological names in Latin	8 (1.7)	8 (5.6)	0 (0.0)
c. Free-floating phrases	3 (0.6)	2 (1.4)	1 (1.0)
d. Authorized by LCSH references	3 (0.6)	3 (2.1)	0 (0.0)
e. Authorized heading added to LCSH-mr	1 (0.2)	0 (0.0)	1 (1.0)
Subtotal	24 (5.0)	18 (12.5)	6 (5.7)
Total nonmatching headings of this length in sample	484 (100.0)	144 (100.0)	105 (100.0)

[a]Percentages may not add to subtotal percentages because of rounding.

version of LCSH-mr on the OCLC Online System. However, these headings were not in the cumulative LCSH-mr used in the compatibility study.

No assigned subject headings occurring in unprinted categories exceed one subdivision. Thus, Table 4.4 contains occurrences of unprinted headings only for unsubdivided and once-subdivided headings. The largest number of unprinted headings are music headings (9 occurrences) followed by biological names in Latin (8 occurrences). Three headings contain the free-floating phrase "in art" or "in literature." Three headings are authorized by notes and general references in LCSH; for example, "Grotesque (The word)" is authorized by the complex *see also* reference under "English language $x Etymology." One assigned heading was not in the version of LCSH-mr used in the project but had been recently established by LC.

Unprinted headings are only 5.0% of the random sample of nonmatching assigned subject headings. Using these figures, we can estimate that unprinted subject headings represent a very small percentage (0.9%) of the unique assigned subject headings in a bibliographic file. By definition, unprinted headings have no corresponding record in the subject authority file and will not be connected with cross-references and other potentially useful information in these records.

4.4.2 Erroneous Subject Headings

Erroneous subject headings are those that contain one or more errors that can be corrected without requiring a human intermediary to refer to the bibliographic record, original item, and/or LCSH to correct the error. The 8.0% sample of nonmatching subject headings yielded the following ten categories of erroneous headings. (Error categories for capitalization, spacing, or punctuation were not established because these types of errors are ignored in the automatic matching procedure.) Descriptions of the ten error categories listed in Table 4.5 for the sample of nonmatching assigned subject headings are:

f. Incorrect MARC tag. The MARC tag applied to the heading is incorrect. For example, the corporate name "Boeing Corporation" is incorrectly tagged 650.

g. *See from* tracing. The assigned subject heading matches an unsubdivided or subdivided *see from* tracing in the eleventh edition of the printed *LCSH*. For example, "Comparative government" is a *see from* tracing in this LCSH edition under the authorized topical subject heading "Comparative politics."

h. Subfield code missing. One or more subdivisions is embedded in the main heading subfield, that is, subfield $a. For example, "Eye Diseases and defects" comprises the entire main heading subfield (subfield $a). The corrected heading is "Eye $x Diseases and defects."

i. Qualifier missing. The qualifier is missing from the main heading subfield. For example, "Bacchus" comprises the entire main heading. The corrected heading is "Bacchus (Roman deity)."

Table 4.5
Erroneous Assigned Subject Headings[a]

	Length of assigned heading			
Unprinted category	Total	a only	a + 1	Exceeding 1 subdivision
f. Incorrect MARC tag	88 (18.2)	23 (16.0)	23 (21.9)	42 (17.9)
g. *See from* tracing	88 (18.2)	3 (2.1)	16 (15.2)	69 (29.4)
h. Subfield code missing	4 (0.8)	1 (0.7)	0 (0.0)	3 (1.3)
i. Qualifier missing	6 (1.2)	2 (1.4)	2 (1.9)	2 (0.8)
j. Addition/omission	56 (11.6)	17 (11.8)	10 (9.5)	29 (12.3)
k. Substitution transposition	19 (3.9)	7 (4.8)	4 (3.8)	8 (3.4)
l. Spelling	7 (1.4)	3 (2.1)	1 (1.0)	3 (1.3)
m. Abbreviation	1 (0.2)	1 (0.7)	0 (0.0)	0 (0.0)
n. Hyphenation	13 (2.7)	1 (0.7)	2 (1.9)	10 (4.3)
o. Combinations	26 (5.4)	8 (5.5)	10 (9.5)	8 (3.4)
Subtotal	308 (63.6)	66 (45.8)	68 (64.8)	174 (74.0)
Total nonmatching headings of this length in sample	484 (100.0)	144 (100.0)	105 (100.0)	235 (100.0)

[a]Percentages may not add to subtotal percentages because of rounding.

j. Addition/omission of one character. One character has been added or omitted from a main heading. For example, the letter "s" has been erroneously added to "Seniority, Employees" and the letter "c" has been erroneously omitted from "Santification." (If more than one character has been added and/or omitted, the heading is categorized as a spelling error.)

k. Substitution/transposition. One character has been substituted for another or two characters have been transposed in a main heading. For example, the letter "a" has been substituted for the letter "o" in "Socialogy" and the letters "c" and "t" are transposed in "Map projetcion." (If more than one character has been substituted and/or two or more occurrences of transposition occur in the main heading, the heading is categorized as a spelling error.

l. Spelling. Multiple occurrences of addition/omission and/or substitution/transposition in a main heading. (If multiple occurrences of such errors result in a nonmatching but correctly spelled heading, the heading is categorized as an unauthorized heading.)

m. Abbreviation error. Unauthorized use of abbreviation(s) for one or more main heading words. For example, the abbreviated word "pts." in "Choruses, Sacred (Mixed voices, 4 pts.) with orchestra" should be spelled out.

n. Hyphenation error. Addition/omission of hyphens. For example, the word "stockroom" in "Stores or stockroom keeping" should be hyphenated, that is, "Stores or stock-room keeping."

o. Erroneous combination. Occurrence of two or more of the above errors (f–n). For example, "U.S." is incorrectly tagged 650 and abbreviated when it should be written out.

Table 4.5 lists the numbers and percentages of erroneous subject headings found in the random sample of nonmatching assigned subject headings.

Two categories tie for the most frequently occurring error: (1) the assignment of a *see from* tracing, and (2) an incorrect MARC tag. Assignment of a subdivided *see from* tracing occurs much more frequently than unsubdivided *see from* tracings. Seven *see from* tracings occur in headings with other errors such as addition/omission and punctuation, so they are included in the "Combinations" category.

Over half (47 of 88) of incorrectly tagged topical headings should have been tagged for geographic names (i.e., MARC tag 651). Addition/omission errors also occur frequently in headings of all lengths. MARC tagging was the second most frequently occurring error found by Lantz *et al.* (1984, 185). These researchers also found more instances of errors for addition/omission than for substitution/transposition.

Frequent types of errors in error combinations are incorrect MARC tag (9 occurrences) and hyphenation (6 occurrences). Five combinations are city flips, which require moving a topical subdivision to the main heading position, converting the original main heading into a geographic subdivision, and inserting an indirect qualifier in between the two. For example, the erroneous heading "Chicago $x Theaters" is converted into the correct heading "Theaters $z Illinois $x Chicago" by transposing topical and geographic elements, adding indirect geographic subdivision, and correcting subfield codes.

Except for two unprinted headings (one deity and one music heading), every main heading of corrected assigned subject headings exactly matches the main subfield element of an LCSH-mr heading. Erroneous headings are 62.2% of the random sample of assigned subject headings. Using these figures, we can estimate that erroneous subject headings represent about 11.0% of the unique assigned subject headings in a bibliographic file. If corrections are made to the main heading of erroneous subject headings, nearly all but a few unprinted headings will have a subject authority record for the main heading in the subject heading string.

4.4.3 Unauthorized Subject Headings

Unauthorized subject headings contain one or more problems that cannot be resolved without requiring a human intermediary to refer to the bibliographic record, original item, and/or LCSH to resolve the problem. A human intermediary has to make an intellectual decision about replacing terms categorized into unauthorized categories with authorized subject headings. Unauthorized subject headings are placed into one of six categories:

p. Split *see from* tracing. The assigned subject heading matches an unsubdivided or subdivided *see from* tracing that requires a human intermediary to make a choice between two or more authorized headings. For example, catalogers can replace the *see from* tracing "Pigs, Wild" with the authorized headings "Feral swine" and/or "Wild boar."

q. Obsolete heading. The assigned subject heading matches an authorized heading printed in the eighth through the tenth editions of *LCSH.* The assigned heading is not listed in the eleventh edition of LCSH as a *see from* tracing or authorized heading. For example, the authorized heading "Electronic data processing in research" is last listed as an authorized heading in the ninth edition of LCSH and is not a *see from* tracing in the eleventh edition of LCSH used in this analysis.

r. Headings created from a multiple heading. The assigned subject heading is in a form authorized by a multiple heading in the eighth through the eleventh editions of LCSH. The practice of multiple headings was discontinued in 1979 (Chan 1986, 173–174; Library of Congress 1987, H330); however, bibliographic records still contain subject headings that were authorized by the practice of multiple headings. For example, the subject heading "Sculpture, Punic" is based on the multiple heading "Sculpture, African [Chinese, Danish, etc.]" printed in the eleventh edition of *LCSH.*

s. Unauthorized addition of a valid qualifier. The qualifier applied to a main heading is used one or more times in an LCSH-mr heading, but not with this particular main heading. For example, the qualifier "(Physics)" is used with "Causality" and "Scattering" in LCSH-mr, but is unauthorized when added as a qualifier to the main heading "Electric welding."

t. No discernible source for validation. Assigned subject headings that are not categorized in p–s above are categorized here. Such terms may have been authorized headings or *see from* tracings in editions prior to the eighth, authorized by previous practice, or local headings incorrectly coded with indicator 2 = 0 (i.e., LC subject heading). Assigned headings bearing the preposition "in" are categorized here when they are not printed in previous or current editions of *LCSH,* for example, "Jews in Tulsa, Okla." and "Negroes in Uruguay." Most headings in this category have no discernible source for validation and are probably made-up subject headings, for example, "Common ridings (Festivals)," "Functionalism (Sociology)," and "O.P. (Old Prices) Riot, 1809."

u. Unauthorized combination. Occurrences of one of the above unauthorized forms (p–t) and one or more errors (f–o) constitute an unauthorized combination. For example, "Pyridoxine defiency diseases" is misspelled and is last used in the eighth edition of LCSH.

Table 4.6 lists the numbers and percentages of unauthorized subject headings found in the sample of nonmatching assigned subject headings.

Only four unauthorized headings (0.8%) are categorized as split *see from* tracings. An example is the *see from* tracing "Boots and shoes," which gives catalogers a

Table 4.6
Unauthorized Assigned Subject Headings[a]

	Length of assigned heading			
Unprinted category	Total	a only	a + 1	Exceeding 1 subdivision
p. Split *see from* tracing	4 (0.8)	1 (0.7)	1 (1.0)	2 (0.8)
q. Obsolete heading	23 (4.8)	5 (3.5)	4 (3.8)	14 (6.0)
r. Multiple heading	21 (4.3)	8 (5.6)	4 (3.8)	9 (3.8)
s. Unauthorized qualifier	1 (0.2)	1 (0.7)	0 (0.0)	0 (0.0)
t. No discernible source	84 (17.4)	37 (25.7)	22 (21.0)	25 (10.6)
u. Combinations	19 (5.4)	8 (5.6)	0 (0.0)	11 (4.7)
Subtotal	152 (31.4)	60 (41.8)	31 (29.6)	61 (26.0)
Total nonmatching headings of this length in sample	484 (100.0)	144 (100.0)	105 (100.0)	235 (100.0)

[a]Percentages may not add to subtotal percentages because of rounding.

choice of three authorized headings from which to choose, namely "Boots," "Shoes," and/or "Footware." To replace this unauthorized heading, catalogers have to review the full bibliographic record, and, possibly, inspect the original document to determine which authorized heading(s) are appropriate. Frost and Dede (1988, 295) also found assigned subject headings that had been split into two or more authorized headings and remarked on the need for "human judgment for conversion."

Obsolete headings average about 4.8% of nonmatching headings. Frost and Dede (1988, 295) found a small number of obsolete headings in their sample. To replace obsolete headings, catalogers may have to inspect the original documents to determine their subjects and assign heading(s) from the current edition of LCSH.

Multiple headings average about 4.3% of nonmatching headings. The headings in this category were authorized by the previous practice of multiple headings. Since 1979, however, LC has been creating individual subject authority records for headings that were once authorized by multiple headings. Multiple headings are maintained in LCSH-mr to indicate that "headings represented by individual authority records and printed in *LCSH* do not necessarily constitute an exhaustive list of valid qualified forms of the heading, and many additional forms of the heading may have been assigned by LC even though they do not yet have authority records and are not printed in *LCSH*" (Library of Congress 1987, H330).

Library staff should develop policies to handle the assigned subject headings in their bibliographic records that were previously authorized by multiple headings. Library staff may decide to keep headings formulated from multiples and wait until

LC creates individual authority records for them. Staff may decide to replace headings formulated from multiples with authorized headings to ensure that topical headings in their databases are traced in subject authority records.

The one heading bearing an unauthorized qualifier is "Electric welding" to which the qualifier "(Physics)" is appended. Since the main heading without the qualifier is listed in LCSH-mr, this heading is relatively easy to correct manually and inspection of the original document is probably not needed; however, if the unqualified and one or more qualified forms exist, a human intermediary must review the original bibliographic record to which the heading was assigned to replace it with an authorized subject heading.

Nonmatching headings placed in the "No discernible source" category account for 17.4% of nonmatching assigned subject headings. Percentages of such categorized headings generally decrease as more subdivisions are appended to the main heading. The largest percentage (25.7%) of these unauthorized headings are unsubdivided. A slightly smaller percentage (21.0%) of "No discernible source" headings are once-subdivided headings. Only 10.6% of the headings in this unauthorized category bear two or more subdivisions.

Some unauthorized headings in the "No discernible source" category are similar to authorized headings. For example, the terms "Utilization of water resources" and "Radio broadcasting industry" are similar to the authorized headings "Water resources $x Utilization" and "Radio broadcasting." Some terms could have been categorized as spelling errors because several letters are added or omitted; however, the words in these phrases are correctly spelled, for example, "Monastic and religious orders" should be "Monasticism and religious orders." Other terms are missing dates, for example, "Franklin, Battle of" should be "Franklin (Tenn.), Battle of, 1864" and "Vietnamese Conflict" should be "Vietnamese Conflict, 1961–1975." Some terms are in a form consistent with previous practice, for example, "Jews in Santa Cruz (Calif.)," "Negroes in Uruguay," and "Sikhs in Great Britain." Frost and Dede (1988, 295) remark on finding such unauthorized headings in their sample and the need for "human intervention" to determine the correct form of indirect geographic subdivision, for example, "Jews $z California $z Santa Cruz."

In Table 4.5, percentages of *see from* tracings increase as the number of subdivisions per heading increases. In Table 4.6, percentages of headings in the "No discernible source" category decrease as the number of subdivisions per heading increases. Why these percentages change with the lengths of assigned headings is not easy to determine. Catalogers may be formulating their own terms to express specific topics that are not specifically addressed by LCSH. Perhaps such individuals formulate their own headings when they cannot find a specific heading in LCSH or are unable to construct a subdivided heading that expresses a specific topic.

Examples of headings placed in the "No discernible source" category that are probably made-up headings are "French language, Books in," "Common ridings (Festivals)," "Omori shellmounds," and "Technical textual discourse." These terms account for two-thirds of the 84 unauthorized subject headings placed in the "No discernible source" category. Thus, made-up headings represent about 2% of unique assigned subject headings in a bibliographic file. Frost and Dede (1988, 295) report this percentage to be 3.9% of the total occurrences of assigned subject headings in their sample.

Of the nineteen unauthorized combinations, one-half are unauthorized headings and the other half are obsolete headings. Most errors (16) in combinations are incorrect MARC tags; other errors are for hyphenation, addition/omission, spelling, substitution/transposition, and abbreviations.

Human intermediaries would be required to review the bibliographic record from which unauthorized headings were extracted to determine the subject matter of the original items. They might have to obtain the items themselves to make an accurate analysis. Then intermediaries would consult current LCSH and SCM:SH editions to find appropriate, authorized subject headings and subdivisions and assign them to replace the unauthorized headings in bibliographic records.

Unauthorized headings are 31.4% of the 8.0% random sample of nonmatching assigned subject headings. Using these figures, we can estimate that unauthorized subject headings represent about 5.5% of the unique assigned subject headings in a bibliographic file. Although computer programs can be used to find nonmatching headings that may be unauthorized, replacing these terms with authorized ones requires human intervention.

4.5 Ensuring a Quality Bibliographic Database

Although, as we have shown, the large percentage (17.6%) of nonmatching headings in the sample bibliographic file (Table 4.2) can be explained, they represent a challenge for maintenance of quality in bibliographic databases. Today's bibliographic databases represent nearly a quarter century of record construction. New editions of the subject headings list and changes in subject cataloging practice often require changes to older cataloging records. The potential for errors to occur in subject heading fields is even greater than in the days of card catalog construction, due to errors in MARC tagging and subfield coding, or in spelling and punctuation that were caught and corrected when technical services staff filed cards in the card catalog.

Changes to older cataloging records have not been done for many reasons, for example, institutional priorities, personnel resources, and system limitations. Libraries recognize that using cataloging records created over a long period of time to build the initial database for their online catalog will result in many inconsistencies between old and new cataloging and the indexes built from them. Consequently, they enlist database services of library automation vendors to improve the quality of older cataloging records, update the name and subject access points in their cataloging records, and create name and subject authority files for their online catalog (Miller 1984). These vendors use authority records in LCSH-mr and LCNAF to update access points and to generate cross-references in local authority records.

The sample of subject headings from the OCLC database described in this chapter was drawn as part of an investigation of database quality. In November 1992, OCLC began a four-month project to correct and update subject headings in its OLUC. A system of computer programs is reviewing all of the LC topical and geographic subject headings in the 25-million record OLUC. Over 750,000 occurrences of headings have been changed; OCLC expects that the total will reach 1.8 million.

The importance of keeping bibliographic and authority files current cannot be underestimated. A study of the access points in the Montana State University's bibliographic database demonstrates that a 25% change in the local authority file occurred over a three-year period because of cataloging for new and withdrawn items (Peterson & Johnson 1990, 15). To keep pace with changes in the database due to new cataloging, cataloging policy changes, and changes to the controlled vocabulary, vendors currently offer customer libraries several approaches to updating their cataloging databases and authority files (Drabenstott 1991, 4–5). However, libraries' local systems have to be able to work in tandem with the updating approaches offered by vendors and bibliographic utilities. In the absence of such capabilities for integrating deleted, changed, and new records into the local system, the access points in libraries' bibliographic databases will become inconsistent with the original local authority file supplied by the library automation vendor, perhaps at the rate of 25% over three years, as cited by the Montana State University researchers.

4.6

Synthesis and Summary

The findings in this chapter underline the need for online systems to help users find the information in subject authority records for the unsubdivided form of the subdivided subject heading they consult in library catalogs. The discussion also demonstrates the need for libraries to budget and plan for ongoing maintenance of their local subject authority file. Many libraries enlist the services of a library automation vendor to improve the quality of older cataloging records when they first build their online catalog's bibliographic database. New cataloging, withdrawn items, and changes in subject cataloging policy and in the controlled vocabulary will affect the subject access points in a library's bibliographic database. To keep their bibliographic and authority files current, libraries can make changes manually or employ the several approaches to updating offered by library automation vendors.

This chapter reports on a compatibility study between the subject headings in LCSH-mr and those in a bibliographic file. Only about seven of every one hundred assigned subject headings are exact matches of LCSH-mr and thus have the potential to be connected with subject authority records that may contain useful information such as cross-references, scope notes, and LC classification numbers for subject searching and browsing (Table 4.2). Systematic removal of subdivisions produces matches of one or more authorized headings in subject authority records for 75.5% of subdivided, assigned subject headings (Table 4.3). About three-fourths of the matching LCSH-mr headings are themselves unsubdivided.

The discussion of orphan headings in Chapter 2 reveals that most of the useful information in subject authority records is contained in records for unsubdivided headings; consequently, even if the best match of an assigned subject heading is a subdivided heading in a subject authority record, the record is not likely to contain useful information about the matched heading or suggest additional subject terms. This finding underlines the need for online systems to help users find and use the information in subject authority records for the unsubdivided form of the subdivided subject heading they consult in library catalogs.

Nonmatching assigned subject headings fall into three categories: (1) unprinted headings (0.9%), (2) erroneous headings (11.2%), and (3) unauthorized headings (5.5%). By definition, unprinted headings have no corresponding authority records in the subject authority file. Unauthorized headings need to be reviewed by human intermediaries and replaced with authorized headings. The occurrence of erroneous and unauthorized headings in libraries' bibliographic files demonstrates the need for libraries to employ the services of library automation vendors to improve the quality of older cataloging records and update access points. An ongoing maintenance program is then needed for the bibliographic and authority files in a library's automated system.

References

Chan, Lois Mai. (1986). *Library of Congress Subject Headings: Principles and application.* Littleton, CO: Libraries Unlimited.

Drabenstott, Karen M. (1991). Introduction. In Karen M. Drabenstott (Ed.), *Subject authorities in the online environment: Papers from a conference program held in San Francisco, June 29, 1987* (pp. 1–8). Chicago: American Library Association.

Frost, Carolyn O., & Dede, Bonnie A. (1988). Subject heading compatibility between LCSH and catalog files of a large research library: A suggested model for analysis. *Information Technology and Libraries,* 7(3), 288–299.

Lantz, Anna E., O'Neill, Edward T., & Vizine-Goetz, Diane. (1984). 'Addrdsses, elctures, esssays' and other variant subject headings. In Suzanne C. Dodson & Gary L. Manges (Eds.) *Academic libraries: Myths and realities: Proceedings of the third national conference of the Association of College and Research Libraries*, 1984 April 4–7, Seattle (pp. 183–186). Chicago, IL: ACRL.

Library of Congress. (1987). *Subject cataloging manual: Subject headings* (Rev. ed.). Washington, DC: Library of Congress.

Library of Congress. (1988). *Library of congress subject headings* (11th ed.). Washington, DC: Library of Congress.

Ludy, Lorene E. (1985). OSU Libraries' use of Library of Congress subject authority file. *Information Technology and Libraries, 4*(2), 155–160.

Miller, Dan. (1984). Authority control in the retrospective conversion process. *Information Technology and Libraries, 3*(3), 286–292.

O'Neill, Edward T., & Vizine-Goetz, Diane. (1988). Quality control in online databases. In Martha E. Williams (Ed.) *Annual Review of information science and technology* (pp. 1–32). Amsterdam: Elsevier Science Publishers.

Peterson, Elaine, & Johnson, Bonnie. (1990). Is authority updating worth the price? *Technicalities, 10*, 5 (May), 1, 15.

Pietris, Mary K. D. (1987). Keynote address: Characteristics of LC subject headings that should be taken into account when designing on-line catalogues. *Cataloguing Australia, 13*(3), 70–80.

5

Studies of the Subject Queries Users Enter Into Online Systems

5.1 Introduction

In the early 1980s, a handful of libraries began offering end users direct access to bibliographic data through local online systems. Recognizing the growth of direct end user access and the need for the library and information science community to share their ideas and experience in this area, the Council on Library Resources (CLR) sponsored a meeting of representatives from institutions that already had some experience with online public access catalogs or were in the final stages of developing such a service (Hildreth 1982, xi). In response to four priority areas identified by conference participants as having highest priority for immediate study and action (Kaske & Ferguson 1980, v), CLR supported five organizations to undertake a nationwide survey of online catalog users to study the first priority area—user requirements and behavior.

At the 1982 Midwinter Meeting of the American Library Association, Ed Brownrigg, one of five principal investigators for the nationwide survey, characterized the preliminary findings by saying, "Sacred cows are being strewn all over the landscape." Brownrigg referred to the unexpected finding about subject access—the high percentage of subject searches conducted by public users of online catalogs, the large number of users who reported difficulties conducting subject searches, and their calls for improvements to subject searching. When Brownrigg's remark reached the library and information science community through Larry Besant's report of the meeting in *American Libraries*, it raised interest in the CLR study (Besant 1982, 160).

The findings of the CLR survey underlined the importance of improving subject access in online catalogs. The prominent subject access researcher Pauline Cochrane called for an entirely new approach to library and information science and new thinking about the primary activity of library catalog users: "Common wisdom since Cutter's time has been that most users of the library want a catalog where they can find a particular item, a known item. . . . But now we have findings from several *online* catalog use studies that dispute this 'truth' " (Cochrane 1983, 3).

Since the nationwide survey and Cochrane's call for a paradigm shift, research in the area of subject access has burgeoned, and dozens of researchers have confirmed the CLR survey findings (Wang 1985; Lewis 1987). In response to recommendations about improving subject searching in online catalogs (Lester 1989, 58–98), system designers have implemented several online catalog improvements, including (1) Boolean-based, keyword searching for subjects, (2) online browsing of alphabetically arranged subject heading indexes, and (3) more online user assistance.

A review of studies conducted since the CLR survey shows that despite a decade of improvements in online catalogs, the difficulties today's users have performing subject searches in online catalogs are similar to those experienced by the earliest online catalog users.

A new study of the subject terms users enter into online catalogs was needed, and is provided in this book. This chapter outlines the methods of this study, which shares two objectives with previous studies, that is, to report the degree of closeness between terms from a controlled vocabulary and terms entered by online catalog users and to recommend online catalog improvements. The present study's unique objective, however, is to further recommend which online catalog capability is best suited to the wide variety of queries users enter into online catalogs.

5.2

Transaction Log Analyses of Users' Subject Terms

The computer's ability to record every system response and user action input into the online catalog provides the researcher with an accurate tool for collecting the subject terms users enter into online catalogs. The record of such user-system interaction is called a transaction log. Logs can be quite voluminous, depending on the amount of user activity on the system, the types of data recorded, and the length of time allowed for data collection.

Standards for transaction logs are still being developed, so the content and format of these logs vary from system to system. Computer programs written to analyze transaction log data from one system must be rewritten to analyze data from a different system.

An important advantage of transaction logs is the unobtrusiveness of this data collection approach. A computer program collects user–system interaction data unbeknownst to catalog users. Consequently, users are not likely to alter their catalog-seeking behavior because they do not know that the terms they are entering into the catalog are being recorded for analysis. Another advantage of transaction logging is the ability to collect voluminous amounts of data in machine-readable form for subsequent analyses using computer programs.

Transaction log analysis also has disadvantages. Two drawbacks pertinent to the new study described in this and subsequent chapters are the researcher's inability to know exactly what users are looking for and when users begin and end their searches. Information about the user's goals can be obtained by supplementing transaction logs with observations of user searches, personal interviews, or a combination of the two. The time problem can be solved by manual analyses of the logs; manual analysis is more accurate than computer analysis because human intermediaries can demarcate individual searches by enlisting changes in both time stamps and the meaning of user queries. These and other disadvantages described by Hildreth (1985) have been a concern to researchers in the United Kingdom who have recently developed a front-end system to overcome many of the limitations of transaction logs through four capabilities: (1) full-screen logging, (2) playback facility, (3) pre- or postsearch, online or offline questionnaire administration, or (4) in-search questionnaire administration (Hancock-Beaulieu, Robertson, & Neilson 1990).

This chapter also reviews what we have learned through transaction log analyses about the subject terms users enter into online catalogs. Transaction log analysis has been used to study user-entered access points since the time of the CLR-supported nationwide survey of online catalogs (Borgman 1983; Larson 1983; Tolle 1983). Comparing the results of individual studies with one another is difficult because the objectives, the categories into which user queries are placed, and the types of subject queries extracted from transaction logs differ from study to study. The following two sections cite only studies in which researchers either selected a random sample of user queries from transaction logs or selected user queries from a transaction log recorded over a certain period of time. Studies in which researchers gave respondents a search task to perform and recorded their activity on a transaction log are not described because of the obtrusiveness of this data collection approach.

Findings about the subject terms users enter into online catalogs can be generalized to increase our understanding of the closeness of these terms to the subject terminology indexed in the catalog. Studies of transaction logs also reveal what questions still need to be answered in new studies about user queries for subjects.

5.2.1 What Have We Learned about User Queries for Subjects?

Twenty generalizations about the subject terms users enter into online catalogs, along with information that supports these generalizations, appear below.

1. A small proportion of the terms users enter into online catalogs are not legitimate subject queries. Studies supporting: (Markey 1984, 66), (Henty 1986, 48), (Walter 1987, 76), (Carlyle 1989, 51), (Lester 1989, 172), (Peters 1989, 270), (Hunter 1991, 400), (Zink 1991, 53).

Queries that are not legitimate subject queries are random configurations (///, HJNVM), data entry errors, and expletives. Such activity could be exploratory, accidental, or indicative of the frustration users are experiencing with their online search. Researchers describe these terms variously as malicious entries, entry errors, graffiti, identifiable obscenities, questions, comments, and so on. A few researchers disregarded such queries from their matching studies (Carlyle 1989, 51; Lester 1989, 172). Most importantly, this activity occurs with much less frequency than the entry of legitimate subject queries: for example, such activity was only 0.4% of the random sample of subject queries extracted from transaction logs at Northwestern University (Lester 1989, 172). This finding demonstrates that online catalog searchers understand enough about the system to enter a legitimate subject search term, that is, a term that has the potential to retrieve bibliographic records.

2. Users include punctuation in their queries. Studies supporting: (Henty 1986, 50), Walter (1987, 78), (Lester 1989, 184).

Examples of punctuation occurring in user queries are possessive forms with an apostrophe, acronyms with periods in between letters, hyphenated words and phrases, and inverted phrases entered with an intervening comma. Of the three studies supporting this generalization, two examined subject queries entered through the URICA online catalog. When the studies were conducted, URICA's indexing software was not performing as expected, causing several user queries to fail when retrievals should have been made. These studies demonstrate the need for double and triple posting of subject headings with punctuation. For example, the subject headings "Coffee-houses" and "Children's art" should be indexed under "coffeehouses" and "coffee houses," and "childrens art" and "children art." The same process applied to subject headings should also be applied to user queries to effect matches of the catalog's controlled vocabulary.

3. Users enter phrases without intervening spaces. Studies supporting: (Henty 1986, 48), (Jones 1986, 6), (Walter 1987, 76).

A small proportion of subject queries fail because words are not separated by spaces. Jones (1986, 6) described an algorithm to find and correct such queries automatically but it would be computationally heavy in the online system he studied. Instead, he suggested that systems display such queries to users and invite them to make corrections on their own.

4. Users misspell words. Studies supporting: (Markey 1984, 66), (Henty 1986, 48), (Jones 1986, 4), (Walter 1987, 76), (Lester 1989, 194, 197) (Peters 1989, 170), (Hunter 1991, 400), (Zink 1991, 53). Study not supporting: (Carlyle 1989, 44).

Spelling errors—substituting, inserting, transposing, and omitting one or more letters—prevent user queries from matching words and phrases indexed in online catalogs. Although spelling errors occur, they are not prevalent in user queries. For example, about 5% of the subject queries examined in separate studies by Lester and

Jones contained spelling errors. Carlyle looked for spelling errors but she encountered none.

5. Users enter abbreviations. Studies supporting: (Henty 1986, 48), (Walter 1987, 76), (Carlyle 1989, 44).

The abbreviated terms that users enter sometimes prevent them from retrieving bibliographic records. Abbreviated terms are not that common; in fact, Carlyle found only one such term in her sample. The inclusion of punctuation or omission of spaces between abbreviated terms is also likely to create retrieval problems.

6. Users preface their queries with an initial article. Study supporting: (Hunter 1991, 400).

In the one study supporting this finding, initial articles were much more likely to occur in title searches than in searches for subject headings. Regardless, these initial articles can prevent systems from retrieving bibliographic records unless systems are programmed to delete initial articles from user queries.

7. Users enter queries in singular form when the authorized form in LCSH is plural and vice versa. Study supporting: (Carlyle 1989, 44).

The example given by Carlyle is the user query "x ray" that is the singular form of the LCSH "X-rays."

8. Users enter queries containing a date that differs in form from the date in the subject heading in the LCSH system. Study supporting: (Carlyle 1989, 44).

Carlyle cited the user-entered query containing the date "20th century." LCSH represents this date as "Twentieth century."

9. Users enter queries containing a different suffix than the subject heading in the LCSH system. Study supporting: (Carlyle 1989, 44).

The example given by Carlyle is the user-entered query containing the suffix "computer programming" that is different from the suffix of the subject heading based on LCSH, namely "Computer programs."

10. Users enter queries using the online catalog's subject search capability that are probably better suited to the catalog's author or title capability. Studies supporting: (Peters 1989, 270), (Hunter 1991, 400), (Zink 1991, 53).

Online catalog searchers enter queries for author names and book titles using the system's subject searching capability. Although such queries are not common, it is not unusual to scan transaction logs and see the same query entered several times using all the different searching capabilities in the catalog. Such users may be unsure which searching capability they should use to enter their query, so they use all of them.

11. Users enter subject queries that match *see* references in LCSH. Studies supporting: (Markey 1984, 66), (Lester 1989, 239).

The more recent study supporting this generalization reported that 9.8% of subject queries entered into the NOTIS online catalog at Northwestern University matched *see* references in LCSH. An additional 0.8% of matches appeared when spelling errors were corrected.

12. Users enter subject queries that exactly match authorized headings in the printed *LCSH*. Study supporting: (Lester 1989, 172).

Lester reported that 40% of the subject queries entered by searchers of the NOTIS online catalog at Northwestern University were exact matches of the subject headings printed in LCSH. (She disregarded capitalization and punctuation, i.e., commas, periods, dashes, hyphens, apostrophes, semicolons, and parentheses, in the matching process.)

13. Users enter subject queries that exactly match subject headings in a bibliographic database based on the LCSH system. Studies supporting: (Markey 1984, 66), (Carlyle 1989, 44), (Peters 1989, 269), (Hunter 1991, 399), (Zink 1991, 53).

The methods used in each of the studies supporting this generalization are different. Markey extracted subject queries from the transaction log of the SULIRS online catalog at Syracuse University that were entered using the catalog's two keyword searching capabilities for subjects. Although only 18% of subject queries matched subject headings in the SULIRS database, 50% of the subject searches users conducted in SULIRS contained at least one subject access point that exactly matched such subject headings. Zink reported that about 10% of the subject searches in the WolfPAC online catalog at the University of Nevada, Reno, would have matched an authorized heading based on the LCSH system had it been assigned to bibliographic records in the database. Of the several different types of subject and known-item search capabilities available to users of the LUMIN online catalog at the University of Missouri, users chose the "official LCSH subject search" capability for 6.9% of their queries. This capability required users to enter an exact match of a subject heading based on LCSH and assigned to a bibliographic record in the LUMIN system (Peters 1989). Forty-eight percent of the user queries that used this approach retrieved bibliographic records. The BIS online catalog at North Carolina State University required users to enter a subject heading based on LCSH to retrieve bibliographic records. About 38% of the subject access points entered into BIS were successful in retrieving bibliographic records (Hunter 1991). Carlyle excluded several categories of queries, including geographic and personal names, from her analysis of subject queries entered into the ORION online catalog at UCLA. She reported that 43% of subject queries exactly matched a listed subject heading in the printed *LCSH* or a subject heading based on the LCSH system to which subdivisions were appended.

14. Queries that are exact matches of the controlled vocabulary are likely to be shorter than nonmatches. Study supporting: (Markey 1984, 67, 70). Study not supporting: (Lester 1989, 176).

Lester reported that exact matches in her study are the same length (1.7 words) as nonmatches. The nonmatches in Markey's study were longer (2.3 words) than exact matches (1.5 words). A related study conducted at The Ohio State University Libraries required users to write down the topics they searched in the LCS online catalog. The researchers noted that all but 20% of the queries represented single-topic subjects or names (Van Pulis & Ludy 1988, 527).

15. The majority of the subject queries users enter into online catalogs using the system's subject searching capabilities are for topical subjects. Study supporting: (Lester 1989, 186).

Over 70% of the queries in Lester's study were for topical subjects. A surprisingly high percentage (44%) of these queries matched subject headings printed in *LCSH.*

16. Queries for names or combinations of names and other words are less likely to match subject headings printed in *LCSH* than queries for topical subjects. Study supporting: (Lester 1989, 188).

Out of the nearly 29% of user queries in Lester's study that contained personal, corporate, or geographic names, only thirty percent were successful in matching a subject heading printed in *LCSH.* The high percentage of nonmatches can be explained by the exclusion from *LCSH* of most headings for personal and corporate names and geographic places that name jurisdictional units. Such headings are more likely to be found in LCNAF than in *LCSH.*

17. User queries are sometimes an amalgamation of two or more subject headings from the LCSH system. Study supporting: (Carlyle 1989, 44).

The example given by Carlyle is the user query "crystallography geometry" that matched two separate subject headings printed in LCSH: "Crystallography" and "Geometry." Queries that are an amalgamation of two or more subject headings are also likely to have the same problems as queries that almost match subject headings based on the LCSH system, for example, spelling errors, missing punctuation, and abbreviations.

18. The retrieval processes in online catalogs can increase the match success rate between user-entered terms and subject headings based on the LCSH system. Study supporting: (Lester 1989).

Lester tested this statement using twenty-two different retrieval processes to effect matches between user queries and subject headings based on the LCSH system. Of the many processes, she demonstrated that right truncation, string searching with adjacency, and keyword searching with an implicit Boolean "and" operator significantly improved match success.

19. Users enter queries containing language not used in subject headings in the LCSH system. Study supporting: (Carlyle 1989, 44).

Five percent of the queries examined by Carlyle contained language not used in the LCSH system.

20. The subject queries users enter into online systems can be used as *see* references to authorized subject headings. Study supporting: (Walker & Jones 1987, 68).

Designers of the experimental Okapi online catalog in the United Kingdom examined transaction logs to find categories of terms to treat as equivalents (Jones 1986). Examples of categories are abbreviations, noun/adjective pairs, variant spellings, and numbers.

5.2.2 What Have We Learned about the Names Users Enter?

Five generalizations about access points for the names users enter into online catalogs are given below, along with information about the studies that support these generalizations. Most of the findings are drawn from studies of name access points entered by users conducting searches for known items. Findings about the personal, corporate, and geographic names users enter in known-item searches can be generalized to subject searches for names because many systems require users to enter name access points for known-item searches in the same form as name access points for subject searches in order to retrieve bibliographic records. Of the generalizations outlined in Section 5.2.1. above, (2) about punctuation and (4) about misspelled words are also true for name access points. Generalization (10) is true with a minor change, that is, users enter queries using the online catalog's capability for finding personal names through an author search, whereas these queries are probably better suited to other catalog capabilities.

Generalizations specific to name access points follow:

1. Users enter personal names in direct form when systems require the entry of inverted forms. Studies supporting: (Dickson 1984, 32), (Taylor 1984, 8), (Henty 1986, 51), (Peters 1989, 270), Hunter (1991, 400), (Zink 1991, 52).

Several studies draw this conclusion about the personal-name access points users enter into online catalogs. In Dickson's study, the percentage of personal names with given names entered first was as high as 37%.

2. Users enter two personal names at the same time. Studies supporting: (Dickson 1984, 32), (Taylor 1984, 8), (Zink 1991, 52).

Such queries demonstrate that users occasionally search for material by or about several persons. Examples of such queries are "berger, peter and luckman, thomas" and "leopold and loeb."

3. Users enter names with other words. Studies supporting: (Taylor 1984, 8), (Lester 1989, 186).

Taylor placed these queries under the rubric "attempt at Boolean search" and gave the example "greenacre, phyllis on creativity." Lester reported that almost 9% of the queries she examined had elements for geographic names and other words and gave the examples "education--united states," "sex--russia," and "catalogs, museum--britain."

4. The middle names or initials users include in their queries for personal names are sometimes counterproductive. Studies supporting: (Dickson 1984, 32), (Walter 1987, 80), (Peters 1989, 270), (Hunter 1991, 400).

Inclusion of middle names or initials is counterproductive for several reasons. Most center on characteristics of the system into which the query is entered. For example, if the indexed heading has no initial and the user-entered term has one, the system places the user in an alphabetical index of personal names following the name desired by the user and offers no capability for browsing backward in the alphabet.

5. The retrieval processes in online catalogs can increase the match success rate between user-entered names and the access points indexed in bibliographic databases much more than the LCNAF. Studies supporting: (Taylor 1984, 15), (Lester 1989, 258).

Taylor and Lester concluded that name authority records would have helped users find the authorized headings for names for only 6% and 1% of the user-entered terms in their respective studies. According to Taylor, a computer program to invert the elements in user-entered names that produce no retrievals would have helped users find an appropriate name heading for 22% of their access points. Both researchers recommended a right truncation program. Lester also recommended string and keyword searching approaches for names.

5.3 Unanswered Questions about the Subject Terms Users Enter into Online Catalogs

The objective of researchers who conduct studies of the subject terms users enter into online catalogs has been to recommend improvements to the subject searching capabilities of online catalogs. Their calls for subject searching improvements have been joined by other experts and spokespersons who have been thinking about, commenting on, and analyzing research findings. In preparation for her dissertation research, Lester (1989, 58–98) reviewed recommendations for subject searching improvements made by both online catalog researchers and other experts. Examples are:

- Automatic detection and correction of spelling errors.
- Automatic detection and correction of search format errors.
- Automatic replacement of user queries with *see* references from LCSH.
- System-supplied truncation.
- Boolean-based, keyword searching of subject-rich fields of bibliographic records.

Such lists of recommendations are limited for several reasons. They do not tell us which capability will most improve the prospects for success for the greatest number of queries entered into online catalogs. Lists do not tell us if certain characteristics of user queries make them better suited for particular subject searching improvements than others. They also do not tell us which subject searching capabilities in our existing online catalogs are currently working satisfactorily.

The closest that any study comes to shedding light on these issues is Lester's empirical study of the subject terms users enter into online catalogs in which she demonstrates that "the retrieval processes of right truncation, string searching, and keyword searching each make significant improvements in match success with the Library of Congress subject headings" (Lester 1989, 267). Still to be answered are these questions: Which retrieval process is best suited to the widest variety of user queries? Will this process not only produce retrievals but also ensure their precision? What happens to user queries when a retrieval process fails? Should user queries that fail through a retrieval process be submitted to another retrieval process?

A single question sums up the issue at hand: How can online systems respond to user queries with the subject searching approach most likely to succeed in providing relevant information? The present study of the subject terms users enter into online catalogs was undertaken to answer this general question. The remainder of this chapter describes its methods.

5.4 Subject Terms Used in the Transaction Log Study

5.4.1 Transaction Log Data

For the empirical study described here, we extracted subject queries from the online catalog transaction logs of three university research libraries: (1) SULIRS at Syracuse University, (2) ORION at the University of California, Los Angeles

Table 5.1
Transaction Log Data

OPAC name	Logging dates	Number terminals	Number access points
SULIRS			
	Apr. 13 through May 11, 1988	22 (public) 16 (staff) 6 (both)	55,136 (public) 1,633 (staff) 11,166 (both)
Total	29 days	44	67,935
ORION			
	Jun. 4 through Jun. 15, 1988	34 (public) 17 (staff)	12,974 (public) 3,022 (staff)
Total	12 days	51	15,996
LS/2000			
	Jan. 31 through Feb. 21, 1989	10 (public) 2 (staff)	6,263 (public) 402 (staff)
Total	22 days	12	6,665

(UCLA), and (3) LS/2000 at the University of Kentucky. Table 5.1 lists the dates, numbers of subject access points, and number of terminals per library.

Nearly 68,000 subject access points were entered into SULIRS over a 29-day logging period in spring 1988. This time period was the concluding third of the university's winter semester and includes examination week. Access points were entered into terminals used primarily by patrons, reference staff, and a combination of the two. Patrons and reference staff users of ORION entered almost 16,000 subject access points over a 12-day logging period in spring 1988. This time period was at the second half of the university's spring quarter and immediately preceded examination week. Subject access points from LS/2000 numbered 6665 and were collected from terminals used by patrons or reference staff during a 3-week period shortly after the university's winter semester began in 1989.

Subject queries submitted to computer analyses were taken from all terminals listed in Table 5.1. Manual analyses were performed on a sample of the subject queries entered into terminals accessed by patrons only.

The empirical study of user queries focuses on defining the optimum response of online catalogs to the variety of subject terms entered by online catalog users. In an effort to obtain a wide variety of subject access points, we sought transaction logs from three online catalogs that offered different approaches to subject searching. Indicators of success of subject searches conducted in SULIRS, ORION, and LS/2000 are the numbers of bibliographic records retrieved in SULIRS and the number of assigned subject headings retrieved in ORION in response to user queries.

Brief descriptions of the subject searching process in each one of these online catalogs follow. Examples of subject searches are given in Appendix A (SULIRS),

Appendix B (ORION), and Appendix C (LS/2000). Descriptions include the type(s) of subject access points that are extracted from transaction logs for computer and manual analyses.

5.4.2 SULIRS

SULIRS has a command-based interface that offers keyword, implicit and explicit Boolean searching. SULIRS subject searchers enter their access points using the commands "lc" or "sb." When "lc" is entered, SULIRS searches for the user-entered terms in subject heading fields of bibliographic records. When "sb" is entered, SULIRS searches for the user-entered terms in title and subject heading fields of bibliographic records. (SULIRS also accepts "wd" or "su" as equivalent forms of "sb.")

When users enter more than one word following these commands, SULIRS performs an implicit Boolean "and" operation. For example, SULIRS interprets the subject access point "sb; surrealist artist" as "sb; surrealist **and** artist." SULIRS then looks for the word "surrealist" in the title and/or subject heading fields of bibliographic records, looks for the word "artist" in the title and/or subject heading fields of bibliographic records, finds records that contain both words, and displays to the user the number of records retrieved and the option to display them. Subject searching in SULIRS is a one-step approach in which the system's retrieval of bibliographic records leads directly to the display of retrieved bibliographic records bearing the terms in user queries.

Appendix A shows the subject search in which the given example is the second access point entered by the user. The first subject access point is an incorrect spelling for René Magritte, a Belgian surrealist painter. SULIRS does not have separate commands for subject searches for personal, corporate, and geographic names; the "sb" and "lc" labels suffice for entering all subject access points.

SULIRS allows explicit Boolean searching through the "and" operator. The system also allows revision of previously entered statements with an additional statement and the Boolean "and" operator. For example, the third access point in the SULIRS search (Appendix A) is "wd; surrealism." This results in 185 retrievals. The user may decide to reduce this result by entering a statement beginning with the Boolean "and" operator, for example, "and wd; belgium." SULIRS would then search for the word "belgium" in title and/or subject heading fields and retrieve records bearing the words "surrealism" and "belgium" in title and/or subject heading fields of bibliographic records.

SULIRS has no online browsing capabilities. To determine whether terms are used in the database, SULIRS users have to enter the terms directly. SULIRS permits explicit truncation; the entry of "sb; surreali+" retrieves the words "surrealist," "surrealists," "surrealistic," "surrealism," and other words with this stem. SULIRS users can also perform keyword searches for titles, authors, LC call numbers, and/or series using the commands "ti," "au," "cn," or "st," respectively.

For computer and manual analyses, we extracted subject access points from SULIRS transaction logs that users entered with the commands "lc," "sb," "su," or "wd." We also extracted subject access points that were entered using one or more of these commands with title, author, and/or series commands. For example, the subject access point "au; sb; mathematic" is extracted from the log for computer and manual analyses. The number of retrievals is also gleaned from transaction logs. When SULIRS yields more retrievals than the display buffer can hold (usually about one thousand bibliographic records), it informs users that they have retrieved too many records and must reduce the number to display retrieved records. When the logs were restructured by the project staff, the number 99,999 was written to logs for these high-posted searches even though the actual number of retrieved bibliographic records may be lower.

5.4.3 ORION

ORION has a command-based interface that offers keyword, implicit Boolean searching. The major difference between the keyword searching of SULIRS and ORION is that the latter system retrieves an intermediary display of single assigned subject headings bearing the words in user queries. ORION users scan the list of retrieved headings, select the one(s) that interest them, and then retrieve the bibliographic records bearing the selected heading. ORION subject searchers enter their access points using the command "browse" (or the shortened form "b") followed by the field label "su" and their terms. When "b su stress" is entered, ORION searches for this word in the main headings and subdivisions of assigned subject headings. Thus, the assigned headings "Job stress" and "Metals $x Stress corrosion" are retrieved by this access point.

When users enter more than one word following the "browse" command and "su" paragraph label, ORION performs an implicit Boolean "and" operation. For example, ORION interprets the subject access point "b su bibliography on stress" as "bibliography and stress." ORION deletes "on" as a stopword, then looks for the word "bibliography" in assigned subject headings, looks for the word "stress" in assigned subject headings, finds headings bearing both words, and displays to users the number of headings retrieved and the option to display them. Subject searching in ORION is a two-step approach in which the system responds to the retrieval of assigned subject headings with an intermediary list of single headings bearing words in the user query. The system encourages users to browse and select listed headings that express their topics of interest to retrieve a summary list of the bibliographic records to which the selected headings are assigned.

Appendix B shows a subject search in which "b su cuba revolution" is the first subject access point entered by the user. ORION responds with a list of over twenty assigned subject headings bearing both words "cuba" and "revolution." The second subject access point is "b su fulgencio batista" which names the president of Cuba during the 1950s revolution in that country. No headings are retrieved because ORION requires users to enter names using different commands. The command names are "find" or "browse" (or shortened forms "f" or "b") followed by the field label "na" and personal name. This same command is used for searching author names. Thus, "f na fulgencio batista" or "b na fulgencio batista" retrieves material written by and/or about this person.

ORION users retrieve assigned headings that contain every word they enter and additional words in main headings and subdivisions that are not in the original access point. By scanning lists of retrieved headings, users may find terms that are more specific than their original query, that express their topics of interest more precisely, or that stimulate them to narrow their original focus.

For computer and manual analyses, ORION systems staff extracted subject access points from ORION transaction logs that were entered using the "browse" command and "subject" field label, that is, "b su." They also extracted the number of assigned subject headings retrieved by subject access points.

Occasionally, ORION users entered personal names using the "browse" command and "subject" field label, as in the "batista" example. Such name entries were considered subject access points and included in both computer and manual analyses. The number of headings retrieved by such access points was usually zero or close to zero because such headings were in ORION's "name" index.

5.4.4 LS/2000

LS/2000 has a menu-based interface and offers both alphabetical phrase searching and keyword, implicit Boolean searching. Library staff can choose the types of searches to offer to patrons, fields of bibliographic records for search and display, indexes for online browsing, and many other parameters. LS/2000 searchers at the University of Kentucky have the following options in the initial menu that begins their searches:

```
Enter the NUMBER of search you wish to perform
        1 — By AUTHOR
        2 — By TITLE
        3 — By SUBJECT
        4 — By SUBJECT — MEDICAL
        5 — For OTHER Searches
                    OR
  Enter a KEY WORD to see possible matches:
        CHOICE:
```

If LS/2000 users select option 3 (by SUBJECT), the system prompts users to enter their terms and responds with an alphabetically arranged list of main headings beginning with the same letters, word, or phrase as the user-entered term. Users are encouraged to choose a main heading from this list. If users select a heading that retrieves bibliographic records over a number determined by the library, LS/2000 encourages users to reduce the number of retrievals by one of several criteria, for example, entering another keyword, limiting by publication year, or limiting by language. LS/2000 searchers can enter topical subjects, geographical names, or personal names using option 3 in the initial menu.

If LS/2000 users enter a keyword or phrase in response to the last (unnumbered) option in the initial menu, the system responds with a list of single words in the alphabetical neighborhood of the first word of the user-entered term. This alphabetical index is composed of single words from nearly all variable-length fields of University of Kentucky's bibliographic records. Users are encouraged to select a word from this alphabetical list. If they choose low-posted words, they can browse retrieved records. Otherwise, LS/2000 encourages them to reduce high-posted searches in various ways.

If LS/2000 users select option 5 (for OTHER searches) in the initial menu, LS/2000 responds with a menu of other searches:

Enter the NUMBER of the search you wish to perform
1 — By COPY CALL NUMBER
2 — By ISBN
3 — By SERIES
4 — By PERSONAL NAME
5 — By CORPORATE NAME
6 — By CONFERENCE NAME
7 — By SUBJECT — GEOGRAPHIC
8 — By SUBJECT TOPICAL AUTHORITY
9 — By NEWSPAPER LOCATION
10 — By MUSIC PUBLISHER'S NUMBER
(MORE)
CHOICE:

Options 7 and 8 enable LS/2000 users to browse subdivided subject headings for geographic names and topical subjects, respectively. Initially, these two options give responses that are the same as choosing option 3 from the initial menu. LS/2000 encourages users to choose a main heading from the matched alphabetical list presented. The system responds to users' selection of a main heading with an alphabetical list of subdivisions appended to the selected main heading. Selection of a subdivided subject heading results in a brief titles display.

Appendix C shows an LS/2000 subject search for "family therapy." This search does not show all the various subject searching options permitted by LS/2000. The user responds to the initial screen by entering the word "therapy." LS/2000 shows the user the two words in its database beginning with this stem. The user selects the word "therapy" when it occurs in subdivisions of assigned headings. Because the user selects a high-posted word, the system asks the user to limit retrievals. When the user tries to limit retrievals by the phrase "family therapy," the result is zero retrievals. The user retraces these steps and is unsuccessful in second and third attempts to retrieve material on "family therapy."

For computer and manual analyses, we extracted subject access points from LS/2000 transaction logs that corresponded to the commands SG (Subject—Geographic), SJ (Subject Topical Authority), SK (Subject—Medical), SU (Subject) and KW (Key Word). Command SU corresponds to initial menu option 3, SK to initial menu option 4, and KW to entry of a keyword. Commands SG and SJ correspond to secondary menu options 7 and 8, respectively, in the "Other Searches" menu.

5.5

Methods Used for Computer Analyses of Subject Terms

Computer analyses of subject terms compared authorized subject headings and *see from* tracings from machine-readable LCSH records to subject access points entered by patrons and staff to determine the extent to which access points match the terminology of LCSH-mr.

Three types of matches were performed: (1) exact matches, (2) normalized matches, and (3) keyword matches. Exact matches were letter-for-letter matches of LCSH-mr excluding capitalization. LCSH-mr fields used for comparisons were authorized heading (MARC tags 1xx) and the *see from* tracing fields (MARC tags 4xx). For example, the subject access points "mathematics" and "real estate" are exact matches of the authorized subject heading "Mathematics" and a *see from* tracing under "Real property," respectively.

Subject access points that were not exact matches of LCSH-mr were then submitted to the computer for normalization, an automatic process that includes several operations: (1) reordering the words in subject access points into alphabetical order, (2) eliminating stopwords, (3) disregarding capitalization, and (4) disregarding punctuation. The same normalizing operations performed on user queries were also performed on authorized subject headings (MARC tags 1xx) and *see from* tracings (MARC tags 4xx) exceeding one word. Stopwords deleted from normalized queries and LCSH-mr were "a," "and," "of," and "the." For example, the authorized subject heading "Chemical reaction, Rate of" was normalized into the form "chemical rate reaction." Normalization transformed the user query "rate of chemical reaction" into "chemical rate reaction," and was thus responsible for effecting a match between the authorized subject heading "Chemical reaction, Rate of" and user query "rate of chemical reaction."

User queries that were neither exact nor normalized matches of the authorized subject headings or *see from* tracings in LCSH-mr were then submitted to the computer for keyword matches. Keyword matches occurred when the computer program found one or more words in the user query and in authorized subject heading or geographic name (MARC tags 150 or 151) fields or *see from* tracings for topical subjects or geographic names (MARC tags 450 or 451). Matches were made of LCSH-mr that contained words in addition to the one(s) entered by users, but the matching LCSH-mr record had to contain *all words* in the user query. Occasionally, more than one LCSH-mr record was a keyword match of user queries. Examples of keyword matches in LCSH-mr records are highlighted below. Except for the query "time and children," matches of one LCSH-mr record were made.

Query	*LCSH-mr record(s)*
cigarette smoking	Authorized heading: Tobacco; *See from* tracings: **Cigarette** habit--Physiological effect; **Cigarette** smoke--Physiological effect; **Smoking**--Physiological effect
fast food	Authorized heading: Convenience food *See from* tracing: **Fast** foods; **Food**, Convenience
leisure and recreation	Authorized heading: Architecture and **recreation**; *See from* tracings: Architecture and **leisure**; **Leisure** and architecture
time and children	Authorized headings: **Children**--**Time** management; **Time** perception in **children**

All user queries were compared with LCSH-mr to determine the number and percentages of exact matches. Queries that were exact matches were counted, then left out of subsequent computer analyses. The remaining queries were normalized and compared with normalized LCSH-mr to determine the number and percentages of normalized matches; the normalized matches were counted, then left out of subsequent analyses. The remaining queries were submitted to keyword matches of LCSH-mr, and keyword matches were counted. After three computer analyses were performed, some queries still failed to match LCSH-mr terminology. The computer analysis of queries is presented in Chapter 6.

5.6 Manual Analyses of Subject Access Points

5.6.1 Using Initial Access Points

We randomly selected several complete days of activity from terminals accessed by library patrons. Computer programs printed transaction logs containing seven columns of data that enabled us to interpret user-system activity. Figure 5.1 shows a portion of user-system activity from the SULIRS online catalog.

```
(1)  (2)     (3)    (4) (5)   (6)   (7)
----------------------------------------------------------------
. . .
41   880426  121525 C17 sb    00483 motivation
42   880426  121548 C17 sb    00005 organizational motivation
43   880426  124320 C17 sb    00000 ford motor co.
44   880426  124345 C17 sb    00248 ford
45   880426  124517 C17 sb    00006 ford automobile industry
46   880426  125417 C17 su    00000 smoking woman
47   880426  125555 C17 su    00001 effects of smoking
48   880426  125638 C17 su    00004 tobacco women
49   880426  125733 C17 su    00000 smoking fetus
50   880426  125754 C17 su    00003 tobacco fetus
51   880426  132946 C17 sb    00000 auther james balfour speeches
     on zionism
52   880426  135523 C17 su    00000 reading integrated with
     writing
53   880426  135539 C17 su    01575 writing
54   880426  135634 C17 su    00085 writing/reading
55   880426  140405 C17 su    00096 antiques
56   880426  141320 C17 ausb  00002 linguistics
57   880426  141529 C17 auwd  00006 language
58   880426  141940 C17 sb    00005 motifs art deco
59   880426  142234 C17 sb    00003 motifs art nouveau
60   880426  142733 C17 sb    00013 medical encyclopedia
61   880426  143914 C17 sb    00000 delacroix and colr
62   880426  143929 C17 sb    00044 gaugin
. . .

Key:
(1)  Line number          (5)  User-entered command
(2)  Date of transaction  (6)  No. of bibliographic records
                               (SULIRS) or
(3)  Time stamp                subject headings (ORION) retrieved
(4)  Terminal identifier  (7)  Subject query
----------------------------------------------------------------
```

Figure 5.1
Portion of a SULIRS log.

Starting on the far left is a column of line numbers in numerical order that the computer program generates for all user–system activity involving the user's entry of a subject-access point. The second column gives the date by reserving two numerical positions for each of the following: (1) year, (2) month, and (3) day. The third column is a time stamp consisting of two numerical positions for each of the following: (1) hour, (2) minute, and (3) second. The fourth column reserves three alphanumerical positions for identifying the terminal at which the activity took place. The fifth column gives one or more two-letter SULIRS commands entered by the user. An example of one command is shown on line number 46 in which the "su" command directed the system to search for the subject query "smoking woman" in title and/or subject heading fields. An example of two two-letter commands is shown on line number 57 in which the user's entry of "au" and "wd" commands directed the system to search and find the subject query "language" in author fields and in title and/or subject heading fields. The seventh column lists the subject queries users entered into SULIRS. The sixth column reports the number of bibliographic records SULIRS found in response to the subject queries in the seventh column.

In manual analyses, our study was limited to the *initial access points* in subject searches. The decision to study initial subject access points in subject searches was guided by our objective, namely, to determine how online systems can respond to user queries with the subject searching approach most likely to succeed in providing relevant information. If this objective is achieved, then subsequent queries users enter may not be necessary.

We scanned printed transaction logs of user activity and demarcated subject searches. Demarcation was based on the period of time between sequentially numbered transactions. It was also based on the context and subject matter of a query with those preceding and following. Determining when one search ends and the next one begins was sometimes difficult. When in doubt, we considered the user query a new search.

In the sample SULIRS log (Figure 5.1), we would have demarcated ten searches, starting on lines 41, 43, 46, 51, 52, 55, 56, 58, 60, and 61. Queries printed on lines 41 through 45 could be the same search, that is, "Organizational motivation at the Ford Motor Company." However, the time stamp indicates that the query on line 43, "ford motor co." was entered into SULIRS almost thirty minutes after the preceding access point on line 42, "organizational motivation." Thus, we determined that queries on lines 41 and 42 were entered in a search separate from queries on line 43 through 45. On occasion, investigators encountered searches on the same topic, sometimes using the same words, that were entered into the same terminal but separated by one or two hours. They considered these separate searches and analyzed them separately.

We recorded answers to five general questions about the initial subject access points in searches:

1. Is this initial access point a legitimate subject term? (Query Control)
2. How closely does this initial subject access point match the catalog's controlled vocabulary? (Original-match Categorization)
3. Is the match satisfactory? (Match Satisfaction)
4. What is the best match of this access point with the catalog's controlled vocabulary? (Best-match Categorization)
5. How can online systems deliver to users the best match in an efficient, effective way? (Best System Response)

To answer questions 3 and 4, we referred to subsequent access points entered in the same search. Occasionally, this information was not available because users only entered one query in the search.

5.6.2 Query Control

Query control refers to summary data about the initial access point and search: (1) line number in log, (2) number of words in the query, (3) number of access points in the search, (4) number of retrievals (in SULIRS or ORION), and (5) legitimacy of the initial access point. These data were specific to the online catalog searched. Other data about access points address the catalog's controlled vocabulary in a general way that is not connected with the representation of this vocabulary in a particular catalog. Legitimacy was divided into subcategories for single- and multiple-element subject queries, known-item access point, or "other" access points, for example, playing, sex words, or gibberish. Queries placed in known-item and "other" access point categories were discarded from manual analyses.

5.6.3 Original-Match Categorization

Original-match categorization refers to the query's closeness to the catalog's controlled vocabulary. The query was first compared to LCSH-mr. An ordered list of ten matching categories described the closeness of user queries to LCSH-mr. The *first-listed* category that described a match of the user query with LCSH-mr was checked regardless of any availability of a more appropriate category describing a match that might appear later. The tag of the matched LCSH-mr was also recorded to distinguish between matches of authorized headings (MARC tags 1xx) and *see from* tracings (MARC tags 4xx) in LCSH-mr.

If the query did not match LCSH-mr, its closeness to assigned subject headings was determined. The same ten categories used for LCSH-mr were used for assigned subject headings, and as above, the *first-listed* category that described a match of the user-entered term with an assigned subject heading was checked. The machine-readable LCSH-mr and eleventh edition of the printed *LCSH*, revised edition of SCM:SH (Library of Congress 1987), and LC Name Authority File (LCNAF) were used to determine the extent to which queries match assigned subject headings.

Unless a known-item command was explicitly entered, entry of personal, corporate, or geographical names was always considered a subject search. We verified personal, corporate, or geographic names on the LCNAF through the OCLC System. Names not found in LCNAF were verified through subject searches of several online catalogs (e.g., SULIRS, ORION, LS/2000, LCS at Ohio State, and MIRLYN at University of Michigan).

Single-heading categories for matches of LCSH-mr and assigned subject headings were used for both original- and best-match categorizations of user queries. Categories and definitions adopted from Carlyle's study of subject terms entered by ORION users are designated by an asterisk in the list that follows (1989, 45–47). When available, examples are taken from this study, otherwise they are taken from Carlyle's study. Single-heading categories for matches of LCSH-mr and assigned subject headings are:

1. Single-Heading Exact Match*

The LCSH-mr or assigned subject heading matches the user query (including subdivision) exactly, including punctuation.

Example: User "down's syndrome"
LCSH "Down's syndrome"

2. Exact Match, Punctuation Variation*

The LCSH-mr or assigned subject heading matches the user query (including subdivision) exactly, but punctuation is disregarded.

Example: User "acting study and teaching"
Assigned heading "Acting--Study and teaching"

3. Exact Match, Word Order Variation*

The LCSH-mr or assigned subject heading contains the same words as the user query, but order and punctuation are disregarded.

Example: User "photography wedding"
LCSH "Wedding photography"

4. Exact Substantive Word Match*

The LCSH-mr or assigned subject heading consists of the same substantive words that are in a user expression, but word order differs, punctuation is disregarded, and the following stopwords are disregarded: an, and, by, for, in, of, on, the, to.

Example: User "psychology of the adolescent"
LCSH "Adolescent psychology"

5. Spelling Variation*

The LCSH-mr or assigned subject heading includes a spelling variant or variants of a word or words in a user query. This general category is split into five more specific categories, as follows:

5a. Correct Spelling Variant Variation

The LCSH-mr or assigned subject heading contains a correct but variant spelling of one word.

Example: User "colour"
LCSH "Color"

5b. One-Word/Two-Word Variation

The LCSH-mr or assigned subject heading contains one word that the user enters as two words or contains two words that the user enters as one word.

Example: User "latch key children"
LCSH "Latchkey children"

5c. Substitution/transposition

The user query differs from the LCSH or assigned subject heading because one character is incorrectly substituted for another or two letters are transposed.

Example: User "midieval art"
LCSH "Medieval art"

5d. Addition/omission

The user query differs from the LCSH or assigned subject heading because one character is incorrectly added to the query or omitted from the query.

Example: User "raquetball" or "healthy food" or "3astrology"
LCSH "Racquetball" or "Health food" or "Astrology"

5e. Incorrect Spelling

The user query differs from the LCSH or assigned subject heading in more than one spelling variation.

Example: User "phptgraphy" or "integer prograramming"
LCSH "Photography" or "integer programming"

6. Singular/Plural Variation*

The LCSH-mr or assigned subject heading differs from the user query in that one contains a word (or words) that is plural (ends in "s" or "es") and the other contains a word (or words) that is singular. This general category is split into two more specific categories, as follows:

6a. Query Singular/LCSH Plural Variation*

The LCSH or assigned subject heading differs from the user query in that the former contains one word that is plural (ends in "s" or "es") and this same word is singular in the user query.

Example: User "light bulb"
LCSH "Light bulbs"

6b. Query Plural/LCSH Singular Variation*

The LCSH or assigned subject heading differs from the user query in that the former contains one word that is singular and this same word is plural (ends in "s" or "es") in the user query.

Example: User "massages"
LCSH "Massage"

7. Abbreviation Variation*

The user query contains an abbreviation of a word in LCSH or an assigned subject heading, or vice versa.

Example: User "mba"
LCSH "Master of business administration"

8. Date or Numerical Variation*

The LCSH or assigned subject heading contains a date that differs from a date in the user query, or LCSH does not include a date that the user requests; or a difference such as "20"/"twenty" occurs.

Example: User "20th century"
LCSH "Twentieth century"

9. Partial Match

The LCSH or assigned subject heading begins with the same words as the user query, but the heading and query end with one or more additional words. This general category is split into six more specific categories, as follows:

9a. Partial Match, Minus Qualifier

The LCSH or assigned subject heading bears a qualifier that is missing from the user query.

Example: User "lexington"
Assigned heading "Lexington (Ky.)"

9b. Partial Match, First Two Words

The LCSH or assigned subject heading starts with the same first two words in the user query.

Example: User "brumble, h." or "art and artists"
Assigned heading "Brumble, H. David" or "Art and anthropology"

9c. Partial Match, Initial Word and 3-Letter Stem of Second Word

The LCSH or assigned subject heading starts with the same first word and three letters of the second word as the user query.

Example: User "chinese refugees" or "preschool testingh" [*sic*]
LCSH "Chinese reference books" or "Preschool tests"

9d. Partial Match, Initial Word

The initial LCSH or assigned subject heading word matches the initial word in the user query.

Example: User "third reich" or "robin"
LCSH "Third grade (Education) or "Robin Cock (Fictional character)"

9e. Partial Match, Two or More Words Contained in a More Complete Heading

Two or more words in a more complete LCSH or assigned subject heading are contained in the user query.

Example: User "future adult education"
LCSH "Adult education"

9f. Partial Match, One Word Contained in a More Complete Heading

One word in a more complete LCSH or assigned subject heading is contained in the user query.

Example: User "good furniture"
LCSH "Furniture"

10. Combined Match

To make a match, the user query is placed into two or more of the above categories (1–9f).

Example: User "seletion policy"
LCSH "Selection of non-book materials" (combination of spelling variation (5d) and partial match (9f))

If the query matched neither LCSH-mr nor an assigned subject heading, the category for "Use of language not in LCSH-mr or assigned subject headings" was checked. Since such queries completely failed to match the catalog's controlled vocabulary, the third question about the nature of the match is irrelevant.

5.6.4 Match Satisfaction

Responses to the question "Is the match satisfactory?" were "Yes," "Sort of," "Not really," and "Don't know." We had the following information to assess whether the match was satisfactory: (1) the initial query, (2) the matched LCSH-mr or assigned subject heading, and (3) subsequent access points in the search. We did *not* mark a satisfaction category based on what users found in the catalog searched.

Under the "Yes" response were four subcategories that described the type of information that online catalogs could provide to satisfy queries: (1) relevant bibliographic records are assigned the matched controlled vocabulary term, or (2) narrower terms, (3) broader terms, or (4) related terms from LCSH-mr are more appropriate than the heading consulted for expressing the topics of interest users are seeking.

"Sort of" response subcategories described two conditions that might overwhelm users: (1) the amount of material on a topic, and (2) the complexity of the strategies users would have to pursue to satisfy their needs. Examples of queries retrieving too many bibliographic records are "education," "israel," and "maps." We were guided in our decision about the amount of material available on a topic by the number of retrievals in SULIRS and ORION and user queries that named countries, continents, states, disciplines, or fields of study, because these terms would usually be assigned to many bibliographic records in a library's catalog. Subject searches might become unduly complex when users have to browse dozens of authorized headings or references in alphabetical lists to find a more appropriate match or when systems explicitly present users with more than one choice. Examples of the latter are close matches of *see from* tracings that direct searchers to more than one heading or matches of headings connected with complex *see* or *see also* references in LCSH-mr that users must read and follow to find material on their topics of interest.

"Not really" response subcategories described situations when close matches were too general or specific for the topics sought by users or were totally unrelated to their interests. When this satisfaction category was marked, the original-match categorization of the query was usually different from the best-match categorization. These particular queries provided important clues for reordering the sequence of match categories and the system capabilities that were responsible for effecting such matches.

In cases where an adequate assessment about the satisfactory nature of the match could not be made, we chose the "Don't know" response. For example, we often found it impossible to determine the topics users were seeking when their searches were composed of one access point. In such situations, we did not answer the fourth question about best-match categorization because our understanding of the user's interests was incomplete.

5.6.5 Best-Match Categorization

We selected the match category that described the best match of the initial access point with the catalog's controlled vocabulary regardless of its order in the sequence of match categories. We had three sets of categories for placing user queries: (1) matches of single LCSH-mr, (2) matches of single assigned subject headings, and (3) matches of multiple-subject headings.

In the study at hand, the six single-heading categories for partial matches precluded the original-match categorization of user queries in multiple-heading categories. Thus, the original categorization of user queries in this study was restricted to matches of a single LCSH or assigned subject heading.

The multiple-heading categories used in the Carlyle study were only enlisted in this study when we determined *best matches* of the catalog's controlled vocabulary. Multiple-heading categories had almost the same definitions as single-heading categories except for the presence of substantive words from two or more LCSH and/or assigned subject headings. Brief definitions of multiple-heading categories are given below. Appendix D gives full definitions and examples of multiple-heading categories.

- Exact Multiple-Heading Match (comparable to single-heading category 1)
- Correct Spelling Variant Variation (comparable to single-heading category 5a)
- One-Word/Two-Word Variation (comparable to single-heading category 5b)
- Substitution/Transposition (comparable to single-heading category 5c)
- Addition/Omission (comparable to single-heading category 5d)
- Incorrect spelling (comparable to single-heading category 5e)
- Singular/Plural Variation (comparable to single-heading category 6)
- Abbreviation Variation (comparable to single-heading category 7)
- Date or Numerical Variation (comparable to single-heading category 8)
- Partial Match (comparable to single-heading category 9e)

Occasionally, the terms entered by users did not match the catalog's controlled vocabulary, but catalogs did have material on the topics users sought. In such instances, there was no "best match" and the answer to the fourth question, namely, "What is the best match of this access point with the catalog's controlled vocabulary?" was simply "none."

5.6.6 Best System Response

Our last task in the analysis of initial access points was to choose system responses that would deliver to users terms in library catalogs that would be the best matches of their queries. Listed system responses described subject searching capabilities implemented in operational online systems. Examples are the alphabetical displays of LCSH-mr or assigned headings that place users close to the terms they enter and the various keyword matches of the assigned subject headings in bibliographic records that contain the words in user queries. An open-ended category for "Other Responses" enabled us to describe subject searching approaches that might not be implemented in operational online systems but that systems could employ to effect matches of the catalog's controlled vocabulary.

Categories were provided for "No Appropriate System Response" that called for users to express their queries with different words or check sources besides the online catalog. We used these categories when there was no available route in the catalog's alphabetical arrangement or no term relationships in LCSH-mr to guide users to the terminology used by the catalog to express the query nor would keyword searches produce single headings or relevant bibliographic records on the topic that interested users. For example, online catalogs cannot guide users to the assigned subject heading "Women—Tobacco use" through their entry of the query "smoking woman." Alphabetical lists of subject headings based on LCSH would satisfy the "smoking" element of the query but not the "woman" element. Keyword searches would also fail until the singular form of "woman" was converted to the plural form. In the original query, converting the singular form of "woman" to the plural form "women" is not as straightforward as adding a trailing "-s" or "-es." It requires an operation analogous to the handling of *see from* tracings in which the plural form "women" is substituted for the singular form "woman."

5.7

Synthesis and Summary

The findings of transaction log analyses of the subject terms users enter into online catalogs demonstrate that despite online catalog improvements, today's online catalog users are experiencing difficulties that are much the same as the difficulties experienced by the earliest online catalog users. Computer and manual analyses were performed on the subject terms entered by users into online catalogs of three university research libraries to determine the extent to which their subject terms match subject headings based on the LCSH system.

Computer programs were used to produce statistics on tens of thousands of queries placed into match categories for exact, normalized, and keyword matches of the authorized headings in LCSH-mr. Manual analyses were limited to a sample of user queries and only took into account the initial access points in searches. If online systems are to be successful in effecting matches between users' queries and the catalog's controlled vocabulary, then systems can take advantage of the existing links between controlled vocabulary terms to help users pursue their topics of interest using this vocabulary. Users might not need to enter additional access points because their initial access points led to relevant information through system capabilities that encouraged them to browse and explore the controlled vocabulary.

In manual analyses of user queries, we answered five general questions about the initial subject access points in searches:

1. Is this initial access point a legitimate subject term?
2. How closely does this initial subject access point match the catalog's controlled vocabulary?

3. Is the match satisfactory?
4. What is the best match of this access point with the catalog's controlled vocabulary?
5. How can online systems deliver to users the best match in an efficient, effective way?

Match categories used to describe the extent to which the user queries matched subject headings were adopted from a previous study undertaken by Carlyle (1989). We selected from ordered lists of match categories for single-subject-heading categories to answer the second question. Underlying the order of match categories is the sequence of subject searching approaches in operational online catalogs that would effect the particular matches of user-entered terms. To answer the fourth question about the best match of a user's query with the catalog's controlled vocabulary, we selected from the same lists of match categories and an additional list of match categories for multiple headings without regard to the order of categories. User queries for which the answers to the second and fourth questions were different provided important clues for reordering the sequence of match categories and the system capabilities that would be responsible for effecting such matches.

References

Besant, Larry. (1982). Early survey findings: Users of public online catalogs want sophisticated subject access. *American Libraries, 13*, 3 (March), 160.

Borgman, Christine L. (1983). *Research report prepared for OCLC on end user behavior on The Ohio State University Libraries' online catalog: A computer monitoring study*. Dublin, OH: OCLC. OCLC Research Report Series OCLC/OPR/RR-83/7.

Carlyle, Allyson. (1989). Matching LCSH and user vocabulary in the library catalog. *Cataloging & Classification Quarterly, 10*, 1/2, 37–63.

Cochrane, Pauline A. (1983). A paradigm shift in library science. *Information Technology and Libraries, 2*, 1 (March), 3–4.

Dickson, Jean. (1984). An analysis of user errors in searching an online catalog. *Cataloging & Classification Quarterly, 4*, 3 (Spring), 19–38.

Hancock-Beaulieu, Micheline, Stephen Robertson, & Colin Neilson. (1990). *Evaluation of online catalogues: An assessment of methods*. London: British Library. British Library research paper No. 78.

Henty, Margaret. (1986). The user at the online catalogue: A record of unsuccessful keyword searches. *LASIE, 17*, 2 (September/October), 47–52.

Hildreth, Charles R. (1982). *Online public access catalogs: The user interface*. Dublin, OH: OCLC.

Hildreth, Charles R. (1985). Monitoring and analyzing online catalog user activity. *LS/2000 Communique*, pp. 3–6.

Hildreth, Charles R. (1987). *Library automation in North America: A reassessment of the impact of new technologies on networking*. New York: K.G. Saur.

Hunter, Rhonda N. (1991). Successes and failures of patrons searching the online catalog at a large academic library: A transaction log analysis. *RQ, 30*, 3 (Spring), 395–402.

Jones, Richard. (1986). Improving Okapi: Transaction log analysis of failed searches in an online catalogue. *Vine, 62* (May), 3–13.

Kaske, Neal K., & Douglas K. Ferguson. (1980). *On-line public access to library bibliographic data bases: Developments, issues and priorities: Final report to the Council on Library Resources.* Dublin, OH: OCLC, Inc., and the Research Libraries Group, Inc. ED195 275.

Larson, Ray R. (1983). *Users look at online catalogs; Part 2: Interacting with online catalogs; Final report to the Council on Library Resources.* Berkeley, CA: University of California. ED 231 401.

Lester, Marilyn Ann. (1989). *Coincidence of user vocabulary and Library of Congress Subject Headings: Experiments to improve subject access in academic library online catalogs.* Ph.D. dissertation, University of Illinois at Urbana-Champaign.

Lewis, David W. (1987). Research on the use of online catalogs and its implications for library practice. *Journal of Academic Librarianship, 13,* 3 (July), 152–156.

Library of Congress. Subject Cataloging Division. (1987). *Subject cataloging manual: Subject headings.*Rev. ed. Washington, DC: Library of Congress.

Markey, Karen. (1984). *Subject searching in library catalogs: Before and after the introduction of online catalogs.* Dublin, OH: OCLC.

Peters, Thomas A. (1989). When smart people fail: An analysis of the transaction log of an online public access catalog. *Journal of Academic Librarianship, 15,* 5 (November), 267–273.

Taylor, Arlene G. (1984). Authority files in online catalogs: An investigation of their value. *Cataloging & Classification Quarterly, 4,* 3 (Spring), 1–17.

Tolle, John E. (1983). *Current utilization of online catalogs: Transaction log analysis.* Vol. 1 of *Final report to the Council on Library Resources.* Dublin, OH: OCLC. OCLC Research Report Series OCLC/OPR/RR-83/2. ED 231 402.

Van Pulis, Noelle, & Ludy, Lorene E. (1988). Subject searching in an online catalog with authority control. *College & Research Libraries, 49,* 6 (November), 523–533.

Walker, Stephen, & Jones, Richard M. (1987). *Improving subject retrieval in online catalogues: 1. Stemming, automatic spelling correction and cross-reference tables.* London: British Library. British Library Research Paper No. 24.

Walter, Dennis R. (1987). The user at the online catalogue: A record of unsuccessful keyword searches—another case study. *LASIE, 18,* 3 (November/December), 74–83.

Wang, Chih. (1985). The online catalog, subject access, and user actions: A review. *Library Review, 34* (Autumn), 143–153.

Zink, Steven D. (1991). Monitoring user search success through transaction log analysis: The WolfPAC example. *Reference Services Review, 19,* 1 (Spring), 49–56.

6

An Overview of User Queries

6.1 Introduction

This chapter is an orientation to the subject terms users enter into online catalogs. It reports the percentages of user queries that are exact, normalized, and keyword matches of authorized subject headings and *see from* tracings in LCSH-mr. Statistics are produced using computer programs that have the advantage of processing voluminous amounts of data. They have the disadvantages of being unable to tell us much more about matches than their tag and leaving us totally in the dark with respect to nonmatches.

Manual analyses of user queries are necessary to answer more sophisticated questions about matches and nonmatches: What subject searching approaches are successful in effecting matches of the catalog's controlled vocabulary? How many access points are legitimate queries for subject searches in online catalogs? What are the reasons for nonmatch? This chapter answers the first two questions through a manual analysis of a sample of user queries. Queries that are not legitimate matches are identified and discarded from subsequent analyses.

6.2 A Computer Analysis of User Queries

Figure 6.1 divides the percentages of user queries entered into terminals by public catalog users into four categories: exact, normalized, and keyword matches of LCSH-mr, and remaining terms. Subject queries were entered into sixty-six terminals accessed primarily by the public catalog users at three university research libraries. Terminals accessed primarily by staff or by a combination of staff and public catalog users are not included in the results reported here. Computer programs processed a total of 74,373 user queries to arrive at the percentages presented in Figure 6.1.

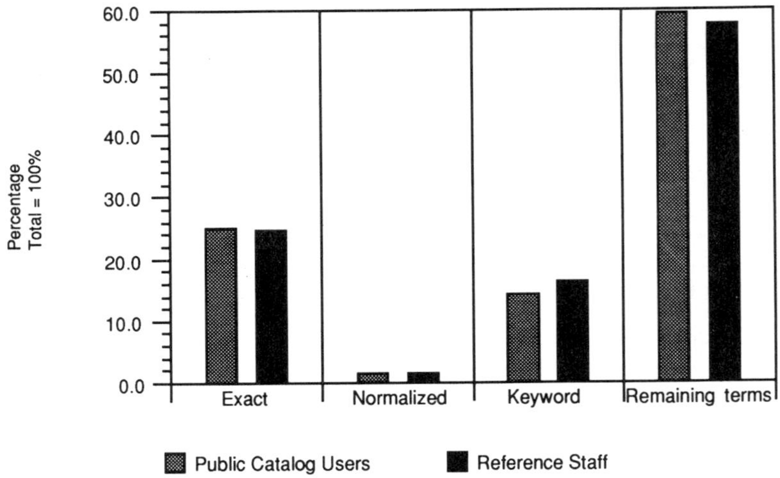

Figure 6.1
Matches of LCSH-mr by public catalog users and reference staff.

Transaction logs supplied for our study also contained queries entered by reference staff. Although we focus on the subject terms entered by public catalog users, results are also given for reference staff queries. Computer programs processed a total of 5057 reference staff queries entered into a total of 35 terminals to arrive at the percentages presented in Figure 6.1.

6.2.1 Exact Matches

One quarter of the subject terms entered by online catalog users are exact matches of LCSH-mr. Percentages for the three groups of online catalog users are the low 22.0% of exact matches entered by SULIRS users, 32.0% of exact matches by ORION users, and the high 36.9% of exact matches by LS/2000 users.

The explanation for the high percentage of exact match by LS/2000 users became evident to us when we performed manual analyses of subject access points. Users repeatedly entered the same access points in searches. Often, these access points were exact matches of LCSH-mr. In the course of the sample LS/2000 search for "family therapy," for example, the user entered five separate access points (Appendix C). If repeated terms are counted, 40.0% of access points were exact matches of LCSH-mr; if they are not counted, 33.3% of access points were exact matches of LCSH-mr. We reviewed several LS/2000 searches like the one shown in Appendix C to determine why users repeatedly enter the same access points.

LS/2000 is a menu-based system that responds to the terms users enter with alphabetical lists of assigned subject headings or single words from selected fields of bibliographic records. When users select headings or words with many retrievals, LS/2000 encourages them to reduce the number of retrievals. The options that the system presents to users for reducing retrievals require them to enter additional terms, browse lists of subject headings or subdivisions in alphabetical proximity to their entered terms, and select headings or subdivisions from alphabetical lists. Using the Boolean "and" operator, the system then combines selected headings or subdivisions with earlier results.

Several user actions during the "reduction" process caused users to end their consultation prematurely and resume the search by reentering the same terms used in their initial access points or terms that they selected from the alphabetical lists. In instances of the latter, such terms are typically main headings that match LCSH-mr. Thus, the subject searching process of LS/2000 itself may be one reason why the percentage of exact match by system users is higher than such percentages by SULIRS and ORION users.

Discarding duplicate access points from subject searches could result in lowering the percentage of exact match by LS/2000 users. To do so would require, however, automatic demarcation of searches and automatic comparison of subsequent access points with the initial access point and with each other, two operations that are not performed in the computer analysis described in this chapter.

In manual analyses, individual searches are demarcated and only the initial access points in these searches examined. The results of subject searches for topical subjects discussed in Chapter 7 demonstrate that the percentage of exact matches for the initial access points entered by LS/2000 is about the same as the percentage for ORION users. We can speculate that the initial access points entered by LS/2000 users are not as likely as subsequent access points to be exact matches of LCSH-mr because users have not been affected by the terminology the system displays to them in the search process.

Overall percentages of matching categories are almost the same for public catalog users and reference staff. One might expect reference staff to enter higher percentages of exact matches than users. However, users sometimes consult reference staff when they themselves have already failed to find their subject queries in the catalog. Reference staff may perform the search using the same subject terms that were unsuccessful for users, then continue the search using their knowledge of the unsuccessful search, the system, and the controlled vocabulary.

In fact, percentages of exact matches entered by reference staff actually vary quite a bit from library to library. Exact matches are lowest at Syracuse (14.9%), highest at the University of Kentucky (51.7%), and about average at UCLA (26.5%). Reference staff at Syracuse probably do not feel pressured to enter exact matches because they know their system retrieves bibliographic records based on matches of words in assigned subject headings and/or titles. Percentages of exact matches are the highest at terminals accessed by reference staff at the University of Kentucky. The previous discussion on problem searches in LS/2000 may hold the key to explaining this high percentage. Problem searches in LS/2000 include those in which users make exact matches of LCSH-mr. Users who have difficulties with the subject searching process may be approaching reference staff and asking them to retrace their steps. Such users may be starting with an exact match of an LCSH-mr or selecting an LCSH-mr in the course of their search. Thus, they have an exact LCSH-mr in mind when consulting reference staff.

Future studies of subject queries could examine terms entered by reference staff to determine the precise reasons why the percentages of exact matches of LCSH-mr are somewhat higher or lower than such percentages for users. Focus group interviews could be used to assess the reference staff's general knowledge about subject searching approaches implemented in the online catalog and how staff utilize these approaches when helping public catalog users.

Exact matches of authorized headings and *see from* tracings in LCSH-mr are enumerated by tag in Figures 6.2 and 6.3. Over 90% of exact matches are given to authorized headings and *see from* tracings for topical subjects. The coverage of authorized headings and *see from* tracings for names in LCNAF is much more extensive in LCNAF than in LCSH-mr; consequently, small percentages of exact matches for names are expected.

6.2.2 Normalized Matches

Figure 6.1 gives percentages of user-entered subject access points that are normalized matches of LCSH-mr. Less than 2% of user-entered terms are normalized matches of LCSH-mr. Percentages hardly vary between systems. Normalized matches do not always produce single LCSH-mr records that are relevant to user queries, as demonstrated in the last three examples below:

User query	*Matching LCSH-mr and/or* see from *tracing*
birth control pill	Pill, Birth Control, USE Oral contraceptives
institutional care children	Children--Institutional care
kindergarten all day	All-day kindergarten
securities and insider trading	Insider trading in securities
bull fighting	Fighting bull
hospitals and the public	Hospitals, Public
the art of war	Art and war

Normalized matches of LCSH-mr are enumerated by tag in Figures 6.2 and 6.3. Percentages of normalized matches are somewhat different than percentages of exact matches with respect to authorized headings and *see from* tracings for topical subjects (MARC tags 150 and 450). Other percentages are unchanged or so small that changes are not noteworthy.

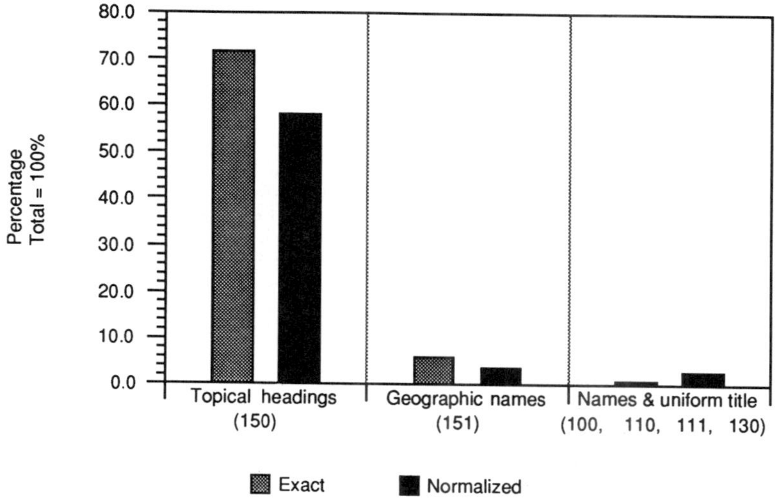

Figure 6.2
Exact and normalized matches by tag for authorized headings (1xx).

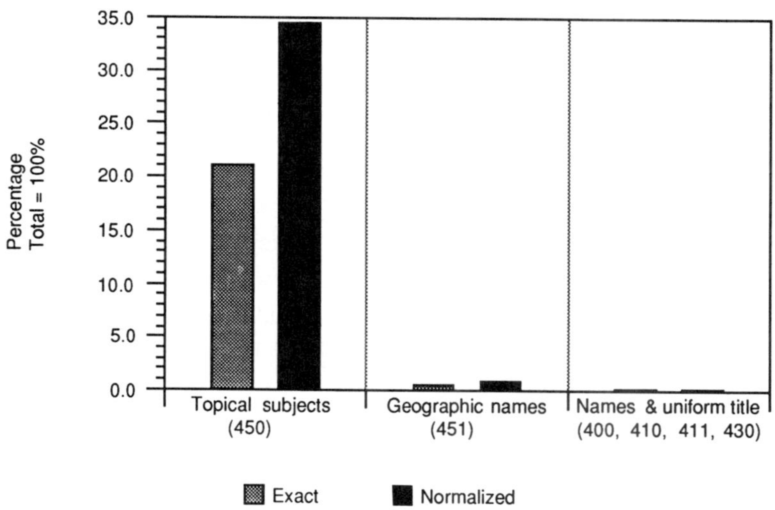

Figure 6.3
Exact and normalized matches by tag for *see from* tracings (4xx).

6.2.3 Keyword Matches

Figure 6.1 gives the percentages of user-entered subject access points that are keyword matches of LCSH-mr. Statistics for keyword matches are based on matching

1% of subject access points entered by SULIRS patrons, and 5% of access points entered by SULIRS staff, ORION patrons and staff, and LS/2000 staff, and 10% of access points entered by LS/2000 patrons, with LCSH-mr headings and references. Overall, 16.2% of user-entered subject terms are keyword matches of LCSH-mr. Percentages hardly vary between systems.

Keyword matches require all the words in user queries to be present in the authorized heading and/or *see from* tracing fields of LCSH-mr records. Keyword matches do not always produce subject headings in the established heading field of LCSH-mr records that are relevant to the topics users are seeking, as demonstrated in the first and last two examples below.

Query	*Authorized heading in matching LCSH-mr record*
aids	Adult education--Audio-visual aids; Hearing aids; Dealer aids; Art--Audio-visual aids; Aids (Disease); and others
cassette	Magnetic recorders and recording--Cassette recorders; Talking books; Talking newspapers
College entrance	College entrance achievement tests; College entrance requirements; and others
fast food	Convenience foods
innocent x	Papal States--History--Innocent X, 1644-1655
leisure and recreation	Architecture and recreation; Leisure counseling
stress	Accents and accentuation; Fishes--Effect of water temperature on; Airframes; Dentists--Job stress; Job stress; and others

A figure for keyword matches by tag similar to Figures 6.2 and 6.3 is not provided because matches are made of more than one LCSH-mr.

6.2.4 Remaining Terms

The majority (57.5%) of subject terms entered by public catalog users are not placed in matching categories. Instead of applying additional automatic techniques such as stemming or spelling correction, we chose to manually examine a sample of initial access points in subject searches to determine the most fruitful techniques for effecting matches of the catalog's controlled vocabulary. The rest of this chapter describes the initial queries in subject searches and their legitimacy as subject terms. Chapters 7–10 focus on the closeness of legitimate subject terms to the catalog's controlled vocabulary.

6.3 Subject Searches and Initial Access Points

Table 6.1 is a fact sheet with details about the total of 1503 searches and initial access points included in manual analyses.

Table 6.1
Fact Sheet for Initial Access Points in Subject Searches

Facts	Total	SULIRS	ORION	LS/2000
Searches				
No. of searches	1503.0	570.0	515.0	418.0
No. of access points	4537.0	1528.0	1690.0	1319.0
Avg. no. of access points per search	3.0	2.7	3.3	3.2
Maximum no. of access points in a search	26.0	18.0	26.0	26.0
Initial access points				
Avg. no. of words per access point	1.8	2.0	1.8	1.5
Maximum no. of words in an access point	10.0	8.0	10.0	7.0
Avg. no. of retrievals per access point	N/A	205.5[a]	352.2[b]	N/A
Percentage of access points with zero retrievals	N/A	30.7	38.8	N/A
Percentage of access points with retrievals > 999	N/A	6.1	5.8	N/A
Avg. no. of words in access points for retrievals > 999	N/A	1.2	1.1	N/A
Avg. no. of access points in searches where initial access point has retrievals > 999	N/A	4.5	4.9	N/A

[a]Number of bibliographic records retrieved. This is an estimate based on substituting 3,000 retrievals for the 99,999 retrievals that is written to logs when number of retrievals exceeds about 1,000.
[b]Number of assigned subject headings retrieved.

Searches average three access points. The longest searches are two searches in ORION and LS/2000 containing twenty-six access points. The ORION user begins with the access point "married people" and enters twenty-five more access points containing variants of the word "marriage" or words for the conditions that marriage brings, for example, "love," "romance," "problems," and/or words about stages, for example, "cycles," "lifecycles," "steps," "process." Phrases are also entered such as "marriage stages," "marriage processes," "marital steps," and "marital problems." The LS/2000 user begins with the access point "career counseling" and enters twenty-five more access points describing related topics such as "high school guidance counseling," "college, choice of," and "student financial aid."

Initial access points average 1.8 words and range from a low of 1.5 words in LS/2000 to a high of 2.0 words in SULIRS. Of the longest initial access points in the three systems, one has several spelling errors and one contains an addition/omission error:

- federal home loan bank system u s periodicalsiii9iu is iiiiiiii (ORION, 10 words)
- women in the work force in the 1900-1950 (SULIRS, 8 words)
- legal cases involving life support systems in humans (SULIRS, 8 words)
- 2a concise history of the middle east (LS/2000, 7 words)

Comparisons between systems with respect to number of retrievals are difficult to make because the two systems that report number of retrievals count different things. SULIRS reports the *number of retrieved bibliographic records*. The number given in the fact sheet (Table 6.1) is an estimate based on substituting 3000 retrievals for the number 99,999 that SULIRS reports to users when the number of retrievals exceeds about one thousand. ORION reports the *number of retrieved assigned subject headings.*

Initial access points entered by SULIRS users *average over two hundred retrievals.* ORION users retrieve an *average of about 350 assigned subject headings* in response to their initial access points. About three in every ten initial access points produce zero retrievals in SULIRS (175 of 570, or 30.7%). Almost four in every ten initial access points produce zero retrievals in ORION (200 of 515, or 38.8%). The initial access points in thirty-five SULIRS searches and thirty ORION searches produce one thousand or more retrievals. In both SULIRS and ORION, access points that produce one thousand or more retrievals are usually composed of one word, which is far below the average of three words. Users whose initial access points are so high posted enter between four and five access points per search in comparison to the average of three access points per search.

6.4 Legitimacy of Subject Terms

To determine the legitimacy of user queries, we placed queries into legitimate subject-term categories for single-element terms and multiple-element terms and into categories for terms discarded from subsequent analyses, that is, known-item access points and "other" access points. Legitimate subject-term and known-item subcategories are named for the topical and name elements present in access points. Examples of queries in the topical-personal name subcategory are "clarence darrow's relegious views" [*sic*] and "hitler's speeches." Both examples have personal-name elements (i.e., "clarence darrow's" and "hitler's") and topical-subject elements (i.e., "relegious views" [*sic*] and "speeches)." Figure 6.4 displays the percentages of initial access points in legitimate subject-term subcategories and in subcategories discarded from subsequent analyses.

About two-thirds (62.2%) of access points consist wholly of elements for topical subjects. Personal name access points are 10.9% of user queries. Of the three different multiple-element combinations occurring in the sample of initial access points, topical subject–geographic name combinations are most common (6.4%). Interestingly, they are more common than single-element queries for geographic names (4.7%). The SULIRS access point "greek mythology's influence on shakespeare" bears three different elements: (1) topical subjects, "mythology's influence," (2) personal names, "shakespeare," and geographic names, "greek."

ORION logs contributed small numbers of queries for personal and corporate names because separate commands (i.e., "find name" or "browse name") were re-

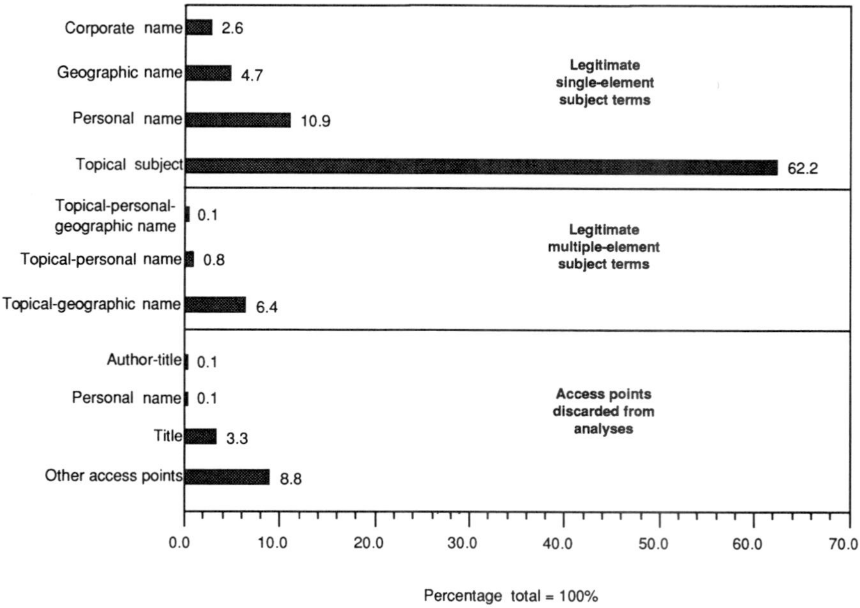

Figure 6.4
Types of access points.

quired for searching names as authors or subjects. The fact that access points for personal or corporate names occur in the sample of ORION access points is in keeping with the generalizations about the subject terms users enter into online catalogs (Chapter 5). Users also enlist the subject searching capabilities of online catalogs to enter known-item access points: between 3 and 4% of subject queries are known-item searches. Under 10% of subject queries are placed in the "other" access points category. Sex words, gibberish, command names, and playing characterize the queries in this category. Queries placed in subcategories for known-item access points and "other" access points amounted to 12.3% of user queries and were discarded from subsequent analyses.

6.5 Access Points Discarded from Manual Analyses

6.5.1 Known-Item Access Points

Queries formulated like a book or journal title and entered into the three systems using their respective subject search commands are categorized as known-item searches. Sometimes we searched one or more online catalogs to verify whether the query actually retrieves a specific known item. Examples of known-item searches are:

- bartlett's quotations (SULIRS)
- dubliners (LS/2000)
- "fireside chats" (LS/2000)
- lcsh (ORION)
- journal of basic enginerring [*sic*] (ORION)
- robinson rusoe [*sic*] (ORION)
- ti = social psychology of fashion (LS/2000)
- two essays on analytical psychology (SULIRS)

Nearly all known-item searches are title searches (49 of 52). The one occurrence of an author–title search comes from SULIRS for "auther [*sic*] james balfour speeches on zionism." Two access points entered into LS/2000 include the system's author search command with the name, that is, "au = adams, ansel" and "au = fujikake," and thus, are categorized as known-item searches. Users must have selected a subject search option from the initial menu, then entered names with an explicit author command, that is, au =. Since users must first choose a subject search option, the system treats the query including author command as a subject term.

Known-item searches average about one access point shorter (2.1) than all queries (3.0) (see Table 6.1). The longest query for a known item is entered by a SULIRS user for "the gospel according to luke" (5 words). Other access points in this search are "the gospel according to matthew," "the book of job," and "the book of ecclesiastes."

The average number of words per known-item access point (2.8) is one word longer than the average (1.8). The longer length of known-item access points may be attributed to the entry of titles.

The number of retrievals is much lower than average for both SULIRS and ORION searches. If the one known-item query that makes SULIRS respond with the prompt of 99,999 items is omitted, the average number of retrievals per SULIRS known-item access points is about twenty-one. SULIRS users can find specific titles using the system's "sb," "wd," or "su" subject searching commands because the system searches words in titles; however, such searches also include bibliographic records containing words from subject heading fields.

The average number of retrievals per ORION known-item access point is six. Five of the six known-item access points in ORION fail to retrieve headings. To find known items, ORION users have to enter different commands.

The transaction logs contained queries users entered using subject commands available in the three systems. Users probably entered known-item access points using known-item search commands. If such searches failed to retrieve items, users might have reentered queries using a subject search command. In another matching study (Markey 1984, 65–73), unabridged transaction logs were examined and it was found that users reenter the same query using several different subject search commands and known-item commands. For example, "surrealist painters" was reentered using commands for subject, title, and author searches. When users enter queries using improper search commands, they may be looking for a manageable number of retrievals or using another strategy following one that produces zero retrievals. Additionally, they may not understand how to use the particular system's different searching commands to meet their information needs.

6.5.2 Other Access Points

The "other" access points category accounts for 8.8% of initial access points (133 of 1503). Average numbers of access points per search and words per access point are well below the averages of 3.0 and 1.8, respectively. The latter may be attributed to the many SULIRS and ORION queries placed in this category that are blank lines, and thus, have zero words per access point. Over two-thirds of the access points in this category produce zero retrievals in SULIRS and ORION, respectively. Blank lines yield no retrievals.

Thirteen different types of initial access points were defined after access points were categorized in the "other" access points category. Types and examples of access points follow. Several of them are connected with the search formulation and operational features of the three online catalogs. Percentages of queries are also cited.

Don't Know What the User Wants (24.1% of other access points).

This category includes word stems (e.g., "ger," "muc," "per," "dans") and incomplete phrases (e.g., "green p"). It also includes terms that we did not understand (e.g., "vignaux," "maldef," "sol gel," "gabins"), were unable to verify (e.g., "cort," "cort thinking program," "brazil bragantina," "rietveld," "group f/64," "framework II," "lsi logic corporation," "parens patriae"), or terms that did not give us enough information to categorize the query (e.g., "directory," "pilates," "interpretations"). Queries categorized here are taken from all three systems.

Blank Line (21.8% of other access points).

Blank lines are entered as access points into all three systems. Entry of blank lines could have been inadvertent or an attempt on the part of the user to get help or induce the system to respond with the ready prompt.

Remote Sign-on Command (21.8% of other access points).

This type of query comes exclusively from University of Kentucky transaction logs. "Liv" is the remote sign-on command to LS/2000 at Kentucky. When online catalog users find an LS/2000 terminal that has been turned off or is in the middle of the last user's search, they sometimes enter the "liv" command in an attempt to restart the system. Instead, LS/2000 resumes operation from the point when the terminal was turned off or the last user left the terminal. If LS/2000 is in subject search mode, it performs a subject search for the user-entered query "liv." Nearly half of LS/2000 queries placed in the "other access points" category were placed in this subcategory.

Command Name (9.8% of other access points).

Occurrences of the SULIRS command name "s" sometimes compose entire queries. SULIRS asks users to begin a new search with the "s" command when the system is in the middle of a search, that is, displaying retrieved citations or reporting the number of citations retrieved. Users' entry of the "s" is probably inadvertent.

To override menus, LS/2000 users can enter search commands directly. Sometimes they enter commands when LS/2000 is expecting a query. Thus, LS/2000 performs a search for the command name entered. Other times they enter incorrect command names with correct command syntax. Examples are "antianri/es," "ls/2000/es," "-/AT," "eses," "3/ti."

Gibberish (6.8% of other access points).

Of the three systems, gibberish is most frequently encountered in LS/2000. Examples are "ba' c," "cu = 508 r152 p p," " p i," and "jqp."

Numbers (5.3% of other access points).

LS/2000 users occasionally enter numbers into the system. When numbers range from 1 to 5, they are probably users' inadvertent reentry of a number corresponding to a particular searching option from the initial menu. Other examples of numbers are "623," "34343434," and "31113131."

Dates (3.0% of other access points).

Dates are encountered as initial access points in SULIRS and LS/2000. Examples are "2019," "1974," and "1983." When access points entered into LS/2000 produce too many retrievals, the system prompts users to reduce the number by date of publication or other criteria. Dates entered at this point would not be the initial access point in searches unless there is considerable time between the entry of the previous access point and the date that causes us to consider the date as a new search, and thus, an initial access point in a search. Additionally, LS/2000 users may begin searches with dates because the system allows users to reduce retrievals by entering dates.

Sex Words (2.3% of other access points).

The context of sex words is important for the investigators to determine whether to include or discard such queries from the study. When sex words started and comprised an entire search, we categorized them here and discarded them from subsequent analyses. Sex words that were exact or partial matches of LCSH-mr or assigned subject headings were included in the analysis. Examples of such queries are "sex," "penis expansion," "erotica," "anal sex." Reviewing lists of access points, we noted that sex words were more likely to occur in the middle or at the end of a search.

Perhaps users enter such words as a diversion during a long search or as an expression of frustration when their searches are not particularly fruitful.

Letters (1.5% of other access points).

Two SULIRS queries are composed entirely of letters that look like abbreviations, that is, dwi and naevc. No heading or *see from* tracing in LCSH-mr or assigned subject heading expresses the former. Investigators are unable to verify the latter.

Playing (1.5% of other access points).

An example of a query categorized as playing is "peter" (followed by "francine"). Often the context of queries helps the investigators categorize them here.

Help (0.7% of other access points).

One SULIRS user entered "help" as his initial query. The correct "help" command in SULIRS is the entry of a question mark (?).

Call Number (0.7% of other access points).

One SULIRS user entered "la227.3.a43" using the system's "lc" command. This subject search is restricted to finding words in LC subject headings. Call numbers are entered into SULIRS using the "cn" command.

Satanic Terms (0.7% of other access points).

The context of satanic words is important to determine whether to include or discard such queries from the study. When satanic words start and comprise an entire search, they are categorized here, and, thus, discarded from subsequent analyses. The one example is "666." Satanic words that are exact or partial matches of headings or *see from* tracings in LCSH-mr or assigned subject headings are included in the analysis. The one example of the latter is "satan."

6.6 Synthesis and Summary

The computer analysis processed almost 75,000 user queries to determine percentages of queries that were exact, normalized, and keyword matches of the authorized headings and *see from* tracings in LCSH-mr. Exactly one quarter of user queries match terms in LCSH-mr. Less than 2% of user queries are matches of normalized terms from LCSH-mr. Keyword matches account for 16.2% of user queries.

Although computer analyses tell us much more about matches than their tag, they leave us totally in the dark about the remaining 57.5% of user queries that are not matched. Computer analyses demonstrate that users are more likely to enter exact matches of topical subject headings in established heading fields of LCSH-mr records (MARC tag 150) than *see from* tracings (MARC tag 450), but they cannot tell us whether matches are made of user queries consisting of two or more elements for topical subjects and names. Computer analyses provide us with promising results from keyword matches but they cannot tell us whether matches are appropriate for the topics users consult in library catalogs. Manual analyses of user queries are necessary to answer more complex questions about matches and nonmatches.

A sample of searches from the transaction logs of the three online catalogs was analyzed manually to answer complex questions about the extent to which user queries match the catalog's controlled vocabulary. The ability of the matched headings to express the topics users are seeking, the characteristics of queries that fail entirely to match controlled vocabulary terms, and the subject searching capabilities required to produce retrievals for such queries were the focus of the manual investigation.

Initial queries are categorized either as legitimate subject queries or as access points discarded from subsequent analyses. Legitimate subject-term categories are composed of single-element and multiple-element subcategories named for the topical and name elements present in access points. Known-item access points and "other access points" together account for less than 10% of the initial access points in subject searches and are discarded from subsequent analyses.

Nearly all known-item access points are titles. When users enter queries using improper search commands, they may be looking for a manageable number of retrievals or using another strategy following one that produces zero retrievals. Additionally, they may not understand how to use the particular system's different searching commands in view of their query.

We divided the "other access points" subcategory into thirteen different types of access points. Several types are connected with search formulation and operational features of the three online catalogs from which transaction log data were derived.

Since computer programs are unable to answer sophisticated questions about matches and nonmatches such as the subject searching approaches that are successful in effecting matches of the catalog's controlled vocabulary and reasons for nonmatch, manual analyses of user queries were performed. This chapter has addressed the first question in the manual analysis: How many access points are legitimate queries for subject searches in online catalogs?

Reference

Markey, Karen. (1984). *Subject searching in library catalogs: Before and after the introduction of online catalogs.* Dublin, OH: OCLC.

7

Queries for Topical Subjects That Are Likely to Succeed

7.1 Introduction

The majority of queries entered into online catalogs consist wholly of elements for topical subjects. Some of these queries express one concept, for example, "motivation," "rap music," and "art." Others express two or more concepts, for example, "reading aloud to children," "sexual abuse in poverty families," and "racism in humor."

The data and analyses presented in this chapter demonstrate that queries consisting wholly of elements for topical subjects are among the most successful in terms of matching the catalog's controlled vocabulary on their own or with the assistance of computer programs for normalization, spelling correction, and other matching techniques. The problem is that matching controlled vocabulary terms are posted in hundreds, and sometimes thousands, of bibliographic records. The number of retrievals goes even higher if records are retrieved based on matches of the words in user queries in title, note, and other subject-rich fields of bibliographic records.

Systems that overwhelm users with large retrievals are penalizing users for making exact matches of the catalog's controlled vocabulary. System responses to the exact matches users enter must ensure the precision of results and effectively manage and limit large numbers of retrievals. In this way, systems would be rewarding users for their exact matches by encouraging them to pursue their search using LCSH terminology.

As the results of the matching study for queries consisting entirely of topical subject elements unfold in this chapter, we must keep in mind system responses to such queries. It matters little whether users exactly match the catalog's controlled vocabulary if they are discouraged from pursuing their searches because systems are unable to manage the results of high-posted searches. Thus, our discussion of user queries for topical subjects that are likely to succeed extends to subject searching capabilities that can effectively manage the results of such searches.

7.2 Subject Searches and Initial Access Points

Table 7.1 is a fact sheet with details about the total of 935 searches initiated by an access point consisting wholly of elements for topical subjects.

Initial access points for topical subjects are about two-thirds of all access points examined in this study; consequently, most summary statistics for these access points are comparable to statistics for initial access points generally (see Table 6.1). Initial access points for topical subjects average about two words but can be as long as eight words. The searches they initiate average about three access points. They retrieve a few more bibliographic records in SULIRS and assigned subject headings in ORION and are less likely to yield zero retrievals than initial access points generally. In both SULIRS and ORION, access points that produce one thousand or more retrievals are composed of one word, which is below the average of 1.8 words per access point. Users whose initial access points are so high posted enter between five and six access points per search in comparison to the average of three access points per search.

7.3 Original-Match Categorization

The original-match categorization of queries for topical subjects is shown in Figure 7.1. The largest percentage (45.7%) of queries for topical subjects are exact matches of LCSH-mr. Percentages vary a little between systems: nearly 50% of user queries for topical subjects entered into ORION and LS/2000 are exact matches of LCSH-mr, and exactly 40% of queries for topical subject entered into SULIRS are exact matches.

The subset of queries consisting of topical subject elements is comparable to the sample of queries examined by Carlyle, because she disregarded queries consisting wholly or partially of proper names and several subcategories of queries not considered legitimate subject queries. Both the Carlyle study (1989, 51) and the study at hand report that 47% of user queries exactly match topical subjects after punctuation is disregarded.

Together, the three manual techniques of disregarding punctuation, word order, and looking for substantive word matches are comparable to normalization procedures used in the computer analysis (Chapter 6). Computerized normalization effected matches of 1.4% of users' queries (see Figure 6.1); however, queries that are not legitimate subject terms were included in the computer analysis. The three manual normalization techniques combined create 1.9% of matches.

The second largest percentage (38.8%) of queries for topical subjects are partial matches. Individual percentages for the six partial match subcategories that make up this category are: (1) minus qualifiers (3.8%), (2) first two words (5.8%), (3) first word

Table 7.1
Fact Sheet for Initial Access Points Consisting of Topical Subject Elements

Summary data	Total	SULIRS	ORION	LS/2000
Searches				
No. of searches	935.0	355.0	361.0	219.0
No. of access points	3094.0	1052.0	1272.0	770.0
Avg. no. of access points per search	3.3	3.0	3.5	3.5
Maximum no. of access points in a search	26.0	18.0	26.0	26.0
Initial access points				
Avg. no. of words per access point	1.8	2.0	1.8	1.5
Maximum no. of words in an access point	8.0	8.0	5.0	6.0
Avg. no. of retrievals per access point	N/A	231.3[a]	362.0[b]	N/A
Retrievals				
Percentage of access points with zero retrievals	N/A	27.3	31.9	N/A
Percentage of access points with retrievals > 999	N/A	4.8	6.1	N/A
High-posted searches				
Avg. no. of words in access points with retrievals > 999	N/A	1.2	1.1	N/A
Avg. no. of access points in searches where initial access point has retrievals > 999	N/A	5.9	5.0	N/A

[a]Number of bibliographic records retrieved. This is an estimate based on substituting 3000 retrievals for the 99,999 retrievals that is written to logs when number of retrievals exceeds about 1000.
[b]Number of assigned subject headings retrieved.

and three-letter stem of the second word (1.7%), (4) first word (25.7%), (5) two words in an LCSH-mr heading (0.5%), and (6) one word in an LCSH-mr heading (1.3%).

No other single category accounts for more than 5% of user-entered topical subjects. No occurrences of date or abbreviation variations were found in the sample. Only 2.4% of the queries for topical subjects entered by online catalog searchers use language not found in LCSH-mr.

The remainder of this chapter discusses queries in original-match categorizations that are likely to succeed in producing useful retrievals. Most attention is given to exact matches of controlled vocabulary terms because they produce so many retrievals that users may be overwhelmed by results.

7.4 Exact Matches

7.4.1 Subject Searches and Initial Access Points

Exact matches are 28.4% of all initial access points in the sample or 45.7% of initial access points for topical subjects (Figure 7.1). Table 7.2 is a fact sheet with

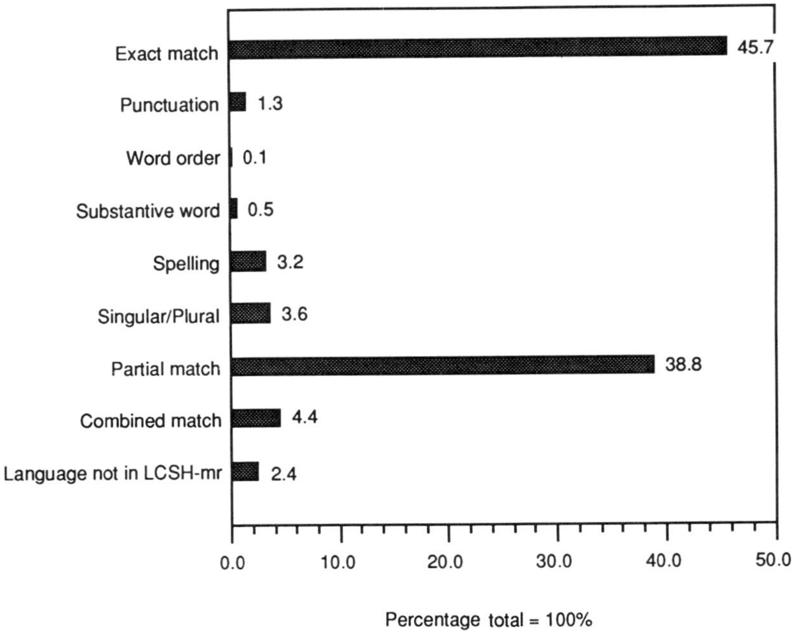

Figure 7.1
Original-match categorization of queries for topical subjects.

details about the total of 427 searches that begin with an access point that exactly matches an authorized heading or *see from* tracing in LCSH-mr. Searches contain about three access points, comparable to the length of subject searches generally (see Table 6.1). Initial access points that are exact matches of LCSH-mr contain fewer words (1.4) than access points generally (1.8). Of exact matches, 68.1% are composed of one word and 27.7% are composed of two words. The two longest initial access points that are exact matches come from ORION users and have four words:

- children of divorced parents
- delivery of health care

Only seventeen queries contain three words that exactly match an LCSH-mr heading. Examples are:

- data base management
- doping in sports
- electron spin resonance
- sickle cell anemia
- strategic defense initiative
- technology and law

Table 7.2
Fact Sheet for Exact Matches

Summary data	Total	SULIRS	ORION	LS/2000
Searches				
No. of searches	427.0	142.0	178.0	107.0
No. of access points	1375.0	391.0	559.0	425.0
Avg. no. of access points per search	3.2	2.8	3.1	4.0
Maximum no. of access points in a search	26.0	14.0	24.0	26.0
Initial access points				
No. matching established subject heading (150)	339.0	108.0	143.0	88.0
No. matching unauthorized heading (150) with complex *see* reference (260)	9.0	2.0	2.0	5.0
No. matching *see from* tracing (450)	79.0	32.0	33.0	14.0
Avg. no. of words per access point	1.4	1.4	1.4	1.2
Maximum no. of words in an access point	4.0	3.0	4.0	3.0
Retrievals				
Avg. no. of retrievals per access point	N/A	1150.0[a]	689.0[a]	N/A
Percentage of access points with zero retrievals	N/A	4.9	7.3	N/A
High-posted searches				
Percentage of access points with retrievals > 999	N/A	12.7	11.2	N/A
Avg. no. of words in access points with retrievals > 999	N/A	1.2	1.1	N/A
Avg. no. of access points in searches where initial access point has retrievals > 999	N/A	4.9	5.3	N/A

[a]Number of bibliographic records retrieved. This is an estimate based on substituting 3,000 retrievals for the 99,999 retrievals that is written to logs when number of retrievals exceeds about 1,000.
[b]Number of assigned subject headings retrieved.

Exact matches retrieve many more bibliographic records and assigned subject headings than topical subjects generally. SULIRS users retrieve 1150 bibliographic records per exact match of LCSH-mr and ORION users retrieve a list of almost 700 assigned subject headings per exact match. In contrast, queries for topical subjects generally result in 231 bibliographic records or 362 assigned subject headings in SULIRS or ORION, respectively (Table 7.1).

Of queries exactly matching LCSH-mr, only 4.9% of SULIRS queries and 7.3% of ORION queries result in zero retrievals. In contrast, between one-fourth and one-third of SULIRS and ORION queries for topical subjects result in zero retrievals (Table 7.1). The fact that exact matches yield many retrievals is also evident in the higher percentages of initial access points retrieving one thousand or more records or headings. Between 11% and 13% of initial access points that are exact matches yield one thousand or more retrievals in SULIRS and ORION, respectively. About 6% of queries for topical subjects generally produce one thousand or more retrievals (Table 7.1). When searches begin with access points that retrieve one thousand or more records or headings, they average more access points than searches that do not begin with large sets.

About 79% of exact matches are authorized subject headings (MARC tag 150). About 19% are *see from* tracings for topical subjects (MARC tag 450) that are connected to single authorized headings. The remaining exact matches (2%) are unauthorized headings connected with complex *see* references (MARC tag 260). Examples of the latter are "defense spending," "socio-economic status," "construction," and "climate."

7.4.2 Match Satisfaction

Most exact matches are topical subject headings that describe the topics users are seeking and thus will retrieve bibliographic records to satisfy the user's information needs. If users are not satisfied, they can enlist the following headings, references, and notes in LCSH-mr to help them refine their search:

- Related terms (i.e., broader, narrower, and related terms).
- Other authorized subject headings that begin with the same term(s) from the alphabetical arrangement of LCSH-mr.
- Subdivisions printed in LCSH.
- Instructions in complex *see* and *see also* references and scope notes.

Occasionally, initial access points match a subject heading connected with a narrower term that is a better expression of the user's interest than the former. For example, a SULIRS user who enters "astrology" but really wants signs of the zodiac could have benefited from a list of narrower terms under "Astrology" in which "Zodiac" would have been listed.

Sometimes a subdivision is printed in LCSH that formulates a subject heading that is a better expression of the user's interest than the initial access point. An example is a search in LS/2000 that starts with the access point "abortion" and includes the access point "catholic view" later in the search. The user could have benefited from the suggested subdivision "Religious aspects" and multiple subdivision "Baptists [Catholic Church, etc.]" in LCSH-mr.

When LCSH-mr provides no useful information for matched subject headings, users can call on the catalog to provide them with additional information to further their search:

- Free-floating form and topical subdivisions appended to the matched heading.
- Topical and form subdivisions from pattern lists appended to the matched heading.
- Geographic subdivisions appended to the matched heading

An example is a long ORION search consisting of sixteen access points. The initial access point is "weddings." Subsequent access points reveal that this user is interested in customs, ceremonies, and etiquette associated with Guatemalan weddings. The user could have benefited from lists of geographic subdivisions appended to the main heading "Weddings."

System reports of large numbers of retrievals will overwhelm many users and cause them to terminate their search prematurely. About one-third of exact matches probably produce too many bibliographic records. Examples of such queries are:

- Fields of study: agriculture, architecture, art, biology, economics, education, engineering, genetics, journalism, linguistics, neuropsychology, social sciences
- Topics: control theory, ideology, japanese art, leadership, mass media, mythology, surrealism
- Age, ethnic, and religious groups: aged, blacks, jews
- Form: maps, photographs, poems, sound recordings, statistics

The authorized subject headings in these categories produce hundreds and thousands of retrievals. They are connected with related terms, headings beginning with the same term(s), subdivisions printed in LCSH, and instructions in LCSH-mr notes and references. Dozens, even hundreds, of subdivided forms of these subject headings occur in library catalogs. Systems must present users with information that stimulates them to narrow or focus their topics of interest. Users would be best served by a summary of the terminology associated with the matched heading and available options for furthering the search, especially options for exploring subject terminology.

Occasionally, users enter exact matches of LCSH-mr headings or references that require them to make two or more actions to ensure the success of their search. Examples are the queries "stock options" and "construction." These queries match *see from* tracings in the authority records of three authorized subject headings. When users enter these terms, systems are going to give them a choice of authorized headings. To further the search, users must read the instructions accompanying suggested headings to choose one, browse nearby headings in alphabetical lists, or, if suggested headings do not adequately express their interest, enter new queries.

Exact matches of terms connected with complex references, *see from* tracings, or scope notes require users to perform several steps to ensure the success of the search. The instructions under complex *see* and *see also* references are themselves complex. For example, the complex *see* reference under "National defenses" is "*see* subdivision 'Defenses' under names of countries, etc." Users reading and following such instructions have to enter a query containing the name of the country that interests them and this particular subdivision, for example, "Israel—National defenses." Depending on the particular system they are using, searchers may have to be concerned about word order and punctuation in the subdivided headings they enter into the catalog.

Several users begin their search by entering exact matches of subject headings that are broader than their topics of interest. Browsing backward or forward in an alphabetical list of subject headings may lead to a display containing a relevant subject heading. Some users may even have to restate their queries to obtain useful results.

Examples below give user queries, subject headings likely to satisfy user needs, and user actions necessary to produce relevant headings.

Entered term	*Topic of interest in a single heading*	*User action*
advertising	Advertising copy	Browse forward in LCSH-mr
amusements	Amusement parks	Browse backward in LCSH-mr
art	Suprematism in art	Restate query
democracy	Human rights--Europe	Restate query
french	Business enterprises--France	Restate query
gods	Gods, African	Browse forward in LCSH-mr
home nursing	Alzheimer's disease--Patients--Home care	Restate query
plays	Chinese drama Chinese literature	Restate query
indians	Indians of . . .--Civil rights	Browse forward in assigned headings
shoes	Shoes--Fitting Shoes--Sizes	Browse subdivided headings printed in LCSH

Several initial access points do not describe users' topics of interest, for example, "democracy," "french," and "plays." The only way for users to continue such searches is to restate their queries. Some access points express one facet of a multifaceted query that is evident from the subsequent access points users enter in the ongoing search, for example, "amusements," "art," "gods," "home nursing," "indians," and "shoes." Other access points are broader than the topics users are seeking, for example, "advertising" and "shoes." With respect to the latter two types of access points, users need to browse a list of subject headings to find terms expressing the topics they have in mind but have not made explicit in their subject queries. Unfortunately, browsing alphabetical lists of assigned subject headings in operational online catalogs to find appropriate subject headings requires luck, patience, or perseverance, or a combination of the three. More efficient browsing techniques need to be devised.

7.4.3 Best-Match Categorization

Of the original-match categorization of initial access points, 415 (97.4%) have the same best-match categorization. The remaining eleven queries have a different best-match categorization that requires users to reformulate their queries using different terminology.

When users enter terms that are exact matches of LCSH-mr, success is not guaranteed. Several examples of queries have been discussed that require users to make several decisions and/or pursue several options before arriving at satisfactory terms. Pursuing searches in one direction may sometimes lead users away from their topics of interest or make it difficult to retrace their steps to move in a different direction. The benefit, however, of entering exact matches of LCSH-mr is that information from both LCSH-mr and the catalog is probably available for search refinement. The problem with exact matches is presenting the hundreds and thousands of retrievals they make to users in a way that encourages them to narrow or focus the search using catalog information connected to the matched heading such as related terms or subdivided forms of matched headings. Chapter 11 introduces a new approach to subject searching—the exact approach—to handle the exact matches of the catalog's controlled vocabulary that users enter into online catalogs.

7.5 "Almost Exact" Matches

About 2% of initial access points for topical subjects fail to match LCSH-mr because of punctuation, word order, or the inclusion of a common word in either the query or LCSH-mr. Examples of queries composed of the same words as headings from LCSH-mr but missing punctuation are:

- accounting examinations (double hyphen missing in between these two words)
- acting study and teaching (double hyphen missing in between first and second words)
- childrens art (apostrophe missing in first word)
- coffee houses (hyphen missing)
- fortune tellers (hyphen missing)
- log linear models (hyphen missing between first two words)
- rap music (parentheses missing around music)
- recreation management (double hyphen missing in between these two words)
- speeches, addresses, etc. american (comma missing in between last two words)

When users omit single or double hyphens, parentheses, or commas, retrieval would not necessarily be adversely affected in keyword-based systems such as SULIRS and ORION because their indexing programs can be programmed to substitute spaces for punctuation, then index single words. For example, single words in subject headings such as "Rap (Music)" and "Speeches, addresses, etc., American" would be separately indexed under "rap," "music," "speeches," "addresses," "etc," and "american," and punctuation would be deleted. Eventually, these words are brought together again during the postcoordination of keyword retrieval. Indexing programs can handle possessive forms and single hyphens by double or triple posting. Keywords indexed in the subject heading "Children's art" are "art," and "children," and "childrens." Normalized forms of this heading are "children art," "childrens art," and "children, art." Keywords in the hyphenated subject heading "Coffee-houses" are "coffee," "coffeehouses," and "houses." Normalized forms of this subject heading are "coffee houses" and "coffeehouses."

Retrieval may be affected in alphabetical-based systems such as LS/2000 when systems place users several entries before or after the desired heading because users have omitted punctuation. For example, a system could place the user entering "recreation management" in between the phrases "Recreation leadership" and "Recreation research" in an alphabetical index of assigned subject headings. The user would have to browse forward to subdivided headings under "Recreation" to find the desired heading "Recreation--Management" because of the double hyphens between the two words. To prevent this from happening, systems need to generate normalized forms of subject headings that are bereft of punctuation. Such terms would be indexed in the local system, but they would not be displayed to users. When users match normalized terms, systems retrieve the authorized heading and information linked to this heading from LCSH-mr, for example, related terms and LC class numbers, and from the catalog, for example, bibliographic records assigned this subdivided heading and subdivided forms of this heading.

Manual analyses yield only six examples of queries that match LCSH-mr regardless of word order and/or stopwords:

Query	*LCSH-mr*
culture personality	Personality and culture
country western music	Western and country music
photography wedding	Wedding photography
projection in	Projection
psychology of the adolescent	Adolescent psychology
the stock market	Stock market

Retrieval would not necessarily be affected in keyword-based systems such as SULIRS and ORION by users' reordering of words, or inclusion or exclusion of common words, because such systems normally index single words and exclude common words using a stopword list. Retrieval would be affected in alphabetical-based systems such as LS/2000 because systems could place users at a location in the alphabetical index far away from the desired heading. For example, users entering "the stock market" would be placed among *see* references beginning with the word "The" such as "The nutcracker (Ballet)" and "The Theatre (London, England)." Generating normalized forms of LCSH-mr headings, references, and assigned subject headings can help prevent such wasted effort.

In the unlikely event that more than one authorized heading is found, systems can present users with a choice, much like a system response that is required when users match *see from* tracings in two or more LCSH-mr records. Systems should not present users with normalized forms of headings to make a choice, because their meaning may be obscured by word normalization, or removal of punctuation or stopwords. Instead, systems should display authorized headings to users with an explanatory message asking them to choose headings that best describe their topics of interest.

When systems effect matches of user-entered terms using normalized forms of headings, success is not guaranteed because many normalized forms of headings will be linked to authorized headings that are high posted in the catalog. The benefit, however, of system-effected matches of LCSH-mr is that information from both

LCSH-mr and the catalog will be available for search refinement. Chapter 11 will present the exact approach to subject searching as a means of managing many retrievals and useful information connected with the controlled vocabulary terms that users enter directly into online catalogs or select with the assistance of online systems.

7.6 Spelling Categories

7.6.1 Spelling Variations

Only 3.2% of initial access points for topical subjects fail to match LCSH-mr because of spelling variations. Individual percentages for the five spelling subcategories that make up this category are: (1) correct spelling variant (0.0%), (2) one word/two word variation (0.3%), (3) substitution/transposition (0.2%), (4) addition/omission (1.8%), and (5) incorrect spelling (0.9%). The most common spelling variation is addition/omission. Of the seventeen terms with addition/omission errors, ten are spelled correctly by users who enter access points later in the search. Examples are "5graduate schools," "peducation," "healthy food," and "consumerds." Only one misspelling, that is, "raquetball," is repeated and never corrected.

Walker and Jones (1987, 76–77, 151) described a soundex algorithm they used to correct misspellings. Five of the seventeen terms with addition/omission errors in this study could have been corrected using their algorithm. Examples are "psychanalysis," "keyenesian economics," and "raquetball." The combination of corrections made by users themselves and corrections from the soundex algorithm could account for corrections to fifteen of the seventeen misspellings. Two misspellings remain, namely "3therapy" and "eduation."

Only two substitution/transposition errors are encountered, that is, "midieval art" and "lactose intolerence." The first user reenters this misspelling three times in subsequent access points. The second user only enters this single access point in the search. The soundex algorithm of Walker and Jones could have corrected both misspellings.

Spelling errors account for almost 1% of initial access points for topical subjects. Examples are "crcreative," "phptgraphy," "integer prograramming," and "transvesticism." Three of the eight spelling errors are corrected by users themselves. The soundex algorithm could have corrected one more. Examples of two of the four spelling errors remaining uncorrected are "psibocylin" (should be "Psilocybin") and "strategic defense iniative" (should be "initiative").

Whether users are able to find the appropriate heading for expressing their topics of interest sometimes depends on the occurrence of the misspelling in the query and the system's response to user-entered terms. For example, the omission error in the query "strategic defense iniative" occurs in the last word of this three-word query. It would not prevent a user from finding the correctly spelled heading in a system that responds to user-entered terms with an alphabetical index of subject headings, because the first two words of this query are sufficient for placing users close to the desired term in the alphabetical index.

When some misspelled terms are corrected, they lead to many retrievals. For example, the correctly spelled queries for "political science," "psychoanalysis," and "education" match authorized headings assigned to thousands of bibliographic records. Subject information from both LCSH-mr and the catalog is available for search refinement.

Of the thirty misspellings, eight could be corrected using a soundex algorithm similar to the one used by Walker and Jones in Okapi, the experimental subject retrieval system developed by the British Library (Walker & Jones, 1987). The disadvantage to spelling correction algorithms is creating and maintaining a sizable dictionary that contains the majority of words that users misspell. Using the words in authorized headings in LCSH-mr may be adequate as a dictionary for correcting queries that are topical subjects.

Over half of the thirty spelling errors are corrected by users in subsequent access points. Walker and Jones recommend programming systems to prompt users to examine and correct words that fail to produce retrievals. Without automatic spelling correction, searches for seemingly simple queries such as "midieval art" and "lyprosy" are bound to fail even though library catalogs contain plenty of material under correctly spelled headings for these topics, that is, "Art, Medieval" and "Leprosy."

7.6.2 One-Word/Two-Word Variations

The three one-word/two-word variations are "stripmining," "politicalscience," and "latch key children;" authorized headings for these queries are "Strip mining," "Political science," and "Latchkey children." Users entering the latter two queries are successful entering the authorized headings in subsequent access points.

Hyphens in authorized headings and *see from* tracings indicate one-word and two-word variations for terms. Systems can automatically generate one-word and two-word variations for such terms and enter them into authority records and searchable indexes as normalized forms of headings. For example, "log linear models" and "loglinear models" are generated from "Log-linear models." Unfortunately, the one-word/two-word variations entered by the users in this study do not come from hyphenated LCSH-mr.

Transaction logs are a likely source of one-word/two-word variations. Systems can be programmed to keep a log of the subject terms that fail to match exact or normalized headings. Library and systems staff can periodically review logs to find one-word/two-word variations that are responsible for the match failure and add them to the system's authority records. Walker and Jones (1987, 68–69) examined

Okapi's transaction log for frequently entered one-word/two-word variations to compile the system's go/see list. Examples of terms taken from Okapi logs are "infra red" and "infrared," "ultra violet" and "ultraviolet," "micro computers" and "microcomputers." Okapi treats one-word/two-word variations as equivalent single words. In Okapi's go/see list, any member of a given equivalence class points to the same set of postings, and thus a search for "microcomputers" retrieves the same items as a search for "micro computers" and vice versa.

Queries placed in this category include words not separated by spaces, for example, "politicalscience." Jones (1986, 6) described an algorithm to automatically find and correct such queries, but he rejected it for use in Okapi because it would have been computationally heavy. Instead, he suggested that systems display such queries to users and invite them to make corrections on their own.

7.7 Plural and Singular Forms

Individual percentages for the two plural/singular variations that make up this category are: (1) query-singular/LCSH-plural variation (2.8%), and (2) query-plural/LCSH-singular variation (0.8%). Examples of these variations are:

Query	*LCSH-mr*
australopithecine	australopithecines
backaches	backache
birth control pill	birth control pills
blue jays	blue jay
communications	communication
equal rights amendment	equal rights amendments
index	indexes
light bulb	light bulbs
massages	massage
national defense	national defenses
tower	towers
sport	sports
viscous flows	viscous flow

Several different and potentially confusing situations arise with queries in plural/singular variation subcategories in terms of their relationship with controlled vocabulary terms. First, consider the query-singular/LCSH-plural situation. Queries can be partial matches of *one* longer authorized heading or *see from* tracing in LCSH-mr that is the plural form of the singular form entered, for example, "birth control pill" matches "Birth control pills" and "equal rights amendment" matches "equal rights amendments." Simultaneously, queries can also be partial matches of one or more longer authorized headings or *see from* tracings that are not the plural form of the singular form entered. For example, "tower" matches "Tower cranes," "Tower clocks," and "Tower of Babel," and "sport" matches "Sport clothes," "Sport clothes industry," and "Sport fishing." The plural forms of these queries are also authorized headings, that is, "Towers" and "Sports."

With respect to the queries examined in this study, most users entering queries in singular form would probably be more satisfied with the plural form of the matched heading even though the catalog contains several other subject headings beginning with the singular form of the word or phrase. For example, the user entering "castle" is interested in French castles and would find the appropriate assigned subject heading "Castles--France" much quicker in an alphabetical list beginning with the plural form "Castles" than with the singular form, for example, "Castle (Chess)." The exception is a user interested in raising frogs who begins a search with the word "frog." This user would find the *see* reference "Frog raising, *see* Frog culture" quicker if the system starts an alphabetical list of subject headings beginning with the singular form than if it starts under the plural/singular variant "Frogs."

Systems cannot read users' minds to determine whether the plural form of the singular term entered into the catalog would serve users better than the latter. When users enter singular forms of authorized headings, the alphabetical approach would place them in the index before the plural form of many English-language words and phrases would be listed. Users could browse forward in the alphabetical index until they reached the desired term, whether it be in the form of a longer phrase or subdivided heading or the plural form of the entered word or phrase. The alphabetical approach may not be as helpful to users who enter singular forms of words and phrases ending in "-y" because the plural form of such words usually ends in "-ies," which files before the singular form. For example, the subject heading "Arteries" in an alphabetical index would file well before the singular form "artery," under which there is no useful subject heading leading the user back to the authorized heading. Finding the correct form of Latin names used in LCSH may be a problem, especially for Latin words in which the stem occurs in several other headings besides the singular and plural forms of the desired word or phrase.

When the query is plural and the LCSH authorized heading is singular, on the other hand, two different and potentially confusing situations arise. The first is when the user enters a word or phrase in plural form that is used in controlled vocabulary terms beginning with the plural form of the word or phrase. The singular form of the entered term is also used. An example is the query "communications" that occurs in several phrases beginning with this word, for example, "Communications industry" and "Communications software." The singular form of the query is an authorized heading, that is, "Communication." It is also the initial word in several authorized subject headings, for example, "Communication, International," "Communication models," and "Communication in the family." Such queries call for the alphabetical approach to enable users to browse backward and forward to find an appropriate subject heading.

The second potentially confusing situation arises when the user enters a word or phrase in plural form that does not begin a longer controlled vocabulary term starting with the plural form of the word or phrase, but the singular form of the entered term is used as a subject heading. An example is the query "costumes." This term does not occur as a subject heading or *see from* tracing in LCSH. Furthermore, this term is not used in a longer subject heading or reference. The singular form of this term is used on its own, that is, "Costume," and as the initial word in several subject headings, for example, "Costume design," "Costume, Islamic," and "Costume jewelry."

Online systems that respond to such queries with the alphabetical approach need to begin the alphabetical list by including a few subject headings before the best match of the user-entered term. If headings beginning alphabetical lists are singular forms of the entered term, the user may be encouraged to browse backward to find an appropriate heading beginning with the singular form of the entered term. If the alphabetical index includes subdivided headings, perseverance becomes an issue because users may tire of displaying subdivided forms of headings before they reach an appropriate subject heading, in particular, the singular form of the term they entered.

There is an alternative to the alphabetical approach in this second query-plural/LCSH-singular situation. When systems detect the trailing "-s," "-es," or "-ies" on user-entered terms, they delete it, then look for a heading beginning with the singular form of the word or phrase in the alphabetical index of subject headings. Finding the singular form, systems then respond with the alphabetical approach to subject searching with an explanatory message telling users why the list begins with the singular form.

We did not encounter queries for topical subjects composed of more than two words that required deletion or addition of plural suffixes in words beginning or embedded in queries to effect a match of controlled vocabulary terms. However, we can imagine users entering queries such as "communications in the family" or "societies and laws." These queries contain plural forms of the singular nouns in the subject headings "Communication in the family" and "Society and law." System-supplied truncation, suffix removal, or keyword searching of subject-rich fields in bibliographic records may be necessary to produce retrievals for such queries.

Users entering queries that are plural or singular variants of controlled vocabulary terms are going to find relevant items under the variant. A few queries such as "automobile" and "sport" lead to hundreds and thousands of retrievals. Once users select authorized subject headings from alphabetical indexes, they have the same options for search refinement as they have when making exact matches of LCSH-mr, for example, related terms, scope notes, and subdivided forms of selected headings. When users select subject headings from the alphabetical index, systems respond with the exact approach to subject searching. The exact approach, to be introduced in Chapter 11, is a method of managing large numbers of retrievals and displays of references and notes connected with controlled vocabulary terms.

An example of how exasperating it must be when the authorized form of heading is a plural/singular variant of the user-entered term is demonstrated in a SULIRS user's search for "australopithecines." The user enters this one access point in a subject search, retrieves nine bibliographic records, and, presumably, leaves the terminal to check nearby bookshelves. About eight minutes later, a SULIRS user approaches the same terminal and enters the following ten access points:

Access point	*Number of retrievals*
australopithecine	0
australopithicine	0
australopithicent	0
australopithicene	0
hominid	8
australopithicus	0
australopithecine	0
australopithicine	0
australopithecine	0
australopithecus	1

Not once does the user enter the plural form "australopithecines," the exact LCSH-mr heading for this topic, which retrieves nine bibliographic records in SULIRS. Is this the same user who performed a successful search for this topic eight minutes earlier, but did not remember that the plural form was originally entered? The second search, however, shows much persistence and an attitude that says, "I just know you're in there." Many online catalog users think their entered terms retrieve concepts and ideas (Walker & Jones 1987, 62; Markey & Demeyer 1986, 249–250). This user, however, recognizes that word variants produce different results in online systems, but just fails to enter the plural form that is the one producing the desired bibliographic records.

Online bibliographic systems should not fail for this particular user or for others who are not as knowledgeable about online retrieval. Handling the singular/plural variants of LCSH-mr that users enter into online catalogs is not a straightforward task. It takes into account the extent to which queries match LCSH-mr and assigned subject headings and, occasionally, requires automatic detection and deletion of suffixes to effect matches of the catalog's controlled vocabulary.

7.8

Partial Matches of LCSH-mr Minus Qualifiers

Into only one partial match subcategory are queries for topical subjects placed that are likely to succeed in matching single-subject headings appropriate for expressing the users' topics of interest. This is the subcategory for partial matches of LCSH-mr headings or references minus qualifiers, which accounts for 3.8% of user queries for topical subjects. Examples are:

Query	*LCSH-mr*
aids	Aids (Disease); Aids (Horsemanship), *see* Riding aids

blues	Blues (Music); Blues (Songs, etc.), *see* Blues (Music)
consumption	Consumption (Disease), *see* Tuberculosis; Consumption (Economics)
expert systems	Expert systems (Computer science)
goals	Goals (Sports), *see* Targets (Sports)
harmony	Harmony; Harmony (Aesthetics); Harmony (Cosmology), *see* Harmony of the spheres; Harmony (Philosophy)
precis	PRECIS (Indexing system)
stress	STRESS (Computer program language); Stress (Linguistics), *see* Accents and accentuation; Stress (Physiology); Stress (Psychology)
waterbeds	Waterbeds (Furniture)

Sometimes, only one qualified LCSH-mr or *see* reference matches the user-entered term. At other times, one unqualified and several qualified terms match the user-entered term. For example, the query "harmony" matches one unqualified subject heading, two qualified subject headings, and one qualified *see* reference.

Only one query in this category produces a single reference that does not describe the user's topic of interest. The user entering "goals" is interested in goals for personnel management. The matched, qualified heading is "Goals (Sports)." The only way for this user to find material on his topic of interest is to restate the query. In the actual search, the user follows the initial access point with the query "personnel management." Not only does this term more adequately describe the user's interests, it is an exact match of an LCSH-mr and is connected to several narrower terms that can be explored to find additional material.

"Aids" is the term most frequently entered by SULIRS, ORION, and LS/2000 users that is not an exact match of LCSH-mr. The appropriate LCSH-mr for this topic is the qualified heading "Aids (Disease)." Keyword-based systems like ORION retrieve hundreds of assigned subject headings containing the subdivision "Audio-visual aids." Keyword-based systems like SULIRS retrieve thousands of bibliographic records bearing this word in subdivisions and titles.

Handling queries such as "aids" that match all but the qualifiers in main headings is straightforward using normalized forms of headings. Systems should generate normalized forms of qualified headings and references in which the qualifier is omitted and add these references to subject authority records. When users enter queries without qualifiers, they will match one or more of the normalized forms of qualified headings that are connected to authorized headings with qualifiers. Systems should then display to users the authorized headings in these subject authority records with a message prompting them to choose the qualified heading that best describes their topics of interest. Such a choice is comparable to the choice users have to make when they match *see* references that suggest two or more authorized headings. The user's selection of an authorized heading invokes the exact approach to subject searching. Chapter 11 will introduce the exact approach to subject searching as a means of managing the retrievals and other useful information connected with the controlled vocabulary terms that users enter directly into online catalogs or select with the assistance of the online system.

7.9 Synthesis and Summary

Of the initial access points in subject searches, nearly two-thirds consist wholly of elements for topical subjects. Initial access points producing one thousand or more retrievals consist of only one word; they also initiate searches that average between five and six access points per search.

Queries for topical subjects are among the most successful in terms of matching single controlled vocabulary terms on their own or with the assistance of computer programs for normalization, spelling correction, and other matching techniques. Initial access points that are exact matches of LCSH-mr headings or references account for 45.7% of queries for topical subjects. They also contain fewer words (1.4) than access points generally (1.8). Exact matches retrieve many more bibliographic records and assigned subject headings than topical subjects generally.

The problem with exact matches is presenting the hundreds and thousands of retrievals they make to users in a way that encourages users to narrow or focus the search using subdivided forms of the matched term or using links to other controlled vocabulary terms provided by LCSH-mr. Chapter 11 will define a new approach to subject searching—the exact approach—to manage the mountain of information connected to the controlled vocabulary terms that users successfully match through the subject terms they enter into online systems.

User queries undergoing normalization procedures will sometimes match more than one normalized form of heading. Systems must then give users a choice among authorized headings accompanied by a message prompting users to choose the heading that best describes their topics of interest. The user's selection of a single controlled vocabulary term would invoke the exact approach to subject searching.

Only 3.2% of initial access points for topical subjects fail to exactly match an LCSH-mr because of spelling variations. Online systems can enlist the aid of users to detect and correct spelling errors. For example, systems can detect words in user queries that fail to match a dictionary of words from authorized headings in LCSH-mr and prompt users to select from a list of alphabetically similar dictionary entries or a list of words that sound like the potentially misspelled word.

System programming can help prevent user queries from failing to match controlled vocabulary terms for which one-word/two-word variations are possible by double and triple posting hyphenated controlled vocabulary terms. Library staff can also study transaction logs to find phrases that users sometimes enter as single words and vice versa and manually enter variations into subject authority records as local *see from* tracings. Queries placed in the one-word/two-word subcategory include words not separated by spaces. Systems with spelling correction assistance will handle these concatenated queries as if they were spelling errors because they fail to match dictionary entries. Such queries may be displayed to users, who will be invited to make corrections on their own.

Plural/singular variations account for 3.6% of user queries for topical subjects. Most user queries in this subcategory match the initial word(s) of a longer subject heading in the catalog's alphabetical index. Simultaneously, the plural or singular form of the user query is used as a controlled vocabulary term. The system response to such queries is similar to its response to potentially misspelled words because users are presented with an alphabetical dictionary of terms indexed in the online catalog. The difference is that the dictionary used for singular/plural variations is the alphabetical index of controlled vocabulary terms. Systems should prompt users to browse the index to find controlled vocabulary terms that best describe their topics of interest. In order to encourage users to browse backward and forward, systems should also begin the alphabetical list by presenting a few subject headings filed before the best match of the user-entered term.

Problems arise with plural forms of user-entered terms that do not match a longer controlled vocabulary term. The singular form of the entered term is used as a subject heading and may be filed in the index considerably before the system's best match of the plural form in the alphabetical index. Users might not have enough perseverance to browse backward until they find the singular form. We suggest an alternative to the alphabetical approach in which systems are programmed to detect plural suffixes ending user queries, delete them, then, on finding a heading beginning with the singular form of the entered word or phrase, respond with the alphabetical approach.

This chapter is limited to queries for topical subjects that are successful in matching single controlled vocabulary terms on their own or with the assistance of computer programs for normalization, spelling correction, and other matching techniques. Most of the remaining 41.8% of queries fall into partial match subcategories. Chapter 9 takes an in-depth look at these queries for topical subjects to determine how systems can produce retrievals for them based on the extent to which they match the catalog's controlled vocabulary.

This chapter singles out initial access points for topical subjects that are successful in terms of matching single controlled vocabulary terms on their own or with the assistance of computer programs for normalization, spelling correction, and other matching techniques. Such access points account for 58.2% of initial access points for topical subjects entered into online systems.

Exact matches are 45.7% of user queries for topical subjects. Matching techniques are described that systems can perform unbeknownst to users to effect matches of their terms with controlled vocabulary terms indexed in the system. The chapter also describes matching techniques in which systems enlist the aid of users to help them effect a match of controlled vocabulary terms. Automatic and user-assisted matching techniques combine to effect an additional 12.5% of matches of controlled vocabulary terms.

The controlled vocabulary terms that users enter or select in their interaction with the system are likely to be high posted. For example, the words in these controlled vocabulary terms retrieve over one thousand bibliographic records in

SULIRS' keyword-in-record searches and nearly seven hundred assigned subject headings in ORION's keyword-in-subdivided-heading searches. To manage large numbers of retrievals, we recommend a new approach to subject searching—the exact approach—which is described in Chapter 11.

References

Carlyle, Allyson. (1989). Matching LCSH and user vocabulary in the library catalog. *Cataloging & Classification Quarterly, 10,* 1/2, 37–63.

Jones, Richard. (1986). Improving Okapi: Transaction log analysis of failed searches in an online catalogue. *Vine,* No. 62 (May), 3–13.

Markey, Karen, & Demeyer, Anh. (1986). *Dewey Decimal Classification Online Project: Evaluation of a library schedule and index integrated into the subject searching capabilities of an online catalog.* Dublin, OH: OCLC. OCLC Research Report OCLC/OPR/86/1.

Walker, Stephen, & Jones, Richard M. (1987). *Improving subject retrieval in online catalogues: 1. Stemming, automatic spelling correction and cross-reference tables.* London: British Library. British Library Research Paper No. 24.

8

Other Queries Likely to Succeed

8.1

Introduction

This chapter takes a look at two categories of legitimate subject queries—geographic names and corporate names—for which users are successful in terms of matching the catalog's controlled vocabulary on their own or with the assistance of computer programs for normalization, spelling correction, and other matching techniques. This chapter also suggests subject searching capabilities that users need to find relevant information on the geographic names or corporate names they seek in library catalogs. Queries consisting wholly of elements for geographic names or for corporate names are not common, accounting for only 4.7% or 2.6% of queries, respectively (see Figure 6.4). All but one of the queries for names in transaction logs express a single place or entity, for example, "europe," "russia," "cia," and "los angeles dodgers." This one query is "nicaragua vietnam."

LCNAF, rather than LCSH-mr, is the primary source of authorized headings for names. Thus, single controlled vocabulary terms that are satisfactory expressions of user queries for geographic names or corporate names are more likely to match the authorized headings in name authority records than such headings in subject authority records. This is particularly apparent with regard to corporate names because only a few corporate name records in LCSH-mr are made for headings that serve to complete the reference structure or serve as pattern headings. LCSH-mr contains many geographic name records for nonjurisdictional units and for jurisdictional units that are necessary to complete the reference structure as well as a few records for pattern headings.

Users who enter queries consisting wholly of elements for geographic names are quite successful in matching the catalog's controlled vocabulary; however, matching controlled vocabulary terms are posted in hundreds, and sometimes thousands, of bibliographic records. The exact approach is again recommended for managing large numbers of retrievals and other information connected with matched terms (Chapter 11).

Many user-entered queries for corporate names begin with terms used in LCSH-mr, but because LCNAF is the authoritative source for such names, LCSH-mr terms are not satisfactory for describing users' topics of interest. Our discussion of queries for corporate and geographic names focuses on the best-match categorization because it includes the primary sources of access points for these names, that is, LCNAF references and assigned subject headings in bibliographic records.

8.2 Queries for Geographic Names

8.2.1 Subject Searches and Initial Access Points

Table 8.1 is a fact sheet with details about the total of seventy-one searches initiated by access points consisting wholly of elements for geographic names.

In SULIRS and ORION, initial access points for geographic names are entered in searches averaging about one access point less than searches initiated by access points for topical subjects (see Table 7.1). Searches initiated by geographic name queries in LS/2000, however, are longer than searches initiated by topical subject

Table 8.1
Fact Sheet for Initial Access Points Consisting of Geographic Name Elements

Summary data	Total	SULIRS	ORION	LS/2000
Searches				
No. of searches	71.0	13.0	22.0	36.0
No. of access points	234.0	29.0	56.0	149.0
Avg. no. of access points per search	3.3	2.2	2.5	4.1
Maximum no. of access points in a search	14.0	5.0	7.0	14.0
Initial access points				
Avg. no. of words per access point	1.3	1.3	1.4	1.2
Maximum no. of words in an access point	3.0	3.0	3.0	2.0
Retrievals				
Avg. no. of retrievals per access point	N/A	299.4[a]	1954.8[b]	N/A
Percentage of access points with zero retrievals	N/A	30.8	18.2	N/A
Percentage of access points with retrievals > 999	N/A	15.4	31.8	N/A
High-posted searches				
Avg. no. of words in access point with retrievals > 999	N/A	1.0	1.0	N/A
Avg. no. of access points in searches where initial access point has retrievals > 999	N/A	1.5	2.4	N/A

[a]Number of bibliographic records retrieved.
[b]Number of assigned subject headings retrieved.

access points in this system. The longest search beginning with a geographic name also comes from LS/2000 and contains fourteen subject access points: it begins with an exact match of the geographic name "Somalia" and contains several other names of countries in Africa, for example, "sudan," "mauritania," "tanzania," "south africa," and persons or topics associated with these countries, for example, "aids," "apartheid," "djibouti," and "revolution." The user may be surveying the catalog on several topics since the search does not have an obvious focus.

The average number of words (1.3) in queries for geographic names is lower than the average for topical subjects (1.8). The longest geographic names are two names composed of three words, that is, "australia barrier reef" and "mt.st.helens." Three words make up the latter if punctuation is replaced with spaces.

User queries for geographic names are high posted. About fifteen percent of SULIRS queries for geographic names produce one thousand or more retrievals. ORION queries for geographic names retrieve almost two thousand assigned headings per initial access point.

8.2.2 Original-Match Categorization

The original-match categorization of queries for geographic names is shown in Figure 8.1. Original matches take into account only the closeness of queries to LCSH-mr headings and references.

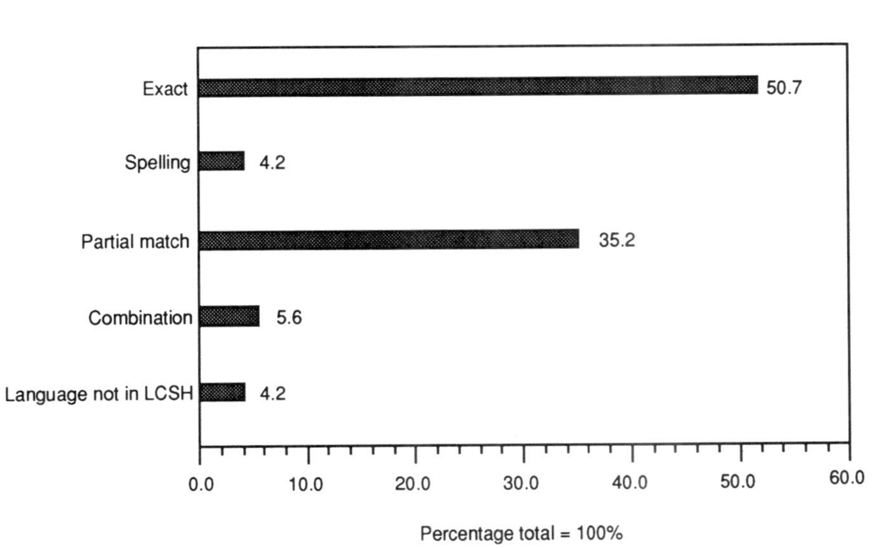

Figure 8.1
Original-match categorization of queries for geographic names.

Over half of the geographic names users enter are exact matches of LCSH-mr. All but five of these exact matches are composed of one word. Examples of exact matches are "africa," "europe," "kentucky," "united states," "appalachian region," and "egypt."

Correction of a few spelling errors is necessary to effect exact matches of geographic names in LCSH-mr records. The spelling correction algorithm used in Okapi (Walker & Jones 1987, 76–77, 151) would correct some errors such as "artic," "austrailalia," "austrailia," "caribbean," and "chernoyble." In searches for all but one of these misspellings, users are successful making corrections on their own.

Partial matches account for 35.2% of user queries for geographic names. Individual percentages for the four partial-match subcategories that make up this category are: (1) minus qualifiers (9.9%), (2) first two words (1.4%), (3) first word and three-letter stem of the second word (1.4%), and (4) first word (22.5%).

8.2.3 Match Satisfaction

Many retrievals characterize subject searches in which users enter an exact match of a geographic name in LCSH-mr. When searches in LS/2000 produce many retrievals, the system prompts users to reduce them by entering another subject term or other criteria. After entering exact matches of geographic names, three-fourths of LS/2000 users refine their searches by combining these results with searches for other subjects. Examples of such refinements are:

Initial access point	*Refinements*
africa	economy
europe	1871-1918
germany	history
guam	climate
japan	high technology
russia	cossack
syria	politics
united states	territorial expansion

SULIRS also allows users to refine the results of previous searches, but the prompt accompanying high-posted search results does not tell users how to refine their search by entering another search term. SULIRS users have to explicitly enter three types of data in the following order to refine previous results: (1) Boolean "and" operator, (2) search type such as subject-heading word (lc) or keyword-in-record (sb), and (3) query. Of the five searchers who enter an exact match of a geographic name, only one continues the search. This searcher, whose initial access point is "israel," does not refine previous results but reformulates the search by entering the access points "israel's wars" and "anwar el sadat."

When users enter terms into ORION, the system responds with the number of headings retrieved. To refine results, users have to reformulate their search. Five of the ten ORION users who enter exact matches of geographic names reformulate their search; all five reenter the initial access point and a topical subject. Although the Boolean "and" operator is implicit, all five users include this operator in their access points.

Initial access point	*Subsequent access points*
england	england and travel
israel	israel and history
israel	israel and mapai
spain	spain and military
wyoming	wyoming and fishing

When users refine their searches for geographic names, the success of the new search depends on several factors including their ability to enter terminology used in controlled vocabulary terms and the subject searching approaches used by the system to produce retrievals. For example, the second and last queries in the above list contain the same substantive words as the assigned subject headings, that is, "Fishing--Wyoming" and "Israel--History," but these queries would fail to produce retrievals in some systems because of improper word order, inclusion of stopwords, and/or exclusion of correct punctuation.

To save users from guessing at the terminology of headings during the refinement process, systems need browsing capabilities that display subdivided forms of assigned subject headings. The exact approach to subject searching that is the system's response to exact matches of controlled vocabulary terms gives users the opportunity to browse in this manner, prompting them to select categories of subdivided forms when too many such forms are retrieved to be displayed on a single screen. The exact approach is discussed in greater detail in Chapter 11.

The inclusion of normalized forms of headings in the index that supports the exact approach would enable users to make exact matches of the substantive words in their queries with assigned subject headings containing the same words but not necessarily in the same order or bearing the same punctuation as the original assigned subject heading. For example, normalizing the queries "israel and history" and "wyoming and fishing" would be necessary to match normalized forms of the headings "Israel--History" and "Fishing--Wyoming" to effect matches for the exact approach.

A browsing capability will be especially helpful to users who enter queries for geographic names because their interests often lie in time periods that are expressed in the period subdivisions under place names. Period subdivisions provide an outline to the history and, occasionally, to the politics, social conditions, and customs of a particular country. Unfortunately, it is difficult for online systems to maintain the chronological order of period subdivisions because the initial element in such subdivisions is text instead of dates and date ranges. Twenty years ago, Lois Chan (1972) suggested modifications to period subdivisions to help automated systems file them in the proper chronological order. The library community's support for Chan's suggested modifications is expressed in the recent recommendations of an ALA subcommittee on the display of subdivisions (American Library Association, 1992) and of the LC Subject Subdivisions Conference (Library of Congress, 1992).

Two queries from the above list, that is, "england and travel" and "spain and military," match words embedded in subdivided subject headings, that is, "England--Description and travel" and "Spain--History, Military," respectively. Users need a keyword search of single subdivided headings to retrieve these subdivided headings. Chapter 12 gives additional details on a keyword-in-subdivided-heading search approach to assist such users.

Examples of queries matching all but the qualifiers in LCSH-mr headings and references are:

User query	*Qualified LCSH-mr*
london	London (England)
lyon	Lyon (France)
venice	Venice (Italy)
usa	Usa (Hindu mythology)

Except for the last example, matching LCSH-mr may be satisfactory for expressing users' topics of interest. However, the users entering "london" and "venice" may be interested in "London (Ont.)" and "Venice (Calif.)," respectively. When users enter queries matching all but the qualifiers in controlled vocabulary terms, systems cannot limit the choice of headings they present to users to LCSH-mr headings and references. They must include subject headings assigned to bibliographic records and LCNAF references. With regard to the last example above, users would have benefited from a *see* reference under "USA" guiding them to the authorized heading "United States."

About one-fourth of user-entered geographic names match the initial word in an LCSH-mr. In the examples that follow, the matching LCSH-mr is listed alongside the geographic names given in LCNAF records that users are probably seeking.

User-entered name	*LCSH-mr*	*LCNAF heading*
amsterdam	Amsterdam (Netherlands) Kinkerbuurt	Amsterdam (Netherlands)
bern	Bern (Switzerland) in art	Bern (Switzerland)
bismarck	Bismarck Archipelago(Papua New Guinea)	Bismarck (N.D.)
hopkins county	Hopkins family	Hopkins County (Ky.)
lake arrowhead	[Complex *see* reference for] Lake	Lake Arrowhead (Calif.)
lexington	Lexington, Battle of, 1775	Lexington (Ky.)
monaco	Monaco Grand Prix Race	Monaco

LCNAF headings are probably more satisfactory for expressing users' topics of interest than the matching LCSH-mr headings and references. When the system response to a user query is the alphabetical approach, the alphabetical index should consist of assigned subject headings from bibliographic records and references from LCSH-mr and LCNAF records.

Remaining queries in partial match categories match the initial words in authorized headings and references in LCSH-mr and LCNAF but both queries and matching terms end in different words. In every case, the matching heading or reference does not satisfactorily describe users' queries. Examples are:

User-entered geographic names	*Matching heading*
australia barrier reef	Australia; Australia Day
modern china	Modern arts; Modern Chinese language, 1919–
soviet russia	Soviet prose literature; Soviet satire

Browsing an alphabetical index of subject headings assigned to bibliographic records and LCSH-mr and LCNAF references would help the user who enters the last query find the authorized heading "Soviet Union" because the desired heading is in close alphabetical proximity to the entered term. Keyword search approaches are likely to produce bibliographic records for these three queries because they retrieve records based on the presence of all words in user queries. For example, a keyword search of subject heading fields for the first query yields records bearing both single headings "Great Barrier Reef (Qld.)" and "Coral reefs and islands--Australia." When online systems perform such keyword searches, they should feature relevance feedback routines to inform users of subject headings common to the majority of retrieved records so that users can further their searches using these headings.

8.2.4 Best-Match Categorization

About half of the geographic names that users enter are exact matches of LCSH-mr. Often exact matches retrieve many bibliographic records, and, as a result of large sets or system prompts, users refine their initial search. The exact approach is recommended as the system response for such exact matches. Not only does this approach manage large retrievals, but it helps users refine their searches by presenting them with terminology used in the catalog in the form of subdivided headings instead of having them guess the terminology used in controlled vocabulary terms and duplicate the word order and punctuation used in such terms.

Spelling is especially important with regard to geographic names because many names of places in the United States and in foreign countries are based on languages other than English. The dictionary for a spelling checker could be composed of words in the main heading (subfield $a) of geographic name records from LCNAF (USMARC tag 151). The problem with such a dictionary is that systems are going to include words from geographic names in lists of suggested corrections to users who are correcting misspelled words for topical subjects because systems cannot determine without the help of a human intermediary whether the misspelled word is an element for a topical subject or a geographic name. Systems could prompt users to make such a decision, but it is doubtful whether public catalog users could distinguish between the two. An alternative approach is for systems to invite users to correct spelling before they supply users with lists of suggested corrections.

LCSH-mr contains subject authority records for many nonjurisdictional units and for jurisdictional units that are necessary to complete the reference structure and a few records for pattern headings. LCNAF is the primary source of authority records for verifying the geographic names in subject headings and providing references from unused to authorized terms. Catalogers can also formulate subject headings for geographic names by following the rules in Chapter 23 of AACR2. LCNAF and LCSH-mr should contribute references to the alphabetical index that users browse to find suitable headings, but most of the index would be given to assigned subject headings from bibliographic records. Browsing alphabetical indexes will help users who enter all but the qualifiers in geographic names and match the initial word(s) in longer geographic names to find an appropriate geographic name or reference for the place that interests them.

8.3 Queries for Corporate Names

8.3.1 Subject Searches and Initial Access Points

Table 8.2 presents details about thirty-nine searches initiated by an access point consisting wholly of elements for corporate names.

Table 8.2
Fact Sheet for Initial Access Points Consisting of Corporate Name Elements

Summary data	Total	SULIRS	ORION	LS/2000
Searches				
No. of searches	39.0	19.0	9.0	11.0
No. of access points	121.0	3.7	2.2	30.0
Avg. no. of access points per search	3.1	12.0	5.0	2.7
Maximum no. of access points in a search	12.0			6.0
Initial access points				
Avg. no. of words per access point	2.2	2.2	2.4	1.9
Maximum no. of words in an access point	6.0	4.0	5.0	6.0
Retrievals				
Avg. no. of retrievals per access point	N/A	170.1[a]	0.0[b]	N/A
Percentage of access points with zero retrievals	N/A	36.8	100.0	N/A
Percentage of access points with retrievals > 999	N/A	5.3	0.0	N/A

[a]Number of bibliographic records retrieved. This is an estimate based on substituting 3000 retrievals for the 99,999 retrievals that is written to logs when number of retrievals is about 1000.
[b]Number of assigned subject headings retrieved.

The average number of words per corporate name is about two, and the longest such name is six words, "united states food and drug administration." Over a third of corporate names entered into SULIRS fail to retrieve bibliographic records. The one SULIRS query that retrieves one thousand or more bibliographic records is "congress." All nine queries entered into ORION fail to retrieve records because they should have been entered using the "name" index for personal, corporate, and conference name searches.

8.3.2 Original-Match Categorization

The procedures we followed to determine how closely the subjects that users enter match the controlled vocabulary are the same ones we followed for matching geographic names, that is, we examined LCSH-mr first, followed by LCNAF and the assigned subject headings in OCLC and several other online catalogs. Nearly three-fourths of user-entered corporate names are partial matches of an LCSH-mr. The remaining quarter are exact or partial matches of corporate names that are assigned headings.

Most partial matches of LCSH-mr are unsatisfactory for retrieving relevant bibliographic records on the topics users seek. The queries "united states food and drug administration" and "civil rights act 1964" are partial matches of the LCSH-mr "United States" and "Civil rights," respectively. However, searchers would have to do a considerable amount of browsing in the alphabetical index beginning with these terms to find relevant subject headings for expressing their topics of interest. Several partial matches are family names; examples are "Samuel family," "Skidmore family," and "Mackintosh family" for the queries "samuel french," "skidmore, owings and merrill," and "mackintosh," respectively. Several partial matches are geographic names; examples are "Philadelphia (Pa.)" and "Kent (Conn.)" for the queries "philadelphia museum" and "kent state," respectively. Several user-entered corporate names have geographic name elements themselves, for example, "united states food and drug administration," "philadelphia museum," "kent state," "los angeles dodgers," "school of american research," and "syracuse univeristy [*sic*]."

8.3.3 Best-Match Categorization

LCSH-mr is unable to satisfy queries for the corporate names users enter into online catalogs. Users would be better served matching the queries they enter for corporate names with LCNAF references and with subject headings assigned to bibliographic records. Figure 8.2 shows that most best-match categorizations for corporate name queries are assigned subject headings.

The best match for 15.4% of the thirty-nine corporate names in our sample is an exact match of an authorized heading or *see from* tracing for a corporate name in

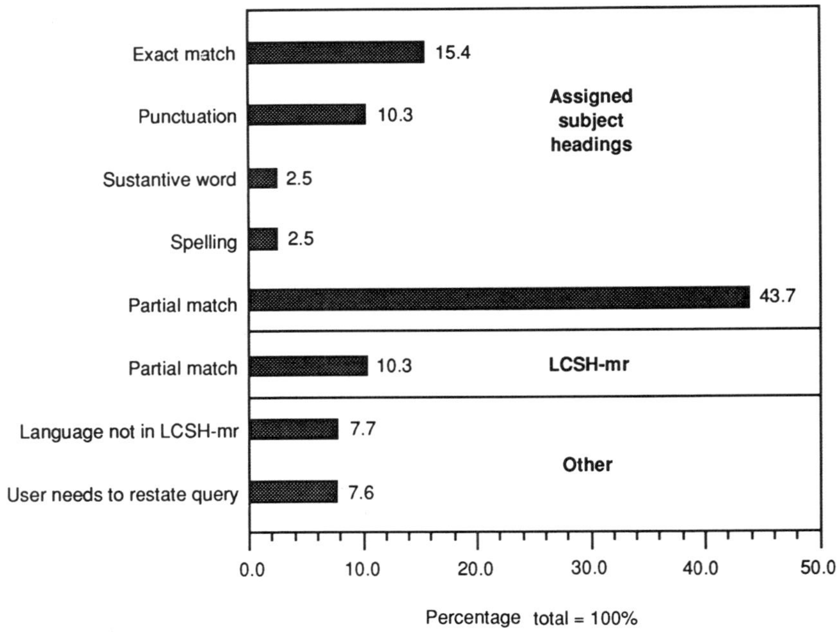

Figure 8.2
Best-match categorization of queries for corporate names.

LCNAF. An additional 12.8% of queries are matches of normalized headings of LCNAF headings and references. Examples are:

User-entered corporate name	*Nature of match*
apple company inc.	Exact match of LCNAF *see from* tracing minus punctuation
colgate-palmolive company	Exact match of authorized heading in LCNAF
erisa	Exact match of LCNAF *see from* tracing
skidmore, owings and merrill	Exact match of authorized heading in LCNAF minus punctuation
the beatles	Exact match of authorized heading in LCNAF minus stopword
united states food and drug administration	Exact match of authorized heading in LCNAF minus punctuation

The percentage of queries in the partial match category is rather high. Individual percentages for partial match subcategories are: (1) minus qualifiers (10.3%), (2) first two words (18.0%), (3) first word (7.7%), and (4) two words embedded in a subject heading (7.7%). Matching headings and references for queries placed in partial best-match subcategories are satisfactory for expressing users' topics of interest when they match all but the qualifier in LCNAF headings or references or a longer LCNAF heading or reference. Examples are:

User-entered corporate name	*Matching LCNAF heading*
coca-cola	Coca-cola Bottling Company United (U.S.); Coca-cola Company
ford motor co.	Ford Motor Company
kent state	Kent State University
los angeles dodgers	Los Angeles Dodgers (Baseball Club)
pantheon	Pantheon (Paris, France : Quarter)
pink floyd	Pink Floyd (Musical quartet)
samuel french	Samuel French Ltd.
school of american research	School of American Research (Santa Fe, N.M.)

Queries that match LCSH-mr are interesting. The query "harvard" matches all but the qualifier in the LCSH-mr *see* reference "Harvard (Training Planes)," but most likely, the user is looking for information on "Harvard University." If so, the user is not going to be satisfied with a system response that presents the qualified heading "Harvard (Training Planes)" to the user. The query "hewlett" matches the first word in the LCSH-mr *see* reference for the personal name "Hewlett family." If personal names are eliminated from subject indexes for topical subjects and corporate names, the query "hewlett" would then match the first word in the LCSH-mr *see* reference "Hewlett-Packard 33E (Calculator)."

If users could identify their queries as consisting wholly of elements for corporate names, then systems could respond more accurately with searches and browsing lists restricted to corporate name fields of authority and bibliographic records. SCM:SH (Library of Congress 1990, H405) lists almost one hundred categories of names that bear USMARC tags for corporate names. It may be easy to convey to users that names of organizations, for example, religious denominations, corporations, broadcasting stations, chambers of commerce, are corporate headings. However, expecting them to know that names of universities, embassies, libraries, monasteries, and city halls are corporate names may be too difficult because they consider these names to be places or topical subjects. Some categories of headings that users may consider to be corporate names are tagged as topical subjects (USMARC tag 650), for example, bus terminals, fire stations, post offices, shrines, and immigration stations. Furthermore, users may confuse the task of distinguishing the elements in queries, for example, topical subjects, personal names, corporate names, with the type of search they intend to perform, that is, subject or known-item search.

The difficulty of determining what is and what is not a corporate name is the major reason for our recommendation that corporate names be included in the same indexes that support subject searching for topical subjects. Most corporate names are represented in direct forms and not inverted like personal names; consequently, the first few words in user-entered corporate names should frequently match the first few words in corporate names. In an online system, topical subjects and corporate names would be interfiled, giving persevering users the opportunity to find corporate names that represent their topics of interest. Thus, the two users interested in "Harvard University" and "Hewlett-Packard Company" are going to find subject headings expressing their topics of interest in an alphabetical index; however, they may have to scan several lists of subject headings before finding desired ones.

A drawback to separating subject indexes for personal names from corporate names is the large number of corporate names that are derived from individuals, for example, "Ford Motor Company," "Deere & Company," "Walt Disney Productions." When users enter subject terms like "ford," "edison," "john deere," "bell," "max factor," "liz claiborne," "calvin klein," are they searching for individuals or the companies associated with these names? Perhaps corporate names should be double posted, that is, added to the alphabetical and keyword indexes that support searches for subjects generally and for personal names.

A few queries need to be reformulated to effect relevant matches of the catalog's controlled vocabulary. An example is the query "head," an exact match of the LCSH-mr heading "Head." The user needs to restate this query because subsequent access points demonstrate a specific interest in the skiing equipment made by a company named "Howard Head." Another example is the query "congress." It matches the initial word in two *see* references about congresses and conventions. A user who browses forward in LCSH-mr in this part of the alphabet and studies listed headings might find subdivided headings like "United States. Congress--Leadership" and "United States. Congress--Ethics" under the *see* references "Congressional leadership" and "Congressional ethics (United States)," respectively. The main heading, "United States. Congress," in these subdivided headings may stimulate the user to enter it directly to find material on the topic of interest.

A few queries placed in the partial-match category match the initial words in authorized headings and references in LCSH-mr and LCNAF, but both queries and matching terms end in different words. In every case, the matching heading or reference does not satisfactorily describe users' queries. Examples are:

User-entered corporate names	*Matching headings*
keystone corporation	Keystone Lake (Okla.); Keystone motion picture camera
league of professional	League of Nations
navy seals	Navy organization; Navy wives
theater women	Theater programs; Theater ticket subscription
toshiba affair	Toshiba Strike, 1949

Partial matches do not ensure that all the words in user queries are found in bibliographic records. Keyword search approaches for such partial matches will probably be more satisfactory in producing relevant information than the alphabetical approach because they retrieve records based on the presence of all words in user queries. Keyword searches should begin with keyword-in-heading approaches because retrievals are produced based on the presence of query words in a single field. In keyword-in-record approaches, retrievals are based on matches of query words in separate data fields.

Corporate names represent less than 3% of the subject terms entered by online catalog users in this study of initial access points. This percentage may be small because of the difficulties users have formulating corporate names. For example, they may have to determine the order of name components for government agencies and subordinate departments within agencies; they may be searching for an organization that has changed its name several times; they could be spelling out the full name of an organization that is commonly expressed with an acronym. The availability of *see* references will help users overcome some of these difficulties. Local *see* references could be generated by selectively rotating the subordinate unit(s) of corporate names into the entry element position. For example, the *see* reference "Sea Air Land Team. United States. Navy" is generated from the authorized heading "United States. Navy. Sea Air Land Team" The rotation algorithm would not need to generate *see* references for all possible combinations. Mischo (1981) made a similar recommendation for assigned subject headings to increase the number of subject access points in alphabetical or derived search key approaches.

Corporate names should be added to the same alphabetical and keyword subject indexes that contain topical subject headings and references from LCSH-mr. When users enter their subject terms, systems look for matches in the following order: (1) exact match, (2) match of normalized forms of headings, and (3) match of a longer heading or reference. Systems would respond with the exact approach (see Chapter 11) to users whose queries fit the first two matching categories and with an alphabetical index of assigned subject headings and authority-file references to users whose queries were longer. Systems could prompt users about the results of exact and normalized matches to determine if they want to continue searching for their query and produce the alphabetical index in response to a positive user reaction. Remaining queries, that is, those that do not fit the above matching criteria, would be submitted to various keyword search approaches, beginning with keyword-in-heading searches.

8.4 Synthesis and Summary

Catalogers can formulate subject headings for corporate names they are unable to verify in LCNAF, the primary source of authorized headings for corporate names, by following rules and guidelines in AACR2 and assigning these headings to the bibliographic record at hand. When users refine their searches for geographic names, the success of the new search depends on several factors, including their ability to enter terminology used in controlled vocabulary terms and the subject searching approaches used by online systems to produce retrievals. To save users from having to guess about the terminology and structure of headings, systems need browsing capabilities that display subdivided forms of assigned subject headings. The exact approach to subject searching is recommended as the system's response to exact matches of controlled vocabulary terms because it gives users the opportunity to browse by prompting them to select from a menu of categories of subdivided forms connected to the matched heading (Chapter 11).

Most partial matches of user queries for geographic names are not satisfactory when matching terms come from LCSH-mr because LCSH-mr has limited coverage of geographic names. To find a relevant controlled vocabulary term, users need to search subject headings for geographic names assigned to bibliographic records by library catalogers and *see* references for these names from LCNAF and LCSH-mr.

Geographic names and corporate names should be added to the same alphabetical and keyword subject indexes that support subject searching for topical subjects.

Corporate names could be double posted, that is, added to alphabetical and keyword indexes for subjects generally and for personal names because a large number of corporate names are derived from the names of individuals and families. This may help some users who enter names into online catalogs to find information on the individuals or organizations associated with the names.

References

American Library Association. (1992). *Headings for tomorrow: Public access display of subject headings*. Chicago, IL.: American Library Association.

Chan, Lois Mai. (1972). The period subdivision in subject headings. *Library Resources & Technical Services, 16*, (Fall), 453–459.

Library of Congress. (1990). *Subject cataloging manual: Subject headings*. Washington, DC: Library of Congress.

Library of Congress. (1992). *The future of subdivisions in the Library of Congress subject headings system: Report from the Subject Subdivisions Conference*, Martha O'Hara Conway (Ed.). Washington, DC: Library of Congress.

Mischo, William H. (1981). *Technical report on a subject retrieval function for the online union catalog*. Columbus, OH: OCLC. OCLC Technical report series OCLC/DD/TR-81/4.

Walker, Stephen, & Jones, Richard M. (1987). *Improving subject retrieval in online catalogues: 1. Stemming, automatic spelling correction and cross-reference tables*. London: British Library. British Library Research Paper No. 24.

9

Queries for Topical Subjects Not Likely to Succeed

9.1 Introduction

This chapter returns to our examination of the sample of transaction log queries that consisted wholly of elements for topical subjects. Many of these queries match single-subject headings in the catalog's controlled vocabulary. The problem is that matching headings are not necessarily satisfactory for expressing users' topics of interest. A few queries express one concept, for example, "junkyard," "widowhood," and "saw horse," while many more express two or more concepts, for example, "teenage sexuality," "black television comedians," and "the computer in reading and language arts."

The discussion of successful queries for topical subjects in Chapter 7 is followed here with a consideration of the remaining 41.8% of topical subject queries that were unsuccessful. Most initially unsuccessful queries are in partial-match categories, although some consist of subject terms not found in the catalog's controlled vocabulary. This chapter also discusses how online systems can make useful responses to these remaining queries even though they do not match controlled vocabulary terms or they do match terms that are not relevant.

9.2 Queries Matching the First Two Words of LCSH-mr

9.2.1 Subject Searches and Initial Access Points

Nearly 4% of all initial access points in the sample, or 5.8% of initial access points for topical subjects, form partial matches of their first two words with terms in LCSH-mr. Table 9.1 presents details about the fifty-four searches in our sample that begin with an access point that matches the first two words in an authorized heading or *see from* tracing in LCSH-mr.

Table 9.1
Fact Sheet for First Two Words in LCSH-mr

Summary data	Total	SULIRS	ORION	LS/2000
Searches				
No. of searches	54.0	25.0	18.0	11.0
No. of access points	210.0	89.0	85.0	36.0
Avg. no. of access points per search	3.9	3.6	4.7	3.3
Maximum no. of access points in a search	19.0	10.0	19.0	10.0
Initial access points				
Avg. no. of words per access point	3.4	3.8	3.1	3.3
Maximum no. of words in an access point	8.0	8.0	5.0	5.0
Retrievals				
Avg. no. of retrievals per access point	N/A	30.7[a]	11.0[b]	N/A
Percentage of access points with zero retrievals	N/A	48.0	27.8	N/A
Percentage of access points with retrievals >999	N/A	0.0	0.0	N/A
Low-posted searches				
Avg. no. of words in access point with zero retrievals	N/A	4.3	3.8	N/A
Avg. no. of access points in searches where initial access point has zero retrievals	N/A	3.5	7.0	N/A

[a]Number of bibliographic records retrieved. Since no searches retrieved more than 527 citations, this number is not an estimate.
[b]Number of assigned subject headings retrieved.

Except for LS/2000, the average number of access points per search is greater than for topical subject queries (see Table 7.1). The number of words in initial access points is greater than average, but by definition these queries have at least two words. They average between three and four words. Examples of queries exceeding four words are:

- problem solving or creativity or
- world war 2 underground movements
- social problems and drugs and unemployment
- women in the work force in the 1900-1950

Numbers of retrievals per access point are considerably lower than such retrievals in SULIRS and ORION for topical subjects generally (see Table 7.1). No query results in one thousand or more retrievals.

9.2.2 Producing Retrievals Based on Query Characteristics

Although queries in this partial-match category contain initial two-word pairs that match terms in LCSH-mr headings and references, the terms they match are not always satisfactory for expressing users' topics of interest. We examined queries that produced satisfactory and unsatisfactory retrievals and placed queries into three more specific subcategories that describe the extent to which they match LCSH-mr. Queries in these specific subcategories are also designated for certain subject searching approaches.

1. *Queries Matching a Longer LCSH Heading or Reference*

User queries consisting of two or more words that exactly match as many words in a longer LCSH-mr usually satisfactorily match authorized headings or *see* references relevant to the topics users seek. However, users typically omit the punctuation in matching headings. Examples of queries and matching controlled vocabulary terms are:

Queries	*Matching LCSH-mr headings or references*
camp sites	Camp sites, facilities, etc.
college education	College education costs, *see* College costs
greenhouse effect	Greenhouse effect, Atmospheric
insider trading	Insider trading movement
late gothic	Late gothic art, *see* Art, Gothic—Late Gothic
meals on wheels	Meals on wheels program
new deal	New Deal, 1933–1939
star trek	Star trek films

A useful system response to such queries would be the alphabetical approach. This approach lets users browse and select subject headings in the alphabetical neighborhood of the entered term. Systems would respond with the alphabetical approach to user queries that exactly match longer inverted headings or headings with commas. They would also disregard punctuation in the matching procedure. Matching controlled vocabulary terms would fail to satisfy users' needs for two of the above queries. Subsequent access points in the search beginning with "late gothic" reveal that the user is interested in late gothic architecture, particularly rayonnant architecture. The query "college education" matches a *see* reference that is more specific than the user's interest in finding information on obtaining a liberal arts education. Both users fail to express their interests in their initial queries, especially in the former query on gothic art. They would be better off reformulating their queries than browsing alphabetical lists or related terms associated with matching LCSH-mr headings or references.

2. *Queries Matching a Two-word* See *Reference*

Queries in this category have two characteristics: (1) they are composed of three or more words, and (2) the first two words match a two-word *see* reference in LCSH-mr. Examples are:

Queries	*See references in LCSH-mr*
group dynamics in the classroom	______ ______, *see* Social groups

labor market cartels	______ ______, *see* Labor supply
mass communication research	______ ______, *see* Communication; Communication and traffic; Mass media; Telecommunication
reading aloud to children	______ ______, *see* Oral reading
real estate and computers	______ ______, *see* Real property
sexual abuse in poverty families	______ ______, *see* Child abuse

When users include words from *see* references in their queries, they increase the possibility that keyword searches will result in zero retrievals because the words in *see* references are not assigned as authorized headings. Systems could check the initial two words in user queries to determine if they are *see* references, then replace *see* references with words from authorized headings to increase the chances of making matches. Such references would be difficult to find when embedded in queries; however, queries beginning with two-word *see* references could be enhanced automatically by systems to include the authorized headings. For example, the words in the authorized heading "Oral reading" could be substituted for the first two words in the query "reading aloud" or combined in a Boolean "or" operation with "reading aloud." The enhanced query would be "((oral and reading) or (reading and aloud)) and children." This automatically reformulated query would increase the user's chances of retrieving bibliographic records in a keyword search for this query. Examples of titles retrieved in The University of Michigan's MIRLYN online catalog in response to keyword searches using this statement are *For reading out loud* and *A parent's guide to children's reading.*

Before enhancing queries and performing various Boolean operations, systems could tell users that a different phrase(s) is used for or added to their words and encourage them to continue the search using this phrase. An example is:

SYSTEM > "Child abuse" is used instead of "Sexual abuse." Press ENTER to search for "Child abuse in poverty families."

Occasionally, several authorized headings are suggested under *see* references. In such instances, systems could offer users a choice of authorized headings.

SYSTEM > Several terms are used instead of "Mass communication." Select term(s) to substitute for "Mass communication":

1. Communication
2. Communication and traffic
3. Mass media
4. Telecommunication

USER > 4

SYSTEM > Searching for "telecommunication research" . . .

In this example, the user selects "Telecommunication." This word is then combined with "research" using the Boolean "and" operation. The system performs keyword searches of subject headings, titles, or combinations of these and other subject-rich fields for bibliographic records bearing these two words.

*3. **Remaining Queries***

User queries that do not have the characteristics of the two previously described subcategories of queries are candidates for keyword searching approaches. However, the brute force of keyword searching of *all subject-rich fields* of bibliographic records is not immediately applied to such queries. Keyword searching approaches are applied successively, beginning with keyword searches of the main headings in assigned subject headings for words in user queries. If keyword searches of main headings produce zero or too few retrievals, systems continue with keyword searches of single subdivided subject headings. For example, keyword-in-main-heading searches fail to retrieve subject headings in response to the query "television stations maps"; however, keyword-in-subdivided-heading searches produce the single assigned subject heading "Television stations--United States--Maps." If successful in retrieving headings, both of these keyword approaches yield single headings bearing every word in user queries.

The sequence of keyword searches performed on users' queries is intended to rank retrieved bibliographic records. That is, records retrieved through the first keyword approach—keyword searches of main headings—are likely to be most relevant to user queries because nearly all of the words in main headings are also in user queries. Bibliographic records retrieved through the second keyword approach—keyword searches of subdivided headings—are also likely to be relevant to user queries. However, the subdivided headings are probably going to contain several additional words in main headings and/or subdivisions that are not found in the original query. Keyword approaches begin with controlled vocabulary fields of bibliographic records because catalogers assign this vocabulary to bibliographic records to represent the subject matter of library materials. Governing their assignment of controlled vocabulary terms is the principle of specific and direct entry. This principle requires catalogers to assign controlled vocabulary terms that are specific to the subject matter treated in the item in hand. If users enter subject terms matching controlled vocabulary terms or several keywords in such terms, there is a good chance they will retrieve material relevant to the topics they seek.

Keyword searches of subdivided LCSH-mr and assigned subject headings can yield long lists of assigned subject headings. For example, nearly three dozen subdivisions are suggested in LCSH-mr under "Automobiles--Motors." Selection of one of these subdivided LCSH-mr headings can lead to dozens of assigned subject headings subdivided by free-floating subdivisions. Recommendations on displaying LCSH-mr and assigned subject headings retrieved in keyword searches will be given in Chapter 12.

If keyword searches of assigned subject headings produce zero or too few retrievals, systems can continue with keyword searches of words in bibliographic records. Title keyword searches should come first in the sequence of keyword-in-record search approaches because retrievals would be restricted to a single field. Furthermore, titles are often indicative of an item's subject contents. If title keyword searches produce an insufficient number of retrievals, systems can continue with keyword searches of subject heading fields. The last keyword approach is the brute force keyword search of all subject-rich fields of bibliographic records. Matches of the words in user queries are made of the words in subject-rich fields of bibliographic records. Matching words will probably be in separate fields because previous keyword searches in the sequence have failed to produce retrievals in searches of single fields, that is, title-keyword searches, or searches of the same field type, that is, keyword-in-subject-heading searches. Examples of queries and the subject-rich fields producing retrievals in keyword searches are:

Query	*Fields producing retrievals*
art and artists	Subject-heading fields: Art; Artists
civil war prints	Civil war from period subdivisions; prints from titles
mass media and politicians	Subject-heading fields: Mass media; Politicians
old age and television	Subject-heading fields: Old age; Television
racism in media	Subject-heading fields: Racism; several headings beginning with Racism; several headings beginning with Media
social change in film	Subject-heading fields: Social change; many headings containing Film
working class history	Working class from titles; history from topical subdivisions

When systems enlist keyword searching approaches, they need a feedback capability that enables users to choose relevant subject headings from retrieved bibliographic records. The system then uses the heading(s) to search for additional records. Effective feedback capabilities are difficult to design and implement because relevant headings found in retrieved bibliographic records are not always combined using one Boolean operator. Feedback capabilities have to let users distinguish between synonymous headings, that is, those that would be combined in a Boolean "or" operation, and headings that are relevant to their interests but not synonymous, that is, those that would be combined in a Boolean "and" operation. Feedback capabilities will also be discussed in greater detail in Chapter 12.

9.2.3 Unsuccessful Searches

Keyword searches do not always produce relevant bibliographic records. When keyword approaches fail, systems can respond with alphabetical lists of assigned subject headings. Often, such lists contain a heading expressing one facet of the user's topics of interest. The partially matched heading may be connected with related terms or subdivided headings that express one or more facets of the original query. Examples are:

Queries	*Relevant assigned headings*
corporate planning and computer	Alphabetical index yields "Corporate planning" and subdivision "$x Data processing"
french literature guide	Alphabetical index includes "French literature"
gallium arsenide transistors	Alphabetical index begins with "Gallium arsenide semiconductors"
racism in humor	Alphabetical index includes "Racism in language"

Some queries are poorly worded. When keyword searching is applied to the query "problem solving or creativity or," it produces bibliographic records on both topics because of the implicit Boolean "and" operation. This user needs to search for "problem solving" and "creativity" separately. The user entering the query "late gothic" is really interested in rayonnant architecture and needs to restate the query.

Even if an authorized heading is substituted for the *see* reference "mass communication" in the query "mass communication and post-industrial society," this query requires that at least four words be present in the same bibliographic record. This requirement may be too stringent and result in zero retrievals. The user may have to restate the query or look for subdivisions appended to a subject heading selected from the alphabetical index to express the "post-industrial society" facet of the query. The query for "french literature guide" probably delivers to the user a high-posted heading, that is, "French literature," which may contribute to the difficulty of finding bibliographic records for guides to French literature. The user's best bet is to compose titles for items of interest, for example, "an introduction to French literature" or "introducing French literature."

Three queries begin with the words "world war 2" or "world war II." If keyword searches produce zero retrievals forcing systems to respond with alphabetical lists of LCSH-mr and assigned subject headings, lists are going to begin long before the heading that users want, for example, "World War, 1939–1945." The only way users can be helped is through the addition of local *see* references for "World War 2" and "World War II." Otherwise, they may have to browse through hundreds of "World War, 1914–1918" headings before arriving at headings for the Second World War.

9.3 Queries Matching the First Word and Three-Letter Stem of Second Word of LCSH-mr

Only sixteen queries (1.7%) for topical subjects begin with one word and a three-letter stem of the second word that matches the same in an LCSH-mr. Examples are:

Query	*LCSH-mr*
chemical bonding	Chemical bonds
computer conferencing	Computer contracts
islamic revitalization	Islamic revolution, Iran, 1979, *see* Iran--History--Revolution, 1979
management compensation plans	Management committees
neural net	Neural networks, *see* Neural circuitry
personal constructs	Personal construct theory
political activism	Political action committees
preschool testingh [sic]	Preschool tests

A few queries make a partial match of an LCSH-mr heading or reference that satisfactorily describes the topics of interest sought by users. These queries exactly match the same characters in a longer controlled vocabulary term, for example, "neural nets," or differ from matching controlled vocabulary terms because of suffixes, for example, "chemical bonding," "personal constructs," and "preschool testingh [*sic*]." If systems respond to such queries with the alphabetical approach, users are likely to find and select appropriate subject headings.

Persevering users may find appropriate subject headings for several other queries listed above by browsing an alphabetical subject heading index, but the search could become quite complicated. For example, nearby "political activism" is the complex *see* reference "Political activity," which, if selected, gives a note telling users to use this phrase as a subdivision under classes of persons. The user then has to compose and enter a query that names the relevant class of persons and includes the phrase "political activity."

The queries in this partial match subcategory should be added to the partial match subcategory for first word matches of LCSH-mr and handled accordingly. These queries should be submitted to various keyword-in-heading and keyword-in-record search approaches because they fail to meet the criteria for the alphabetical approach.

The analysis of queries in this subcategory suggest two refinements to subject searching approaches. First, queries are candidates for the alphabetical approach when they exactly match the same characters in a longer controlled vocabulary term. This subtle change would enable systems to respond with the alphabetical approach to the query "neural net" with an alphabetical index containing the *see* reference "Neural networks." Second, systems could generate normalized forms of the main heading subfield in topical subject headings minus frequently occurring suffixes. When keyword searches fail to produce retrievals, systems could extend their searches to such normalized forms of topical subject headings. Of course, systems would also have to perform the same procedures on user queries as they perform on topical subject headings to create the normalized forms bereft of suffixes.

9.4 Queries Matching the First Word of LCSH-mr

9.4.1 Subject Searches and Initial Access Points

Except for exact matches of LCSH-mr, the partial-match subcategory for matches of the first word of an LCSH-mr accounts for the largest percentage (25.7%) of user queries for topical subjects. Table 9.2 is a fact sheet with details about the total of 240 searches initiated by an access point matching the first word in an LCSH-mr heading or reference.

The number of access points per search (3.3) is the same as the number of access points in searches for topical subjects generally (see Table 7.1). The longest search in this category contains eighteen access points. It starts with "distribution," and subsequent access points show that the user is interested in exporting and distributing frozen food in Venezuela. Following several nonrelevant subject headings printed in *LCSH* that begin with the word "Distribution" is the *see* reference "Distribution channels." This reference suggests the authorized heading "Marketing channels" that expresses one facet of the user query. The alphabetical approach could

Table 9.2
Fact Sheet for First Word in LCSH-mr

Summary data	Total	SULIRS	ORION	LS/2000
Searches				
No. of searches	240.0	108.0	90.0	42.0
No. of access points	792.0	350.0	343.0	99.0
Avg. no. of access points per search	3.3	3.2	3.8	2.4
Maximum no. of access points in a search	18.0	18.0	17.0	12.0
Initial access points				
Avg. no. of words per access point	2.1	2.2	2.1	1.6
Maximum no. of words in an access point	8.0	8.0	4.0	6.0
Retrievals				
Avg. no. of retrievals per access point	N/A	116.0[a]	71.0[b]	N/A
Percentage of access points with zero retrievals	N/A	36.1	57.8	N/A
Percentage of access points with retrievals > 999	N/A	4.6	2.2	N/A
Low-posted searches				
Avg. no. of words in access point with zero retrievals	N/A	2.8	2.5	N/A
Avg. no. of access points in searches where initial access point has zero retrievals	N/A	3.9	3.6	N/A

[a]Number of bibliographic records retrieved. This is an estimate based on substituting 3,000 retrievals for the 99,999 retrievals that is written to logs when number of retrievals exceeds about 1,000.
[b]Number of assigned subject headings retrieved.

have helped the user find "Marketing channels," and, eventually, geographic subdivisions to express the second facet of the user's topic.

The average number of words per access point (2.1) is a little higher than the average generally (1.8). The longest access point in this partial-match subcategory is entered by a SULIRS user and contains eight words. This long access point and others entered in the same search are:

- legal cases involving life support systems in humans
- legal involvement in life support systems
- legal involvement in critical care
- cutting off life support systems
- should people be kept alive by life support systems

LCSH-mr contains the heading "Life support systems (Critical care)." The alphabetical approach would not help the user because the initial access point begins with the first word in several nonrelevant LCSH-mr headings, for example, "Legal advertising," "Legal aid," and "Legal assistance to abused wives." The user needs to begin the query with "life support systems" or "critical care" to find relevant headings using the alphabetical approach. Keyword approaches could retrieve bibliographic records if the searcher uses fewer words and/or words from an appropriate subdivision, for example, "legal status, laws, etc."

SULIRS and ORION searches for queries in this category retrieve fewer bibliographic records or assigned subject headings than queries for topical subjects generally (see Table 7.1). Over one-third of SULIRS searches and one-half of ORION searches fail to produce retrievals. Queries in searches failing to produce retrievals contain between two and three words. Users do not persevere because these searches average about the same number of access points as searches overall.

9.4.2 Producing Retrievals Based on Query Characteristics

Although queries in this partial-match subcategory contain the same initial word as LCSH-mr headings and references, the terms they match are not always satisfactory for expressing users' topics of interest. We examined queries producing satisfactory and unsatisfactory retrievals, then placed them into two more specific subcategories that describe the extent to which they match LCSH-mr. Queries in these two specific subcategories are also designated for certain subject searching approaches.

1. One-Word Queries.

By definition, one-word queries match the initial word in a longer LCSH-mr heading or reference. About one-fourth (61) of the 240 partial-match queries are composed of one word. Some words are quite specific, for example, "fibonacci," and match only the initial word of one LCSH-mr, that is, "Fibonacci numbers."

Others are not so specific, for example, "crime," so they match the initial word of many LCSH-mr headings. Different forms of these words, for example, "crimes," "criminal," "criminologists," may also lead to hundreds of other headings and *see* references.

When users enter a one-word query matching the first word of an LCSH-mr heading or reference, the alphabetical approach usually places them in a list of assigned subject headings and LCSH-mr references that includes a relevant heading nearby. Examples are:

Query	*LSCH-mr headings and references*
addicts	Addicts, Narcotic
fitness	Fitness, physical, *see* Physical fitness
grocery	Grocery trade
kalman	Kalman filtering
mergers	Mergers, conglomerate, *see* Conglomerate corporations
pinball	Pinball machines
space	Space, Outer, *see* Outer space
speeches	Speeches, addresses, etc.
wholesale	Wholesale price indexes

Occasionally, users will have to browse backward or forward to find heading(s) of interest. Examples of queries requiring considerable browsing of an alphabetical index of assigned subject headings are:

Query	*Initial LCSH-mr match*	*Desired LCSH-mr*
aztec	Aztec architecture	Aztecs
basal	Basal body temperature	Basal reading instruction
instruments	Instruments, Acoustic impedance, *see* . . .	Instruments, Musical, *see* . . .
lobbies	Lobbies, Hotels, *see* . . .	Lobbying; Lobbyists
rights	Rights, Abuse of	Rights, Human, *see* Human rights
robin	Robin, Cock (Fictitious character)	Robin Hood (Legendary character)

Several queries are composed of one word, and subsequent access points, if there are any, are too vague to enable us to determine the users' topics of interest. In such instances, the alphabetical approach may help users. They may realize the breadth of their topics because so many LCSH-mr headings are listed in close alphabetical proximity to their entered term, and, if so, rephrase their queries. Examples of such queries are given along with the first of many LCSH-mr headings or references beginning with the same word entered by users.

Query	*LCSH-mr headings and references*
baroque	Baroque altarpieces, *see* . . .
detective	Detective and mystery films
egyptian	Egyptian alfalfa weevil
export	Export and import controls, *see* . . .
graph	Graph grammars
jew	Jew family
illustration	Illustration, Biological, *see* . . .

marine	Marine accidents
safety	Safety, Industrial, *see* . . .

If keyword approaches are used for these queries, they produce hundreds of retrievals that come from words in subject headings, titles, and other subject-rich fields of bibliographic records. For example, the query "marine" can lead to thousands of bibliographic records on topics such as "Marine algae," "Marine biology," "Marine fishes," and "Marine painting." Plural forms of these queries can produce even more retrievals, for example, headings beginning with "aztecs" or "jews."

When queries are composed of one word that matches the first word in a longer LCSH-mr, systems should respond with an alphabetical index of assigned subject headings that enables users to browse forward and backward to find a heading that interests them. Sometimes, they will use such lists to survey the amount of material written on topics, then enter a query that more specifically addresses their topics.

2. Queries Exceeding One Word.

Keyword approaches are the recommended system response for queries composed of two or more words that match only the first word of an LCSH-mr heading or reference. Keyword approaches are applied in the same order as recommended earlier in this chapter for queries composed of two or more words that match the first two words of an LCSH-mr. The order is: (1) main headings, (2) subdivided headings, (3) titles, (4) subject-heading fields, and (5) all subject-rich fields of bibliographic records. Keyword searches of controlled vocabulary fields are performed first to ensure the precision of retrieved output. Should keyword approaches fail to produce retrievals or a satisfactory number of retrievals, truncation could be applied to query words and keyword searches repeated in the order given above.

Examples of queries retrieving relevant unsubdivided and subdivided subject headings in response to keyword-in-heading search approaches are:

Query	*LCSH-mr*
cross-cultural marriage	Marriage--Cross-cultural studies
diseases trees	Trees--Diseases and pests
legends of the Bible	Bible--Legends
gait analysis	Gait in humans--Analysis
media and violence	Violence in mass media
music history	Music--History and criticism
peer tutoring	Peer-group tutoring of students
telecommunication congresses	Telecommunication--Congresses
sales training	Sales personnel--Training of

The advantage of matching authorized headings in LCSH-mr is the possibility that related terms are connected to matched headings. For example, under "Trees--Diseases and pests" are several narrower terms and a complex *see also* reference directing searchers to names of specific trees with this same subdivision, for example, "Elm--Diseases and pests."

9.4.3 Identifying Relevant Subject Headings in Retrieved Output

When searches of single headings fail to produce retrievals, title keyword searches often yield relevant bibliographic records. Systems can analyze the results and report single-subject headings common to retrieved records to help users further the search. Examples of queries for which title searches produce relevant bibliographic records and single headings express users' topics of interest in their entirety are:

Query	*Possibly relevant subject headings*
black leaders	Afro-American Leadership
cognitive process	Cognition
discrete signal analysis	Signal theory (Telecommunication)
marijuana cultivation	Marihuana--Growth
teacher as professional	Teachers--Training of; Teachers--In-service education
teenage sexuality	Youth--Sexual behavior; Teenagers--Sexual behavior
trademarks logos	Trademarks
transnational organizations	International business enterprises

The relevant headings produced by the various keyword-in-record searches do not contain the same words as those in user queries. Thus, systems must enlist users to provide information about retrievals to help further the search. When two or more subject headings are common to retrieved bibliographic records, systems need users to tell them whether two or more such headings must be present in retrieved records for users to deem output relevant. For example, the system reports to the user entering the query "teenage sexuality" that the subject headings "Youth--Sexual behavior" and "Teenagers--Sexual behavior" may retrieve additional relevant records. The system needs to know whether these headings are synonymous with one another, and, thus, would be combined in a Boolean "or" operation, or relevant but not synonymous, and thus combined in a Boolean "and" operation.

Keyword searches of subject-heading fields produce several queries yielding two or more relevant subject headings that have to be present in the same record to ensure relevance. Examples are:

Query	*LCSH-mr and assigned headings*
aids advertising	Aids (Disease); Advertising
chaotic dynamics	Chaotic behavior in systems; Dynamics
sensory and perception	Sensory stimulation; Visual perception
segregation of public housing	Segregation; Public housing
software engineering and artificial intelligence	Software engineering; Artificial intelligence
speech and reading	Speech; Reading
zen in archery	Zen Buddhism; Archery

Keyword-in-record search approaches may yield relevant bibliographic records but not necessarily usable subject headings. For example, users who enter the queries "advertising principles" and "basic psychology" may be guessing at the titles of items they would want to retrieve. Subject headings assigned to retrieved items may be high posted and not necessarily limited in assignment to introductory works on these topics. Examples of such queries are:

Query	*Relevant titles*
advertising principles	*Advertising, its principles and practice; Advertising age*
basic psychology	*Psychology: Studying the behavior of people*
introduction to polymer science	*Introduction to polymer science*
the computer in reading and language arts	*Microcomputers in reading and language arts*
the depression of 1990	*The great depression of 1990*

Keyword searches for several remaining queries retrieve relevant bibliographic records in keyword searches for truncated query words. Asterisks mark truncated stems in the examples that follow. Two truncated queries are the same as the original queries, but truncation enables systems to make retrievals on plural forms of query words.

Original query	*Truncated query*
child stereotyping	child stereotyp*
cognitive process	cognitive process*
condom advertisement	condom* advertis*
refugee resettlement	refugee* resettlement
surrealist painters	surrealis* paint*

9.4.4 Queries Failing to Produce Relevant Retrievals

Although several queries match the initial word in an LCSH-mr heading or reference, they fail to retrieve relevant bibliographic records or subject headings for different reasons. Here are some examples. The query "city director" is entered by a user wanting a city directory, and it needs to be restated in the form of a city name and words in relevant subdivisions, for example, "directories" and/or "telephone." The queries "farm aid" and "secondary smoke" may be more appropriate for searches in magazine indexes because these sources cover current events quicker than the monographs and books that are accessible in library catalogs. Three misspellings cause keyword searches to fail. If spelling is corrected in the query "black playwrites," keyword searches for this query yield relevant bibliographic records and the relevant subject heading "Afro-American dramatists" that users can enter to retrieve additional material. A few queries contain misspellings, which, when corrected, still fail to retrieve relevant bibliographic records or headings in keyword searches, for example, "black fraternaties and sororities" and "seletion policy." The technical terminology in a few queries for science and medical topics may have been too specific for library catalogs to produce retrievals, for example, "congenital dyerythropoietic anemia," "myeloid cell lines," "silicone adheisives [*sic*]," "stuttering psychogenic," "technique in neutralizations," and "ventricular arrthymia [*sic*]."

The best bet for users entering the following queries is to reformulate their queries:

- computer su dissertation
- lampoon comedy
- notions of buddha
- plants geotropism
- race g
- saw horse

An estimated one-fourth of the 240 queries in this partial-match subcategory should be reformulated to produce useful retrievals for users. No amount of keyword or alphabetical searching would help them find material on their topics of interest.

A few users would benefit from the alphabetical approach when keyword approaches for their queries produce zero retrievals. Even though these queries are composed of two or more words, the alphabetical approach lists relevant assigned subject headings or references in close alphabetical proximity to the initial word that the query matches. Examples of such queries are:

Query	*LCSH-mr headings and references*
aids: facts and issues	Aids (Disease)
architecture in the 16th to18th centuries [*sic*]	Architecture; browse headings with period subdivisions
abestos chemistry	Asbestos
colloquial sayings	Colloquial English, *see* English language--Conversation and phrase books or --Spoken English, or browse forward to Colloquial Language
golgi body	Browse backward to Golgi apparatus
kwakiutl potlach	Kwakiutl Indians
neanderthal man	Neanderthal race
oglala sioux	Oglala Indians
penis expansion	Penis

When systems exhaust keyword approaches, systems could prompt users to continue with the alphabetical approach. This approach will not always direct users to relevant headings, but it may save them from rephrasing their queries or terminating their search prematurely.

9.5

LCSH-mr Words Embedded in Queries

Words from an LCSH-mr heading or reference are embedded in 1.8% of queries for topical subjects. Examples of queries placed in the two partial-match subcategories and possibly relevant LCSH-mr headings containing query words are:

Query	*Possibly relevant LCSH-mr headings*
cardiothoracic surgery	Chest--Surgery; Heart--Surgery
denotational semantics	Programming languages (Electronic computers)--Semantics
future adult education	Adult education

motifs art deco	Art deco--Themes, motives
polyaromatic hydrocarbons	Polycyclic aromatic hydrocarbons
severely physically handicapped	Physically handicapped

Several queries lead to relevant bibliographic records using the sequence of keyword searching approaches recommended for queries in other partial-match categories. For example, a title keyword search "future adult education" produces several titles including *Adult Education in the United States: its scope, nature, and future direction.* Users could further the search using the subject heading assigned to this book, that is, "Adult education--United States."

Although queries in embedded-word subcategories contain words from LCSH-mr, subject headings formed by the matching words are often broader than queries, not relevant to queries, or they express one facet of multifaceted queries. Examples of such queries and LCSH-mr headings containing query words are:

Query	*LCSH-mr headings and references*
domination	A chronological subdivision, that is, Turkic-Mongol domination, 1045–1522
outcome based education	Headings beginning with Education
squeeze state	Headings beginning with State, for example, State birds
supported work for handicapped	Handicapped
the governor's job	Headings beginning with Governor's, for example, Governor's Palace (Williamsburg, Va.); headings beginning with Job
what companies look for	*see* references beginning with and including Companies

Keyword searches for several queries including "reaist artists [*sic*]," "good furniture," and "rayonnant architecture" do not produce retrievals. Dropping the nonmatching initial word in these queries results in exact matches of "Artists," "Furniture," and "Architecture," broader subject headings that produce hundreds and thousands of retrievals. These headings could also lead to narrower terms or subdivided headings that better express the topics of interest users are seeking.

Keyword searches will help users find bibliographic records and relevant subject headings for about half of the queries in partial-match subcategories in which one or more words from LCSH-mr headings or references are embedded in queries. When such queries are entered into online systems, systems should respond with the recommended sequence of keyword search approaches, starting with the keyword-in-main-heading search.

9.6

Queries Composed of Words Not Found in LCSH-mr

Only 2.5% of queries for topical subjects do not match the terminology of LCSH-mr. Most queries in this category are one-word queries. Examples are:

Query	*Close matches of LCSH-mr*
advertisers	Advertising
classicalism	
clauddau	
critique of ironwood	
dsm	
euromarkets	Euro-dollar
gnatting	
graphwriter	
junkyard	
l'arche	
mcat	
mrp	
nira	
nmr	
rioting	Riots
sci fi	
sociopath	sociopathic personality, *see* . . .
walkman	
widowhood	Widows

A few of these one-word queries match the first two syllables in a longer LCSH-mr heading or reference that users may want to pursue. They would have to persevere by browsing forward or backward in alphabetical lists to find the appropriate heading(s).

Title keyword searches for terms that look like abbreviations, that is, "mcat," "mrp," "dsm," and "nmr," are successful. Abbreviations are given and spelled out in titles, subtitles, or notes of several retrieved bibliographic records, for example, "management resource planning" for "mrp," "diagnostic and statistical manual" for "dsm," and "nuclear magnetic resonance" for "nmr." Title keyword searches for "graphwriter" produce the assigned subject heading "Lotus Graphwriter II (Computer program)" in a retrieved bibliographic record. This heading may more adequately describe what the user is looking for than the original query.

Alphabetical and keyword approaches that fail to produce useful results for several queries are "l'arche," "classicalism," "walkman," "nira," "clauddau," and "gnatting." The query "nira" looks like an abbreviation; however, it is misspelled because it is followed by the query "nra" for the National Rifle Association.

Keyword searches of titles produce the most useful results for queries composed of words that are not in LCSH-mr. If systems are unable to produce retrievals for title keyword searches, they should prompt users to review their queries and correct misspelled words. If users do not correct spelling but still want to pursue the search, systems should respond with the alphabetical index of subject headings.

9.7 Combinations of Categories

A small percentage (4.4%) of user queries for topical subjects require changes, for example, addition of punctuation or spelling correction, before they can be categorized in one of the matching categories. For example, the query "chippecwa" has an addition error that must be corrected to effect a match of the initial word in the LCSH-mr "Chippewa, Battle of, 1814."

Over a third of the queries in the combined-match category require spelling corrections. Some queries have an additional problem that needs correction before a match of an LCSH-mr heading or reference can be made. For example, the query "periodicala publishing" needs correction of the substitution error and missing punctuation (i.e., insertion of a comma) before a match of the first two words in an LCSH-mr can be made. Additional examples are:

Query:	ardennese battle of the
Spelling error:	addition
LCSH-mr/Type of match:	Ardennes, Battle of the, 1944–1945/partial match of the same characters in a longer LCSH-mr minus punctuation
Query:	green house effect
Spelling error:	one-word/two-word
LCSH-mr/Type of match:	Greenhouse effect, Atmospheric/first two words
Query:	philoctetess
Spelling error:	addition
LCSH-mr/Type of match:	Philoctetes (Legendary character)/normalized form minus the qualifier
Query:	servomechnism
Spelling error:	omission
LCSH-mr/Type of match:	Servomechanisms/partial match of the same characters as a longer LCSH-mr
Query:	women and facism
Spelling error:	omission
LCSH-mr/Type of match:	Fascism and women/normalized form minus stopword and disregarding word order

When the individual words in queries fail to produce retrievals in keyword searches, there is a good chance that such words are misspelled. Systems that do not have automatic spelling correction could show these words to users and ask them to check for misspellings. In most of the above examples, spelling errors occur toward the middle or end of the first word. If online systems place users at an alphabetical location that is close to the term they intended, they are still going to have to browse backward or forward to find the desired heading.

Almost one-fourth of the queries in the combined-match category require conversion of a query word(s) into its plural or singular form before a partial match can be made. Examples are:

Query:	mathematic theory correctness
LCSH-mr/Type of match:	Mathematics/partial match of first word of LCSH-mr
Query:	slope stability
LCSH-mr/Type of match:	Slopes (Soil mechanics)/partial match of first word of LCSH-mr
Query:	stereotypes of disease
LCSH-mr/Type of match:	Stereotype (Psychology)/partial match of first word of LCSH-mr
Query:	times series analysis
LCSH-mr/Type of match:	Time-series analysis/exact match of normalized form minus punctuation

Every query in the above examples contains two or more words. The word that requires conversion to plural or singular to effect a match of LCSH-mr is embedded in the query. If this word had been the trailing word of the query, partial matches of a longer LCSH-mr heading or reference could be made in a few cases. Since these queries do not fit the criteria for alphabetical searching, they should be submitted to keyword searches in the recommended sequence of approaches. System-supplied truncation could be applied to queries that still fail to produce retrievals, and the sequence of keyword searches could be repeated. For example, keyword search approaches will probably fail to produce retrievals for the query "times series analysis" until words are truncated to effect a match of the single heading, "Time-series analysis."

Users need perseverance and patience to review and evaluate the results of several system approaches. For example, keyword searches for the two trailing words in the query "on line compter systemss" yield zero retrievals. System prompting may induce users to correct spelling to form the revised query "on line computer systems." If keyword searches still fail to produce retrievals, persevering users may find the relevant heading "On-line data processing" when browsing the alphabetical index of subject headings beginning with the word "On."

Some queries do not contain enough information for human intermediaries to determine users' interests. Queries for "chippecwa [*sic*]," "control," "demographics," and "domination" are open to several interpretations. To effect matches, spelling errors need to be detected and plural forms of terms converted to the singular. When alphabetical searches produce lengthy alphabetical lists of headings beginning with these words, users may realize the open-endedness of their topics and reformulate their queries.

Several queries are specific to users' topics of interests but they are expressed in terms other than those used by the controlled vocabulary for the same topic or by bibliographic records included in the catalog. Examples are the queries "legaalization of drug usee [*sic*]," "peace movement in the 1960," and "physciological [*sic*] aspects of cocaine use." Even after spelling errors are corrected, systems may fail to produce retrievals. LCSH-mr provides relevant subject headings for these topics, for example, "Cocaine--Physiological aspects," "Vietnam Conflict, 1961–1975--Protest movements," and "Drugs--Law and legislation," but neither queries nor subject headings are alike in form or structure.

9.8 Synthesis and Summary

Users are quite successful entering queries for topical subjects that match one or more words in LCSH-mr headings or references. Next to exact matches, partial matches of LCSH-mr headings and references account for the largest percentage of user queries in the various matching categories. Individual percentages for the six partial-match subcategories that make up this category are: (1) minus qualifiers (3.8%), (2) first two words (5.8%), (3) first word and three-letter stem of second word (1.7%), (4) first word (25.7%), (5) two words embedded in an LCSH-mr (1.3%), and (6) one word embedded in an LCSH-mr (0.5%). The problem is that systems cannot respond in the same way to queries in each of these subcategories. Systems must be programmed to identify specific subsets of queries in certain categories in order to respond with a subject searching approach that is likely to produce useful retrievals.

Systems should generate normalized forms of qualified headings and references that are bereft of qualifiers. The system response to user queries that match all but the qualifier is a list of qualified headings and references. The user's selection of a listed term would invoke the exact approach (see Chapter 11), which then displays retrievals and other useful information connected with the selected controlled vocabulary term such as related terms, subdivided forms of the selected heading, and so on. Should a listed or selected term not be satisfactory for representing users' topics of interest, systems should continue with the alphabetical approach, in which a browsing list of assigned subject headings and LCSH-mr references begins with terms in the alphabetical neighborhood of the entered term.

The alphabetical approach is recommended for queries in the next three partial-match categories, that is, first two words, first word and three-letter stem of second word, first word, in which the user-entered term matches the same characters as those in a longer assigned subject heading or reference. For example, the system response to the partial matches "neural net," "hydroelectric power," and "mergers" is the alphabetical approach because it would include LCSH-mr headings and references such as "Neural networks," "Hydroelectric power plants" and "Mergers, Conglomerate" that are satisfactory expressions of users' topics of interest.

Systems can be programmed to detect plural suffixes on one-word queries. Suffix removal may enable systems to effect an exact match of an LCSH-mr heading or reference or a partial match of a longer controlled vocabulary term. In the latter instance, systems would respond with the alphabetical approach. Title keyword searches are recommended for the remaining one-word queries in the first word, partial-match subcategory. Queries failing to produce retrievals at this point are probably misspelled and should be presented to users with a prompt asking them to check spelling.

Remaining queries in these three partial-match subcategories and all queries in subcategories for word(s) embedded in LCSH-mr headings and references should be submitted to keyword searches. First, the individual words in these queries should be submitted to keyword-in-record searches. If one or more words fail to produce retrievals, they are probably misspelled and systems should enlist the assistance of users to correct spelling. The results of keyword-in-record searches would not be shown to users at this time. Instead, systems would follow a sequence of keyword searches until retrievals are made: (1) keyword-in-main-heading, (2) keyword-in-subdivided-heading, (3) title keyword, (4) keyword-in-subject-heading fields, and last, (5) keyword-in-record searches.

The sequence of keyword searches performed on users queries is intended to rank retrieved bibliographic records. That is, records retrieved through the first keyword approach—keyword searches of main headings—are likely to be most relevant to user queries because nearly all of the words in main headings are also in user queries. Bibliographic records retrieved through the second keyword approach, that is, keyword searches of subdivided headings, are also likely to be relevant to user queries. However, the subdivided headings are probably going to contain several additional words in main headings and/or subdivisions that are not found in the original query. Keyword approaches begin with controlled vocabulary fields of bibliographic records because this vocabulary is assigned by library catalogers to represent the subject matter of library materials.

Should keyword search approaches fail to produce retrievals, systems can apply truncation or suffix removal to query words to effect matches. However, the same procedures used to truncate or remove suffixes from query words must be applied to controlled vocabulary terms. Such procedures may require systems to double post words and subject headings in bibliographic records. With respect to truncation, systems could add entries for exact words and truncated word stems to keyword indexes. With respect to suffix removal, systems could generate and add normalized forms of subject headings and references minus suffixes to the alphabetical index of subject headings; however, normalized forms would not be displayed to public catalog users during retrieval.

Systems could also be programmed to detect multiple-word queries beginning with two words that exactly match a two-word *see* reference in LCSH-mr. They could substitute the authorized heading in place of the *see* reference before conducting a keyword search for the query. The substitution would increase the chances of retrieving bibliographic records in a keyword search for such queries because the authorized heading and words in the heading are more likely to be posted in the catalog than the *see* reference.

When systems enlist keyword searching approaches, they need a feedback capability to enable users to choose relevant subject headings from retrieved bibliographic records. The system would then use the heading(s) to search for additional records. Effective feedback capabilities are difficult to design and implement because relevant headings found in retrieved citations are not always combined using one Boolean operator. Chapter 12 discusses feedback capabilities in greater detail.

Recommendations for effecting matches of user queries with the catalog's controlled vocabulary will not yield relevant retrievals for every user query. Some queries do not contain enough information to get the system started in the right direction. Some queries do not adequately express the topics users have in mind. Other queries may produce more satisfactory retrievals in magazine indexes than in library cataloging databases. The benefit of recommended search approaches is to place the responsibility of determining which approach produces useful results on the system rather than on the user.

What distinguishes queries covered in this chapter from those covered in the preceding one is that matching headings are not always satisfactory for expressing users' topics of interest. This chapter presents data and analyses to support recommendations for the online catalog's choice of subject searching approaches to user queries for topical subjects. Systems respond with an approach based on system-identifiable characteristics such as the number of words in queries and the extent to which they match the catalog's controlled vocabulary and produce retrievals. The system-selected approach should place users in the situation where they have a choice of relevant subject headings or references to pursue or retrieve bibliographic records that describe their topics of interest and bear relevant subject headings they can use to further the search.

10

Other Queries Not Likely to Succeed

10.1 Introduction

This chapter takes a look at the one remaining single-element category of legitimate subject queries—queries consisting wholly of personal-name elements. It also examines the three multiple-element categories of legitimate subject queries consisting of combinations of name and topical-subject elements.

Queries for personal names rank second behind queries for topical subjects in terms of frequency of occurrence in subject searches. Less than 1% of queries consist of personal-name and topical-subject elements. Only one query containing three elements for personal names, geographic names, and topical subject occurs in the sample of transaction log data under consideration here, and it is added to the multiple-element combination for personal names and topical subjects. Topical-subject–geographic-name combinations are more common (6.4%) than single-element queries for geographic names (4.7%).

LCNAF, rather than LCSH-mr, is the primary source of authorized headings for names. Thus, single controlled vocabulary terms that are satisfactory expressions of user queries for personal names and combinations of personal names and topical-subject elements should come from the authorized headings in name authority records instead of subject authority records. However, few user queries containing personal-name elements match LCNAF headings and references because users are unable to duplicate the structure and content of these terms. This chapter discusses how online systems can nonetheless make useful responses to such queries.

Users who enter queries for combinations of geographic names and topical subjects also find it difficult to match their terms with controlled vocabulary terms that fully express their topics of interest for a different reason: the order of elements in controlled vocabulary terms is so unpredictable. This chapter recommends several subject searching approaches impervious to word order that would best serve users entering these queries.

Table 10.1
Fact Sheet for Personal Name Queries

Summary data	Total	SULIRS	ORION	LS/2000
Searches				
No. of searches	163.0	72.0	28.0	63.0
No. of access points	387.0	141.0	53.0	193.0
Avg. no. of access points per search	2.4	2.0	1.9	3.1
Maximum no. of access points in a search	16.0	12.0	8.0	16.0
Initial access points				
Avg. no. of words per access point	1.8	1.8	1.7	1.8
Maximum no. of words in an access point	5.0	5.0	4.0	4.0
Retrievals				
Avg. no. of retrievals per access point	N/A	82.5[a]	0.7[b]	N/A
Percentage of access points with zero retrievals	N/A	18.1	89.3	N/A
Percentage of access points with retrievals > 999	N/A	1.4	0.0	N/A
Low-posted searches				
Avg. no. of words in access points with zero retrievals	N/A	1.8	2.0	N/A
Avg. no. of access points in searches where initial access point has zero retrievals	N/A	2.0	2.0	N/A

[a]Number of bibliographic records retrieved. This is an estimate based on substituting 3,000 retrievals for the 99,999 retrievals that is written to logs when the number of retrievals is about 1,000.
[b]Number of assigned subject headings retrieved.

10.2 Queries for Personal Names

10.2.1 Subject Searches and Initial Access Points

Table 10.1 is a fact sheet with details about the total of 163 searches beginning with an access point consisting wholly of elements for personal names.

ORION contributes the fewest number of names (28) because users must enter personal-name queries specifying the system's "name" index. Subject terms specifying ORION's "subject" index are only written to the transaction logs used in this study. If ORION is being used correctly, personal-name elements should be excluded from search statements entered with the "browse subject" command. The names ORION users enter into the system are included in our discussion of personal-name queries, but these names have been incorrectly entered, and may be more likely to contain errors because users are using ORION incorrectly. Searching personal names in SULIRS and LS/2000 does not require use of commands, menu options, or indexes that are different from those for general subject searching.

The average number of words per personal-name query is the same as queries for topical subjects (1.8) (see Table 7.1). The longest name has five words: "dr. martin luther king jr." The average number of retrieved bibliographic records in SULIRS for personal names (82) is much smaller than the number of retrieved records in SULIRS searches for topical subjects (231) (see Table 7.1). ORION searchers should be browsing the "name" index for personal, corporate, and conference name access points; consequently, personal names entered using the "subject" index retrieve less than one assigned subject heading per search. Except for LS/2000, searches initiated with queries for personal names average almost one access point less than searches for topical subjects (see Table 7.1). The longest such search contains sixteen access points, begins with the surname "lovelace," and includes several access points revealing the user's interest in seventeenth century English poetry, for example, "cavalier poetry," "seventeenth century poetry," "english poetry," "english lit," and "cavalier oets [*sic*]."

10.2.2 Form of Name Entered

Subject searching for personal names is handled in two different ways in the three online catalogs from which transaction log data were obtained for this study. LS/2000 features a two-step approach that requires users to enter inverted forms of names, for example, "shakespeare, william," or "lincoln, abraham," or enter the surnames, for example, "copernicus" or "gauguin." LS/2000 responds with an alphabetical list of assigned subject headings in alphabetical proximity to the term entered. A user action to select a listed subject heading can be followed by display of bibliographic records assigned the selected heading. SULIRS and ORION perform keyword-in-record and keyword-in-subdivided-heading searches, respectively, in response to the personal names users enter; consequently, the order of elements in personal-name queries is not a concern. SULIRS features a one-step approach in which the system retrieves bibliographic records bearing the entered terms. When users enter surnames only using terms that are also given names, for example, "grant," "kelly," "thomas," the number of retrieved records can be quite high because SULIRS retrieves records bearing these words irrespective of their use as given names or surnames. Although ORION performs keyword searches, the system features a two-step approach in which the system responds with a list of assigned subject headings bearing the words in user queries. A user action to select a listed subject heading can be followed by display of bibliographic records assigned the selected heading.

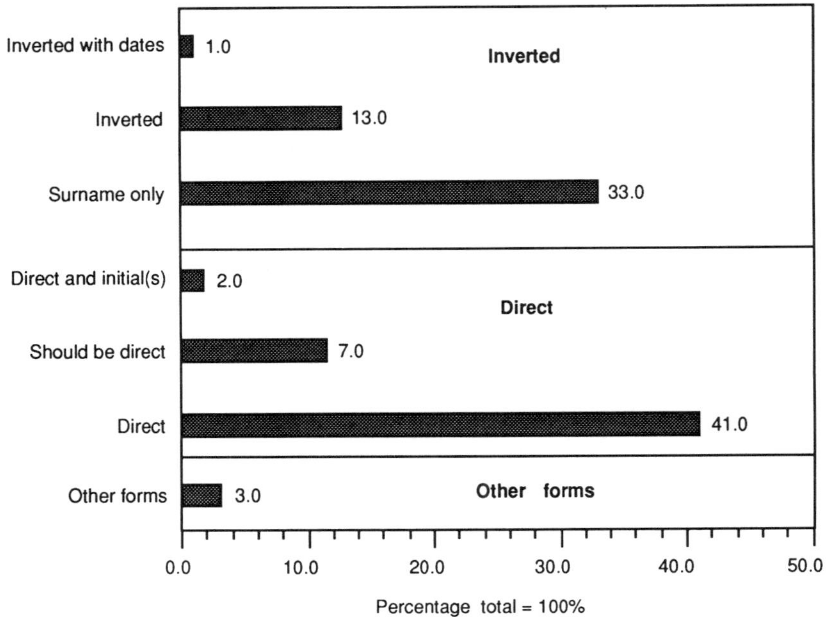

Figure 10.1
Form of personal name entered into SULIRS and ORION.

Figures 10.1 and 10.2 summarize the forms of names entered into the two online catalogs featuring keyword searching, SULIRS, and ORION, and the one online catalog featuring alphabetical searching, LS/2000.

It is reassuring that over 80% of queries for personal names entered into LS/2000 are entered correctly, that is, they are in inverted form or are direct forms of names for persons whose names are in direct form in authorized headings. In SULIRS and ORION, where order of elements in personal-name queries is not a concern because of keyword retrieval capabilities, queries are divided almost equally into direct and indirect form categories.

The entry of surnames and direct and indirect forms of names are frequently entered forms of names. About 5% of personal names entered by online catalog users are in and should be in direct form. Examples are "aristotle," "black elk," "ovid," and "el greco." Only one personal name is accompanied by dates, that is, "bach alexander 1813–1893." The dates are correct. Two names contain initials, for example, "abrahams r d."

A discussion of the seven names placed in the "other forms" category is interesting. One name consists only of initials, that is, "fdr." LCNAF provides a *see* reference under these initials to direct users to the authorized form of name. The given name "vincent" is entered in a search where the user is probably interested in the

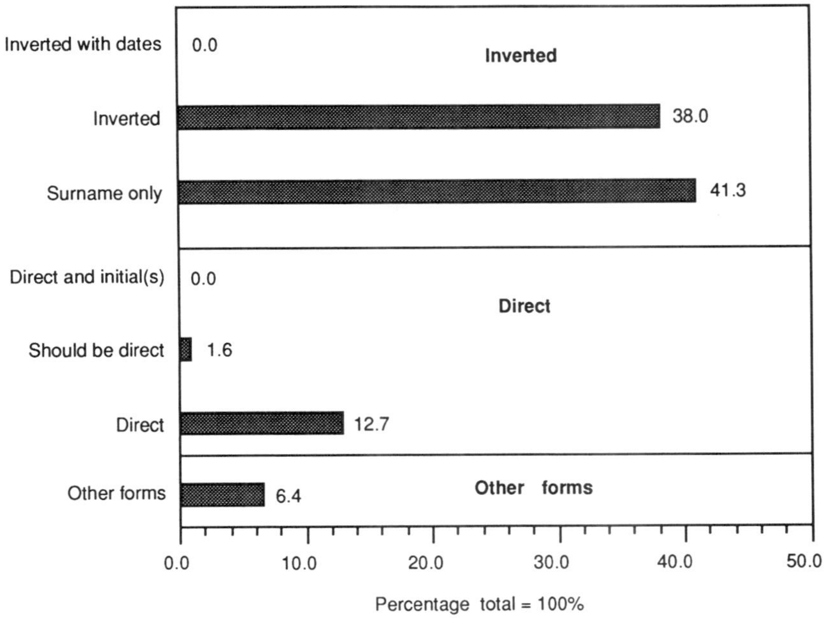

Figure 10.2
Form of personal name entered into LS/2000.

artist "Vincent van Gogh." Name access points connected with the Boolean "and" operator come from LS/2000, which does not have an explicit "and" operator: "nietzche and kierkegard" and "sacco and vanzetti." Searches in the LCNAF and several online catalogs fail to verify "n scribner richard." A *see* reference would have helped the user entering "le roi soliel" find information on the French king Louis XIV. The user needs to enter the surname "bruegel" to find a shelf to browse for "the large red bruegel book."

10.2.3 Best-Match Categorization

Comparing user queries for personal names with authorized headings and references in LCSH-mr produces few satisfactory matches because LCNAF, rather than LCSH-mr, is the authoritative source for name headings. Surprisingly, there are a few instances when partial matches of LCSH-mr headings and references would satisfy searchers. Examples are queries for "goya," "joyce,j," "hitler," "sacco," and several queries beginning with "shakespeare." Authority records exist for these individuals in LCSH-mr. The subject authority record for "Shakespeare, William,

1564–1616" serves as the pattern heading for individual literary authors. The personal name "sacco" is the first word in the topical-subject heading "Sacco–Vanzetti case."

In the best-match categorization, we match user queries with LCNAF headings and references. If no match is made, we search several online catalogs, including OCLC's Online Union Catalog, SULIRS, LCS, LS/2000, and MIRLYN to verify personal-name queries. Name authority records are not available for many personal names; however, library catalogers can formulate assigned subject headings for these names by following rules and guidelines in AACR2 and previous LC cataloging. Figure 10.3 gives best-match categories for user queries consisting wholly of elements for personal names.

Two categories account for more than 80% of best-match categorizations: (1) partial matches of LCNAF headings or references or an assigned subject heading, and (2) combinations of categories. The partial-match category can be further divided into three subcategories: (1) first two words (11.7%), (2) first word (30.1%), and (3) word(s) embedded in LCNAF or assigned subject headings (4.3%). When searchers match the first two words of an assigned heading, they are entering an inverted name with proper punctuation. Examples are "poe, edgar" and "wittgenstein, ludwig"; the matching assigned headings bear a longer name and/or date(s). When searchers match the initial word of an assigned heading, they are entering a

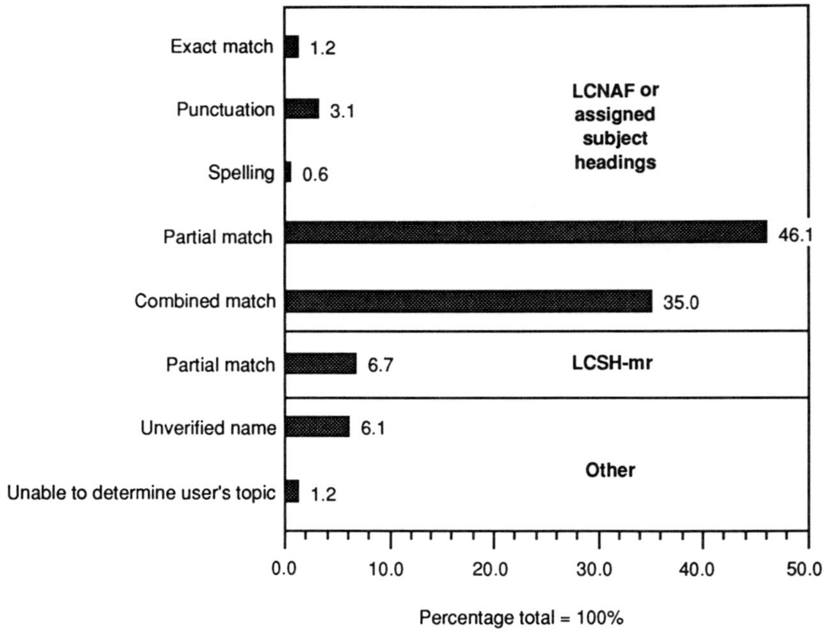

Figure 10.3
Best-match categorization of queries for personal names.

surname used in the catalog. Examples are "pollock," "vatter," and "lovelace." When searchers match words embedded in LCNAF or assigned subject headings, they are entering names in direct form and prefacing names with titles. Examples are "senator lloyd bentsen," "sir lawrence olivier," and "lady jane grey."

The second-largest percentage (35.0%) of queries for personal names requires more than one category to effect a match. Although over a dozen different category combinations occur, three different combinations account for most queries:

1. Punctuation and first two words in a personal-name heading. Queries match the surname and given name of a longer personal-name heading that includes a comma between these two elements, and a middle initial, middle name, and/or date. Examples are "picasso pablo," "metz william," and "morisot berthe."
2. Punctuation and two words embedded in a personal-name heading. Queries match inverted personal-name headings bearing a comma in between surname and given name and date(s). Examples are "christina rossetti," "richard pryor," and "ernest hemingway."
3. Spelling and partial match of a personal-name heading. Queries are various partial matches of personal-name headings after spelling is corrected. Examples are "rene margrite" and "farakan louis."

Only two personal names entered by users are exact matches of personal-name headings, that is, "puig, manuel," and "aristotle." When users enter exact matches of personal-name headings minus punctuation, they are matching authorized headings in LCNAF that do not have dates; examples are "bellow saul" and "sobell morton." Ten names (6.1%) could not be verified in LCNAF or several online catalog databases.

10.3 Queries for Personal Names with Topical Subjects

Only thirteen initial access points are composed of elements for personal names and topical subjects. Examples are "delacroix and colr [*sic*]," "the life of william faulkner," "paintings of pollock," and "architect irving gill." Determining what subject-searching approach successfully produces retrievals for these queries gives clues for handling user queries for personal names generally.

The one query containing elements for personal names, geographic names, and topical subjects, "greek mythology's influence on shakespeare," is added in this category for analysis. Thus, the fact sheet for the personal-name–topical-subject combination gives details for a total of fourteen initial access points (Table 10.2).

Most of these queries are entered into SULIRS, in which the average number of access points and words per access point exceeds these numbers for subject searches generally (see Table 6.1). The longest search of this type is entered into SULIRS; it begins with the query "clarence darrow's relegious [*sic*] views." Almost every access

Table 10.2
Fact Sheet for Initial Access Points Consisting of Personal Names and Topical Subjects

Summary data	Total	SULIRS	ORION	LS/2000
Searches				
No. of searches	14.0	9.0	3.0	2.0
No. of access points	49.0	43.0	4.0	2.0
Avg. no. of access points per search	3.5	4.8	1.3	1.0
Maximum no. of access points in a search	13.0	13.0	2.0	1.0
Initial access points				
Avg. no. of words per access point	3.3	3.1	3.0	4.5
Maximum no. of words in an access point	5.0	5.0	4.0	5.0
Retrievals				
Avg. no. of retrievals per access point	N/A	11.3[a]	0.7[b]	N/A
Percentage of access points with zero retrievals	N/A	55.6	66.7	N/A
Percentage of access points with retrievals > 999	N/A	0.0	0.0	N/A
Low-posted searches				
Avg. no. of words in access points with zero retrievals	N/A	3.8	2.5	N/A
Avg. no. of access points in searches where initial access point has zero retrievals	N/A	6.8	1.5	N/A

[a]Number of bibliographic records retrieved.
[b]Number of assigned subject headings retrieved.

point in this search contains elements for personal names and topical subjects, for example, "clarence darrow and religion," "darrow and religion," "darrow and his religious beliefs," and "darrow and the scopes trial." The user enters the name "darrow" and retrieves nine bibliographic records but does not seem to be satisfied with these records because the search continues. The only result that would satisfy this user might be titles bearing elements for both personal names (e.g., "darrow") and topical subjects (e.g., "religious views"). Such a result would seemingly convince the user that the item deals with Clarence Darrow's religious views.

Seven of twelve queries result in zero retrievals in SULIRS and ORION. When initial access points in SULIRS searches produce zero retrievals, searches average almost seven access points. A discussion of retrievals in ORION is not worthwhile because the system requires users to enter subject queries for personal names using a different command and index than are used for subject searches generally.

The best-match categorization should provide more useful results than the original-match categorization because the former takes LCNAF into account when effecting matches of user queries. In fact, neither LCSH-mr nor LCNAF is particularly helpful in effecting matches because matching terms express only one facet of multifaceted user queries. Examples of these queries and matching terms in LCSH-mr or LCNAF follow.

Query:	chaucer criticism
Type of partial match:	first word of LCNAF heading
Matching term:	Chaucer, Geoffrey, d. 1400
Query:	descartes future prediction
Type of partial match:	first word of LCNAF heading
Matching term:	Descartes, René, 1596–1650
Query:	paintings of pollock
Type of match:	exact LCSH-mr reference
Matching term:	Paintings, *see* Painting
Query:	religion tolstoy
Type of match:	exact LCSH-mr heading
Matching term:	Religion
Query:	themes and fnt shakespeare
Type of partial match:	first word of complex *see* reference
Matching term:	Themes, motives, etc.

When the initial query word is a topical subject, it typically matches a topical-subject heading or reference in LCSH-mr that expresses the topical-subject element of users' queries. An example is "religion tolstoy" in which the topical subject, "religion," satisfies the topical-subject element of the query; however, records retrieved bearing the LCSH-mr "Religion" will be too general because they do not address the user's interest in Tolstoy. When the initial query word is the surname of a personal name, it typically matches a surname in an LCNAF heading that expresses the personal-name element of users' queries. An example is "chaucer criticism" in which the LCNAF heading beginning with the name "Chaucer" satisfies the personal-name element of the query; however, the user may not be satisfied with records retrieved with this heading until one that mentions criticism of Chaucer's works appears.

When surnames are the initial words in access points, the alphabetical approach helps users find an appropriate assigned heading for the name, then gives them the opportunity to browse retrieved records or subdivided headings to find ones that satisfy the topical-subject element of the query. Keyword searches of subdivided headings or of all subject-rich fields of bibliographic records are promising approaches when users precede personal-name elements with elements for topical subjects. It is difficult, however, for online systems to distinguish between the individual elements in user queries without obtaining this information from users explicitly.

10.4 System Requirements for Personal Name Searching

The content and structure of assigned subject headings for personal names must be considered when determining how to improve the performance of user queries for personal names and for combinations of personal names and other elements.

Personal-name headings come from the assigned subject headings in libraries' bibliographic records. Catalogers establish these headings by following AACR2 rules and guidelines and previous LC practice. They refer to LCNAF to verify personal names. References are generated from LCNAF records for names used in libraries' bibliographic records. Catalogers also refer to the *Subject cataloging manual* to add subdivisions to personal-name headings. The results are single assigned subject headings bearing elements for personal names, topical subjects, and geographic names. The order of elements, when applicable, in such headings is: (1) surname, (2) given name or initial, (3) a middle name or initial, (4) one or more dates, (5) topical subdivisions, and (6) geographic subdivisions. Subdivisions appended to personal-name headings are usually for topical subjects; however, several subdivisions under names of persons authorize use of geographic subdivisions (Library of Congress 1990, H1110).

As we have seen, users rarely express all six elements of personal-name headings in their queries. Furthermore, when two or more elements are included, users rarely enter elements in the sequence prescribed by personal-name headings. When searching for user queries bearing personal-name elements, systems need information about the particular elements included in queries to distinguish personal-name elements from topical-subject elements. Systems could then accommodate the rigid structure of personal-name headings by searching for as many elements as needed to provide useful retrievals.

Systems need answers to questions about the presence of elements for personal names in user queries and the identity of the individual elements in such queries. To obtain answers, systems can require users to enter personal-name searches with a command that is different from the command used for entering topical subjects. ORION does just that. As we have seen, users will enter queries containing personal-name elements using the incorrect command.

Another approach combines menu and form-filling modes. Windows could be substituted in place of menus. The initial menu gives users a choice of conducting known-item or subject searches. Choosing the latter, users are presented with a second menu (or window) offering a choice of subject searches for named persons or topics. Users who then conduct a search for named persons are presented with a simple form asking them the person's surname, given name or initial, and topic. Instead of a form, systems could elicit these three criteria from users in a successive manner, that is, asking one question, obtaining the answer, recording it, then asking the second question, obtaining the answer, recording it, then asking the third question, and so on. How systems manipulate the information users give them is geared toward the structure of assigned subject headings for personal names and the system's ability to produce retrievals for certain combinations of elements.

Separating searches for topical subjects from those for personal names requires users to distinguish between queries for "what" and "who." SCM:SH identifies four simple categories of personal-name headings: names of persons, families, clans, and named Biblical characters. Public catalog users would search for names of persons most frequently. A large proportion of queries entered into online catalogs at institutions with genealogical collections would be family and clan names. A short definition of names included in the separate subject search option for personal names could be added to the online help capability of library catalogs.

Table 10.3 lists three subject searching approaches that systems can enlist for personal-name queries. The approaches systems undertake depend on the elements users offer. Systems present results for only those approaches that produce postings in the library catalog.

Personal-name headings are given USMARC tag 600 in bibliographic records; references are given USMARC tag 400 in authority records. Headings and references bearing these tags would compose the keyword-in-subdivided-heading and alphabetical indexes to support subject searching for personal names in online catalogs.

At the most, systems need three elements—last names, first names, and topics—to perform keyword searches of single subdivided headings. If such searches yield zero retrievals, systems should drop first names and perform keyword-in-subdivided-heading searches for the remaining two elements. Keyword searches of

Table 10.3
Sequence of Subject Searching Approaches for Personal Names

	Available elements			
Approach	Last name	First name	Middle name	Topic
Queries with topics				
1 Keyword-in-subdivided-heading	X	X		X
2 Keyword-in-subdivided-heading	X			X
3 Keyword-in-record	X	X		X
4 Keyword-in-record	X			X
Queries without or omitting topics				
5 Alphabetical	X	X	X	
6 Alphabetical	X	X		
7 Alphabetical	X			

all subject-rich fields of bibliographic records may yield retrievals for queries that are combinations of personal names and topics. If keyword approaches fail to produce retrievals, systems should drop the topic element and perform an alphabetical search using as many name elements as match assigned subject headings and references in the catalog.

For example, the three elements "faulkner" (surname), "william" (given name), and "life of" (topic), would probably not successfully retrieve single assigned subject headings bearing these words, that is, approaches 1 and 2, because the topic element is not used in subdivisions under subject headings for personal names. Keyword-in-record approaches may yield bibliographic records bearing the topic element and name element(s) because titles and/or note fields may contain the topic element, "life." Retrieved records may have the assigned subject heading "Faulkner, William, 1897–1962--Biography." A feedback capability is recommended for keyword-in-record approaches so that users can find additional information using relevant headings in retrieved records. If users are not satisfied with the results, systems should continue with the alphabetical approach but omit the topical element of the query to effect a match of a personal-name subject heading.

When users do not enter a topic element, the alphabetical approach is recommended. Systems respond with an alphabetical list of assigned subject headings for personal names in the alphabetical neighborhood of the entered name. Alphabetical lists are limited to the name subfields of personal-name subject headings, that is, subfields $a, $q, $b, $c, and $d. To reduce the amount of information on screens, subject headings subdivided by topical or geographic subdivisions should be excluded. Alphabetical indexes of personal-name subject headings that are limited to name subfields are sufficient to help users find and verify the name they are looking for. Once users select a main heading, systems can then display the topical and geographic subdivisions appended to it. The exact approach, discussed in Chapter 11, would give users access to topical and geographic subdivisions.

When users enter a surname only, systems also respond with the alphabetical approach. Alphabetical lists are also the last resort when systems are unable to find matches of two or more query elements. For example, a query with two elements "delacroix" (surname) and "colr [*sic*]" (topic) may not retrieve single headings or bibliographic records, but an alphabetical search for the surname "delacroix" will probably place the user at a location in the index from which to browse forward to find the assigned subject heading "Delacroix, Eugène, 1798–1863." Selecting this heading will give the opportunity to display assigned headings with subdivisions such as "Criticism and interpretation" or "Catalogues raisonnés," which may be appropriate to this topic.

The alphabetical approach recommended here is similar to approaches described by other researchers who have studied personal name queries (Dickson 1984, 36; Taylor 1984, 15). They recommend that systems first find assigned headings that match surnames and given names in user queries. If they fail, systems then look for assigned headings that match surnames and the first letter of given names. Finally, systems look for assigned headings that match the surnames users enter.

Previous studies also report that users do not enter inverted forms of names. Researchers recommend an approach that flips names when queries fail to produce retrievals (Dickson 1984, 36; Taylor 1984, 14). These approaches demonstrate that systems can be programmed to accommodate the different forms of personal-name queries users enter and effect matches of controlled vocabulary terms.

Subject searches containing personal-name elements are 11.8% of the queries entered by SULIRS, ORION, and LS/2000 searchers in our sample. This percentage increases to 14.8% when ORION queries are ignored because ORION searchers used an incorrect search command. This means that about one in seven queries is a subject search for a personal name. On their own, online systems cannot distinguish between query terms that are topical subjects and terms that are personal names. Systems need to enlist users' assistance to identify the various elements of personal-name queries. They can then make useful responses to user queries even though the structure of controlled vocabulary terms and user queries differ.

10.5 Queries for Geographic Names with Topical Subjects

10.5.1 Subject Searches and Initial Access Points

Combinations of geographic names and topical subjects are 6.4% of initial access points. Table 10.4 is a fact sheet with details about the total of ninety-six searches beginning with an access point consisting of elements for geographic names and topical subjects.

Searches bearing elements for both geographic names and topical subjects average between three and four access points. Subject searches generally consist of three access points (see Table 6.1). Access points bearing both elements average almost one word more than access points for these elements alone (see Tables 7.1 and 8.1). Most access points contain at least two words, that is, a geographic name and topical subject consisting of one word each. Examples are "japanese art," "chinese reforms," "israel conflict," and "singapore health." Some are much longer like "united states military bases abroad," "psychiatric clinics of north america," and "coins of the united states in 1943." The latter is the longest query of this type.

The longest search beginning with both elements comes from ORION and contains nineteen subject access points. It begins with the one-word query "spanish" and contains several access points that express the user's interest in learning Spanish, for example, "spanish and language," "spanish and language and tape," "spanish and learn," and "language and spanish and program." The initial access point in this longest search is difficult to characterize because it could refer to the Spanish language, Spanish people, or the many aspects of Spanish culture. Queries similar to this one are "afro-american" and "oorrientalism [*sic*]."

Table 10.4
Fact Sheet for Initial Access Points Consisting of Geographic Names and Topical Subjects

Summary data	Total	SULIRS	ORION	LS/2000
Searches				
No. of searches	96.0	31.0	60.0	5.0
No. of access points	322.0	75.0	230.0	17.0
Avg. no. of access points per search	3.4	2.4	3.8	3.4
Maximum no. of access points in a search	19.0	8.0	19.0	7.0
Initial access points				
Avg. no. of words per access point	2.8	2.9	2.8	2.4
Maximum no. of words in an access point	10.0	7.0	10.0	5.0
Retrievals				
No. of retrievals per access point	N/A	119.6[a]	107.8[b]	N/A
Percentage of access points with zero retrievals	N/A	35.5	33.3	N/A
No. of access points with retrievals > 999	N/A	3.2	1.7	N/A
Low-posted searches				
Avg. no. of words in access points with zero retrievals	N/A	3.0	3.3	N/A
Avg. no. of access points in searches where initial access point has zero retrievals	N/A	3.5	3.6	N/A

[a]Number of bibliographic records retrieved. This is an estimate based on substituting 3,000 retrievals for the 99,999 retrievals that is written to logs when number of retrievals is about 1,000.
[b]Number of assigned subject headings retrieved.

Average numbers of retrievals in SULIRS and ORION are much lower than the numbers obtained in searches for each element alone in these systems (see Tables 7.1 and 8.1). One-third of these access points fail to produce retrievals in SULIRS and ORION. High-posted searches are not typical for queries of this type.

10.5.2 Original-Match Categorization

The results of the original-match categorization of queries consisting of elements for geographic names and topical subjects are not encouraging because of the preponderance of partial matches (Figure 10.4).

Only four queries exactly match an LCSH-mr heading. These queries are "japanese art," "italian language," "paleosiberian languages," and "new york stock

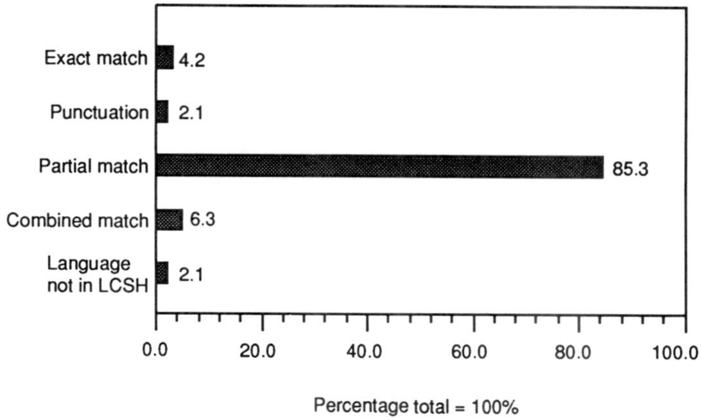

Figure 10.4
Original-match categorization of queries for geographic names and topical subjects.

exchange." National or geographic adjectives are used in all four terms. Two ORION users enter queries that match all but the punctuation in LCSH-mr. These are the queries "indians literature" and "egypt history" that match all but the punctuation in the subdivided reference "Indians--Literature" and heading "Egypt--History." The two queries matching all but the qualifier in the LCSH-mr reference "Indian music (American Indian)" and heading "Syrian Temple (Rome, Italy)" appear to be satisfactory because of the ethnic and national adjectives in the matching terms.

Partial matches account for 85.3% of queries. Individual percentages for the five partial-match subcategories are: (1) minus qualifiers (2.1%), (2) first two words (26.0%), (3) first word and three-letter stem of second word (3.1%), (4) first word (53.1%), and (5) one word embedded in LCSH-mr (1.0%).

The largest percentage (53.1%) of partial matches is for first-word matches. Unfortunately, many of these matches are too general or unsatisfactory because the matching word expresses only the geographic or topical subject element of the query. Matches of the former are "Romania" in the query "romania religion," "Brazil" in "brazil and politics," and "Italy" in "italy architecture." Matches of the former include matches of a longer LCSH-mr heading or reference that has nothing to do with the user's query. Examples are "Southern Africa" in the query "southern literature" and "Greek abbreviations" in the query "greek drama characters." The same things happen when the first query word is the topical subject of the query. Examples are "Adoption" in the query "adoption brazil," "Economy" in "economy africa," and "Upper air temperature" in "upper education in spain."

Another partial-match subcategory with a large percentage is the first two words in an LCSH-mr heading or reference. Most matches are two-word, adjectival, topical-subject headings, or two-word geographic names. The matching heading, however, expresses only one facet of a multifaceted query. Examples are "Psychiatric clinics" in the query "psychiatric clinics of north america," "Soviet Union" in "soviet union military," and "Air force chaplains" in "air force bases american."

A few two-word queries match the first two words of an LCSH-mr heading or reference that is a satisfactory expression of user queries or that is in alphabetical proximity to the desired term in an alphabetical index of subject headings. Examples are the queries "vietnamese conflict," "korean war," and "afro-american." These are close matches of the topical-subject headings "Vietnamese Conflict, 1961–1975," "Korean War, 1950–1953," and several headings beginning with the term "Afro-american."

All three queries that match the first word and three-letter stem of the second word in an LCSH-mr heading or reference have nothing to do with the matched LCSH-mr. The queries and matching LCSH-mr are "chinese reforms" and "Chinese reference books," "japanese automobile honda" and "Japanese authors," and "french history chronology" and "French historical drama."

10.5.3 Best-Match Categorization

When users enter queries bearing elements for geographic names and topical subjects, the best match of their query and the catalog's controlled vocabulary could be the following:

- A topical-subject heading or reference in the form of an ethnic, national, or geographic adjectival heading in direct form (USMARC tags 650 or 450), for example, "French historical drama," "Jewish etiquette," and "Turkish wit and humor."
- A topical-subject heading or reference in the form of an ethnic, national, or geographic adjectival heading in inverted form (USMARC tags 650 or 450), for example, "Folk art, Jewish," "Manuscripts, Old Norse," and "Sculpture, Greek."
- A topical-subject heading with a geographic subdivision (USMARC tag 650 and subfield $z), for example, "Fishing--Wyoming," "Landforms--Ohio," and "Weddings--Guatemala."
- A geographic name with topical subdivision (USMARC tag 651 and subfield $x), for example, "Egypt--History," "Nepal--Description and travel," and "Romania--Religion."

The best match of user queries is not restricted to fields specifically reserved for geographic names, that is, USMARC tag 651. For this reason, subject searches for query combinations of geographic names and topical subjects have to include topical-subject headings and references, that is, MARC tags 650 and 450. They also have to be impervious to word order because users cannot be expected to know which of the four forms of headings described above will be used for the subject they have in mind. Users also cannot be expected to know whether the ethnic, national, or geographic element in their query is expressed as an adjective, for example, "Egyptian history," "Swiss universities," or noun, for example, "Egypt--History," "Universities and colleges--Switzerland."

10.5.4 System Requirements for Searching Queries with Topical-Subject and Geographic Elements

The sequence of subject searching approaches recommended for topical subjects generally should be applied to query combinations for geographic names and topical subjects. Systems would first look for exact matches of assigned subject headings or LCSH-mr references, then try to effect exact matches using normalized headings that eliminate punctuation, stopwords, qualifiers, and are insensitive to word order. Examples of matches are:

Query:	greek sculpture
Type of match:	normalized form of LCSH-mr heading minus punctuation, disregarding word order
Matching term:	Sculpture, Greek
Query:	indian music
Type of match:	normalized form of LCSH-mr reference minus punctuation and qualifier
Matching term:	Indian music (American Indians), *see* Indians--Music
Query:	romania religion
Type of match:	normalized form of assigned subject heading minus punctuation
Matching term:	Romania--Religion
Query:	titles of nobility and honor spain
Type of match:	normalized form of assigned subject heading minus punctuation, disregarding stopwords
Matching term:	Titles of honor and nobility--Spain

Systems would then respond to queries matching the same characters in a longer assigned subject heading or LCSH-mr reference with the alphabetical approach. Examples of queries for which systems would produce an alphabetical index of subject headings containing terms desired by users are given below, along with partially matched controlled vocabulary terms.

Query	*Longer matching headings or reference*
afro-american	Headings and references beginning with "Afro-american"
korean war	Korean War, 1950–1953
spanish	Headings and references beginning with "Spanish"

Remaining user-entered terms bearing elements for geographic names and topical subjects would be submitted to keyword searches in the following sequence: (1) keyword-in-main-heading, (2) keyword-in-subdivided-heading, (3) title keyword, (4) keyword in subject-heading fields, and (5) keyword-in-record matches. To detect misspellings, systems can first submit these queries to the last keyword approach and prompt users to check and correct the spelling of words failing to produce retrievals. Queries producing retrievals in keyword-in-main-heading searches and matching LCSH-mr headings and references follow.

Queries	*LCSH-mr headings*
battle of stalingrad	Stalingrad, Battle of, 1942–1943; Stalingrad, Battle of, 1942–1943, in literature
battle of the nile	Nile, Battle of the, 1798
irish humor	Irish wit and humor; Irish wit and humor, Pictorial
march on washington	March on Washington for Jobs and Freedom, 1963
southern literature	Southern states in literature

Examples of queries that are likely to produce retrievals in response to keyword-in-subdivided-heading searches are:

Queries	*Single subdivided headings*
australia retail	Retail trade--Australia
brazil and politics	Brazil--Politics and government
great britain stuarts	Great Britain--History--Early Stuarts, 1603–1649; Great Britain--History--Stuarts, 1603–1714
human experimentation and germany	Human experimentation in medicine--Germany; Human experimentation in psychology--Germany
singapore health	Many headings beginning with Public health subdivided by Singapore
southern literature	American literature--Southern states
soviet union military	Soviet Union--History, Military
travel and nepal	Nepal--Description and travel

Title keyword searches would retrieve relevant bibliographic records for several queries. A feedback capability is needed to enable users to choose relevant subject headings from retrieved bibliographic records. They could use such headings to retrieve additional records. Feedback capabilities need to enlist the assistance of users to determine whether subject headings are satisfactory expressions of their topics of interest or must be used with other headings or criteria. Examples of queries that produce relevant retrievals and subject headings in title keyword searches are:

Query	*Relevant headings in retrieved records*
alaska natives	Eskimos--Alaska; Aleuts; Indians of North America--Alaska
chinese culture	China--Civilization
disabled united states	Handicapped--United States
economy africa	Africa--Economic conditions; Africa--Foreign economic relations
ussr government	Soviet Union--Politics and government

The various keyword search approaches do not always give useful results. Examples of queries for which keyword searches are ineffective are given below, along with more effective searching strategies.

Query	*Keyword results/other strategy*
asian americans lifestyle and income	Zero retrievals. Find subdivisions under "Asian americans" expressing "lifestyle" or "income" facets.

coins of the united states in 1943	Zero retrievals. Rephrase query and leave out "1943."
french history chronology	Zero retrievals. Rephrase query using "france" instead of "french."
french revolution varenes	Zero retrievals. Correct spelling and rephrase query using "france."
greek drama characters	Zero retrievals. Find subdivisions under "Greek drama" expressing "characters" facet.
illinois power	"Black power--Illinois" is not relevant to the user's interest in Illinois utilities. Rephrase query.
japanese automobile honda	Zero retrievals. Rephrase query and leave out "japanese."
swiss universities	Zero retrievals. Rephrase query using "switzerland" instead of "swiss."

Several capabilities developed for the experimental Okapi system could produce retrievals for these difficult queries. Walker and Jones (1987, 68) treat the adjectives for selected proper names as equivalent terms. For example, "switzerland" and "swiss" retrieve the same bibliographic records. This technique could have helped users find relevant records for two of the queries listed above. Okapi's spelling correction algorithm could have corrected the misspelling of "Varennes" (Walker & Jones 1987, 74) and searched "france" along with "french." This system's combinatorial approach does not require every word in user queries to be present in retrieved bibliographic records. This approach may be the most fruitful for retrieving relevant bibliographic records for several queries instead of requiring that users determine on their own which words to leave out of rephrased queries (Walker & Jones 1987, 77–83).

10.6 Synthesis and Summary

This chapter describes matching user queries with the catalog's controlled vocabulary for the following elements: (1) personal names, (2) personal names and topical subjects, and (3) geographic names and topical subjects. Few matching controlled vocabulary terms express the topics users are seeking. Thus, much of the discussion is given to determining useful responses that online systems can give to these queries.

Rather different objectives underlie recommendations regarding searching approaches suited to queries bearing personal-name elements and queries bearing geographic and topical-subject elements. In personal-name queries, the system's objective is to elicit from users the identity of the individual elements. The system can then try to fulfill the user's request for both name and topical-subject elements. Failure to fulfill the request does not mean that the search has failed entirely. The system can restrict itself to the personal-name element(s). Finding the desired name may eventually lead users to a subdivided form of personal-name heading that expresses the topical-subject element of the query; however, the subdivided form for personal-name subject headings will probably use different terminology to express the topical-subject element than was used in the original query. With respect to query combinations of geographic names and topical subjects, systems need not elicit from users the identity of the individual query elements because the order of these elements is unpredictable. The system's objective is to apply subject searching capabilities to user queries that are impervious to word order to accommodate the unpredictable order of geographic name and topical-subject elements in assigned subject headings.

Online catalogs need a separate subject searching option for personal-name queries to enable the systems to distinguish such queries from queries for subjects generally. Systems also need to prompt users about the identity of the individual elements of personal-name queries so they can try to satisfy both name and topic elements. Three subject searching approaches are recommended for personal-name queries: (1) keyword-in-subdivided-heading, (2) keyword-in-record, and (3) alphabetical searches. The approaches systems undertake depend on the elements users offer and the use of these elements in the bibliographic database. Keyword searches are recommended for queries bearing the topic element(s). If they fail to produce retrievals, systems omit the topic element and enlist the alphabetical approach using as many name elements as match assigned subject headings and references in the catalog. The alphabetical approach is the sole approach recommended for queries containing only personal-name elements.

System requirements for handling user queries consisting of geographic name and topical-subject elements are the same as those for handling user queries consisting wholly of elements for topical subjects, geographic names, or corporate names. Systems look first for exact matches of assigned subject headings and LCSH-mr references and for normalized forms of these terms. The system response to exact matches is the exact approach. If an exact match is not made, systems try to find a partial match of the same characters in a user query as in a longer assigned subject heading or LCSH-mr reference. The system response to such partial matches is the alphabetical approach. If a partial match is not made, systems follow a sequence of keyword searches until retrievals are made: (1) keyword-in-main-heading, (2) keyword-in-subdivided-heading, (3) title keyword, (4) keyword in subject heading fields, and last, (5) keyword-in-record searches.

References

Dickson, Jean. (1984). An analysis of user errors in searching an online catalog. *Cataloging & Classification Quarterly, 4*, 3 (Spring), 19–38.

Library of Congress. (1990). *Subject Cataloging manual: Subject headings*. Washington, DC: Library of Congress.

Taylor, Arlene G. (1984). Authority files in online catalogs: An investigation of their value. *Cataloging & Classification Quarterly*, *4*, 3 (Spring), 1–17.

Walker, Stephen, & Jones, Richard M. (1987). *Improving subject retrieval in online catalogues: 1. Stemming, automatic spelling correction and cross-reference tables*. British Library Research Paper No. 24. London: British Library.

11

The Exact Approach to Subject Searching

11.1

Introduction

When public catalog users enter exact matches of the catalog's controlled vocabulary, online systems could respond with the alphabetical approach to subject searching. Unfortunately, the alphabetical approach is no longer capable of managing large numbers of subdivided forms of subject headings. Recent studies of online catalog searching demonstrate just how little perseverance searchers have when faced with large numbers of retrievals (Van Pulis & Ludy 1988; Wiberly & Daugherty 1988).

Several researchers have recognized the difficulty of displaying long lists of subdivided forms of headings to users and suggested methods for reducing such lists (Holley & Killheffer 1982, 130; Cochrane 1986, 62; Markey 1984, 112–113; and Chan 1986, 355–358). More recently, Massicotte (1988, 374) commented on the inadequacy of the alphabetical approach:

> The problem we are faced with is the undue display length of a browse list under a given search term. Scanning an alphabetically arranged list of indexed terms is simply not sufficient to assist the user. New character strings are added daily to the index, and indexes will continue to expand at an ever-increasing rate. This factor alone will eventually make browsing the alphabetical index less and less viable as a method of searching.

New browsing approaches must be invented. Such approaches must draw system users into the matched topic, provide a conceptual framework of the entire topic, and enable users to be selective about exploring its particular aspects.

This chapter describes such a new approach to subject searching—the exact approach. This new approach is merely a variation of the alphabetical approach to subject searching. We advocate the implementation of the exact approach in online catalogs as the system response to user-entered queries that are exact matches of the catalog's controlled vocabulary. The exact approach anticipates the user's selection of the exact match from an alphabetical list, and thus begins with a report of the results of such exact matches. The report includes a summary of subdivided forms of the matched subject heading, and, if available, options for browsing related terms and other information about the matched heading. The challenge here is to convey to users the range of available opportunities in a single screen.

User queries may be normalized matches of two or more controlled vocabulary terms or a combination of exact and normalized matches. Before the system responds with the exact approach, the user may be asked to make a choice among controlled vocabulary terms. The exact approach is also the system's response to the user's selection of a controlled vocabulary term from the alphabetical index of subject headings.

The exact approach can be implemented in existing online catalogs; however, without further developmental work, it would be limited in usefulness because only three broad categories could be constructed from the three different types of subject subdivisions used with subject headings. This chapter describes the editorial and developmental work efforts needed to fully implement the exact approach in online bibliographic systems.

11.2 Generating Entries for the Searchable Index

The searchable index for the exact approach contains entries for the exact forms and normalized forms of assigned subject headings from bibliographic records and *see* references from LCSH-mr records. Exact forms are controlled vocabulary terms bereft of capitalization, punctuation, and subfield codes. Normalized forms of headings and tracings have punctuation, stopwords, subfield codes, and main-heading qualifiers removed, and word order regularized. Separate entries are also made for one-word/two-word variations of hyphenated words and for possessive forms of nouns with and without the trailing "s." These various forms are added to the searchable index for the exact approach to improve the chances of matching user queries with controlled vocabulary terms in the catalog. Examples of exact and normalized forms for an assigned subject heading from a bibliographic record follow:

Assigned subject heading:	Arms and armor, Islamic
Exact form:	arms and armor islamic
Normalized form:	armor arms islamic
Assigned subject heading:	Autonomy (Psychology)
Exact form:	autonomy psychology
Normalized form:	autonomy
Assigned subject heading:	Cut-out craft
Exact forms:	cut out craft; cutout craft
Normalized forms:	craft cutout; craft cut out
Assigned subject heading:	Lundy's Lane, Battle of, 1814
Exact forms:	lundys lane battle of 1814; lundy lane battle of 1814
Normalized forms:	1814 battle lane lundys; 1814 battle lane lundy
Assigned subject heading:	Lexington (Ky.)

Exact form:	lexington ky
Normalized forms:	ky lexington; lexington
Assigned subject heading:	Library science $x Periodicals
Exact form:	library science periodicals
Normalized form:	library periodicals science

Normalization techniques are appropriate for the following controlled vocabulary terms: (1) topical-subject headings (USMARC tag 650), (2) *see from* tracings for topical subjects (USMARC tag 450), (3) subject headings for geographic names (USMARC tag 651), and (4) *see from* tracings for geographic names (USMARC tag 451). These techniques could also be applied to assigned subject headings and tracings for corporate names and uniform titles (USMARC tags 610, 410, 630, and 430); however, we are reluctant to generalize these normalization techniques to other access points because we encountered so few queries for corporate names and uniform titles in our study of a sample of the subject terms users enter into online catalogs. Additional research is needed to determine whether corporate names and uniform titles require a different set of normalization techniques.

Many online systems create a Local Subject Authority Record (LSAR) for every unique subject heading assigned to bibliographic records. A computer program generates normalized forms of the assigned subject headings and adds them to LSARs. Exact and normalized forms are placed in the searchable index for the exact approach accompanied by pointers referring to LSARs. LSARs themselves contain pointers to bibliographic records bearing the assigned subject heading in subject-heading fields (USMARC tags 6xx). It is not necessary to add exact and normalized forms to locally defined fields of LSARs; however, their presence in LSARs would speed catalog maintenance when subject headings or tracings are changed or deleted.

LCSH-mr records may contain *see from* tracings for between 7% and 10% of the subject headings in LSARs (see chapter 4). A computer program can add *see from* tracings for these subject headings from LCSH-mr records to LSARS. Normalization techniques can also be extended to *see from* tracings. For example, normalization techniques could add four normalized forms to LSARs for the two *see from* tracings in the LCSH-mr records for the authorized subject heading "Autonomy (Psychology)":

See from tracing:	Freedom (Psychology)
Exact form:	freedom psychology
Normalized form:	freedom
See from tracing:	Independence (Psychology)
Exact form:	independence psychology
Normalized form:	independence

Systems would never display normalized forms to public catalog users. Most normalized forms would not make sense because they are derived automatically by online systems and are missing punctuation, stopwords, and qualifiers, and their word order has been regularized.

In a searchable index, exact and normalized forms of subject headings and tracings are accompanied by pointers to the LSARs bearing the authorized form of the heading. For example, the pointer for the normalized form "autonomy" would refer to the LSAR for the authorized subject heading "Autonomy (Psychology)." This pointer would be different from the pointer for the exact form of the unqualified, authorized heading "Autonomy." The user query "autonomy" would match one exact form and one normalized form pointing to two different LSARs. In such a situation, online systems would present users with the following choice:

> Enter subject to search > autonomy
> Choose 1 of the 2 headings used in this catalog to express **autonomy:**
> 1. Autonomy
> 2. Autonomy (Psychology)
>
> Enter your choice >

Generating normalized forms of authorized headings and *see from* tracings increases the number of access points to authorized subject headings. For example, normalized forms double the number of access points for the authorized heading "Autonomy (Psychology)." One authorized heading and two *see from* tracings generate three exact and three normalized forms.

When user queries match normalized forms of *see from* tracings, the terminology of the authorized subject heading is likely to be different from user queries. Systems should inform users of the matching heading and give them the option to reject the heading if it is unsuitable. In the following example, the system has applied normalization techniques to the user query "independence in psychology" to effect a match of the exact form of the *see from* tracing "Independence (Psychology)." The system prompts the user about continuing the search based on the matched heading:

> Enter subject to search > independence in psychology
> Closest match pertinent to this subject is **Autonomy**.
> Press RETURN to continue searching for **Autonomy**.

In another example, the user enters "independence" and matches an exact form of a *see from* tracing and a normalized form of a *see from* tracing. The system again presents a choice of headings to the user:

> Enter subject to search > independence
> Choose 1 of the 2 headings used in this catalog to express **independence**:
> 1. Autonomy
> 2. Autonomy (Psychology)
>
> Enter your choice >

In both searches, users would benefit from scope notes that define the scope and coverage of these headings. Unfortunately, few subject headings (2.4%) have scope notes (see Table 2.1). Most of the time, users will have to choose subject headings and display bibliographic records to determine the scope and coverage of headings.

These situations are similar to the choice-of-headings situation that occurs when *see from* tracings refer users to two or more authorized subject headings used to express the topic. For example, the *see from* tracing "Boots and shoes" is given in three different subject authority records, that is, "Boots," "Footwear," and "Shoes." Users entering the query "boots and shoes" or variants of this *see from* tracing would be offered a choice:

Enter subject to search > boots and shoes
Choose 1 of the 3 headings used in this catalog to express **boots and shoes**:
1. Boots
2. Footwear
3. Shoes

Enter your choice >

Every unique assigned subject heading in a library's bibliographic database has its own LSAR. LSARs are made even for headings with multiple subdivisions, for example, "Automobiles--Motors--Maintenance and repair--Periodicals--Bibliography--Catalogs" and "Telecommunication--Switching systems--Design and construction--Data processing--Congresses." LCSH-mr contributes *see from* tracings and three types of related terms to LSARs. Exact and normalized forms of both authorized subject headings and *see from* tracings are system generated; such forms increase the number of access points to LSARs.

11.3 Preferring the Exact Approach to Alphabetical Browsing

Browsing the alphabetical subject heading index is rapidly becoming unfeasible in large bibliographic databases. A recent study of alphabetical searching in LCS demonstrates just how little browsing searchers do in an online catalog that features the alphabetical approach. About three-fourths of LCS searchers reported that they entered an exact match of a controlled vocabulary term in the catalog. Only one-eighth of these searchers reported that they browsed preceding or succeeding lists even though 90% of matched subject headings were followed by subdivided forms (Van Pulis & Ludy 1988, 529).

The LCS study tells us that the subdivided forms that most system users scan are those at the beginning of the alphabet. In Figure 11.1, subdivisions following the one-word query "weather" begin with "Abstracts" and end with "Bibliography." These are the only subdivided forms of main headings that most LCS users are browsing even though an additional thirty subdivided forms of this main heading are available. (Phrase headings are also listed in Figure 11.1 because LCS interfiles the different forms of headings in alphabetical lists.)

```
sub/weather

TBL/ TITLES-------------------------------------------- SAL/
> 1    91 Weather                                           1
  2     1 Weather--Abstracts
  3     1 Weather analysis--Congresses
  4       Weather and crime
  5            SEARCH UNDER:  Crime and weather
  6       Weather and industry
  7            SEARCH UNDER:  Industry and weather
  8     1 Weather--Bibliography--Catalogs
  9     8 Weather broadcasting                              9

For MORE subjects: PS+        For related SUBJECTS: SAL/number
PREVIOUS subjects: PS-                  For TITLES: TBL/number
```

Figure 11.1
Subdivisions under "Weather" in LCS.

Browsing alphabetical lists may be manageable to LCS users interested in weather because a half-dozen lists are needed to display subdivided and unsubdivided subject headings beginning with the word "Weather." For LCS users interested in agriculture, the system contains approximately 2300 unique subdivided forms of this authorized subject heading. To browse all subdivided forms of this heading, LCS users would have to display 230 screens consisting of ten subdivided headings at a time. (In fact, the number of screens is much higher because LCS interfiles subject headings beginning with the same word(s) and subdivided forms of headings.)

We can speculate on the reasons why users are not browsing alphabetical lists of assigned subject headings. Users may find lists unduly long and tedious. Operational systems do not yet have navigational tools to enable users to predict how many lists of subdivided forms are yet to be displayed. Furthermore, research findings from two separate studies demonstrate that some users do not understand what they are looking at (Markey 1989; Janosky, Smith, & Hildreth 1986). Regardless of the reasons, we know that users are not browsing alphabetical displays.

Following the entry of exact matches of LCSH-mr, users typically enter subsequent access points that are more specific than the initial access point and/or include geographic or topical elements that are not in the initial access point. Examples are:

Initial access point	*Subsequent access points*
etiquette	etiquette and central america
lexington	lexington ky history
marijuana	drugs and pregnancy
plant diseases	chemicals [*sic*] extractions of plants in the treatment of diseases
spain	spain and military
trees	planting tree
wyoming	wyoming and fishing

If users browse subdivided forms of their initial access points, they may find subdivided headings that express the specific topic that interests them. However, research shows that they do not browse subdivided headings using the alphabetical approach. New browsing approaches must be invented that draw users into their topic and provide a conceptual framework of the entire topic.

Massicotte recommends a "metaindex: a conceptual, rather than alphabetical, index of the individual index entries grouped under a particular search term or stem" (1988, 375). One method of constructing such a metaindex is to use existing subfield codes to distinguish between the various types of subdivisions. Unfortunately, only three such codes are available in bibliographic records: (1) topical ($x), (2) period ($y), and (3) geographic ($z). Period and geographic subdivisions may be sufficiently specific to be able to convey to users the scope and coverage of material with these subdivisions. However, topical subdivisions include just about anything that is not obviously geographic or chronological.

Massicotte notes that topical subdivisions represent "legal, technical, mathematical, scientific, economic, sociological, and political aspects of a subject" (1988, 377). She suggests constituting broad categories of subdivisions to represent aspects of topics in the metaindex. Topical subdivisions would have to be mapped to appropriate broad categories, then given a subfield code representing the particular broad categories to which they belong. When the number of subdivided headings is unduly long, the subfield codes of broad categories would be used to group together and summarize subdivided forms. For Massicotte, unduly long lists of subdivided headings are lists that surpass one screen (1988, 373).

Massicotte's ideas build on the work of several others involved in improving browsing displays of subdivided forms of headings (Holley & Killheffer 1982, 130; Cochrane 1982, 5; Cochrane 1986, 62; Markey 1984, 112–113; Chan 1986, 355–358). We have drawn upon the ideas of these researchers to fuel our ideas about managing the undue length of browsing displays through the exact approach to subject searching.

11.4 Browsing Using the Exact Approach

User queries that match exact or normalized forms of assigned subject headings or *see from* tracings result in the retrieval of a single assigned subject heading. The result of the user's selection of an assigned subject heading or *see from* tracing from the alphabetical subject-heading index is also a single assigned subject heading. Occasionally, systems are going to offer users a choice among several authorized subject headings. However, the exact approach takes over when users identify a single assigned subject heading.

When users enter or select one assigned subject heading from the thousands, or in some databases, millions of unique headings, a complex situation occurs giving users several opportunities to pursue their topics of interest. They can display:

- Bibliographic records bearing this subject heading.

- Subdivided forms of the subject heading.
- Related terms.
- Other potentially useful information about the heading, for example, LC class numbers, or complex references.

It is difficult for users to determine which opportunity holds the most promise. The challenge here is to convey the range of opportunities available to users in a single screen.

The exact approach presents users with a conceptual map to subdivided forms of the entered (or selected) heading. It also gives users the option of browsing related terms and other subject information associated with that heading. The conceptual framework manages subdivided forms of authorized headings that express specific aspects of the topics that users may have in mind but have not made explicit in their queries.

Using Massicotte's idea of an metaindex, we manually reviewed every unique subdivision appended to the high-posted subject heading "Agriculture" in Ohio State's LCS online catalog and formulated the fourteen broad categories of subdivided forms. Table 11.1 lists these broad categories and gives examples of subdivided subject headings placed in each category.

Table 11.1
Broad Categories under "Agriculture"

Broad categories	Examples of categorized subdivisions under "Agriculture"
Business and economics	Economic conditions; Finance; Forecasting; Labor productivity
Collecting and collection aspects	Literary collections
Computers	Automation; Computer-assisted instruction; Computer programs; Data processing
Education	Computer-assisted instruction; Curricula; Scholarships, fellowships, etc.; Study and teaching; Text-books
Energy and environment	Energy conservation; Energy consumption
General aspects	Abbreviations; Bibliography; Dictionaries; Indexes; Societies; Text-books
Geography	Indiana; New York (State); Soviet Union; United States
History	Folklore; History; Origin
Medicine	Accidents; Hygienic aspects; Safety measures
Politics	International cooperation
Research	Mathematical models; Research; Simulation methods; Statistics; Survey methods
Science and technology	Effect of radiation on; Remote sensing; Systems engineering
Society, ethics, and religion	Moral and religious aspects; Philosophy; Social aspects
Visual aspects	Charts, diagrams, etc.; Maps; Pictorial works; Tables

Arrays of broad categories are expected to draw users into their topic by providing a conceptual map to the treatment of the entire topic. Postings are not included in such arrays because they may dissuade users from selecting high-posted categories. Users should make decisions based on their interests and exploration of specific aspects, not on numbers of bibliographic records.

The array should be accompanied by additional subject information about the entered (or selected) headings to give users the opportunity to explore other terminology used to express their topics of interest. This is where LCSH-mr makes a contribution to subject searching because it is the source from which related terms, LC class numbers, complex references, and scope notes are generated and added to LSARs. The availability of such information for the entered (or selected) heading may give users more suitable terms for the ideas they have in mind than the terms they originally entered or selected from alphabetical browsing lists. The challenge here is to stimulate users to pursue such information for a particular heading and distinguish it from the array of broad categories that conveys different information about the heading.

In Figure 11.2, three search options are given that lead to the display of information on this particular heading. "General works" results in the retrieval and display of bibliographic records bearing the unsubdivided heading "Agriculture." "Notes" gives scope notes, complex notes, and LC class numbers connected with the subject heading. The "Related Topics" option produces lists of narrower, related, and broader terms.

In Figure 11.2, the broad-category arrays and options summarize the range of opportunities available to users for the subject heading "Agriculture." Of the broad categories in this figure, "Business and economics" is the highest posted broad category; however, this is not apparent to users because of the absence of postings from the display. Figure 11.3 shows the system response to a user's selection of this broad category from the array in Figure 11.2.

Nine of the fourteen unique subdivisions are enumerated; postings per unique subdivision are as low as one record and as high as 2904 records. Selecting a low-posted subdivision leads to a list of titles. Selecting a high-posted subdivision results in a list of subdivided forms under the selected subdivision, unless too many subdivided forms are available to fit on a single screen, in which case the system once again summarizes subdivided forms by broad categories. The high-posted subdivision "Economic aspects" leads users to additional broad categories describing subdivisions appended to the main heading–subdivision combination "Agriculture--Economic aspects" (Figure 11.4).

In Figure 11.4, the broad-category array and options summarize the range of opportunities available to users for the subdivided subject heading "Agriculture--Economic aspects." "Geography" is the highest posted broad category; however, this is not apparent to users because the numerous postings are absent from the display. A user's selection of this broad category would result in a list of geographic subdivisions appended to this subdivided heading. Certain subdivisions, for example, "India,"

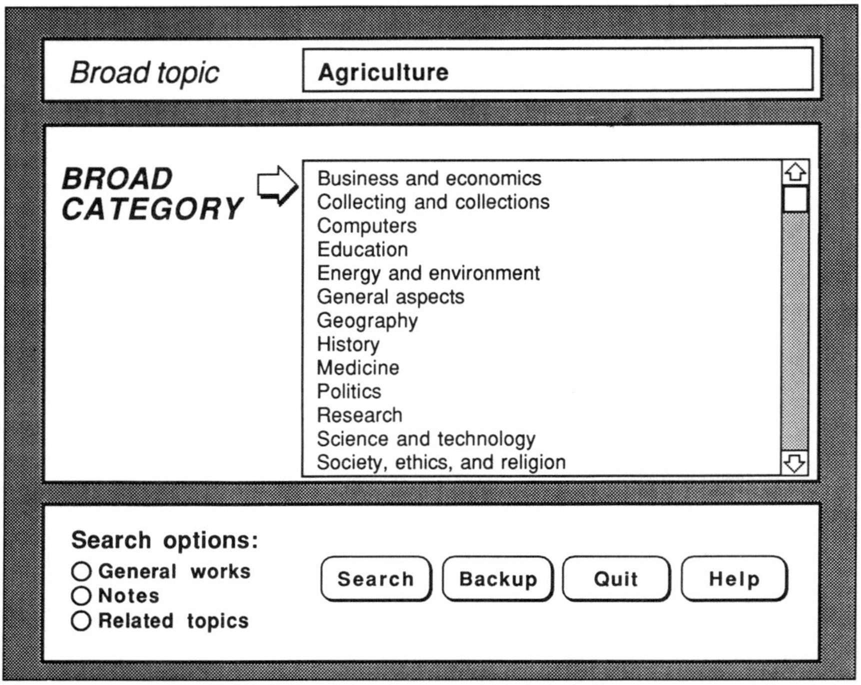

Figure 11.2
Broad category array and options under "Agriculture."

"Soviet Union," and "United States," are themselves subdivided by so many subdivisions that broad categories may be necessary to summarize them. Other broad categories are not as high posted; for example, as in Figure 11.5, the user selects the low-posted broad category "Research," which results in a list of subdivisions.

Except for the subdivision "Mathematical models," less than thirty titles are retrieved by individual subdivisions. The user's action to select this subdivision could result in a list of titles or subdivided forms of the subdivided subject heading "Agriculture--Economic aspects--Mathematical models." Systems need a threshold below which no further summarization by broad categories or subdivided headings is possible.

The broad topic "Television" presents another example of the exact approach. In LCS, unique subdivisions appended to the assigned subject heading "Television" are described by the ten broad categories listed in Figure 11.6.

Broad categories under "Television" are not as highly posted as those under "Agriculture." Thus, the user's action to select any of the broad categories listed in Figure 11.6 would lead to lists of as many subdivisions as fit on a single screen. Fig-

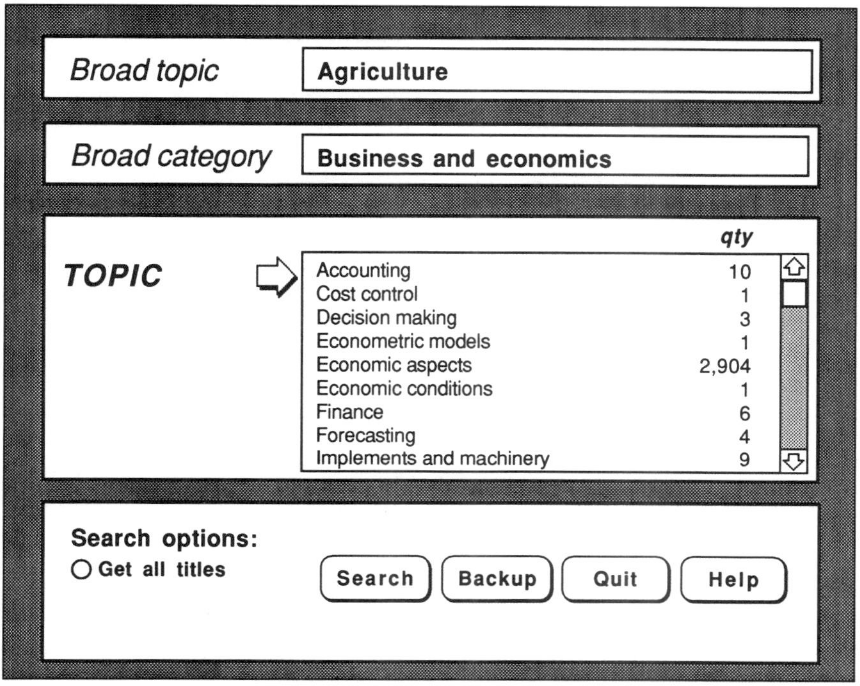

Figure 11.3
Selecting a broad category under "Agriculture."

ure 11.7 shows lists of subdivisions that are a result of the user's selection of the "General aspects" broad category.

If the user scanning the broad-category array in Figure 11.6 selects the "Related Topics" option, as many as six screens of terms related to "Television" could appear, depending on use of these terms in a library's database. Since there are too many related terms to fit on one screen, the first terms that should be displayed are ones coded "narrower" in subject authority records and used in bibliographic records. Related terms listed in Figure 11.8 are limited to the first thirteen "narrower" terms that would be shown to a searcher of Ohio State's LCS online catalog under "Television." The user can browse forward in the alphabetized list of narrower terms using the scroll bar.

If twenty or fewer related terms are available, it probably makes no sense to divide them into separate screens for narrower, broader, and related terms. Such separation would only create more work for users who have to navigate from screen to screen and keep track of their place. If more than twenty related terms are available, it may make sense to separate them into two sets, a set of "narrower" terms and another including "broader" and "related" terms.

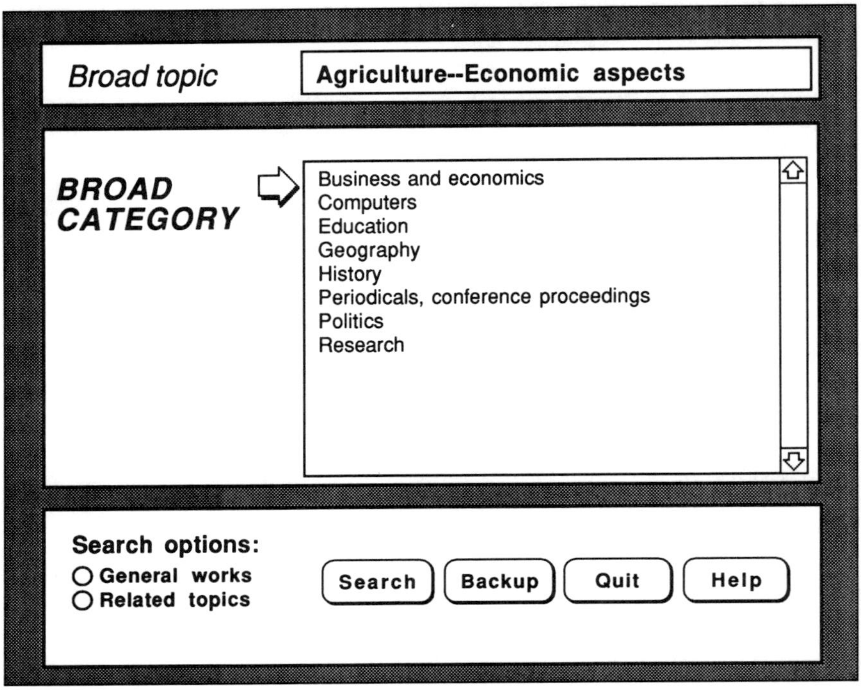

Figure 11.4
Broad category and options under "Agriculture--Economic aspects."

"Narrower" terms should be shown before other types of relationships because many users approach library catalogs with a specific topic in mind but consult a term in the catalog that is broader than this specific topic (Knapp 1944; Bates 1977; Markey & Demeyer 1986, 156–158; Hancock-Beaulieu 1990, 325). If such users browse lists of narrower terms, they may select a listed term that is not as broad as their initial access point to use in place of it.

11.5 The Exact Approach for Personal Names

The exact approach figures into searches for personal names as a follow-up to searches that begin with the alphabetical approach. Systems also respond to user queries for personal names with the alphabetical approach when users supply name and topic elements that fail to produce retrievals using various keyword search ap-

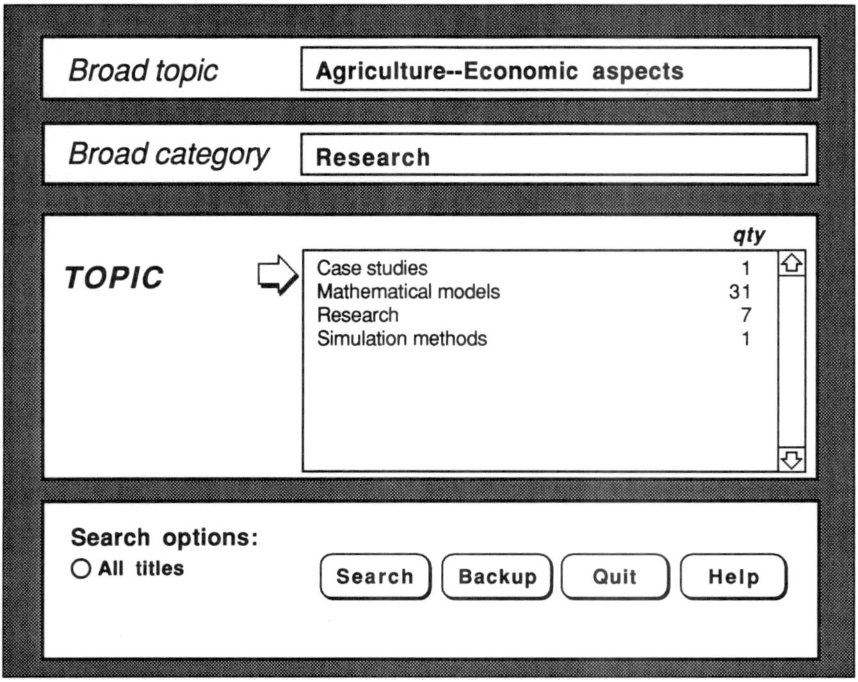

Figure 11.5
Selecting a broad category under "Agriculture--Economic aspects."

proaches. Systems invoke the exact approach upon the user's selection of a listed entry from the alphabetical index of personal names. In Figure 11.9, the online system responds to the user's entry of the surname "marx" with the alphabetical index of personal names in the neighborhood of "marx."

When the user selects a listed name, the system responds with the exact approach giving subdivided forms of the selected name. If too many subdivided forms are available to fit on a single screen, the system enlists broad categories to convey the subject matter of available subdivided forms. The user's selection of "Karl Marx" results in too many subdivided forms; consequently, the system responds with broad categories (Figure 11.10).

Selection of a broad category leads directly to a list of subdivided subject headings. For example, the user's selection of the "Philosophy" broad category results in the five subdivided headings in Figure 11.11.

Selection of one of the listed subdivided forms under the broad category "Philosophy" leads directly to bibliographic records.

The alphabetical and exact approaches work hand in hand to satisfy user queries for personal names as subjects. The alphabetical approach allows the user to browse

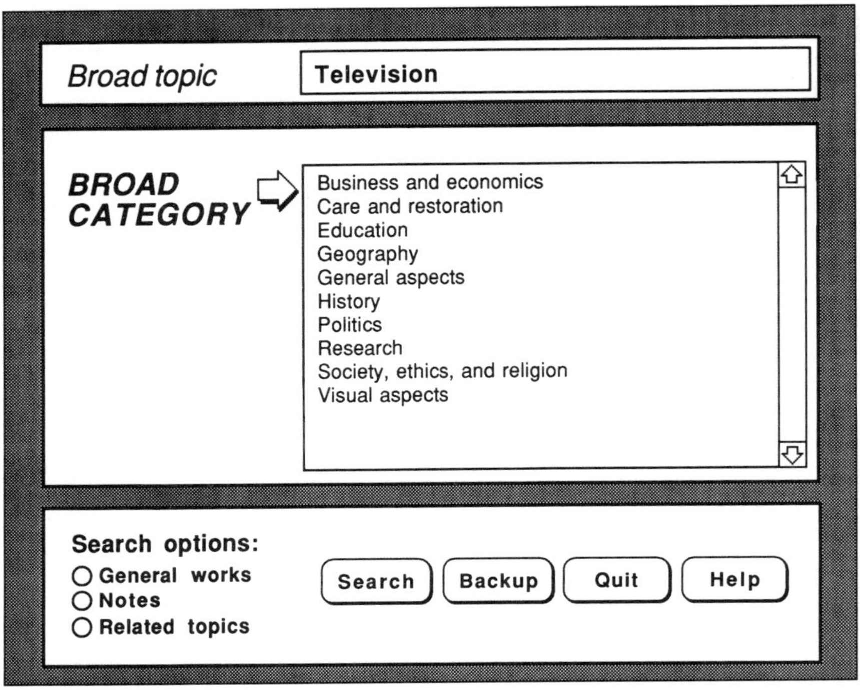

Figure 11.6
Broad category array and options under "Television."

in the neighborhood of the entered name to find the appropriate one, and the exact approach manages retrievals for the selected name.

11.6 Implementing the Exact Approach in Online Systems

Four work efforts are needed to implement the exact approach in online bibliographic systems:

1. Identify Broad Categories of Subdivisions

Arrays of broad categories that characterize the exact approach in online catalogs can be created by online systems using existing machine-readable files of bibliographic records or subject-authority records. However, only three broad categories can be constructed using the available subfield coding for subject subdivisions. Unless we are to be burdened with long lists of undifferentiated subdivisions, subfield coding

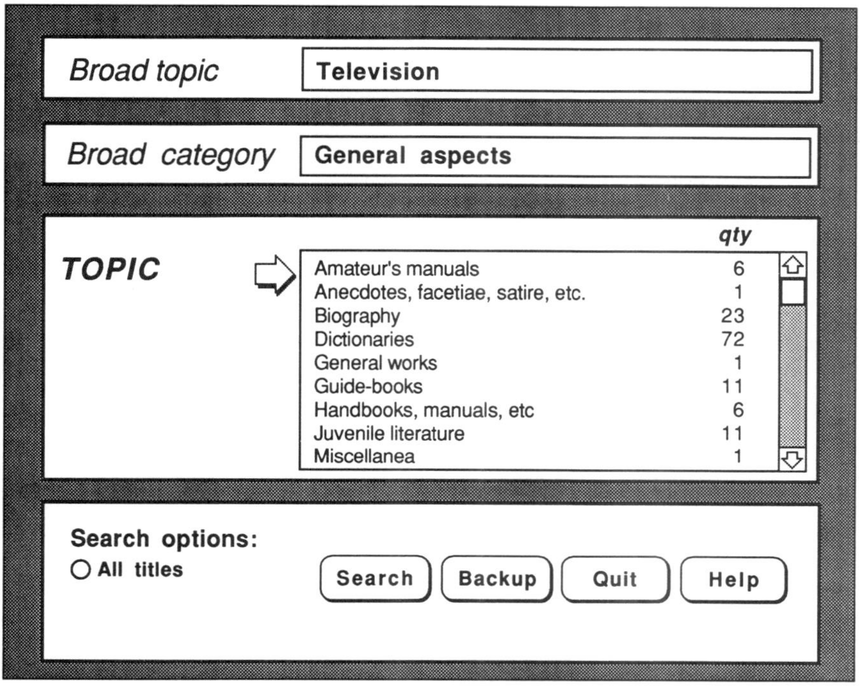

Figure 11.7
Selecting a broad category under "Television."

must be enhanced with additional coding to distinguish between the many different aspects of a subject heading that subject subdivisions express. Enhancements need to be made to these tools and new machine-readable files need to be designed and created. Broad categories of subdivisions must be defined and given names. Free-floating subdivisions and subdivisions based on pattern headings must be reviewed to determine what broad categories they belong to. Subdivisions can be placed in more than one category. The tag of the main heading and/or the pattern heading that the main heading follows sometimes designate the appropriate category. For example, the subdivision "Chronology" is used from a historical perspective with topical-subject headings and applies to the life of a person when used with subject headings for personal names (USMARC tag 600). Thus, this subdivision belongs to the "History" or "Life" broad category when used with topical-subject headings (USMARC tag 650) or personal names (USMARC tag 600), respectively.

A working group could be formed to review subdivisions based on free-floating and pattern headings. The working group could be coordinated by both the Subject Analysis Committee (SAC) of the Association for Library Collections and Technical Services (ALCTS) of the American Library Association (ALA) and LC's

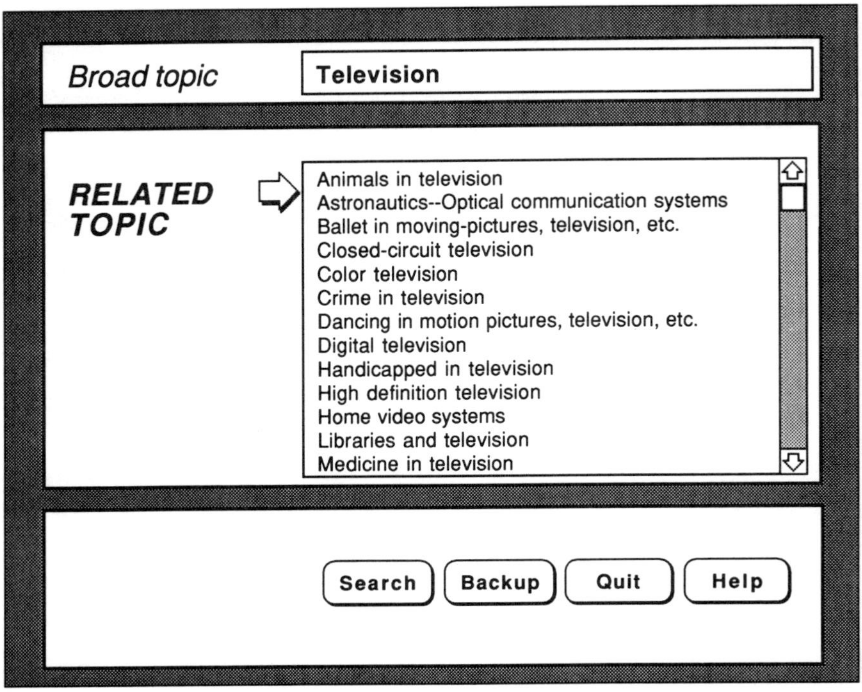

Figure 11.8
Terms related to "Television."

Subject Cataloging Division (SCD). Members could come from the library cataloging community at large and from the Library of Congress. Membership should also be extended to the library reference community because these staff interact with library patrons. Ultimately, library patrons will be users of the broad categories that are established by the working group.

When formulating broad categories for certain pattern headings, working-group membership should be extended to subject specialists or scholars. The researchers in this study found that formulating broad categories for such pattern subdivisions as "Wars," "Christian Denominations," and "Organs and Regions of the Body" required subject knowledge and expertise.

The working group should consult the publication entitled *An introduction to Library of Congress Subject Headings* (Library of Congress 1975). The syndetic structure under many headings may give working-group members an idea of subdivisions that belong in the same category. For example, the "Business and economics" category could include the free-floating subdivision "Economic aspects" and the three subdivisions given as *see also* references under this subdivision, that is, "Commerce," "Economic policy," and "Finance" in *An introduction.*

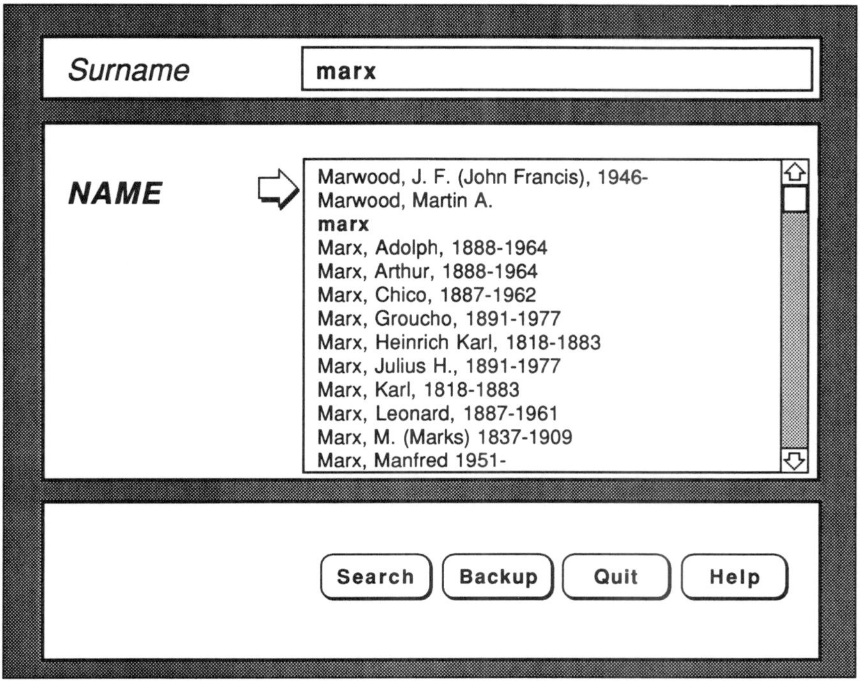

Figure 11.9
Alphabetical approach to "marx."

Although *An introduction* is now out of date, the working group should consider reintroducing information from this publication in machine-readable subdivision records. Scope notes, *see* references, and the syndetic structure under subdivisions could be added to such machine-readable records to help both library catalogers and public users of online systems.

Broad category names should be pretested with end users. It makes no sense to formulate categories without knowing whether the terminology used to represent categories is understandable to the individuals who will ultimately use them.

2. Identify Headings in LCSH-mr That Follow Pattern Headings

Subdivisions used with a particular subject heading from a pattern sometimes belong to a different broad category when used with a subject heading from a different pattern. For example, the subdivision "Contraction" used with a subject heading from the "Languages" pattern has a totally different meaning from its use with a different heading from the "Organs of the Body" pattern.

USMARC coding is not present in subject-heading fields of bibliographic records (MARC tags 6xx) or authorized heading fields of LCSH-mr records

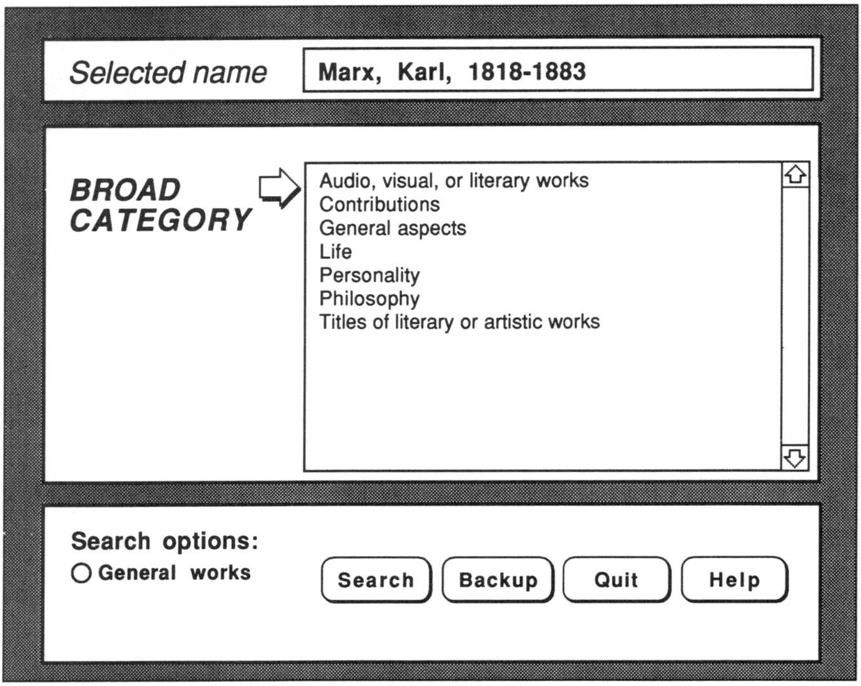

Figure 11.10
Exact approach to "Karl Marx."

(MARC tags 1xx) to identify headings that follow pattern headings. Such coding needs to be established and added to machine-readable files to ensure that broad categories can be identified properly.

Every heading in LCSH-mr must be reviewed to determine whether it follows a pattern. We may be able to call on the Library of Congress, other libraries, and library automation vendors that may have maintained a card or computer file of assigned subject headings that follow pattern headings. Such a file would enable headings in LCSH-mr that follow pattern headings to be enhanced with coding that identifies the pattern. Once this coding is in LCSH-mr, library systems staff can add the coding to their machine-readable bibliographic files either when they create a Local Subject Authority File (LSAF) or when they contract with a vendor to verify the subject headings assigned to bibliographic records and create a LSAF for them to load into their local system.

If files of pattern headings do not exist, a second working group has to be formed to identify LCSH-mr headings that follow a pattern. Since this task documents previous and current cataloging practice, library and LC catalogers are the most likely members of the second working group.

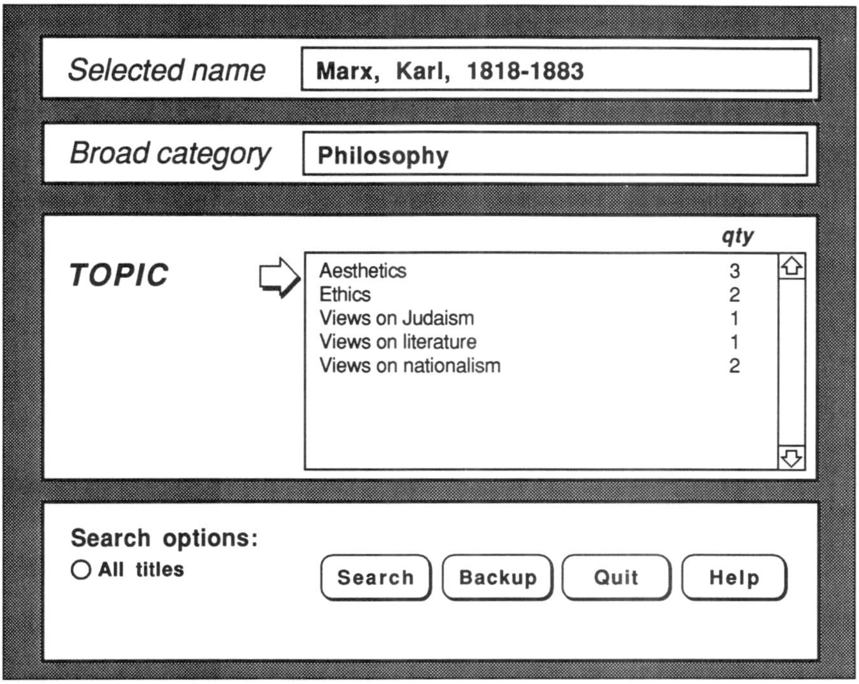

Figure 11.11
Selecting a broad category under "Philosophy."

3. Create Machine-Readable Subdivision Records

The records in libraries' bibliographic files have been created over a long period of time. Older records do not have subfield coding for broad categories. When staff create new bibliographic records, broad category coding needs to be included. Then subject searching capabilities such as the exact approach can utilize this coding in the construction of broad categories.

To aid in the conversion of older records and creation of new ones, a file of machine-readable subdivision records should be made bearing subfield coding for broad categories. To enable libraries to add subfield coding for broad categories to existing bibliographic records, authority records in such a file should contain: (1) authorized subdivisions, (2) subfield code(s) of the broad category(ies) to which the particular subdivision belongs, (3) tag(s) to indicate the types of subject headings that are authorized with the particular subdivision, and, (4), if applicable, the code that designates the pattern heading(s) associated with the particular subdivision. The contents of subdivision records would be a direct result of the first working group's efforts.

Machine-readable subdivision records could be used by library systems staff and library automation vendors to add subfield coding for broad categories to existing bibliographic databases. Bibliographic services could mount the records into their cataloging subsystems to help catalogers who are composing subdivided headings to add the correct subdivision and broad category coding to bibliographic records.

4. Enhance LCSH-mr with Coding for Headings following a Pattern

The fourth work effort follows on the heels of the second working group, which is charged with identifying LCSH-mr headings that are governed by pattern headings. The codes that the working group defines should be added to authorized headings in LCSH-mr that follow a pattern. These codes will enable systems to automatically identify the correct broad category code for a particular subdivision. For example, a code for the "Organs of the Body" pattern would be added to the LCSH-mr record for the authorized subject heading "Stomach." A different code for the "Languages" pattern would be added to the LCSH-mr record for the authorized heading "English language." Broad category codes accompanying the subdivisions in the subdivided headings "Stomach--Contraction" and "English language--Contraction" would be different because the subdivision has a different meaning when appended to these two headings. Thus, these two subdivisions would belong to different categories. Systems would automatically distinguish between the two different broad categories because of the presence of pattern heading coding in LCSH-mr records.

Many subdivisions are printed in LCSH. These subdivisions will not go in the machine-readable subdivision file. Most are topical subdivisions, for example, "Law and legislation," "Message processing," and "Switching systems" under the main heading "Telecommunication." These subdivisions need their own subfield coding that identifies them as special or unique topics with respect to the subject-heading string to which they are appended. They would be given a name such as "Special topics" and placed in a separate broad category.

11.7

Synthesis and Summary

When searchers enter terms that exactly match an assigned subject heading or a normalized form of a controlled vocabulary term or select controlled vocabulary terms from a system-supplied alphabetical index, systems should respond with the exact approach because it gives a conceptual map of the topic in the form of a broad category array. The array sums up the various aspects of the topic and/or the various perspectives from which the topic can be treated. The array can be accompanied by options to browse related terms, suggested LC classification numbers, or scope notes, that is, information from LCSH-mr. Whether users explore the unique subdivisions under broad categories or information supplied by LCSH-mr, finding a suitable subject heading to express their topic of interest depends on a number of factors including luck, perseverance, and their ability to use system capabilities.

The alphabetical approach gives assigned subject headings that are in the same alphabetical neighborhood as the subject terms users enter. When assigned subject headings are listed alphabetically, sometimes the headings preceding or following the matched heading are related to one another or express a specific aspect of a topic that users have in mind but have not made explicit in their queries. For example, the following assigned subject headings precede and follow "Agriculture" in the alphabet.

Preceding headings	*Following headings*
Agricultural administration	Agriculture, Cooperation
Agricultural assistance	Agriculture and energy
Agricultural chemicals	Agriculture and politics
Agricultural education	Agriculture and state
Agricultural extension work	Agriculture publishing
Agricultural laborers	Agriculture teachers
Agricultural pests	Agriculturists

If a user is interested in education aspects of agriculture, a system could respond to the query "agriculture" with the exact approach because the user has made an exact match of the assigned heading "Agriculture." The system would produce the arrays of broad categories and options shown in Figure 11.2. Choosing the broad category "Education" would lead the user to bibliographic records under the subdivisions "Curricula," "Computer-assisted instruction," "Outlines, syllabi, etc.," "Study and teaching," "Scholarships, fellowships, etc.," and "Text-books." The exact approach does not feature lists of subject headings in the same alphabetical neighborhood as the matched heading. Thus users may miss potentially relevant records under "Agricultural education," "Agricultural extension work," and "Agriculture teachers," that is, assigned subject headings that would precede and follow the exact match "Agriculture" in alphabetical lists of assigned headings produced by the alphabetical approach.

Users would find some of the subject headings in the alphabetical neighborhood of the matched heading by exploring related terms under "Agriculture" and under a few subdivided forms of "Agriculture." For example, related terms under "Agriculture--Study and teaching" suggest subdivided and unsubdivided terms: "Agricultural experiment stations," "Agricultural students," "Agriculture--Scholarships, fellowships, etc.," "Agriculture teachers," and "Forestry schools and education." The scope note under this subdivided heading suggests "Agricultural education."

Users cannot rely on LCSH syndetic structure to find all relevant terms for their topics of interest. Headings that express similar topics may be separated from one another because they are composites of subject headings that have been established as separate terms. Dykstra (1988) recommends that terms in single headings be identified, extracted, and established as separate authorized headings. Thus, subject headings like "Television and children," "Agriculture and state," and "Agricultural wastes as fuel," would become "Television," "Children," "Agriculture," "State," "Agricultural wastes," and "Fuel," respectively. This process would require editorial review of LCSH and its syndetic structure. Until such a review is undertaken and completed, users performing comprehensive searches in online systems will have to use other searching approaches, such as keyword and alphabetical approaches, to satisfy their information needs.

We recommend the exact approach over the alphabetical approach because it consolidates subdivided forms of the matched subject heading through broad categories describing aspects of the matched subject. The display of broad categories is intended to stimulate users to find and select an aspect that is not made explicit in their original queries. When users select a broad topic, subdivided forms that address the subject of the broad topic will come from many parts of the alphabet. In the alphabetical approach, subdivided forms on a broad topic of interest would be separated from one another because they come from all parts of the alphabet. Users would have to browse through the entire alphabetical arrangement of subdivided headings to find those addressing an aspect of the matched subject pertinent to their interests. Under high-posted subject headings such as "Agriculture" and "Television," browsing could take a long time. Research findings demonstrate that few users browse past the initial screen that lists a main heading that is the same as or close to the term they entered and subdivisions beginning with the first letter(s) of the alphabet. Consequently, the alphabetical approach is not an effective way of presenting users with controlled vocabulary terms in response to the queries they enter that match such terms.

The exact approach is not possible without considerable editorial work. Broad categories of subdivisions must be identified and named. Subject headings following a pattern must be identified. The exact approach is also not possible without enhancement of existing machine-readable files and the creation of new ones. Existing machine-readable files of bibliographic records must be enhanced with broad category coding. Development of a machine-readable file of subdivision records and enhancement of the existing machine-readable file of subject authority records with broad category codes would facilitate conversion of existing bibliographic files.

Without editorial work and the development of new machine-readable tools, we are left with a paltry selection of three subdivision codes for summarizing a wealth of subject matter on broad topics, that is, topical subdivisions ($x), period subdivisions ($y), and geographic subdivisions ($z). Figure 11.12 shows broad categories for the assigned subject heading "Agriculture" when broad category codes are limited to the three existing subdivision codes.

In Figure 11.12, broad categories refer to geographic, period, and topical subdivisions, respectively. Comparing Figure 11.12 with Figure 11.2, which gives the complete array of broad categories under "Agriculture," note that several categories such as "Business and economics," "Education," "Politics," and "Society, ethics, and religion" are missing from Figure 11.12. These missing categories are consolidated

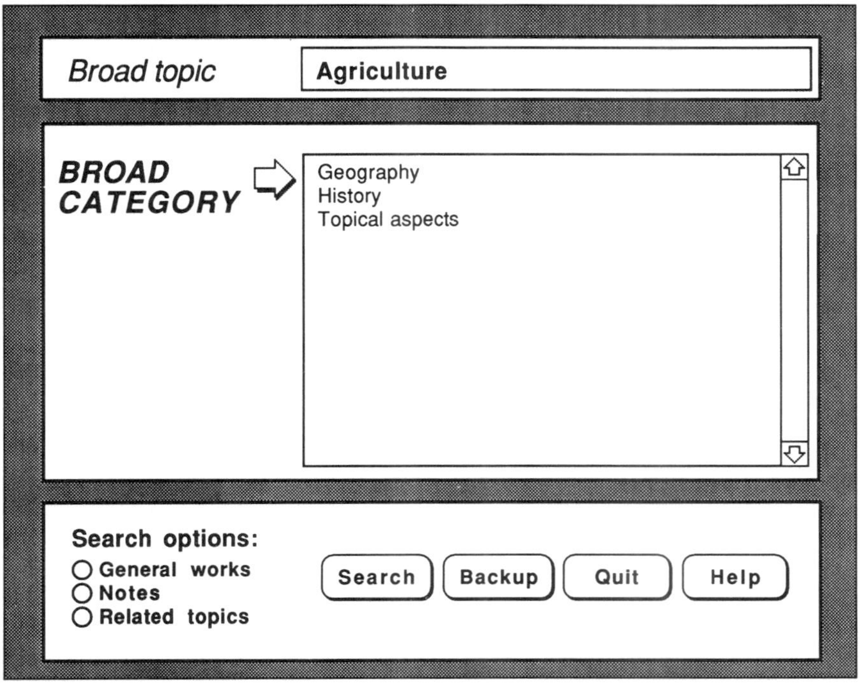

Figure 11.12
Broad category array and options under "Agriculture" using existing subfield codes.

under "Topical aspects" in Figure 11.12, which is composed of all topical subdivisions. Selection of this broad category would lead users to hundreds of unique subdivisions, and, thus, require many screen displays.

Responding to the recommendations of the Library of Congress Subject Subdivisions Conference, the Library of Congress could introduce a separate subdivision code for form subdivisions (Avram 1992). Thus, subdivisions such as "Abbreviations," "Abstracts," "Anecdotes, facetiae, satire, etc.," "Bibliography," and "Biography" will be given a unique subfield code that is different from the existing $x, $y, and $z codes. The availability of a separate code will reduce long displays of topical subdivisions. In the "Agriculture" example (Figure 11.12), the availability of different coding for form subdivisions would reduce the number of unique subdivisions in the "Topical aspects" category by 25%. A recent study of subject heading compression suggests that specifically coding form subdivisions may reduce long lists of subdivided forms by only 10% (McGarry & Svenonius 1991). Specifying form subdivisions in machine-readable bibliographic and authority files is a step in the right direction, but it will not entirely solve the problem of lengthy screen displays.

Alternatives to additional subfield codes for managing the many subdivided forms of assigned subject headings can be drawn from the suggestions of researchers who have been studying the problem of large retrievals (Larson 1989; Lesk 1989; Prabha 1989, 1990; Lynch 1990). Systems could prompt users to summarize or reduce retrievals by criteria that do not necessarily touch on their subject matter, for example, date of publication, language, bibliographic format, library branch. Limiting results by format may not substantially reduce retrievals if the format sought by users is the predominant format in the library's bibliographic database. At academic institutions, reducing retrievals by branch libraries could touch on the subject matter of retrievals because many institutions have branch libraries corresponding to academic disciplines, for example, art library, chemistry library, engineering library, physics library.

Library classifications may hold the most promise for summarizing the results of high-posted searches in terms of their subject matter. Systems could use broad ranges of classification numbers to consolidate retrievals and captions from the classification schedules to describe the subjects of consolidated retrievals. When users selected a consolidated set of retrievals, online systems would respond with a display of subdivided forms using the available three or four types of coded subdivisions, that is, topical, period, geographic, and, possibly, form. Depending on the number of retrievals, captions used to represent broad ranges of classification numbers could be taken from the almost two dozen alphabetical characters (A–Z) for the Library of Congress Classification (LCC), the ten numerical characters (0–9) for the Dewey Decimal Classification (DDC), or from smaller ranges within these larger ranges. A problem with this approach arises from the current LC policy that calls for catalogers to assign classification numbers based on the first-listed subject headings in bibliographic records. Subject headings relevant to users may not be the first-listed headings in retrieved bibliographic records; consequently, the classification caption used to summarize retrievals may not be indicative of the subjects users are seeking. Users may disregard some consolidated sets of retrievals because the classification caption summarizing them does not describe the topics that interest them.

In recent years, hypertext, graphic user interfaces, and pointing–clicking devices such as the mouse have given system designers new tools for improving the usability of online catalogs. We could place our hopes on the possibility that future computer systems have navigational techniques to facilitate browsing of textual material in ways that we have not yet dreamed of.

Managing the wealth of subdivided forms and conveying their essence to catalog users can be best accomplished through broad category arrays. However, editorial work is needed to sort topical subdivisions into pertinent broad categories and to identify the pattern headings that govern subject headings printed in *LCSH*. A machine-readable subdivisions file must be created. This new file and the existing file of subject authority records must be enhanced with broad category and pattern heading coding so system designers can use information in these files to construct arrays of broad categories.

References

Avram, Henriette D. (1992). Cataloging modifications at the Library of Congress, Collections Services. 2 January (Photocopy).

Bates, Marcia J. (1977). System meets user: Problems in matching subject search terms. *Information Processing and Management, 13*(6), 367–375.

Chan, Lois Mai. (1986). *Library of Congress Subject Headings: Principles and application.* Littleton, CO: Libraries Unlimited.

Cochrane, Pauline A. (1982). Subject access in the online catalog. *Research Libraries in OCLC: A quarterly,* 5 (January): 1–7.

Cochrane, Pauline A. (1986). *Improving LCSH for use in online catalog: Exercises for self-help with a selection of background readings.* Littleton, CO: Libraries Unlimited.

Dykstra, Mary. (1988). Can subject headings be saved? *Library Journal, 113,* 15 (September 15, 55–58.

Hancock-Beaulieu, Micheline. (1990). Evaluating the impact of an online library catalogue on subject searching behaviour at the catalogue and at the shelves. *Journal of Documentation, 46,* 4 (December), 318–338.

Holley, Robert P., & Killheffer, Robert E. (1982). Is there an answer to the subject access crisis? *Cataloging & Classification Quarterly,* 1(2/3), 125–133.

Janosky, Beverly, Smith, Philip J., & Hildreth, Charles R. (1986). Online library catalog systems: An analysis of user errors. *International Journal of Man-Machine Studies, 25,* 573–592.

Knapp, Patricia B. (1944). The subject catalog in the college library. *Library Quarterly, 14*(3/4), 108–118, 214–228.

Larson, Ray R. (1989). Managing information overload in online catalog subject searching. In *ASIS 89: Proceedings of the 52nd ASIS annual meeting* (pp. 129–135). Medford, NJ: Learned Information.

Lesk, Michael, (1989). What to do when there's too much information. *Hypertext '89 Proceedings,* (November), 305–318.

Library of Congress. (1975). *An introduction to Library of Congress Subject Headings.* Washington, DC: Library of Congress.

Library of Congress. (1990). *Subject Cataloging manual: Subject headings.* Washington, DC: Library of Congress.

Lynch, Clifford. (1990). Large database and multiple database problems in online catalogs. In *Annual Review of OCLC Research, July 1989–June 1990* (pp. 51–55). Dublin, OH: OCLC.

McGarry, Dorothy, & Svenonius, Elaine. (1991). More on improved browsable displays for online subject access using records from ORION. *Information Technology and Libraries, 10* (September), 185–191.

Markey, Karen. (1984). *Subject searching in library catalogs: Before and after the introduction of online catalogs.* Dublin, OH: OCLC.

Markey, Karen. (1989). Alphabetical searching in an online catalog. *Journal of Academic Librarianship, 14,* 6 (January), 353–360.

Markey, Karen, & Demeyer, Anh. (1986). *Dewey Decimal Classification Online Project: Evaluation of a library schedule and index integrated into the subject searching capabilities of an online catalog.* Dublin, OH: OCLC. OCLC Research Report Series OCLC/OPR/RR-86/1.

Massicotte, Mia. (1988). Improved browsable displays for online subject access. *Information Technology and Libraries,* 7, 4 (December), 373–380.

Prabha, Chandra. (1989). Managing large retrievals: A problem for the 1990s? In *OPACs and beyond; Proceedings of a joint meeting of the British Library, DBMIST, and OCLC* (pp. 33–38). Dublin, OH: OCLC.

Prabha, Chandra. (1990). Managing large retrievals. In *Annual Review of OCLC Research, July 1989–June 1990* (pp. 24–26). Dublin, OH: OCLC.

Van Pulis, Noelle, & Ludy, Lorene E. (1988). Subject searching in an online catalog with authority control. *College & Research Libraries, 49,* 6 (November), 523–533.

Wiberley, Stephen E., & Daugherty, Robert Allen. (1988). Users' persistence in scanning lists of references. *College & Research Libraries, 49,* 2 (March), 149–156.

12

Choosing among Existing Subject Search Approaches as Responses to User Queries

12.1 Introduction

Most user queries are not exact or normalized matches of controlled vocabulary terms, so the exact approach will not be an appropriate system response to such queries. This chapter discusses the use of alphabetical and keyword searching approaches for handling nonmatches.

Whether systems respond to user queries with alphabetical or keyword approaches, their responses will include catalog information that contains the terms users enter and additional terms that may or may not address the topics users have in mind. For example, the alphabetical approach will give an alphabetical index of assigned subject headings containing controlled vocabulary terms that begin with the same words in the user query and end in different words.

The catalog information provided by alphabetical and keyword approaches should stimulate users to find suitable controlled vocabulary terms to express the topics they seek. Systems could overwhelm users with the large amounts of catalog information they produce in response to queries. For example, the alphabetical index of subject headings given in response to the user query "differential" could contain dozens of subject headings beginning with this word and hundreds of subdivided forms of these headings. This chapter discusses the contents of subject-heading displays produced by alphabetical and keyword search approaches and suggests methods of limiting the amount of catalog information systems display to keep from overwhelming users.

Discussions of alphabetical and keyword search approaches for personal-name queries and for subject queries generally are kept separate in this chapter because of the different factors that govern systems' selection of a particular approach. Online systems should encourage users to distinguish their queries for personal names from queries for subjects generally. Systems should prompt users for name and topic elements of personal-name queries; users should not be expected to replicate the prescribed order of these elements in subject headings for personal names. Systems are governed in the choice between alphabetical and keyword search approaches by their ability to produce retrievals for combinations of selected name and topic elements. Name elements figure into only the alphabetical approach. Systems would choose the alphabetical approach when users give personal-name queries consisting of name elements only or personal-name queries consisting of a combination of name and topic elements for which keyword search approaches fail to produce retrievals.

User queries for subjects generally are submitted to alphabetical and keyword subject searching approaches. Systems are governed in the choice between alphabetical and keyword approaches by the extent to which user queries match controlled vocabulary terms and produce retrievals. Queries that fail to exactly match controlled vocabulary terms or their normalized forms are candidates for the alphabetical approach. Systems respond with the alphabetical approach to queries matching the same characters in longer controlled vocabulary terms. User queries matching two or more words in single controlled vocabulary terms are submitted to keyword-in-heading approaches. Keyword-in-record searches are suitable for user queries that fail to produce retrievals through other approaches.

Of the subject searching approaches presented in this chapter, we prefer approaches that enlist the catalog's controlled vocabulary. If users find controlled vocabulary terms for expressing their topics of interest, they can refine their searches using related terms, subdivided forms of the matched heading, or controlled vocabulary terms in close alphabetical proximity to the one entered into the catalog. Controlled vocabulary terms also ensure precision of search results because they are assigned to bibliographic records by catalogers to express the subject matter of original items. Subject searching approaches that enlist the catalog's controlled vocabulary are two-step approaches insofar as they present users with intermediary steps involved with browsing controlled vocabulary terms, explanatory information about these terms, or relationships between terms.

One-step subject searching approaches are enlisted only as a last resort because retrievals come from fields other than single-subject heading fields. The outcome of one-step approaches is a set of bibliographic records bearing query words in one or more subject-rich fields. This outcome has limited potential for helping users explore the catalog's controlled vocabulary to find specific subjects they have in mind but have not made explicit in their queries. If relevance feedback capabilities are available, systems could use the subject headings in retrieved records to gain a foothold into the controlled vocabulary to help users find additional material for their topics. This chapter places emphasis on subject searching approaches that enlist the catalog's controlled vocabulary because of the many links this vocabulary provides to other catalog entries that can help users find information on the topics they seek.

Table 12.1
One-Word Queries and the Closest Matching Controlled Vocabulary Terms

Queries	Controlled vocabulary terms
Satisfactory matches	
actuator	Actuators
advertisers	Advertisement writing; Advertising; Advertising, Classified; Advertising and children
biocompatilityt	Biocompatibility
consumerds	Consumers
cotyledons	Cotyledon (Anatomy)
philoctetess	Philoctetes (Legendary character)
sociopath	Sociopathic personality
widowhood	Widows
Unsatisfactory matches	
bibiography	Bibionidae
domination	Dominator (Bomber); Dominance (Psychology)
eduation	Educability
hadicapped	Hadia (African people); Hadith
mcat	MC6800 (Computer)
mrp	MRDS (Information retrieval system; Mrung language)
psychanalysis	Psychagogy

12.2 The Alphabetical Approach to Subject Searching

12.2.1 Extent of Match between Queries and Controlled Vocabulary Terms

The alphabetical approach to subject searching for user queries for subjects generally is featured here. The alphabetical approach is also appropriate for personal-name queries but discussion of this approach for personal-name queries is given later in the chapter.

The alphabetical approach is the system response to user queries that match the same characters in a longer controlled vocabulary term. This approach could also be recommended for one-word queries that match two or more syllables in longer controlled vocabulary terms. Queries that are candidates for the alphabetical approach are presented in Table 12.1.

Several one-word queries are misspelled in Table 12.1. When misspellings occur near or at the end of the query, the closest matching controlled vocabulary term is satisfactory, for example, "biocompatilityt," "consumerds," and "philoctetess." When the misspelling occurs near the beginning of the word, the matching controlled vocabulary term is unsatisfactory, for example, "bibiography," "eduation," and "hadicapped." A few queries and matching terms are the same except for singular or

```
Enter subject to search > peducation
CAN'T FIND peducation.  Please check spelling.
Enter a new word to search > education
```

Figure 12.1
Checking for spelling errors.

plural suffixes; closest matching controlled vocabulary terms are satisfactory for expressing the topics users are seeking.

The larger number of unsatisfactory matches makes us skeptical about enlisting the alphabetical approach as the system response to one-word queries that match two or more syllables in controlled vocabulary terms. Although users would eventually find their topics of interest, they would have to perform a considerable amount of browsing. Instead, we recommend that systems first perform title keyword searches for these words. For example, one-word queries such as "mcat," "mrp," "graphwriter," and "controls" will probably match words in title fields, and may be appropriate for title keyword searches. If title keyword searches fail to retrieve bibliographic records, systems should show users their queries and ask them to check for spelling errors. Walker and Jones (1987, 96) use this strategy in Okapi and note users' receptivity to it. Figure 12.1 is based on Okapi and shows how systems can ask users to check for spelling errors.

If queries are misspelled and users do not correct spelling, the only available system response is the alphabetical approach because keyword approaches will not produce retrievals.

To summarize the types of user queries that are candidates for the alphabetical approach: (1) user queries that match the same characters in a longer controlled vocabulary term, and (2) one-word queries that fail to produce retrievals through the title keyword search.

12.2.2 Displaying Alphabetical Lists of Controlled Vocabulary Terms

The objective of displaying alphabetical lists of controlled vocabulary terms to users is to spark their interest in a term that is in close alphabetical proximity to their query. When users select a term that interests them, systems respond to their selection with the exact approach (see Chapter 11). The exact approach gives users access to the unique subdivided forms of matched headings, related terms, and other information about the matched heading from LCSH-mr.

The alphabetical approach is not effective for displaying the unique subdivided forms of assigned subject headings because so many subdivided forms are connected with such headings. Previous research has shown that users do not browse headings that occur before or after the first screen of headings shown to them. The alphabetical

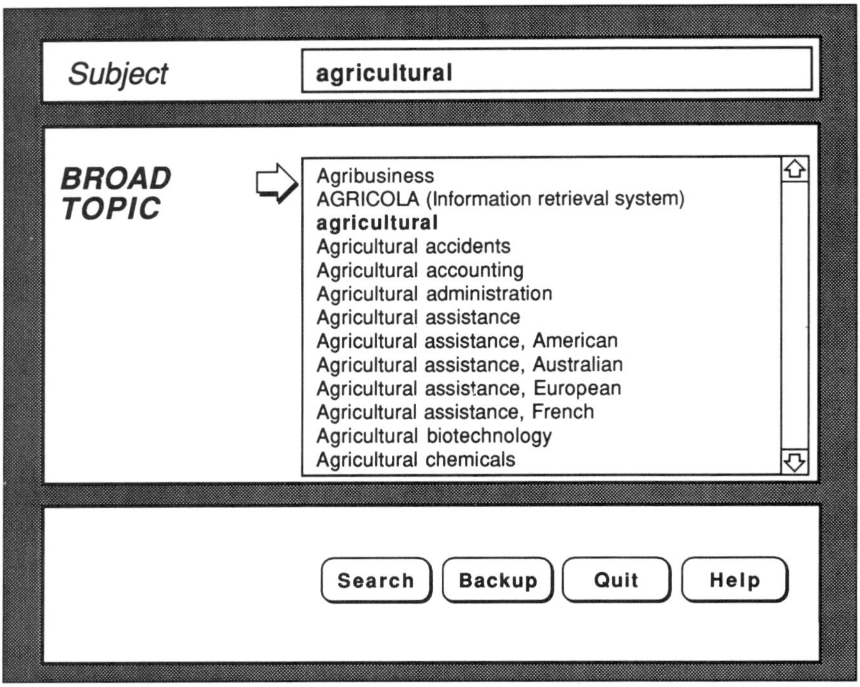

Figure 12.2
Alphabetical index under "agricultural."

approach is best treated as an opportunity to stimulate users with the controlled vocabulary. The alphabetical approach is featured in Figure 12.2. Displayed controlled vocabulary terms are limited to the main headings in assigned subject headings and *see* references.

The user is prompted to select a term other than "agricultural," for which there is no exact match in the index. When users select assigned subject headings, systems respond with the exact approach by providing a broad category array and options for selecting related terms and other information about listed subject headings. This system response would be the same for users selecting "Agricultural assistance" from the alphabetical index as for users whose queries exactly match this assigned subject heading.

In Figure 12.2, *see* references like "Agribusiness," "Agricultural accidents," and "Agricultural accounting" are provided as additional choices. If users select *see* references, systems respond by telling them that a different term(s) is used to express the topic in the catalog. For example, the system responds to the user's selection of the *see* reference "Agribusiness" with the explanatory message shown in Figure 12.3A.

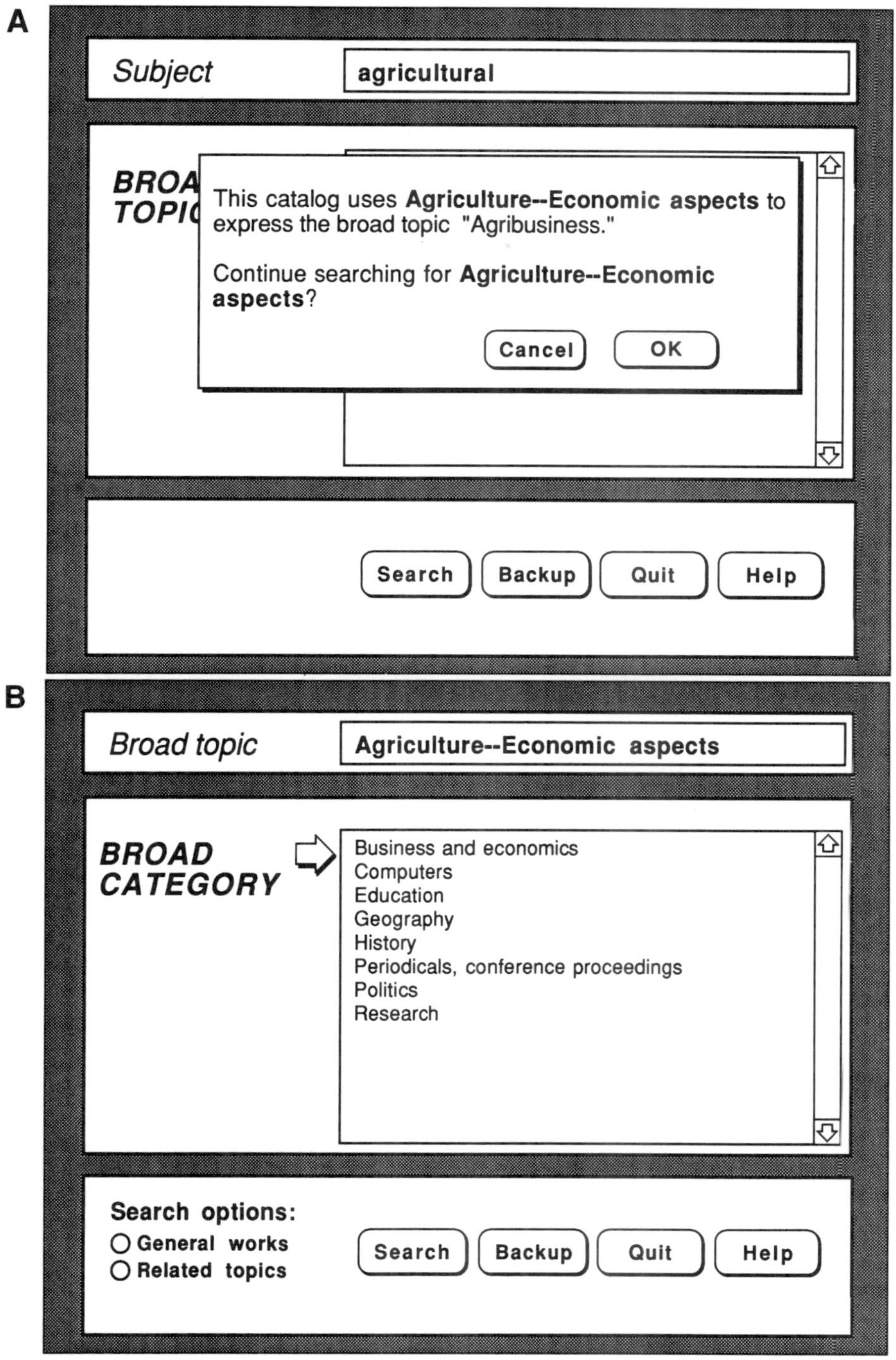

Figure 12.3
Selection of *see* reference in the alphabetical approach.

In Figure 12.3B, the user accepts the authorized heading in place of the *see* reference and continues the search. The system responds with the exact approach, which yields eight broad categories and several options.

In the alphabetical index of subject headings (Figure 12.2), we have intentionally listed *see* references alone, that is, without the authorized heading(s) that are used to represent this topic in the catalog. This simplifies the display and leaves a lot of blank space. It may help users focus on choosing a listed term to represent their topic of interest. If they choose a *see* reference, a system message can interpret what they have selected. When *see* references are accompanied by authorized headings, users must perform two operations simultaneously, that is, browse listed terms and interpret their function. It may be best to limit users to one operation at a time. When users select an unauthorized heading, then the system interprets their action for them (Figure 12.3A).

12.2.3 Alphabetizing Subject Headings in Browsing Displays

The ALA-sponsored Subcommittee on the Display of Subject Headings in Subject Indexes in Online Public Access Catalogs recently completed guidelines for the alphabetization of controlled vocabulary terms (American Library Association 1992). The report does not prescribe a particular approach to alphabetization. It explains the pros and cons of different alphabetization approaches. The report's contents are not summarized here, but its authors urge system designers to read and study it when making decisions about alphabetical arrangement.

In this book, controlled vocabulary terms are alphabetized in the following sequence: (1) unqualified headings, (2) qualified headings, (3) inverted headings, and (4) phrase headings. The alphabetization sequence used here results in a list of headings beginning with a particular word or phrase. Listed headings bearing this word or phrase become increasingly more specific. Qualified headings are a more restrictive case than the unqualified headings that precede them. Inverted headings come next because they are a form of qualified headings (Chan 1986, 56). Phrase headings come last; they include adjectival, conjunctive, and prepositional phrase headings. Conjunctive and prepositional phrase headings often precoordinate two topics that could be expressed using two different headings into specific headings, for example, "Stock-exchange and occultism," "Television broadcasting of news," and "Police services for the mentally ill." This sequence results in the following alphabetical list of assigned subject headings and *see* references beginning with "Preaching":

Preaching
Preaching (Canon law)
Preaching, Afro-American
Preaching, Buddhist
Preaching, Extemporaneous

Preaching, Islamic
Preaching, Jewish
Preaching, Lay
Preaching, Methodist
Preaching, Muslim
Preaching friars
Preaching to children
Preaching to youth

Subdivided headings printed in *LCSH* should not be included in the alphabetical subject heading index. If subdivided headings were included in the index, users might immediately narrow their topics based on these subdivisions. Subdivided forms of matched headings should be accessible through the exact approach under the "Special topics" broad category. In the alphabetical approach, the only subdivided forms that systems should display to users are subdivided *see* references. In the following list of alphabetized terms under "Reading," users would see two subdivided *see* references:

Reading
Reading--Study and teaching
Reading--Therapeutic use
Reading (Adult education)
Reading (Elementary)
Reading (Higher education)
Reading (Primary)
Reading (Secondary education)
Reading, Psychology of
Reading comprehension
Reading devices for the disabled

The filing approach used here could be criticized because it results in several separate sequences of alphabetized terms. These sequences may discourage users from browsing past the first sequence. For example, three sequences are given under the list of "Preaching" headings: (1) "Preaching" to "Preaching (Canon law)," (2) "Preaching, Afro-American" to "Preaching, Muslim," and (3) "Preaching friars" to "Preaching to youth." These three alphabetized sequences might not be readily apparent to users because so few subject headings are given here beginning with the word "Preaching." If the first sequence had taken up an entire screen of subject headings, users might not browse forward to the next screen of subject headings because they may think the first screen displayed all available controlled vocabulary terms. Yet the alphabetization sequence used here may actually facilitate browsing. Controlled vocabulary terms formulated in the same way are placed together. If they were dispersed throughout the list, users would have to take time to interpret individual headings because of the interfiling of different forms of headings. In addition, headings are organized in a logical sequence, beginning with broad terms and ending with specific phrase headings.

An argument can be made for listing assigned headings in strict alphabetical order; this listing can be done by disregarding the forms of headings and punctuation during alphabetization. One could contend that users can quickly scan words or phrases following the initial word "preaching" to find the type of preaching that interests them. "Preaching" headings are filed in strict alphabetical order below:

Preaching
Preaching, Afro-American
Preaching, Buddhist
Preaching (Canon law)
Preaching, Extemporaneous
Preaching friars
Preaching, Islamic
Preaching, Jewish
Preaching, Lay
Preaching, Methodist
Preaching, Muslim
Preaching to children
Preaching to youth

So far, alphabetical lists have been composed of topical subject headings. Ultimately, alphabetical searches for general subject searches will produce alphabetical lists containing topical subject headings, geographic names, corporate and conference names, and uniform titles. System designers will have to make decisions about interfiling the different types of subject headings in a single alphabetized list or separating them into separate sequences of alphabetized headings by type. The SAC Subcommittee Report on the Display of Subject Headings also addresses this issue by giving the pros and cons of each approach (American Library Association 1992).

Strict alphabetical order disperses broad headings, that is, qualified and inverted headings, throughout the alphabet. Alphabetizing headings by form helps to keep these broad headings at the beginning of the alphabetical list. System designers who choose this approach may find that the punctuation in controlled vocabulary terms is not always indicative of the form of heading. For example, commas do not always designate inverted forms of topical subject headings, for example, "Law reports, digests, etc." and "Speeches, addresses, etc." Programming automated systems to distinguish between "meaningful" punctuation in inverted controlled vocabulary terms and "meaningless" punctuation in conjunctive phrase headings would be necessary.

Alphabetization is also an issue with respect to the exact approach. When users select broad categories, subdivisions are listed in alphabetical order. The same forms used in the topical-subject element, that is, subfield $a of topical subject headings, are also used in subdivisions: (1) single-word subdivisions, for example, "Curricula,"

"History," and "Bibliography," (2) qualified subdivisions, for example, "Education (Elementary)" and "Motors (Diesel)," (3) inverted phrases, for example, "Antiquities, Slavic," "Maps, Tourist," and "Personal narratives, Confederate," and (4) phrase subdivisions, for example, "Job descriptions," "Juvenile literature," and "Study and teaching." Like main headings, some subdivisions contain "meaningless" punctuation that makes them look like inverted headings when they are not, for example, "Outlines, syllabi, etc.," "Comic books, strips, etc.," and "Anecdotes, facetiae, satire, etc."

Period subdivisions are accessible through the "History" broad category. Of the six different forms of subdivisions (Chan 1972), one frequently occurring form cites an event followed by a date or date range. This form of period subdivision makes it difficult for online systems to preserve the correct historical sequence when period subdivisions are listed in alphabetical order. The two lists below give alphabetical and chronological arrangements of period subdivisions under "Albania--History":

Alphabetical order	*Chronological order*
1501–1912	To 1501
1878–1912	Turkish Wars, 15th century
18th century	1501–1912
1912–1944	18th century
1944–	19th century
19th century	1878–1912
Axis occupation, 1939–1944	Uprising, 1912
Peasant uprising, 1914–1915	1912–1944
To 1501	Peasant uprising, 1914–1915
Turkish Wars, 15th century	Axis occupation, 1939–1944
Uprising, 1912	1944–

Except for abbreviated century names, subdivisions beginning with dates are in order. They could be placed in chronological order if the date range preceded abbreviated century names, for example, "1801–1900 (19th century)." Subdivisions beginning with words are out of order. They could be placed in chronological order and correctly interfiled with period subdivisions beginning with dates if the date or date ranges at the end of the subdivision were the first element of the subdivision and the date ranges were substituted for or given in addition to abbreviated century names, for example, "1939–1944, Axis occupation" and "1401–1500 (15th century)." Twenty-two years ago, Chan (1972) made such recommendations to facilitate correct chronological filing of period subdivisions in library catalogs. In response to the library community's support for Chan's recommendations (American Library Association 1992; Library of Congress 1992), the Library of Congress could make dates the first element in period subdivisions (Avram 1992). Without this and additional changes to period subdivisions, online systems will construct lists of period subdivisions that are hopelessly out of order.

Online systems staff and their advisors will ultimately make decisions about alphabetization for their own systems. They must consider the objective of alphabetical searching and how this approach supports other subject searching approaches in their systems. They can also consult the SAC Subcommittee Report on the Display of Subject Headings, which surveys alphabetization schemes that are used in online bibliographic systems and explains the pros and cons of each scheme.

12.3 Keyword-in-Heading Approaches to Subject Searching

12.3.1 Characteristics of Queries

Subject queries submitted to keyword-in-heading approaches have the following characteristics: (1) they are composed of two or more words, (2) they are neither exact nor normalized matches of controlled vocabulary terms, and (3) if they match the first one or more words of controlled vocabulary terms, they contain additional words that are different from the closest matching controlled vocabulary term. Keyword-in-heading approaches for queries for subject searches generally are discussed here. These approaches for personal names are discussed later in this chapter.

Two keyword searches of assigned headings are possible: (1) keyword-in-main-heading search approach, and (2) keyword-in-subdivided-heading search approach. Both keyword approaches are two-step approaches, since they present users with intermediary steps.

Systems first search for the words in user queries through the keyword-in-main-heading approach. If they produce no retrievals or too few retrievals, systems search for the words in user queries through the keyword-in-subdivided-heading approach. Keyword-in-subdivided-heading searches sometimes produce large numbers of retrievals. This section discusses the contents of subject heading displays produced by this approach and, to keep from overwhelming users, suggests methods of limiting the amount of catalog information displayed.

12.3.2 Keyword-in-Main-Heading Search Approach

The keyword-in-main-heading search approach is limited to a searchable index of the words in main headings of topical and geographic subject headings (USMARC tags 650 and 651, subfield $a). The index could include words from *see from* tracing subfields for topical subjects and geographic names (USMARC tags 450 and 451, subfields $a, $x, $y, and $z). The result of keyword-in-main-heading searches is an intermediary list of topical and geographic subject headings and tracings bearing the words in user queries. If more than one heading or tracing is retrieved, the system gives users a choice of terms, comparable to presenting users with two or more *see* references and asking them to choose one. When users make a choice between terms, systems respond with the exact approach. If the results of the keyword-in-main-

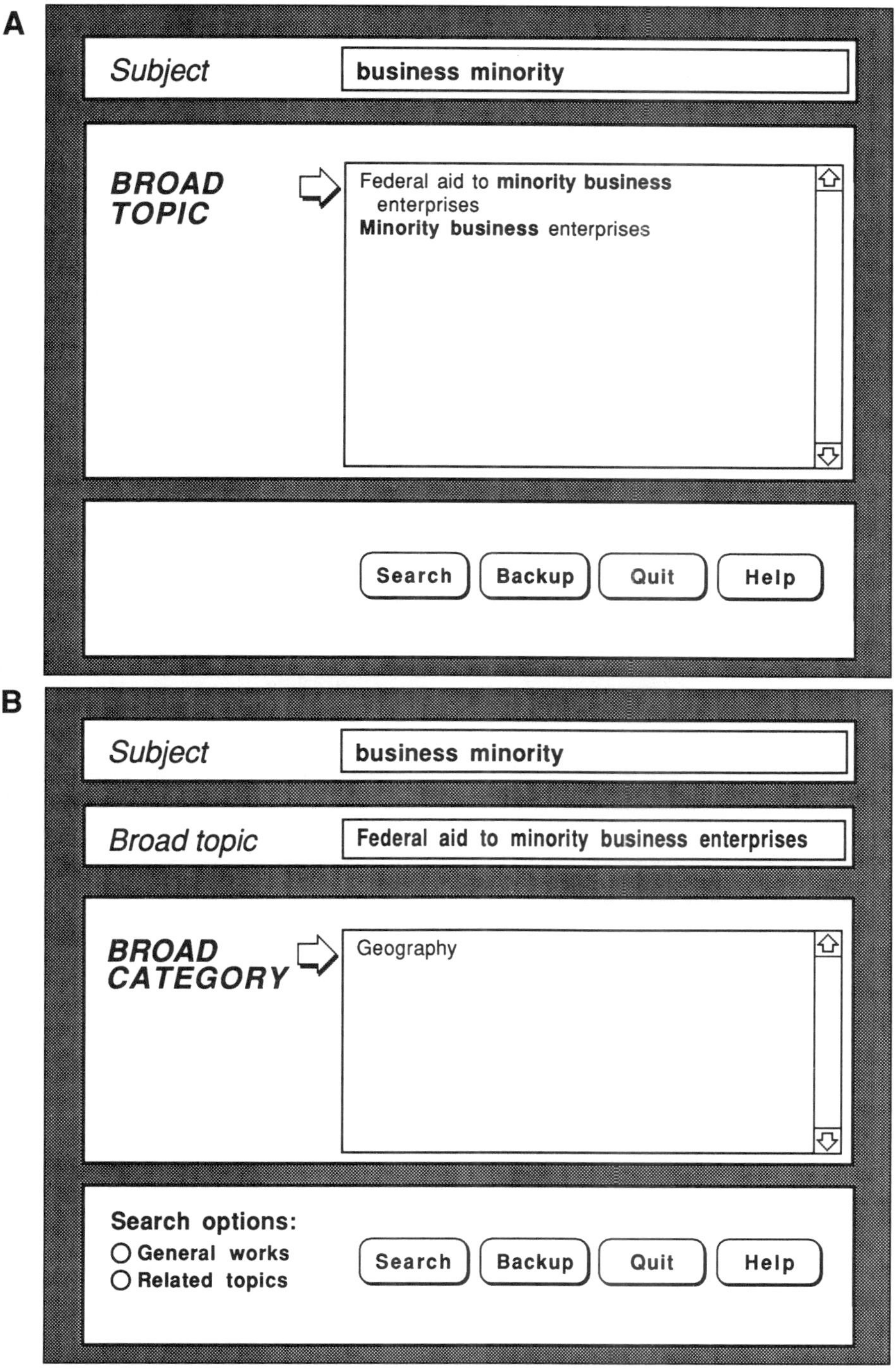

Figure 12.4
Keyword-in-main-heading search approach for "business minority."

heading search approach do not satisfy users, systems can continue searching for the original query using the keyword-in-subdivided-heading search approach.

The user–system interaction for the query "business minority" is shown in Figure 12.4. This query matches two words in two separate topical-subject elements. Thus, the system presents the user with a choice of topical-subject headings (Figure 12.4A). The user's selection of the first heading on the list, "Federal aid to minority business enterprises," results in the exact approach to subject searching for this assigned subject heading (Figure 12.4B). The system cannot fit all subdivided forms of this heading on a single screen; consequently, the system gives an array of one broad category and several options.

To find additional information about the selected heading, users could pursue the "Related topics" option. For the heading selected in Figure 12.4 (i.e., "Federal aid to minority business enterprises"), the catalog would give the related terms "Grants-in-aid" and "Minority business enterprises--Finance." For users who continue their search, systems would display the results of the keyword-in-subdivided-heading search approach using the original query.

12.3.3 Keyword-in-Subdivided-Heading Search Approach

The keyword-in-subdivided-heading search approach retrieves controlled vocabulary terms bearing the words in user queries. Retrievals come from words in

Table 12.2
Queries for the Keyword-in-Subdivided-Heading Search Approach

Query	Examples of subdivided headings
afro american history (96)	**Afro-American** art--**History; Afro-American** press--**History**--19th century; American literature--**Afro-American** authors--**History** and criticism
business france (43)	Big **business--France**--History; Master of **business** administration degree--**France**; Women in **business--France**
humanities study (21)	**Humanities--Study** and teaching; **Humanities Study** and teaching (Higher)--Poland
japanese management (10)	Corporations, **Japanese--Management**; Banks and banking, **Japanese**--Personnel **management**
middle east and United States (26)	**Middle East**--Military relations--**United States; United States**--Foreign relations--**Middle East**
mexican history (107)	Cookery, **Mexican--History**; **Mexican** americans--**History**; Spain--**History**--Civil War, 1936–1939--Participation, **Mexican**
retail directories (11)	**Retail** trade--California--Los Angeles--**Directories**; Stores, **Retail--Directories**
trade canada (144)	Fish **trade--Canada**; Food industry and **trade--Canada**--Statistics; **Trade** secrets--**Canada**; **Trade**-unions--Postal service--**Canada**

main headings and words in subdivisions in topical-subject headings, geographic names, corporate names, meeting names, and uniform titles (USMARC tags 650, 651, 610, 611, and 630). Occasionally, matches come exclusively from words in subdivisions. Most of the time, several subdivided headings are retrieved. The difficulty with this approach is managing large numbers of assigned headings.

Examples of queries composed of words that match words in subdivided subject headings are given in Table 12.2. Accompanying each query is the number of retrievals that keyword-in-subdivided-heading searches produce in ORION and examples of matching subdivided headings. Words in main headings and subdivisions that are the same as the words in user queries are highlighted.

The number of unique assigned subject headings retrieved ranges from a low of 10 headings for "japanese management" to a high of 144 headings for "trade canada." When the number of retrievals is a dozen or fewer, all retrieved headings can be displayed on one screen. For example, a single screen of retrieved subdivided headings is given in Figure 12.5 for the low-posted query "japanese management."

The problem with this display is the length of subdivided headings. They take up a large amount of space, and the screen becomes cluttered and difficult to read

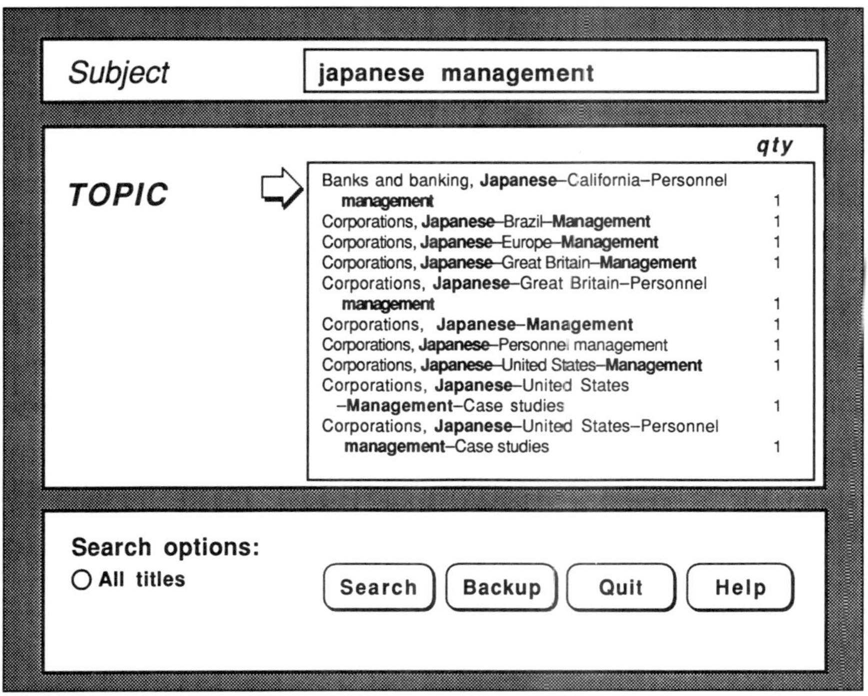

Figure 12.5
Keyword-in-subdivided heading search approach for "japanese management."

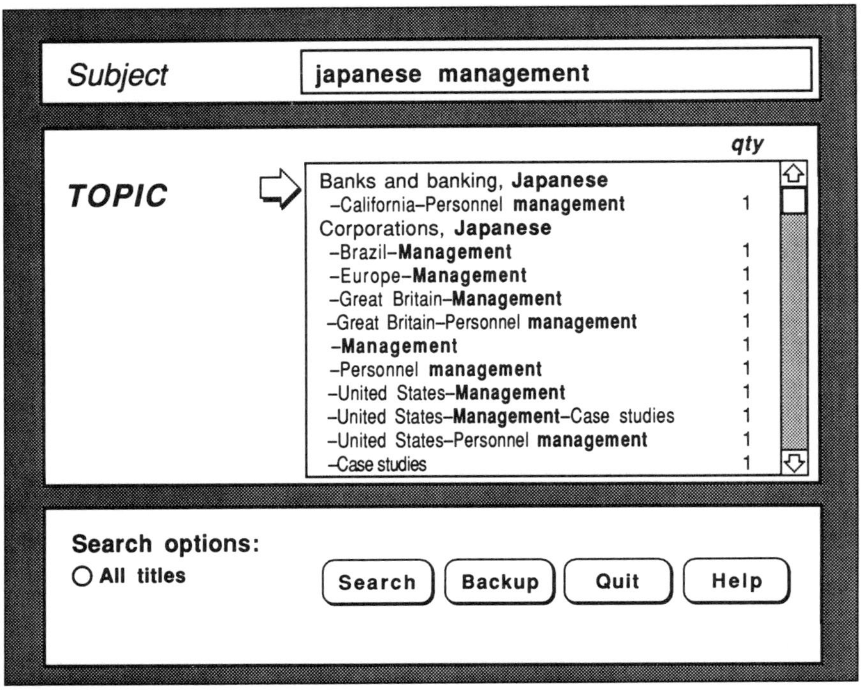

Figure 12.6
Simplified display of subdivided headings for "japanese management."

and study. The display needs to be simplified so that users are encouraged to browse. An alternative to the display of subdivided headings is shown in Figure 12.6. Main headings are listed once. Users can select only the subdivided forms that follow main headings.

A user initiating a subject search on the history of musical instruments enters the query "instruments history." In a keyword-in-subdivided-heading search, this query retrieves more nonrelevant headings than relevant headings. The results of keyword-in-subdivided-heading searches should be summarized in such a way that users can quickly determine which, if any, retrieved headings are satisfactory.

One approach to summarizing retrieved headings is to limit the display to main headings. Users can scan the main headings to see if a listed heading(s) expresses a portion of their query. Figure 12.7A shows main headings retrieved for the query "instruments history" using the keyword-in-subdivided-heading search approach. An explanation accompanies listed headings telling users that the terms may satisfy only part of their topics of interest (Figure 12.7B).

Selection of any main heading listed in Figure 12.7A leads to the subdivided portion of the selected heading. The user who completes the search by selecting

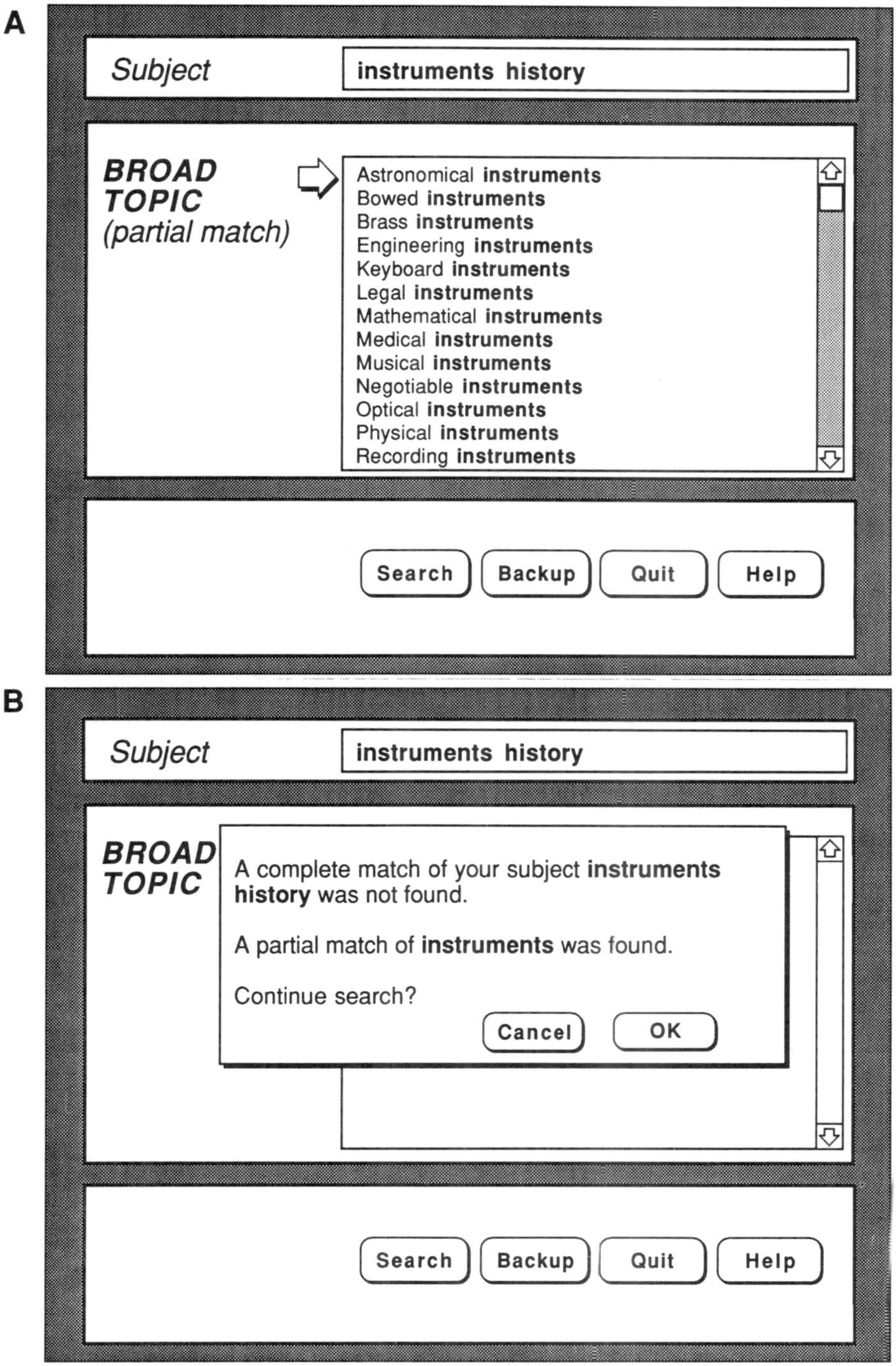

Figure 12.7
Keyword-in-subdivided-heading approach for the query "instruments history."

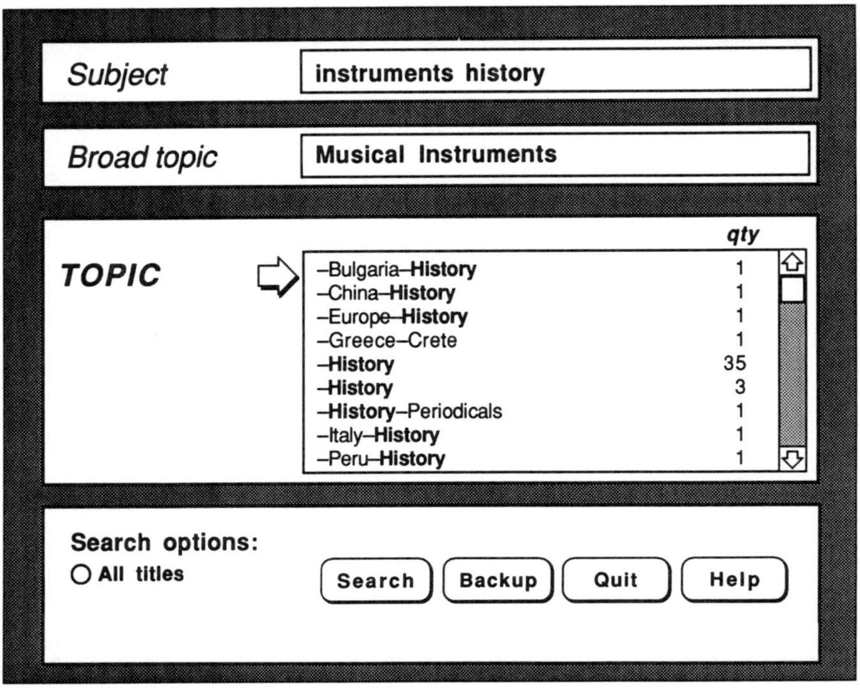

Figure 12.8
Completion of the keyword-in-subdivided-heading search for "instruments history."

"Musical instruments" (Figure 12.8) should return to the main heading display by clicking on the "Backup" button in Figure 12.7 and scroll forward to find potentially relevant subdivided headings toward the end of the alphabet, that is, "Stringed instruments," "Wind instruments," and "Woodwind instruments."

Lists of subdivided segments appended to a particular main heading will not always be as short as the list in Figure 12.8. To summarize large numbers of subdivided forms, systems could turn to broad categories. For example, the query "brazil politics" is high posted with respect to both main headings and subdivided segments. The user's first task is to select among the four dozen unique main headings satisfying part of the query. In the alphabetical list of the first twelve headings (Figure 12.9A), some main headings contain the query word "brazil" and other main headings contain the query word "politics."

The user's selection of the main heading "Brazil" (Figure 12.9B) results in a list of sixty subdivided segments that are appended to this main heading and bear the second query word "politics." Broad categories could be used to summarize these subdivided segments. For example, Figure 12.10A gives a broad category array under "Brazil."

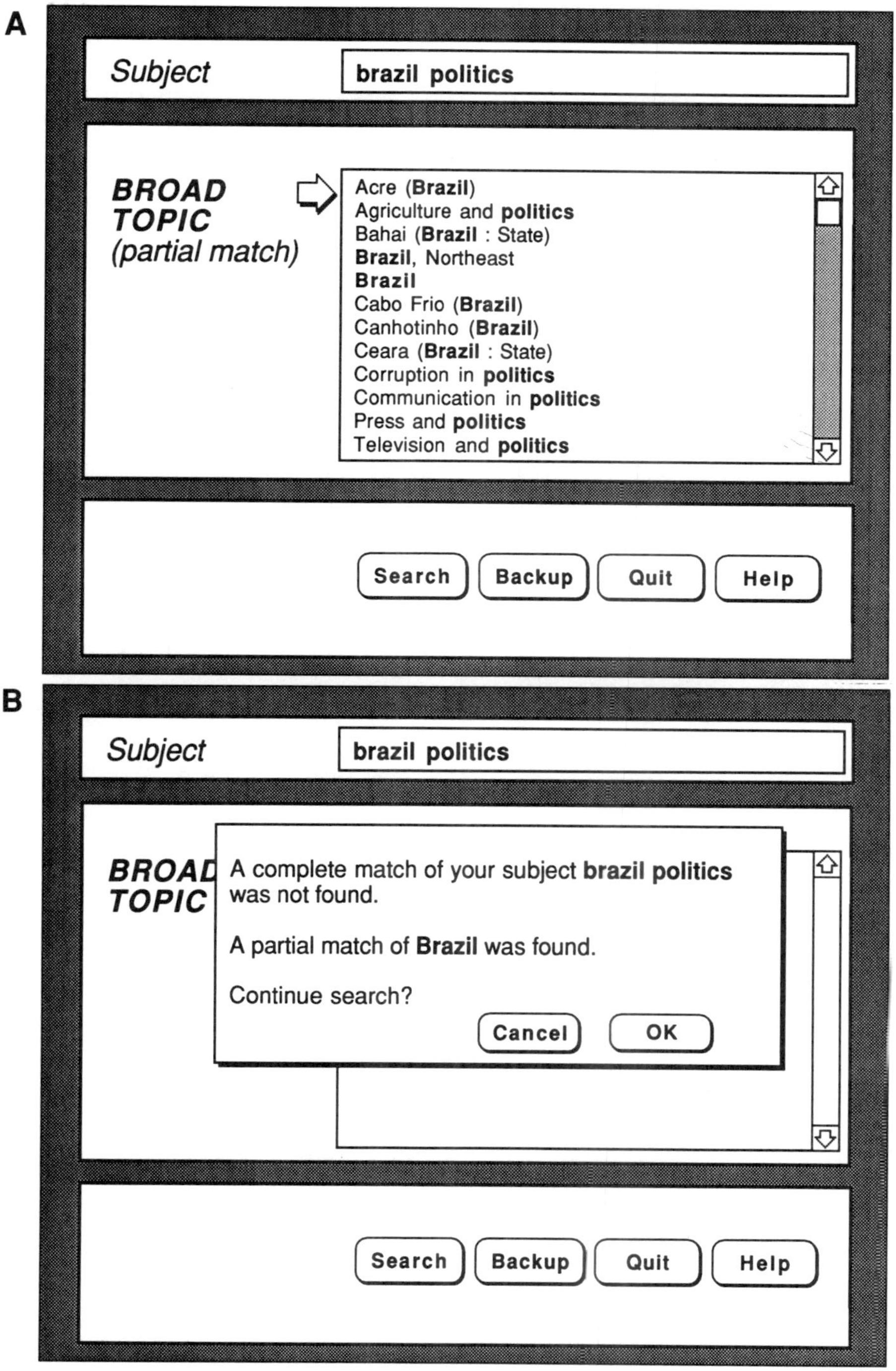

Figure 12.9
Keyword-in-subdivided-heading approach for the query "brazil politics."

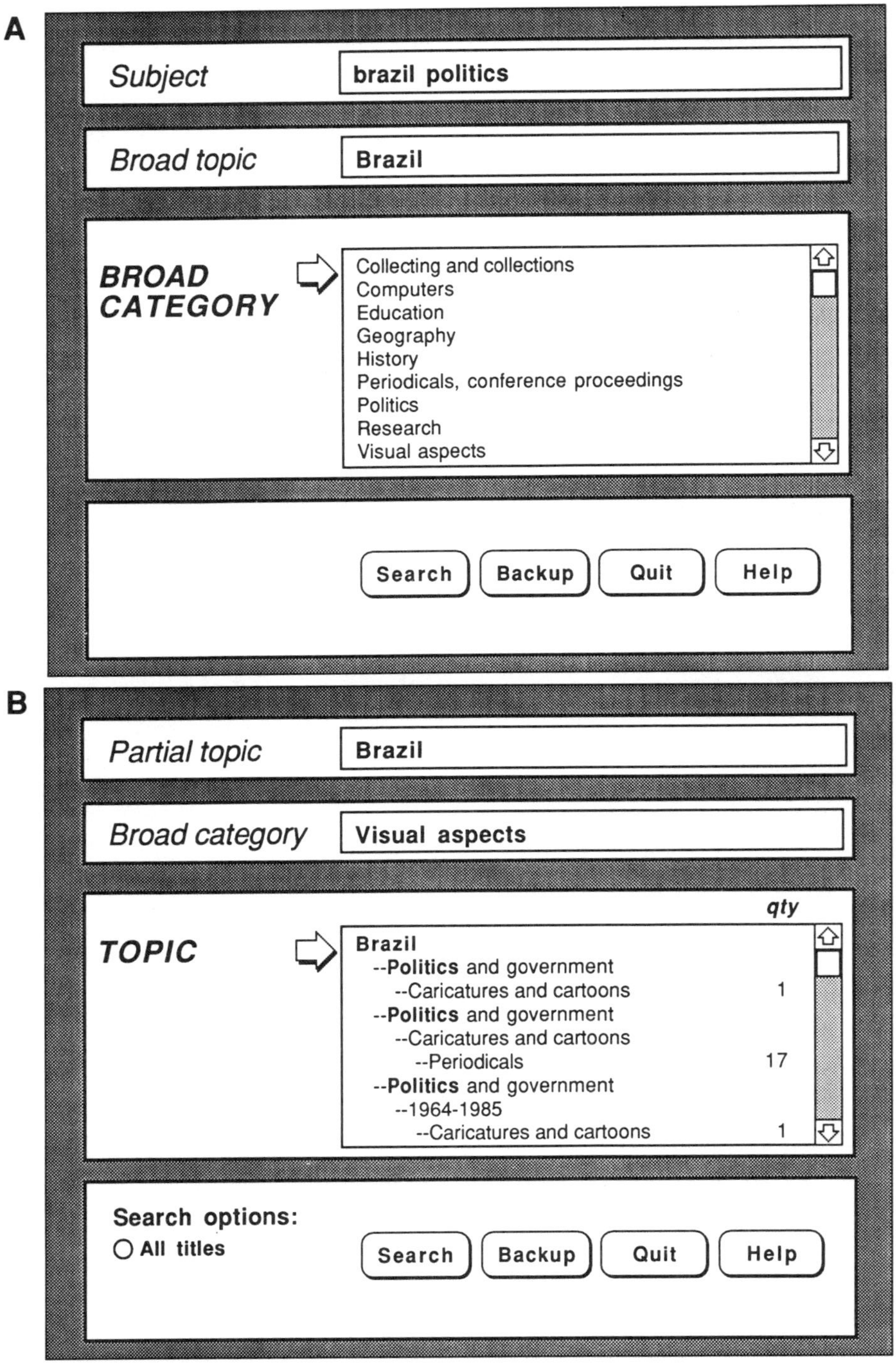

Figure 12.10
Using broad category coding to summarize subdivided headings.

Browsing listed subdivided segments, the user selects the "Visual aspects" broad category (Figure 12.10B). The system responds with a list of subdivided segments bearing the query word "politics." Listed subdivisions express a visual aspect of the topic "Brazil--Politics and government."

Summarizing subdivided segments by broad categories reduces long lists except for the category where the match occurs. In the example (Figures 12.9 and 12.10), the user selects a main heading satisfying the word "brazil" in the query. The query word "politics" comes from subdivided segments placed in the "Politics" broad category. If the user selects this broad category, all sixty subdivided segments will be retrieved because they bear the word that matches part of the original query. If systems exclude the broad categories that retrieve all subdivided segments from the broad category array, some subdivided segments may never have an opportunity for systems to display them because they are placed in the excluded category by virtue of broad category coding.

12.4 Keyword-in-Record Approaches to Subject Searching

12.4.1 Characteristics of Queries

When user queries fail to produce any retrievals or a sufficient number of retrievals through keyword-in-heading approaches, they are submitted to keyword-in-record approaches. Thus, queries submitted to keyword-in-record approaches have the same characteristics as queries submitted to keyword-in-heading approaches: (1) they are composed of two or more words, (2) they are neither exact nor normalized matches of controlled vocabulary terms, and (3) if they match the first one or more words of a controlled vocabulary term, they contain additional words that are different from the controlled vocabulary term. Keyword-in-record approaches are recommended for queries for both subject searches generally and personal names. The former are discussed below.

Three keyword-in-record approaches are possible: (1) title keyword searches, (2) keyword searches of subject-heading fields, and (3) keyword searches of all subject-rich fields of bibliographic records. Systems first search for the words in user queries through the title keyword approach. If they produce no retrievals or too few retrievals, systems search for the words in user queries in subject-heading fields, followed by all subject-rich fields. Keyword-in-record approaches are one-step subject searching approaches. In response to subject queries, systems respond with bibliographic records bearing query words in two or more record fields.

Single-subject headings in bibliographic records retrieved through keyword-in-record approaches will not have the same words as user queries because retrievals come from two or more fields. For example, the query "free trade canada" matches words in two separate headings, that is, "Free trade" and "Canada," because the former heading cannot be subdivided geographically. This chapter discusses how online systems can enlist the aid of public catalog users to identify relevant subject headings in retrieved records. These subject headings can be used to find additional information on the topics users seek.

12.4.2 Title Keyword Searches

The title keyword approach is recommended for two types of queries: (1) one-word queries that fail to match the first word in a longer controlled vocabulary term, and (2) queries composed of two or more words that fail to produce retrievals for exact and keyword-in-heading approaches. When title keyword searches for the former queries produce zero retrievals, there is a good chance that queries are incorrectly spelled. Figure 12.1 demonstrated how systems can enlist user assistance to check and correct spelling.

Examples of queries with characteristics for title keyword searches and relevant titles retrieved in such searches are given in Table 12.3.

Some queries may be title searches that users are entering through the subject searching capabilities of the three systems studied. Possible title searches from the examples above are the queries "dsm," "graphwriter," and "nutritional anthropology." Queries matching titles are expected, for example, "teenage sexuality" and "logical thinking," because the terminology of authors writing about technical topics will be similar to experts researching the same topics.

Some users will be satisfied with the results of keyword title searches. Others will want additional material. Since title keyword searches are one-step subject searching approaches, they provide no intermediary steps that would give users ideas

Table 12.3
Queries for Title Keyword Searches

Query	Relevant title(s)
dsm	*The DSM-III-R casebook: A learning companion to the diagnostic and statistical manual of mental disorders*
graphwriter	*Lotus graphwriter II*
the judicial system	*Courts and Politics: The federal judicial system*
logical thinking	*Logical thinking: An integrated approach; Logic and logical thinking: A modular approach*
mrp	*MRP II: Unlocking America's productivity potential*
nutritional anthropology	*Nutritional anthropology; Nutrition: Monitoring and assessment*
teenage sexuality	Several titles called *Teenage sexuality*
widowhood	*Left alone: A book on widowhood; Life after Harry: My adventure in widowhood*

of related terms for subject searching or specific terms in the form of subdivided headings to represent aspects of the topics they have in mind but have not made explicit in their queries. A strategy for extending one-step subject searching approaches is to use the controlled vocabulary in retrieved, relevant bibliographic records to find additional ones. Two basic problems appear in this strategy. First, many searchers do not know that they can use these terms to find additional records. Second, several elements, that is, headings and/or title words, may have to be present to ensure the relevance of retrieved records.

To overcome the first problem, systems have to explicitly prompt users about the headings assigned to the bibliographic records they have retrieved. This prompting can be done in several ways: one is to ask users whether displayed records are relevant to their topics of interest. Thus, following every bibliographic record display, users would have to respond to a prompt such as "Is this item relevant to your interests (Y/N?)." Systems would keep a record of the first-listed subject headings in records judged relevant by users. The first-listed subject heading describes the predominant topic of the item in hand (Library of Congress 1990, H80). When users stop displaying records, systems would respond with a list of such headings and ask users to select the most relevant ones to continue the search.

Using the query "elizabethan music," we performed a title keyword search in Michigan's MIRLYN online catalog. Fifteen records were retrieved. Judging all fifteen relevant to this query, we found the following subject headings assigned to retrieved records in order of occurrence:

1. Music--England--History and criticism
2. Jonson, Ben, 1573?–1637
3. Chamber music
4. Harpsichord music
5. Lute music
6. Music--England--16th century--History and criticism
7. Music and literature--16th century
8. Shakespeare, William, 1564–1616--Musical settings

The sixth heading, "Music--England--16th century--History and criticism" is the most specific heading to describe the query "elizabethan music." This heading leads to ten additional records on music of the particular period. The first heading occurs in three of the fifteen records but it leads to almost eighty additional records, most of which are comprehensive histories of music in England and not necessarily specific to the Elizabethan period. Other queries for which title searches are successful in retrieving relevant bibliographic records and headings are "book banning," "dog training," "drilling mud additives," "graduate medical education," "mosquito control," and "third reich."

A less obtrusive approach is possible in systems that display brief titles in response to title keyword searches. Users who select brief titles to obtain full bibliographic records have performed a preliminary relevance assessment of the brief titles. Systems would keep track of the first-listed subject headings assigned to the records that users have chosen for full displays. When users make a move to terminate the search, systems would then present users with the list of subject headings in these records. Underlying this approach is the assumption that the full bibliographic records users display are relevant, which is not necessarily accurate: users may display full records when they are curious about an item or uncertain about its relevance because the brief title display does not provide enough subject information on which to make a relevance assessment.

Another approach that requires a minimum of user input, features a system capability that identifies the most frequently occurring subject headings in retrieved bibliographic records. For example, a title keyword search for "college loans" retrieves over three dozen records in MIRLYN. Frequently occurring subject headings are "Student aid--United States--Directories," "Student loan funds--United States--Directories," and "Scholarships--United States--Directories." Systems could present users with frequently occurring subject headings and ask users which one(s) they want to use to find additional information on the topics they seek.

So far, our examples of relevant subject headings gleaned from bibliographic records retrieved in title keyword searches are single headings that express users' topics of interest in their entirety. On occasion several elements, for example, two or more subject headings and/or title words, are often required to ensure the relevance of bibliographic records. Examples of title keyword searches that yield two assigned subject headings that must be present in records to ensure their relevance follow.

Query	*Relevant headings*
landscape artists	Landscape painting; Artists--Biography
segregation of public housing	Segregation; Public housing
sensory and perception	Sensory stimulation; Visual perception
zen in archery	Zen Buddhism; Archery

When several headings and/or title words have to be present in records to ensure their relevance, the strategy for identifying these elements is much more complex. Systems cannot determine on their own whether subject headings from relevant bibliographic records describe all facets of the topics users seek or describe them partially.

Keyword-in-record approaches retrieve records bearing subject headings with the following relationships to the topics users seek: (1) headings are not relevant, (2) headings are relevant but express one facet of a multifaceted user query, or (3) headings are relevant and entirely express the user query. Can users make distinctions about the subject headings in retrieved records and their relationship to the topics they seek? How can systems obtain this information from users?

A handful of online systems do not need answers to these questions because they enlist probabilistic retrieval methods including term weighting, combinatoric searching, and ranked output. When probabilistic retrieval methods are used for relevance feedback, they do not require all designated elements to be present in retrieved bibliographic records. Retrieved records are ranked in order of decreasing relevance based on term weights and/or the number of query (or relevance feedback) words found in records. Probabilistic methods help overcome the rigidity of Boolean retrieval methods that require explicit instructions as to the exact words and phrases that are being retrieved and the logic with which sets of records bearing these words and phrases are combined.

Hildreth (1989, 51–109) discusses probabilistic retrieval methods and relevance feedback capabilities in operational and experimental online catalogs. We urge readers interested in probabilistic retrieval methods for relevance feedback to review Hildreth's work and to study systems that feature these methods to determine how they could be incorporated in Boolean-based retrieval systems to provide relevance feedback in title keyword and other keyword-in-record search approaches.

12.4.3 Other Keyword-in-Record Approaches

Keyword searches of words in subject-heading fields of bibliographic records are recommended following title keyword searches. Queries that produce relevant bibliographic records will be composed of words in separate assigned headings. Examples of queries bearing two relevant assigned headings follow.

Queries	*Relevant assigned subject headings*
capital punishment and terrorists	Capital punishment; Terrorists
erosion sand	Erosion; Sand
free trade Canada	Free trade; Canada
mass media and politicians	Mass media; Politicians
simulation and neural	Computer simulation; Neural circuitry
zen in archery	Zen Buddhism; Archery

Keyword searches of all subject-rich fields of bibliographic records are recommended following keyword searches of words in subject-heading fields. Examples of queries and fields contributing matching words are given in Table 12.4.

Relevance feedback will be especially difficult for these queries because matches come from two or more different fields of bibliographic records. In the absence of probabilistic retrieval methods for relevance feedback capabilities, systems could ask users to highlight particularly relevant words or phrases in relevant records using a pointing and clicking device such as a mouse. Systems would search for additional bibliographic records using the words and phrases designated by users. If several elements are highlighted, keyword-in-record approaches using an implicit Boolean "and" operation to retrieve and combine retrievals for highlighted words and phrases would probably be the most successful retrieval technique.

12.5 When Existing Approaches Fail

Existing subject searching approaches may fail to produce retrievals or fail to produce useful retrievals. Both situations are difficult for users to diagnose and fix on their own.

When queries fail to produce retrievals for keyword-in-record approaches, they typically contain spelling errors. Online systems can be enlisted to help users correct such errors. Examples of such queries are:

- existentalism and human emotion
- graphics inyerchane files
- legaalization of drug use
- on line compter systemss
- organizational developement
- servomechnism
- silicone adheisive
- women and facism
- zinc oxside

One-word queries would be handled differently from queries composed of two or more words. When one-word queries fail to match exact or normalized forms of controlled vocabulary terms or the first word in a longer controlled vocabulary term, they would be candidates for the title keyword approach. If this approach fails to produce retrievals, queries probably contain spelling errors. For example, the one-word queries "mcat," "mrp," "graphwriter," and "controls" produce retrievals in title keyword searches. The one-word queries "philoctetess," "servomechnism," and "aagenda3" do not produce retrievals because they contain spelling errors. Spelling errors in queries composed of two or more words would remain undetected until systems perform searches through the keyword-in-record approach. Systems should

Table 12.4
Queries for Keyword-in-Record Searches

Queries	Words/Fields
caste system	"caste" from heading "Caste"; "system" from titles
fast fourier transforms	"fast" from title; "fourier" from heading "Fourier transformations"; "transforms" from title
homeless people	"homeless" from heading "Homeless persons"; "people" from titles
motifs art deco	"art" and "deco" from heading "Art deco"; "motifs" from titles
psychology basic	"psychology" from heading "Psychology"; "basic" from titles
supported work for handicapped	"handicapped" from heading "Handicapped" and headings beginning with this word; "supported" and "work" from titles
trademarks logos	"trademarks" from heading "Trademarks"; "logos" from titles

show users the word(s) that fail to produce retrievals and ask them to check it for spelling errors. Walker and Jones (1987, 96) use this strategy in Okapi and note users' receptivity to it. Figure 12.1, based on Okapi, shows how systems can ask users to check for spelling errors.

Sometimes users do not know the correct spelling of words. We have scanned a few searches containing the same spelling error entered over and over again, for example, the words "lyprosy" and "midieval" in SULIRS and ORION searches, respectively. If words in queries still fail to retrieve bibliographic records after users have checked for spelling errors, systems could try to correct spelling using spelling correction dictionaries.

The individual words in queries may retrieve bibliographic records on their own; however, the query fails to retrieve records when treated as a unit with an implicit Boolean "and" operator inserted between query words. Such queries are candidates for automatic system truncation of searchable words. When truncation is applied to queries composed of two or more words, systems should start looking for matches with the exact approach and continue through the sequence of keyword-in-subdivided-heading and keyword-in-record approaches until a match is found. Examples of truncated queries are given in Table 12.5 along with the first approach that produces retrievals; question marks indicate the point at which the word is truncated.

Automatic truncation is appropriate only when systems fail to produce retrievals for queries composed of two or more words through conventional subject searching approaches, that is, exact, alphabetical, and keyword approaches. CITE, Okapi, and the other systems that have automatic system stemming capabilities invoke these capabilities at different points in searches (Doszkocs 1983; Walker & Jones 1987, 57–67). The combinatoric, term weighting retrieval method that characterizes CITE and Okapi is another approach that could be applied to such queries. This method

Table 12.5
Existing Approaches Producing Retrievals for Truncated Queries

Original query	Truncated query	Successful approach
architecture modernist	architecture modernis?	keyword-in-record
child stereotyping	child stereotyp?	keyword-in-record
collegiate sports recruiting	colleg? sport? recruit?	title keyword
condom advertisement	condom? advertis?	title keyword
future prices commodities	future? prices commodit?	keyword-in-record
refugee resettlement	refugee? resettlement	keyword-in-record
surrealist painting	surrealis? paint?	keyword-in-record

retrieves bibliographic records even though they do not contain all words in user queries (Hildreth 1989, 78):

> In the combinatoric, term weighting retrieval method, matches on all combinations of the translated query terms are retrieved and ranked for output in decreasing order of relevance. Documents estimated to be most relevant are output at the top of the list.

Several queries entered into the three systems we studied fail to retrieve bibliographic records through conventional approaches and truncation of query words. Such queries are candidates for the combinatoric retrieval method:

- black television comedians
- kwakiutl potlach
- love and marriage in islam
- oglala sioux
- organizational unit planning
- penis expansion
- regular education initiative
- suicide in mass communications

Online searches that produce retrievals sometimes fail because retrievals are not useful to public catalog users. Most of the time, users have to reenter their queries using different words. Retrieval performance can be improved for a subset of these queries containing proper adjectival phrases. Examples are the queries "afro-american history," "mexican history," and "swiss universities." These queries produce many retrievals through the keyword-in-subdivided-heading approach, but retrievals are not relevant to the topics users seek. If users continue to search for the queries "afro-american history" and "mexican history" through the title keyword approach, they will find relevant bibliographic records because this phrase is common usage for these topics. For example, title keyword searches in MIRLYN for the former produce three dozen records; about one third of them use the exact words in the user query, for example, *The state of Afro-American history: Past, present, and future*, *Black mosaic: Essays in Afro-American history*, and *Afro-American history: Past to present.* Several relevant titles bear the relevant heading "Afro-Americans--History." An exact search for this assigned subject heading produces hundreds of additional records. Subject headings used to express both queries are not in a form that is common usage, that is, "Afro-americans--History" and "Mexico--History."

Keyword-in-record approaches to the query "swiss universities" fail to produce relevant bibliographic records. Material on this topic is given the heading "Universities and colleges--Switzerland." In most online systems, the only way that users will retrieve bibliographic records on this topic is to reformulate the query using different words than the initial query.

The Okapi researchers anticipated the problem of proper adjectival headings and included noun/adjective pairs for proper names in the system's go/see list. This list forces Okapi to treat proper nouns and adjectives such as "switzerland" and "swiss," "wales" and "welsh," and "florence" and "florentine" as equivalent terms (Walker & Jones 1987, 68).

Go/see lists could assist online searchers who enter proper nouns when adjectives are required and vice versa or who enter singular forms when plural forms are required and vice versa. Such lists could include country, regional, provincial, state, and selected city names and adjectives such as "Britain" and "British" and ethnic groups such as "Scandinavian American" and "Scandinavian Americans."

During retrieval, the existence of equivalent terms on go/see lists does not mean that systems will be able to immediately pinpoint the assigned subject headings that are relevant to users' topics of interest because output will contain retrievals for both proper adjective and noun forms. For example, the keyword-in-subdivided-heading approach in ORION produces over one hundred assigned subject headings for the query "mexican history." Even more assigned subject headings will be retrieved through the keyword-in-subdivided-heading approach to the query "mexico history." Users may have to browse through long lists of retrieved subject headings to find relevant ones. In the absence of go/see lists, systems could help users by prompting them to continue their search using a different approach or to identify a relevant subject heading in a retrieved bibliographic record.

12.6 Subject Searching Approaches for Personal Names

12.6.1 Eliciting the Elements of Personal-Name Access Points from System Users

Queries for personal names as subjects consist of single personal names, personal names and topics, and, infrequently, two personal names at a time. Users enter queries for personal names using several different forms, for example, direct forms, indirect forms, surnames only, or surnames with initials. When they enter a form of name that is different from the one mandated by the online catalog they are searching, most online catalogs process their access point as if it is the form expected, and give an inappropriate response. For example, systems requiring inverted forms of personal names respond to a direct form of name with an alphabetical list of personal names beginning with the given name of the person. Thus, the user entering "george washington" will be placed in alphabetical index under surnames beginning with the letter "g."

The unpredictable nature of the queries users enter for personal names contrasts with the predictable form of personal-name headings. Names are inverted with the surname in first position, followed by a comma, given name, middle name or initial, comma, and, possibly, dates, for example, "Washington, George, 1732–1799." If a topic is associated with a name, it follows the personal name in the form of a topical subdivision, for example, "Washington, George, 1732–1799 $x Headquarters."

If online systems could elicit the elements of personal-name queries from users, then online searches for these queries would be comparable to putting together a jigsaw puzzle. That is, systems would match the surnames, given names, middle names, and topics entered by users to these same elements in personal name headings. Obviously, the difficulty here is to elicit the different elements of personal-name headings from users and make sure that users enter the correct elements in response to system prompts. A form-filling mode or "pop-up" windows could be used. Prompts connected to the form-filling mode have to be subtle enough to elicit elements that users have in mind. A pointing and clicking device such as a mouse could be used to help searchers pick and choose among the various personal-name elements for which they choose to provide information. Users should not feel pressured to give information just because it is requested. System designers will want to test prompts with online catalog users to make sure they are obtaining accurate responses from users and not extracting information from users that they would not have otherwise given.

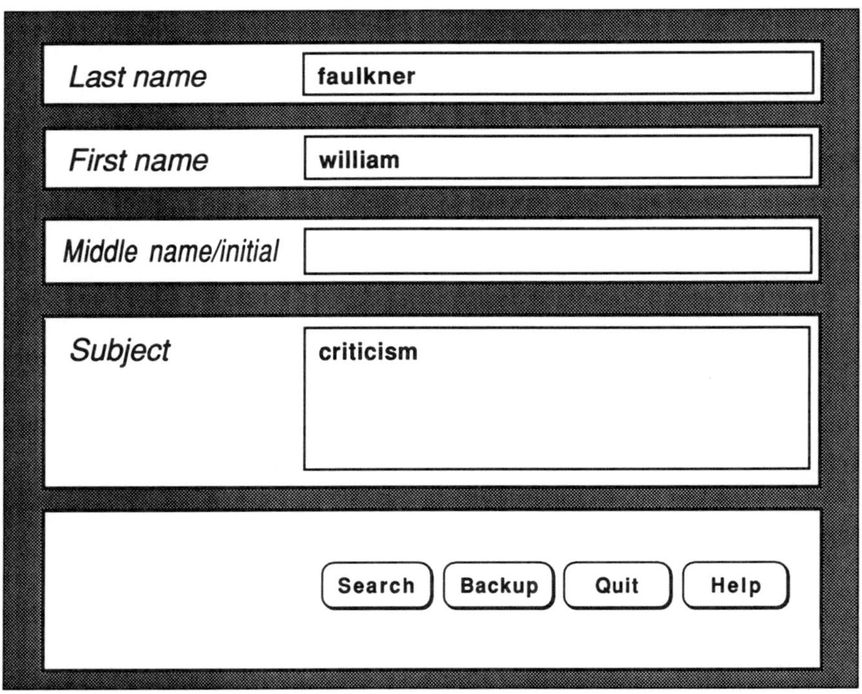

Figure 12.11
Eliciting the elements of personal-name queries from users.

On paper, it is difficult to reproduce the dynamic interaction between systems and users. Figure 12.11 shows four elements that systems could request from users. The next box appears when the user completes the preceding box.

The boxes request name elements in inverted form, that is, last name first, followed by first and middle names. This sequence should be familiar to users because it appears in published telephone directories, in personal phone directories, and on printed forms and applications. The sequence of elements presented is not suggested because it follows the sequence of elements in personal-name headings, but because so many users enter personal names that are just last names (see Figure 10.1). Thus, users need to complete only the first box and enter RETURN three times. Users will probably be stumped by names that are represented in direct form in catalog headings, for example, "black elk," "aristotle," "ovid;" consequently, they will probably enter the name elements familiar to them in the first box.

Users enter personal-name queries that include topics; however, they do not enter elements in any particular sequence. Examples of queries can be found beginning with first or last names and ending with topics, for example, "clarence darrow's relegious [*sic*] views," "hitler's speeches," and "descartes future prediction." Other examples show that users enter the topic before the name, for example, "paintings of pollock" and "religion tolstoy." In Figure 12.11, the system prompts users last for the topics they have in mind.

Testing interfaces for eliciting the elements of personal-names queries from online catalog users is imperative. Tests should determine whether users understand the information that is being requested and whether they feel pressured to respond. System designers may have to try several designs before they find one appropriate to their catalog's users. Users will benefit greatly from the definition of an interface that elicits usable information for the elements of personal-name queries.

12.6.2 Subject Searching Approaches for Personal Names

Subject searching approaches for personal names are limited to keyword-in-subdivided-heading, keyword-in-record, and alphabetical approaches. The exact approach is implied in the alphabetical approach because the user's selection of a name from an alphabetical list of assigned headings invokes the exact approach from systems.

The particular subject searching approach that the personal-name query invokes in online systems depends on the type(s) of elements that users offer and the system's ability to produce retrievals for these elements. Table 10.3 shows the sequence of subject searching approaches for personal-name queries.

Systems first try to produce retrievals for the name and topic elements of personal name queries through keyword-in-heading and keyword-in-record approaches. Even though some users will offer all four elements, that is, last, first, and middle names, and topics, systems may ignore first and middle name elements to effect a match. In Figure 12.12, the online system is able to find subdivided headings containing the two name elements and one topic element entered by the catalog user.

If keyword approaches fail to produce retrievals using name and topic elements, the systems ignore the topic elements and respond with the alphabetical approach. The alphabetical approach is also suggested for personal-name queries without topic elements. The alphabetical approach places users in the alphabetical index of personal names where their entered names are or would be listed in the alphabet. Systems always provide a response to subject searches for personal names through the alphabetical approach. It is important that users enter the correct element for last names because the system's placement at a particular point in the alphabetical index nearby the desired personal name depends on this element.

If the system is unable to find the topic element in a personal name query, it will respond with names in alphabetical proximity to the personal name elements entered by the user (Figure 12.13).

In Figure 12.13, the system is unable to satisfy the topic element of the query, so it ignores this element and places the user in an alphabetical directory of personal name headings. The user's selection of a listed name from the alphabetical index

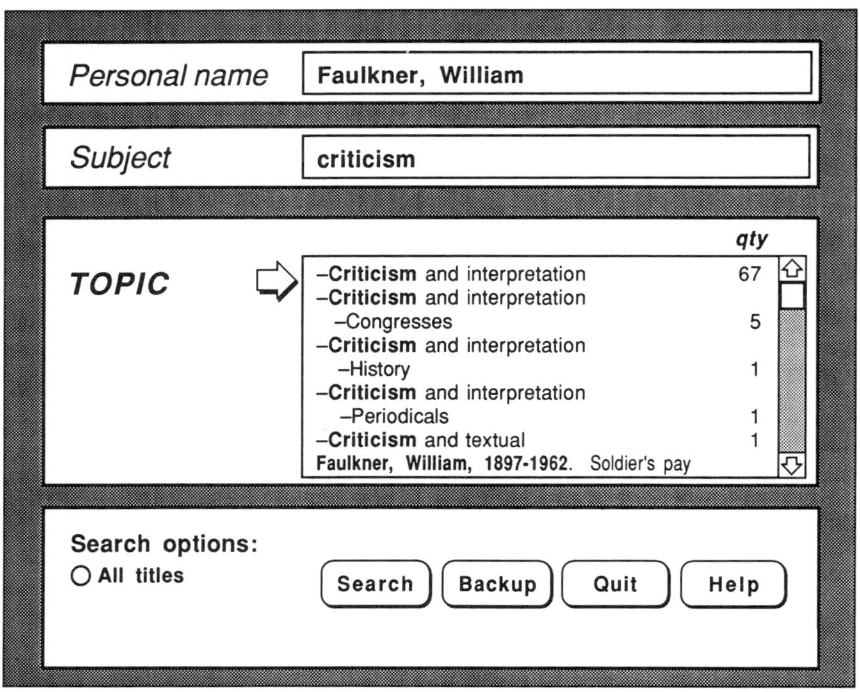

Figure 12.12
Keyword-in-subdivided-heading approach to the query "william faulkner criticism."

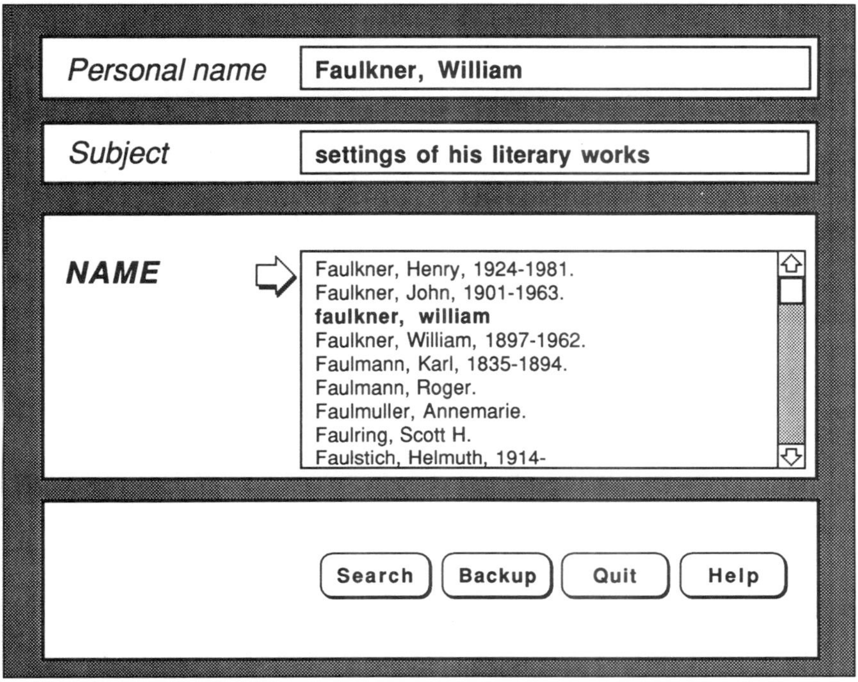

Figure 12.13
Alphabetical approach to a personal-name query.

invokes the exact approach to subject searching. If no subdivided forms of the name exist, the system merely responds with the number of bibliographic records retrieved and as many brief records as fit on one screen. If subdivided forms exist, the system responds with the following: (1) a list of as many subdivided headings as fit on one screen, or (2) a broad category array. In Figure 12.14, the system responds to the user's selection of a listed personal name heading with a broad category array.

The exact approach is not an explicit approach to subject searching for personal names, because users seldom include in their queries dates and date ranges that are needed to make exact matches of personal-name headings. The alphabetical approach is much like scanning the telephone directory because it gives names and a little more information, for example, dates, honorary titles, literary titles, to help users identify the particular name they have in mind.

Methods used to enhance entry vocabulary for topical subjects and geographical names are not recommended for personal names because the objective of these methods is to increase users' chances of making exact matches and invoking the exact approach. Since the exact approach does not figure into the sequence of subject

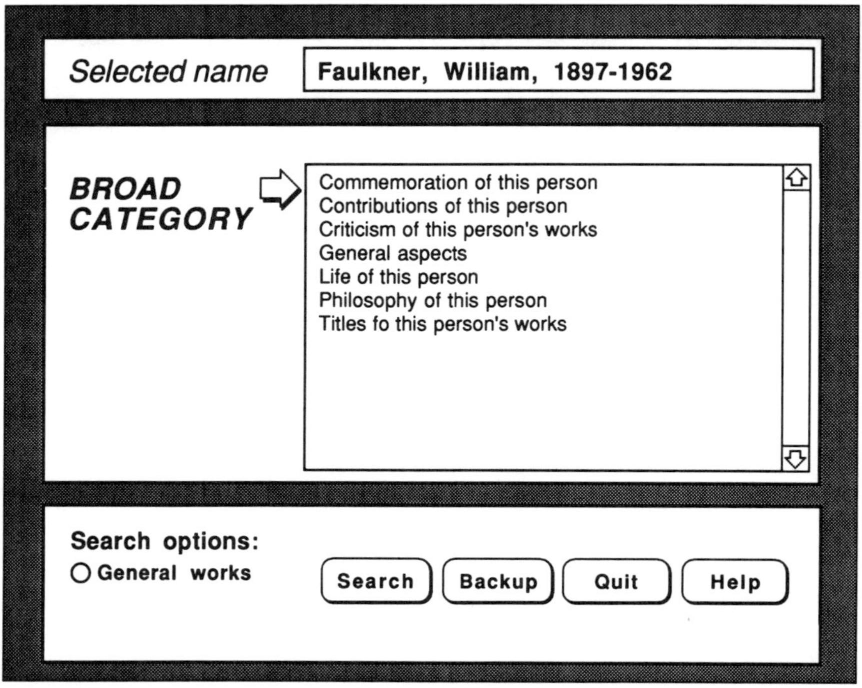

Figure 12.14
Broad category array under a personal-name heading.

searching approaches for personal names (see Table 10.3), these methods are not applicable to personal-name searches.

12.7 Synthesis and Summary

The majority of user queries are not matches of exact or normalized forms of controlled vocabulary terms. This chapter singles out various alphabetical and keyword approaches as appropriate system responses to such queries based on the number of words they have, whether they match longer controlled vocabulary terms, and their ability to produce retrievals.

Unlike the exact approach, alphabetical and keyword approaches will present catalog users with terms they enter and additional terms that may or may not address the topics users have in mind. These approaches have to facilitate browsing to enable users to find suitable terms for the topics they seek, but the problem with these approaches is that the large amounts of catalog information they provide may be overwhelming.

In the alphabetical approach, subject subdivisions are excluded from listed assigned subject headings. Often, there are dozens of subdivided forms for individual subject headings. Including these forms in the alphabetical index requires users to perform two tasks simultaneously: (1) find an appropriate subject heading for their topics of interest, and (2) refine their topics using available subject subdivisions. Excluding subdivided forms from the alphabetical index simplifies searching because users can concentrate on one task, that is, finding an appropriate subject heading. When they select a listed subject heading, the exact approach gives them access to subdivided forms of the selected heading to refine their search.

Many retrievals characterize keyword-in-subdivided-heading searches. Some of the words in user queries may be found in many different main headings. Main headings can be connected to many subdivided forms containing the other words in user queries. Subdivided forms of main headings may be composed of many subdivisions.

The results of keyword-in-subdivided-heading searches need to be summarized in such a way that users can quickly determine which, if any, retrieved headings are satisfactory. Systems can limit the initial display to main headings with an explanation that the headings displayed may satisfy only part of the topics users seek. Systems can limit subsequent displays of subdivided headings that satisfy the other part of the topics users seek using broad category coding. They can also simplify such displays by using the main heading as a caption for displays and listing subdivided forms connected to the main heading under the caption.

Of the subject searching approaches presented in this chapter, systems prefer the alphabetical and keyword-in-heading approaches because they are two-step approaches. Users can refine their searches using related terms, subdivided forms of the selected heading, or controlled vocabulary terms in close alphabetical proximity to query terms users enter into catalogs. Controlled vocabulary terms also ensure precision of search results because these are assigned to bibliographic records by catalogers to express the subject matter of original items.

Keyword-in-record approaches are enlisted only as a last resort because they are one-step subject searching approaches. Relevance feedback capabilities should be available to users to help them find the controlled vocabulary terms used for their topics of interest. Users can then use these terms to gain a foothold into the controlled vocabulary used for their topics. Throughout this chapter, emphasis is placed on subject searching approaches that enlist the catalog's controlled vocabulary because of the many links it provides to other catalog entries that can help users find information on the topics they seek.

Subject searching approaches in operational online catalogs can handle most user queries in terms of providing controlled vocabulary terms to express the topics users seek. Techniques associated with probabilistic retrieval methods, for example, automatic stemming, combinatoric retrieval, are needed for a small portion of user queries. Probabilistic methods would be especially useful as a means of providing relevance feedback for queries submitted to keyword-in-record approaches. Systems could prompt users to identify relevant words and phrases in various bibliographic record fields that would be used by probabilistic methods to find additional controlled vocabulary terms and bibliographic records. Probabilistic methods help overcome the rigidity of Boolean retrieval methods, which require explicit instructions as to the exact words and phrases that are being retrieved and the logic with which sets of records bearing these words and phrases are combined.

References

American Library Association. (1992). *Headings for tomorrow: Public access display of subject headings.* Chicago, IL: American Library Association.

Avram, Henriette D. (1992). Cataloging modifications at the Library of Congress, Collections Services." 2 January (photocopy).

Chan, Lois Mai. (1972). The period subdivision in subject headings. *Library Resources & Technical Services, 16,* 453–459.

Chan, Lois Mai. (1986). *Library of Congress Subject Headings: Principles and application.* Littleton, CO: Libraries Unlimited.

Doszkocs, Tamas E. (1983). CITE NLM: Natural-language searching in an online catalog. *Information Technology and Libraries, 2,* 4 (December), 364–380.

Hildreth, Charles R. (1989). *Intelligent interfaces and retrieval methods for subject searching in bibliographic retrieval systems.* Washington, DC: Library of Congress. Advances in Library Information Technology 2.

Library of Congress. (1990). *Subject cataloging manual: Subject headings.* Washington, DC: Library of Congress.

Library of Congress. (1992). *The future of subdivisions in the Library of Congress Subject Headings System: Report from the Subject Subdivisions Conference,* Martha O'Hara Conway (Ed.). Washington, DC: Library of Congress.

Walker, Stephen, & Jones, Richard M. (1987). *Improving subject retrieval in online catalogues: 1. Stemming, automatic spelling correction and cross-reference tables.* London: British Library. British Library Research Paper No. 24.

13

Search Trees for Subject Searching

13.1

Introduction

The subject terms users enter into online systems possess certain characteristics that reveal the subject searching approaches most likely to produce assigned subject headings and bibliographic records on the topics users seek. Computer systems can be programmed to identify many of these characteristics without the aid of a human intermediary: for example, characteristics associated with success are the number of words in user queries and the extent to which they match controlled vocabulary terms. Programming computer systems to identify these characteristics will enable systems to respond to the subject queries users enter with the subject searching approaches most likely to succeed.

This chapter describes how online systems choose between exact, alphabetical, and keyword approaches. Users do not explicitly choose a particular approach. Rather, systems respond with an approach based on the characteristics of user queries and their ability to produce retrievals. When systems select an approach yielding zero or too few retrievals, they continue searching using another approach. Systems are governed by search trees in their selection of one subject searching approach over others. Search trees are a set of paths with branches or choices that enable systems to carry out the most sensible search approach at each stage—a definition adopted from one given to search trees by the Okapi designers who first introduced them (Mitev, Venner, & Walker 1985, 94).

Six search trees for subject searching are presented in this chapter. The search trees implemented in Okapi are different from those recommended in this chapter for two important reasons. First, only half of the bibliographic records in Okapi's database contained subject headings. When formulating search trees, the Okapi designers did not place as much emphasis on subject headings as on other subject information that was present in most of the system's bibliographic records (Mitev *et al.*, 1985, 40). The vast majority of bibliographic records created by American libraries are assigned subject headings based on the LCSH system (O'Neill & Aluri 1979), so the search trees presented in this chapter are based on this system.

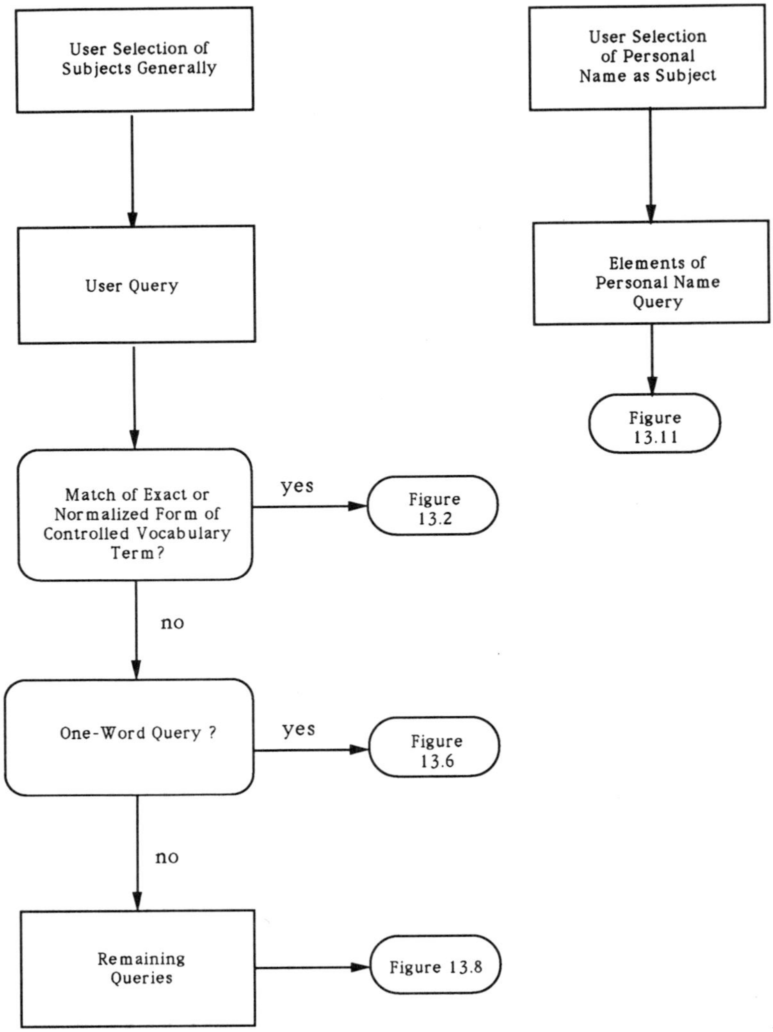

Figure 13.1
Initial search tree.

The second reason that our search trees differ from those of the Okapi designers stems from how the trees were developed. Okapi's designers noted that the sequence of search functions or approaches "evolved through a process of discussion and trial and error" (Mitev *et al.*, 1985, 94). We formulated search trees as a result of an empirical study of the subject terms users enter into online catalogs (see Chapters 5–10). This chapter presents search trees and tests their ability to retrieve relevant subject headings or titles using queries that are frequently entered into online catalogs.

13.2 Initial Search Tree

The user's selection of the subject searching option in online catalogs sets into motion the initial search tree, which serves as a filter insofar as it dispatches user queries to a particular search tree that favors the selection of certain subject searching approaches over others (Figure 13.1).

The initial search tree lets users distinguish their queries for personal subjects from queries for topical subjects generally and, based on summary characteristics that systems determine about topical subject queries, dispatches them to a particularly appropriate search tree. All user queries for subjects generally are candidates for the exact approach. To effect an exact match, systems manipulate queries in the same way that controlled vocabulary terms are manipulated to establish exact and normalized forms, for example, ignoring capitalization and removing punctuation and stopwords. In the event an exact match is found, the initial search tree dispatches the query to the search tree that governs the exact approach (Figure 13.2).

If it is unable to find an exact match, the initial search tree dispatches the user query to one of two search trees based on the number of words in the query. One-word queries are given to a search tree that favors the alphabetical approach (Figure 13.6). The extent to which remaining queries match controlled vocabulary terms determines whether they are submitted to a search tree that favors the alphabetical or keyword approaches (Figures 13.8 and 13.10, respectively).

Systems prompt users entering personal-name queries for the name elements and topic element of personal-name queries (see Figure 12.11). Personal-name queries are handled by a search tree that is separate from search trees for subjects generally (Figure 13.11). Systems choose between alphabetical and keyword approaches depending on the types of elements users enter and the ability of these elements to produce retrievals.

13.3 Search Tree Featuring the Exact Approach

Systems respond with the exact approach to user queries for subjects generally that match exact or normalized forms of controlled vocabulary terms. Generally, the exact approach presents a conceptual map to subdivided forms of the matched heading, and, if available, gives users the option to browse related terms and other information about the matched heading (see Chapter 11).

13.3.1 Frequently Entered Queries for the Exact Approach

The initial search tree passes queries that are matches of exact or normalized forms of controlled vocabulary terms onto the search tree for the exact approach (Figure 13.2).

If systems retrieve two or more exact or normalized forms of controlled vocabulary terms, they present retrieved terms and ask users to make a choice. If systems retrieve a single controlled vocabulary term, or if users select a single term from a list of matching controlled vocabulary terms, systems respond with the exact approach. Users can refine their searches using subdivided forms of the matched heading or related terms connected to it. When users terminate the search, systems prompt them to continue. Systems respond to users who want to continue searching by answering the original query with the alphabetical approach. Users can refine their searches using subject headings in the alphabetical neighborhood of their entered term.

In the search tree for the exact approach, the alphabetical approach follows the exact approach (Figure 13.2). Subject headings in the alphabetical neighborhood of the matched heading may be given in a different form than the matched heading. They may express topics that broad categories conveyed through the exact approach or subdivided forms of the matched heading that were displayed following the selection of a broad topic. To demonstrate this process, consider again the example used in Chapter 11 in which the initial and subsequent user queries suggest an interest in agriculture and education. The query "agriculture" exactly matches the subject heading "Agriculture" and thus invokes the exact approach. Users can refine their search by browsing subdivided forms of the topical subject heading "Agriculture" under the "Education" broad category to find subdivisions such as "Curricula," "Outlines, syllabi, etc.," and "Study and teaching." They can also refine their searches through the alphabetical approach by selecting subject headings in the alphabetical neighborhood of "Agriculture" that convey education subtopics, for example, "Agricultural education," "Agricultural extension work," and "Agricultural teachers." The original query entered into the catalog did not have to contain a word or phrase to express the educational aspect of agriculture to enable users to find relevant subject headings through the exact or alphabetical approach.

Table 13.1 lists frequently entered queries that match exact or normalized forms of controlled vocabulary terms. Systems would respond to these queries with the exact approach. Queries are placed into categories such as "Current events," "Drugs," and "Fields of study." The list is selective and could be expanded to include categories for "Fine and performing arts," "Computers," and "Sex." Annotations in the middle column indicate the type of term matched; unless designated, all matches are authorized subject headings. An "X" in the right-hand column designates queries composed of terms that also occur as a free-floating or pattern subdivision. User queries entered most frequently in all three systems that are candidates for the exact approach are "aids" and "sex."

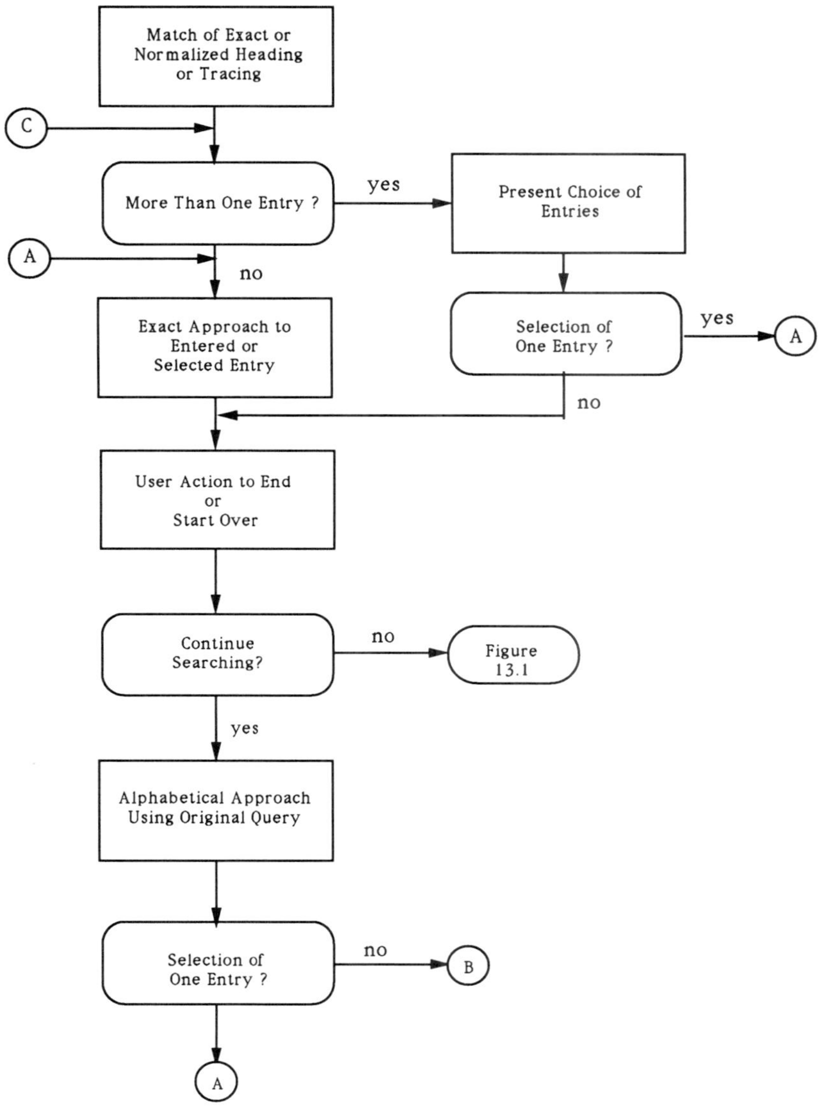

Figure 13.2
Search tree for the exact approach.

Several queries match two or more entries because of the removal of qualifiers in controlled vocabulary terms. In such instances, systems would give users a choice of headings before responding with the exact approach. For example, the query "korea" matches exact and normalized forms of authorized headings, that is,

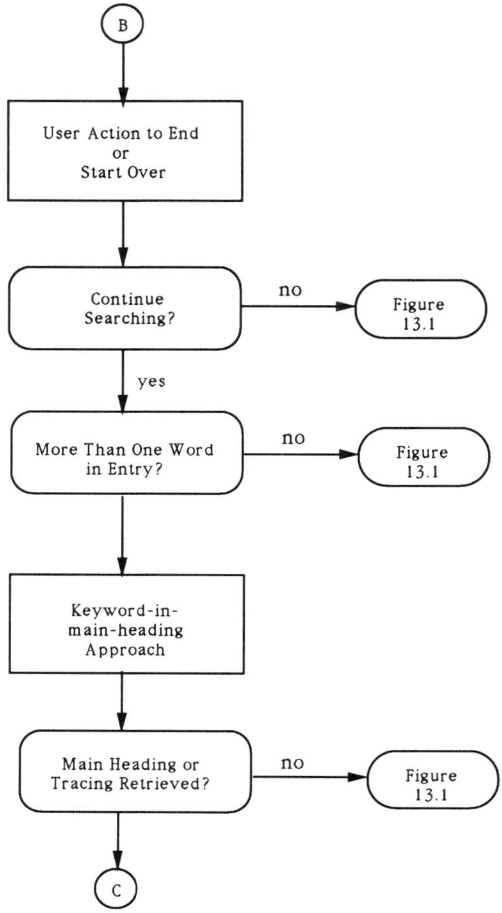

Figure 13.2 (*continued*)

"Korea," "Korea (North)," and "Korea (South)," and normalized forms of tracings, that is, "Korea (Democratic People's Republic)" and "Korea (Republic)." The two tracings refer searchers to the two qualified headings, respectively. Thus, systems would give users a choice of three terms:

Enter subject to search > **korea**
Choose 1 of the 3 headings used in this catalog to express **Korea**:
1. Korea
2. Korea (North)
3. Korea (South)

Enter your choice > 2

Table 13.1
Frequently Entered Queries for the Exact Approach

Category/query	Type of match	Subdivision
Broad fields of study		
art	exact form	
computers	exact form	
education	exact form, normalized form (minus qualifier)	X
german	normalized form (minus qualifier)	
management	exact form	X
marketing	exact form, normalized form (minus qualifier)	X
psychology	exact form	X
Current events		
abortion	normalized form (minus qualifier)	
aids	normalized form (minus qualifier)	
child abuse	exact form	
food additives	exact form	
inflation	normalized form (minus qualifier)	
stress	normalized form (minus qualifier)	
suicide	exact form	
Drugs		
cocaine	exact form	
drugs	exact form	
steroids	exact form	
Places		
africa	exact form	X
central valley	normalized form (minus qualifier)	X
japan	exact form	X
korea	exact form; tracing: normalized form (minus qualifier)	X
vietnam	normalized form (minus qualifier)	X
Other		
blues music	normalized form (minus punctuation)	
feminism	exact form	
motion pictures	tracing: exact form	
real estate	tracing: exact form	
sex	exact form	
sports	exact form; normalized form (minus qualifier)	X
translation	normalized form (minus qualifier)	X
women	heading: exact form, normalized form (minus qualifier); tracing: normalized form (minus qualifier)	X

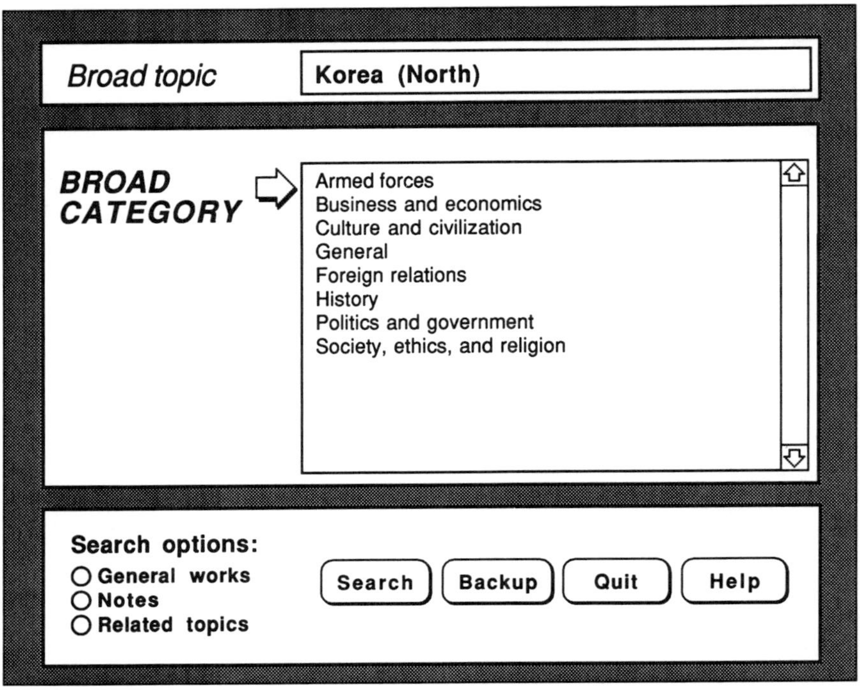

Figure 13.3
Broad category array and options under "Korea (North)."

The user's selection of "Korea (North)" directs the system to respond with the exact approach. This approach presents a conceptual map to subdivided forms of the selected heading, and options to browse related terms and other information about the selected heading. Figure 13.3 shows arrays of broad categories and options for the selected term.

The user's selection of a broad category leads to a list of subdivided headings. It could have also led to an intermediary screen of broad categories if there had been many subdivided forms under a broad category. Figure 13.4 shows subdivided forms under the broad category for "Politics and government."

Most of the frequently entered queries in Table 13.1 match headings assigned to thousands of bibliographic records and connected to hundreds of subdivided forms. Users entering these queries may have more specific topics in mind, but they have not made them explicit in their queries. The exact approach provides a framework for managing the retrievals of high-posted headings. It enables systems to summarize results to users in one or two screens. It also encourages users to explore and refine their topics by browsing subdivided forms of headings under broad categories to find ones that touch on the topics users seek.

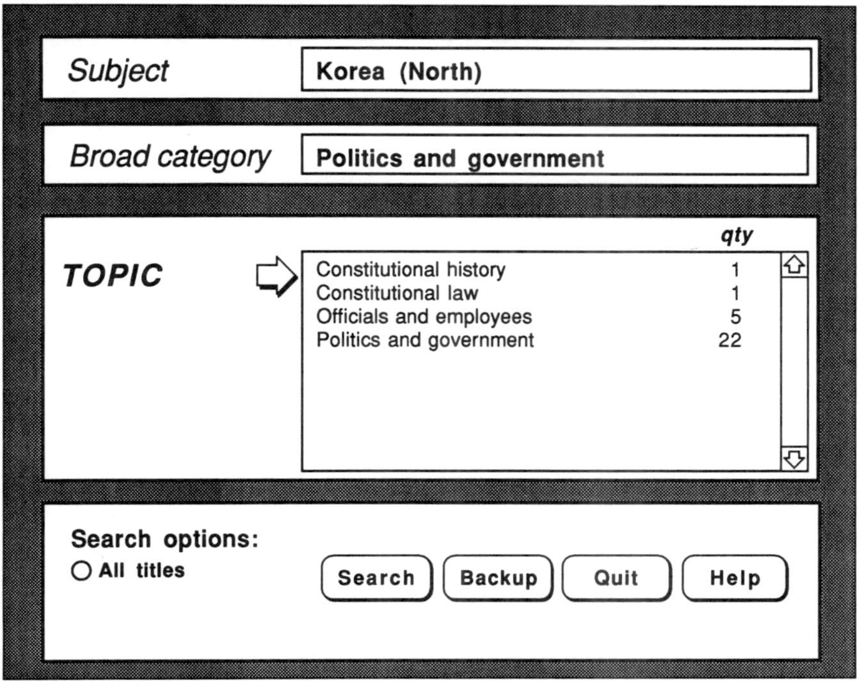

Figure 13.4
Selecting a broad category under "Korea (North)."

13.3.2 Following the Exact with Other Approaches

User queries may match controlled vocabulary terms that do not express the topics users seek. Examples from the most frequently entered queries list are "german" and "translation" that match the qualified assigned heading "German (Dance)" and the qualified tracing "Translation (Genetics)," respectively. With the former, users are probably interested in the German language or people or other topics about Germany; in the latter, users are probably interested in translations from one language into another. When users terminate the search, systems should prompt them to continue searching and respond with the results of the alphabetical approach. Figure 13.5 shows how this response looks.

User queries that make systems respond with the exact approach are words and phrases that are assigned subject headings or tracings in their own right. Often, these queries are also the initial word(s) in inverted headings or longer phrase headings. In its emphasis on drawing users into more specific aspects of their topic using broad categories and subdivided forms of the matched term, the exact approach does not

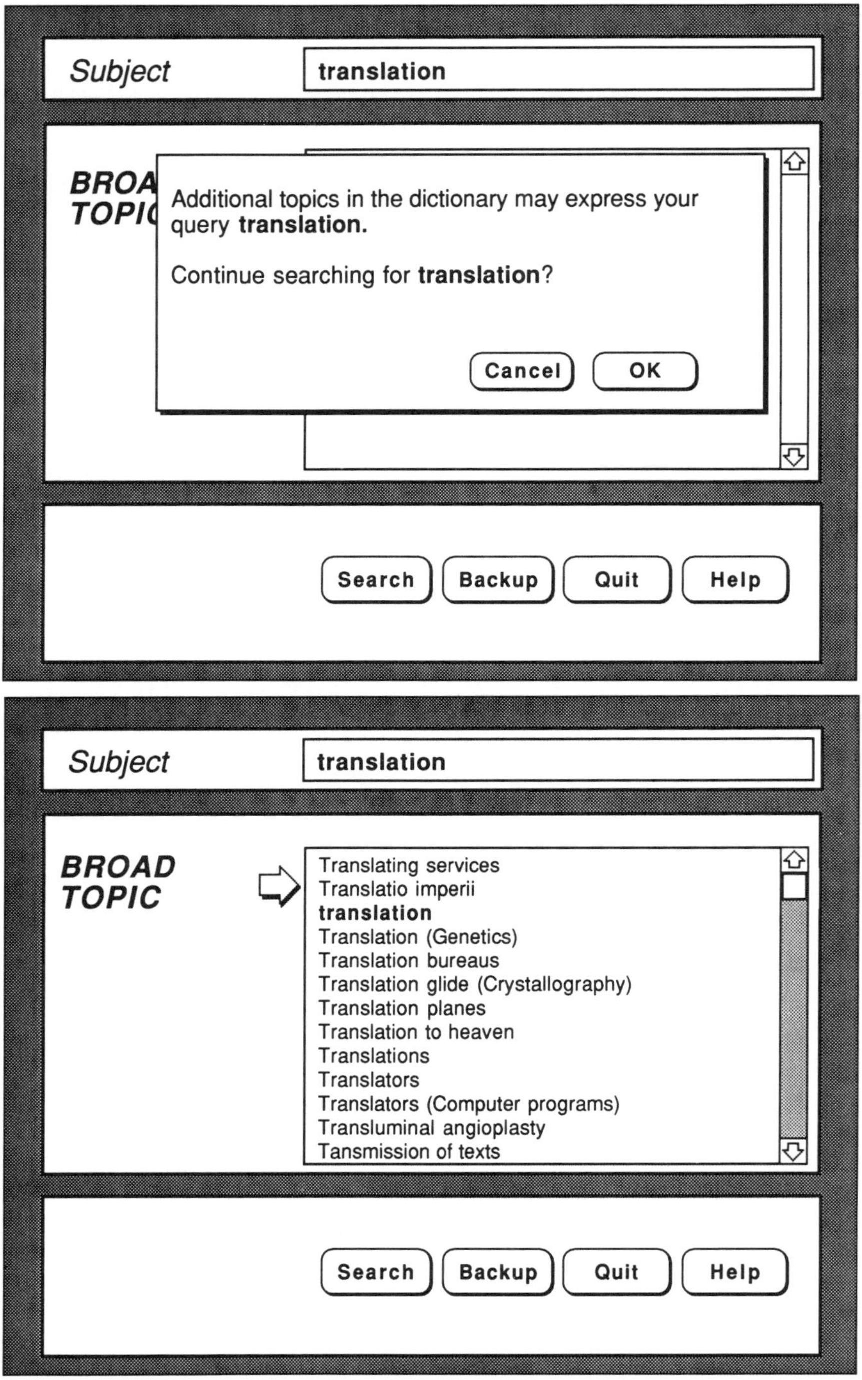

Figure 13.5
Alphabetical approach following the exact approach.

show users terms in the same alphabetical neighborhood as the user query. Following the exact approach with the alphabetical approach overcomes this limitation.

When users are done with the alphabetical approach, systems could continue searching by following a particular sequence of keyword-in-heading approaches. Systems would start with the keyword-in-main-heading approach. For example, the user entering "jazz music" would retrieve a list of assigned subject headings bearing words in the user query:

- Double-bass and piano **music** (**Jazz**)
- Guitar **music** (**Jazz**)
- Monologues with **music** (**Jazz** ensemble with chamber orchestra)
- Piano **music** (**Jazz**)
- Saxophone **music** (**Jazz**)

None of these subject headings would be in the alphabetical neighborhood of the original query "jazz music"; consequently, they would not be accessible through the alphabetical approach that follows the exact approach. Since they are not listed among the related terms listed under the topical-subject heading "Jazz music," they would not be accessible through the exact approach either.

The problem with expanding the search tree to include keyword approaches for queries that initially induce online systems to respond with the exact approach is the sheer number of main headings and subdivided headings bearing the words in the original query and the increasing possibility of retrieving false drops and large quantities of nonrelevant retrievals. For example, the exact approach to the query "aids" retrieves the main heading and subdivided forms of "Aids (Disease)." The keyword-in-subdivided-heading approach to this query produces hundreds of non-relevant headings bearing the subdivision "Audiovisual aids." Consider the hundreds of subject headings that would be retrieved in keyword-in-heading searches for the following frequently entered queries:

- art
- education
- japan
- management
- motion pictures
- music
- sex
- women

Results may be more manageable for the query "jazz music" than for the above-listed queries because it contains two words. Thus, the search tree that features the exact approach limits keyword searches to queries composed of two or more words.

The search tree for the exact approach could feature the keyword-in-subdivided-heading search in place of the alphabetical approach for user queries that match geographic names. Many topics associated with geographic names are expressed in the form of topical-main headings with geographic subdivisions, for example, "Food supply $z Africa," "Industrial management $z Japan," "Small business $z Ontario $z London." Users cannot be expected to know when the geographic names they enter are used as main headings or geographic subdivisions. Before responding with the alphabetical approach, systems could be programmed to check the tag of the matched heading. Queries matching a geographic name (i.e., MARC tag 651) would be submitted to the keyword-in-subdivided-heading approach instead of the alphabetical approach. There is the potential for retrieving hundreds of subdivided headings as a result of keyword-in-subdivided-heading searches because systems are retrieving any heading bearing the user-entered geographic name in a subdivision.

At the present time, the search tree should not be enhanced to include this strategy for geographic names because many of them require the interposition of an indirect geographic qualifier. Online systems cannot automatically convert the direct form of geographic names into the indirect form used in geographic subdivisions because many exceptions to indirect subdivision affect the form used for the indirect geographic qualifier. The availability of indirect forms of geographic names in a cross-reference field of geographic name authority records would make it possible for online systems to substitute one form for another in subject searches. Indications that this field may be a future enhancement of the USMARC format for authority data come from a recent proposal to MARBI (Library of Congress 1989) and the recommendations of the LC Subject Subdivisions Conference (Library of Congress 1992).

13.4 One-Word Queries

The search tree for one-word queries is given in Figure 13.6. One-word queries that match the initial characters in longer controlled vocabulary terms are submitted to the alphabetical approach. The user's selection of a listed controlled vocabulary term invokes the exact approach. Remaining one-word queries are submitted to title keyword searches. When title keyword searches produce retrievals, systems invoke relevance feedback routines to help users find additional material. When title keyword searches fail to produce retrievals, systems ask users to check their queries and correct spelling. If users correct spelling, systems submit revised queries to the initial search tree (Figure 13.1) because revised queries may now match exact or normalized forms of controlled vocabulary terms.

Table 13.2 is a list of one-word queries entered most frequently into the online catalogs of three university libraries. Since these queries match the initial characters or word in longer controlled vocabulary terms, systems would respond to them

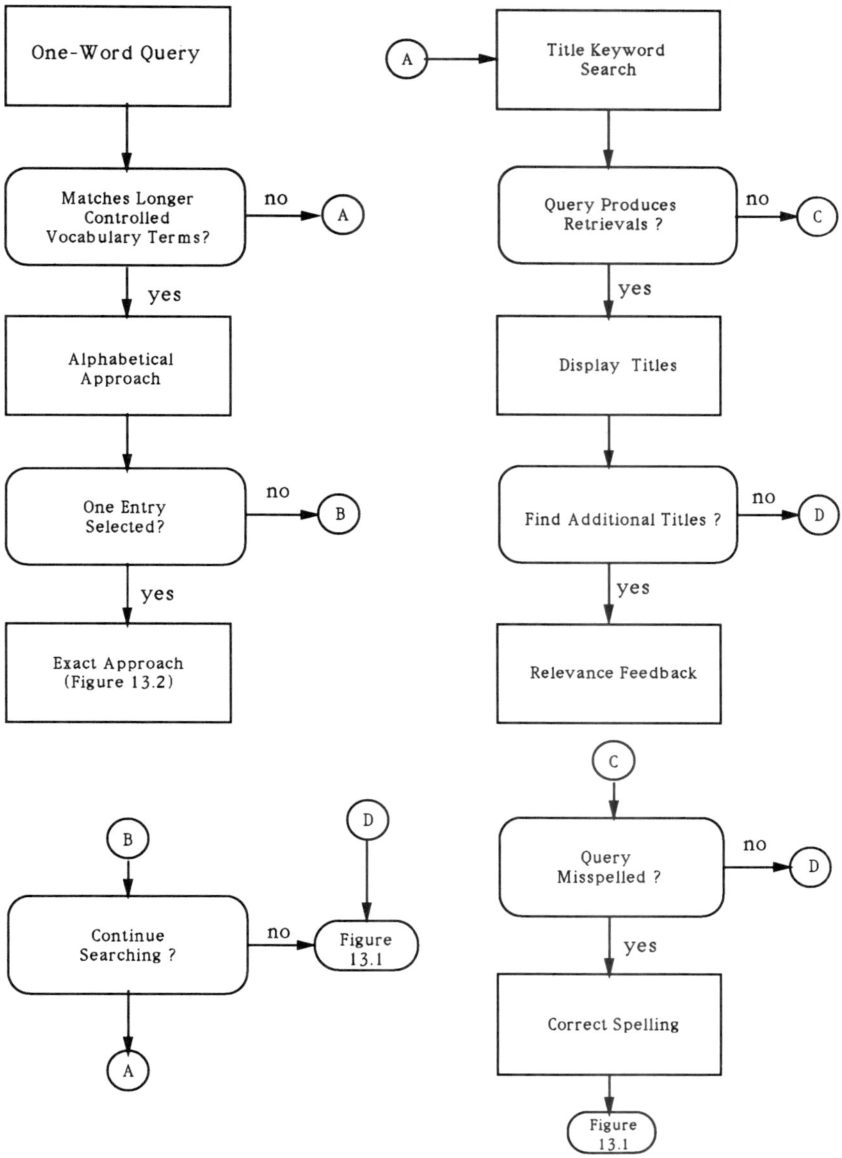

Figure 13.6
Search tree for one-word queries.

Table 13.2
Frequently Entered One-word Queries

Query	Nearby headings and tracings
college	College, Choice of; College, Electoral; College administrators
crime	Crime; Crime and age; Crime and criminals
depression	Depression, Mental; Depression, Postnatal; Depression in children
economic	Economic anthropology; Economic assistance
encyclopedia	Encyclopedias and dictionaries
film	Film actors; Film audiences; Film collections
homeless	Homeless persons; Homeless women
law	Laws, Local; Laws of the mean (Calculus)
media	Media, Condensed; Media centers (Education)
phobia	Phobias; Phobias in children
regulation	Regulation of blood circulation; Regulation of body weight
resume	Resumes (Employment)
spanish	Spanish abbreviations; Spanish American drama
western	Western Africa; Western and country music; Western art; Western bean cutworm

with the alphabetical approach. Examples of matching terms accompany queries in Table 13.2.

Queries that match the initial characters in longer controlled vocabulary terms are "encyclopedia," "phobia," and "resume." Terms in the same alphabetical neighborhood would be satisfactory for expressing the topics users seek. Other queries match the initial word in longer controlled vocabulary terms. Figure 13.7 shows the system's response to the query "regulation."

Listed terms address medical topics. Users interested in economic topics would have to browse forward to find suitable terms, for example, "Regulation of prices," "Regulation of trade," "Regulatory agencies." The alphabetical approach will also place users in an index of controlled vocabulary terms covering many different topics beginning with the words "college," "economic," "laws," and "media." They may eventually find terms on the topics they seek but only after a considerable amount of browsing. Users entering queries matching the first few letters of longer controlled vocabulary terms, for example, "comm," "a," and "descr," will also have to browse.

Among most frequently entered queries is "mccarthyism." This query is submitted to title keyword searches because it does not match a longer controlled vocabulary term. In MIRLYN, such searches produce almost two dozen titles including two different books entitled *McCarthyism.* If users want to find additional material, systems could present them with a list of assigned subject headings common to retrieved records and ask them to select relevant ones. For example, subject headings common to several bibliographic records retrieved in the title keyword search for "mccarthyism" are "McCarthy, Joseph, 1908–1957," "Subversive activities--United States," and "Internal security--United States." Systems could ask users to select relevant headings and search separately for the subject headings users select or they

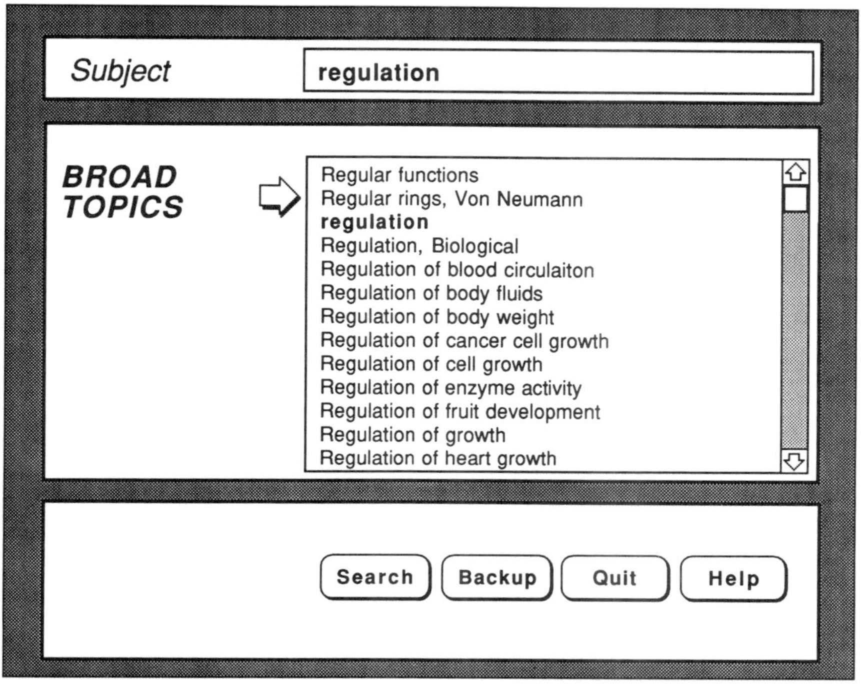

Figure 13.7
Alphabetical approach to "regulation."

could combine the results of searching selected subject headings using the Boolean "and" operator. However, few subject headings (1.4) are assigned to bibliographic records; systems would seldom be able to produce retrievals for combinations of two or more selected subject headings. Combinatorial retrieval methods would probably produce the most useful results because they would search for the words in selected subject headings, but all the words in these headings would not have to be present for retrievals to be made.

13.5 Remaining Queries

Remaining queries for subjects generally are composed of two or more words. Some queries match the initial words of longer controlled vocabulary terms. These queries are submitted to the alphabetical approach (Figure 13.8). The rest are submitted to a series of keyword searches that begins with the keyword-in-main-

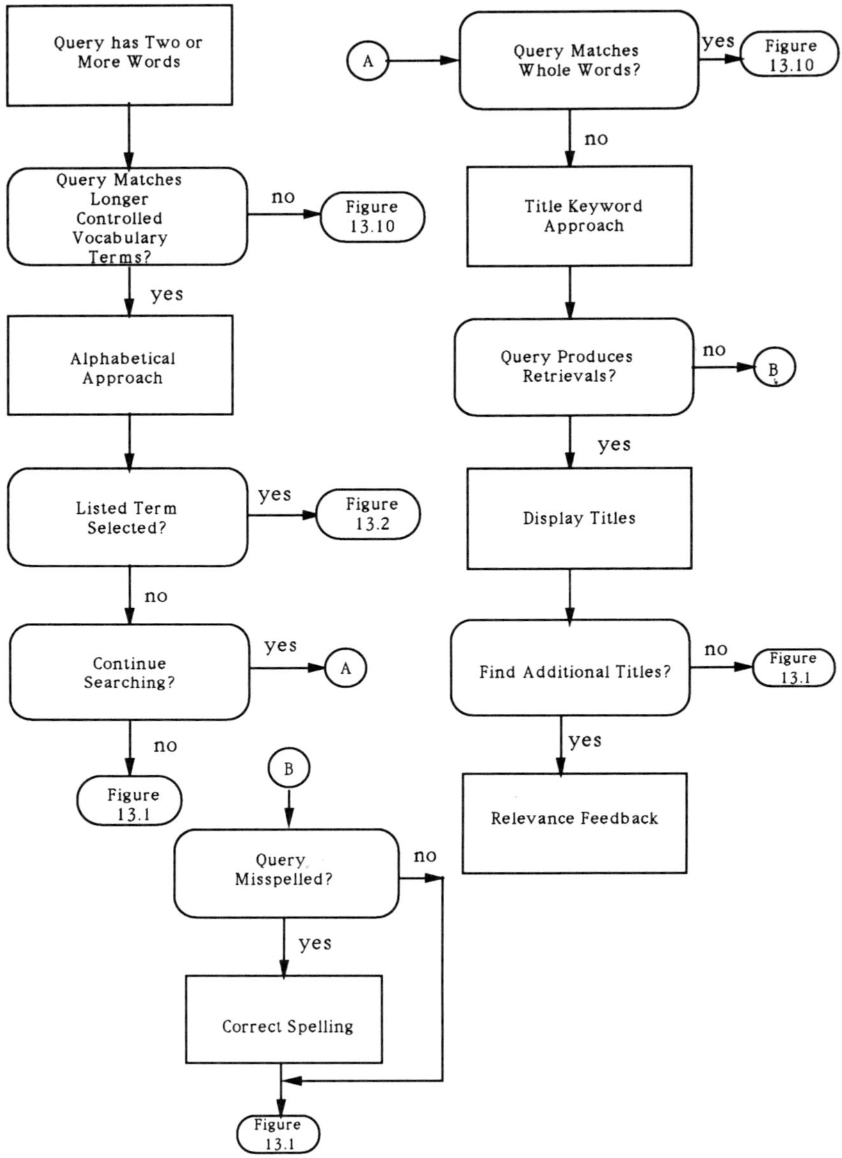

Figure 13.8
Search tree for multiword queries featuring the alphabetical approach.

heading search (Figure 13.10). When the particular keyword search produces zero or too few retrievals, systems continue searching using the next keyword approach in the series.

13.5.1 Multiword Queries for the Alphabetical Approach

Figure 13.8 is a search tree for queries composed of more than one word. Systems respond with the alphabetical approach to queries that match longer controlled vocabulary terms. To find additional material, systems continue searching using the keyword-in-main-heading search.

The search tree takes into account that some queries are partial matches of controlled vocabulary terms. For example, the query "civil rights movement" matches the first two words and part of the third word in the heading "Civil rights movements." The initial system response to such queries is the alphabetical approach. When users respond to system prompts to continue searching using the original query, systems continue with the results of title keyword searches.

Table 13.3 is a list of queries composed of two or more words from "most frequently entered" lists. These queries match the initial words of longer controlled vocabulary terms. The term that would immediately follow the query in an alphabetical index of controlled vocabulary terms is given in this table.

The alphabetical approach is appropriate for the queries in Table 13.3 because it is likely to place users close to the term that expresses their topics. Two of the closest matching headings are hyphenated. Systems should ignore punctuation in user queries and controlled vocabulary terms when placing users in the alphabetical index.

Figure 13.9 shows the system's response to the "civil rights movement" query in which the alphabetical list begins with two terms that precede the user-entered term in the alphabetical index.

Table 13.3
Multiword Queries for the Alphabetical Approach

Query	Controlled vocabulary term
afro american	Afro-American actors
civil rights movement	Civil rights movements
food industry	Food industry and trade
greenhouse effect	Greenhouse effect, Atmospheric
home care	Home care services
korean war	Korean War, 1950–1953
mail order	Mail-order antique business
nuclear war	Nuclear warfare
supreme court	Supreme courts
vietnam war	Vietnam war, 1961–1975

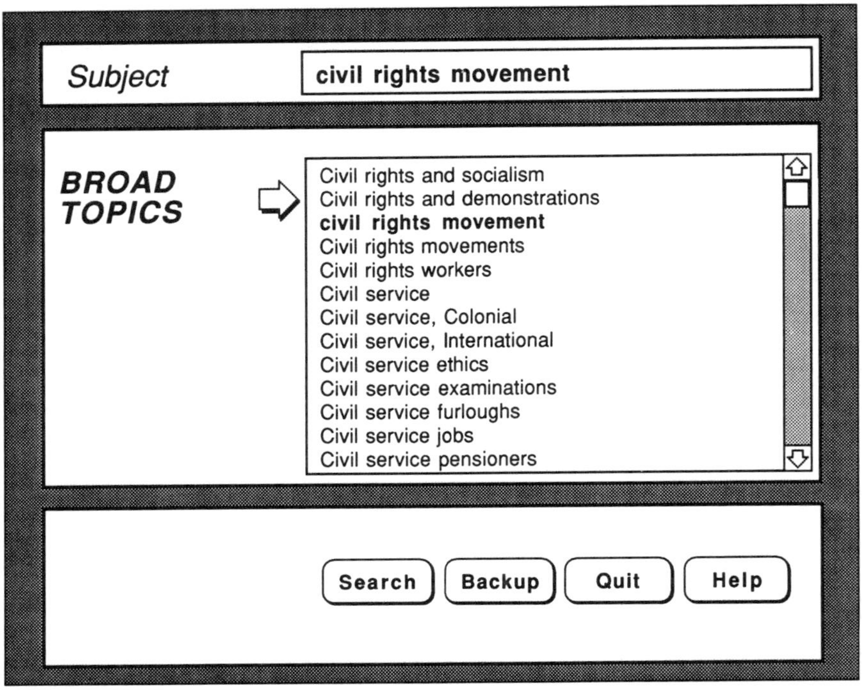

Figure 13.9
Alphabetical approach to "civil rights movement."

In Figure 13.9, terms listed immediately before and after the query may interest users. Selection of a term invokes the exact approach in online systems. When users attempt to terminate the search, the system prompts them to continue searching for the original query. Since the query "civil rights movement" does not match whole words of longer controlled vocabulary terms, the system would continue searching using the title keyword approach. When queries match whole words in longer controlled vocabulary terms, systems continue searching with the keyword-in-main-heading approach (Figure 13.10).

13.5.2 Multiword Queries for Keyword Approaches

Remaining queries composed of two or more words are submitted to a search tree for keyword approaches (Figure 13.10). Systems first use the keyword-in-record search to ensure that individual query words are posted in the catalog. If one or more query words fail to produce retrievals, the entire series of keyword searches will fail. Systems ask users to check the spelling of their queries and correct them if necessary.

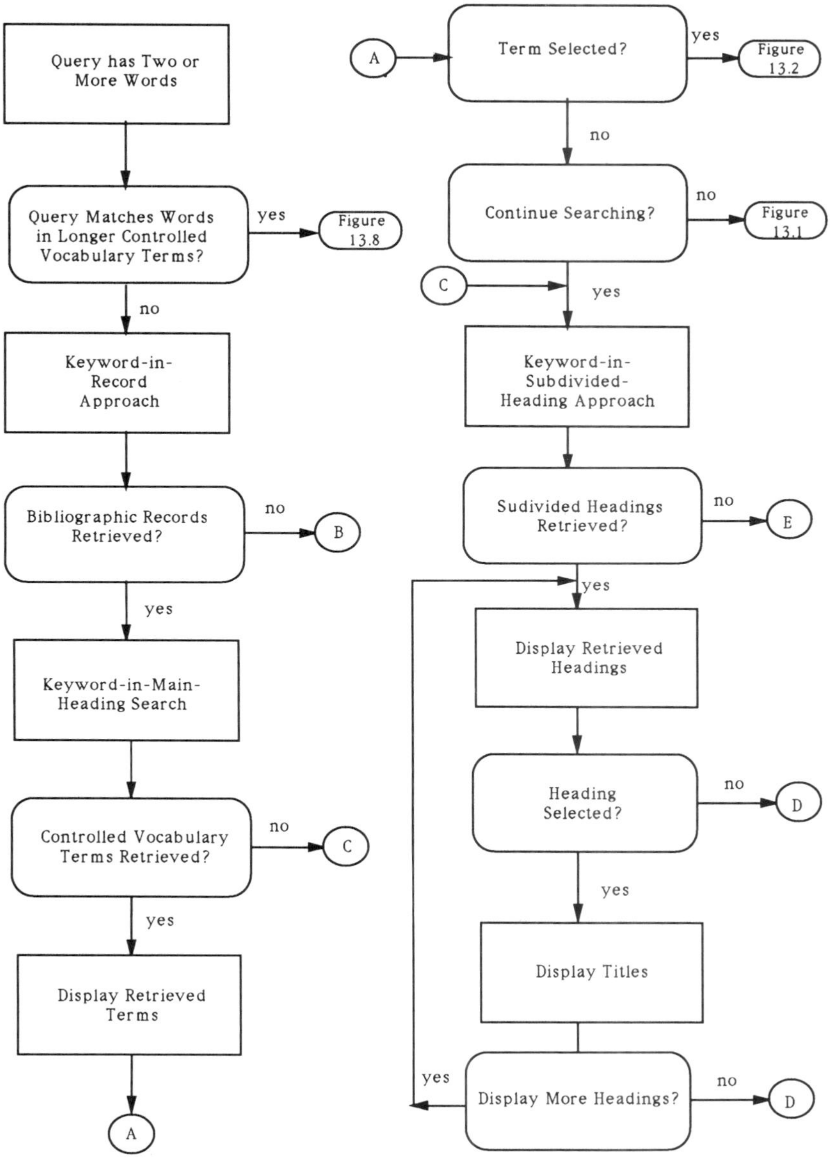

Figure 13.10
Search tree for multiword queries featuring keyword approaches.

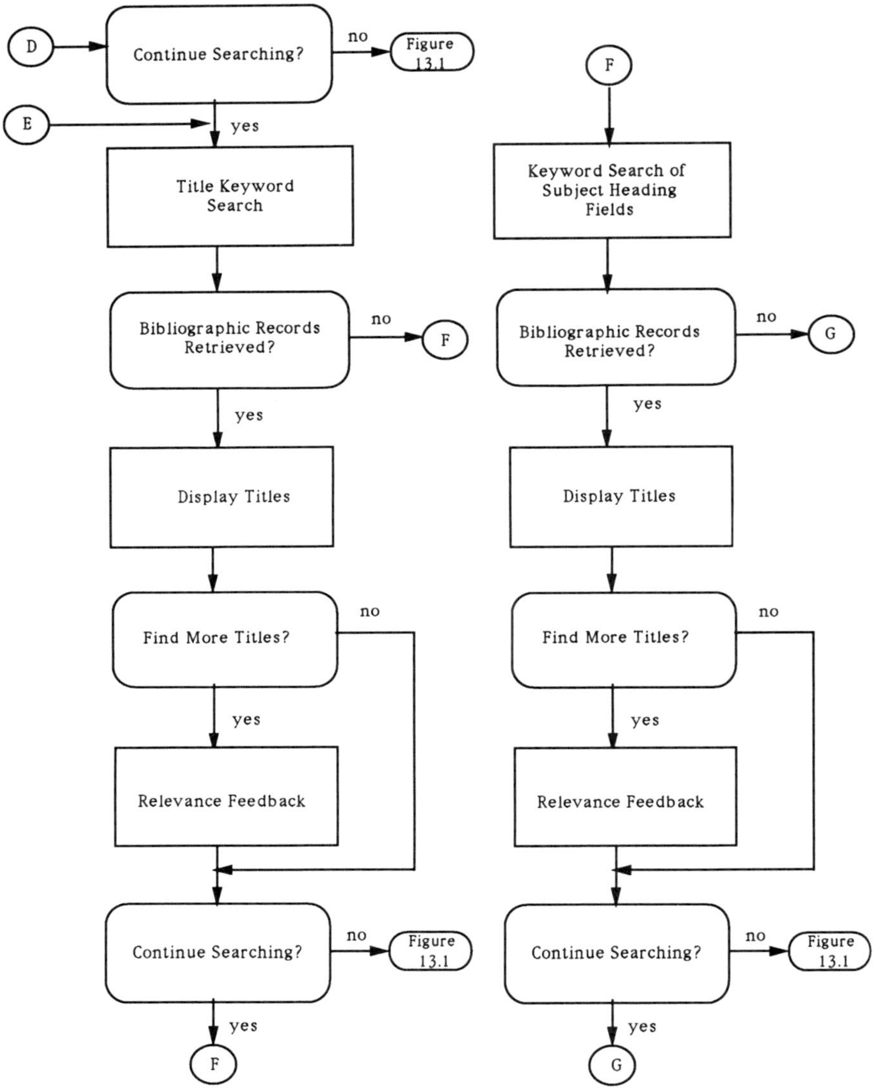

Figure 13.10 *(continued)*

If users make changes, systems start at the beginning of the subject-searching process, that is, looking for matches of exact and normalized forms of controlled vocabulary terms. If changes are not made, systems could try to correct spelling using automatic spelling correction algorithms. Otherwise, systems have to ask users for a different query because the original one fails to produce retrievals using any keyword approach.

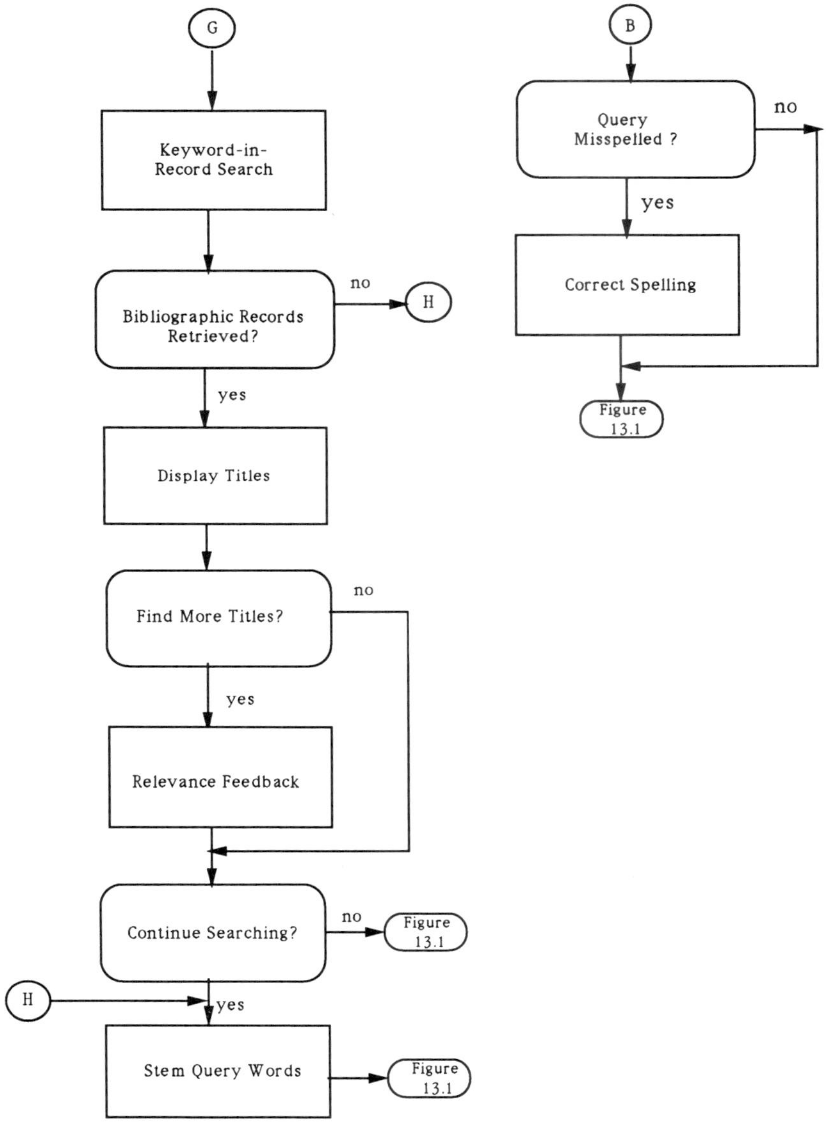

Figure 13.10 *(continued)*

Retrievals produced through the initial keyword-in-record search are not shown to users. Instead, systems continue searching beginning with the keyword-in-main-heading search. The initial keyword-in-record search is meant to save systems additional steps searching for a query that does not retrieve any bibliographic records through the entire series of keyword searches.

Table 13.4
Frequently Entered Queries for Keyword Approaches

Query	Headings/titles
Keyword-in-main-heading	
garden art	Garden of love in art; Public Garden (Boston, Mass.) in art
jewish humor	Jewish wit and humor
mont saint michel	Le Mont-Saint-Michel (France)
Keyword-in-subdivided-heading	
english grammar	English language--Grammar; and many headings with the subdivision combination Grammar, Comparative--English
medals badges	Several geographic names subdivided by Medals, badges, decorations, etc.
music britain	Music--Great Britain; Punk rock music--Great Britain; and several more Music phrase headings subdivided by Great Britain
soviet union constitution	Soviet Union--Constitution
Title keyword	
environmental art	*Art in the land: a critical anthology of environmental art*
financial ratios	*Financial ratios for the prediction of corporate failure; Financial ratios for monitoring corporate sickness*
garden art	*The garden art of Japan; The garden art of China; Garden art and architecture*
scopes trial	*The roots of bias: An empiricist press and coverage of the Scopes trial*
social phobia	*Unwillingly to school: School phobia or school refusal, a medico-social problem*
world war ii	*World War II in photographs; World War II from an American perspective*
Keyword-in-record	
scopes trial	*The great monkey trial; The Scopes case; Bryan and Darrow at Dayton*

Table 13.4 is a list of queries composed of two or more words from "most frequently entered" lists. These queries do not match exact or normalized forms of controlled vocabulary terms, nor do they match the initial characters of longer controlled vocabulary terms, so they are submitted to the search tree for keyword approaches beginning with the keyword-in-main-heading approach (Figure 13.10). Controlled vocabulary terms or titles retrieved in online catalogs with these various keyword approaches are listed in the order in which systems invoke these approaches to produce retrievals.

When a keyword approach produces zero retrievals, the system continues with the next approach in the sequence. For example, the keyword-in-main-heading approach fails to produce retrievals for the query "music britain" and continues with the keyword-in-subdivided-heading approach that yields several subdivided headings. The keyword-in-main-heading approach produces the main heading "Le Mont-Saint-Michel (France)" for the query "mont saint michel." If too few titles are assigned this main heading, users can continue searching for the original query through the next keyword approach in the sequence, that is, keyword-in-subdivided-heading approach. This query would probably retrieve subdivided headings with the query words occurring in geographic subdivisions.

The first approach that retrieves headings or bibliographic records does not always produce relevant ones. For example, the keyword-in-main-heading approach produces the assigned subject headings "Garden of love in art" and "Public Garden (Boston, Mass.) in art" in response to the query "garden art." The title keyword approach yields records with the titles *The garden art of Japan* and *Garden art and architecture* that may be more suited to the topic sought than were the retrieved subject headings. At first, users may be hesitant to continue searching when prompted by systems, but they gain confidence in this strategy when it leads to satisfactory results.

For several queries on most frequently entered lists, the keyword-in-subdivided-heading approach retrieves many subdivided headings. For example, searches in ORION using this approach yielded over 150 assigned subject headings for "english grammar" and over 70 assigned subject headings for "music britain." In Chapter 12, suggestions are given for displaying large sets using broad category codes.

The title keyword approach is particularly successful, retrieving relevant bibliographic records for the queries "environmental art," "garden art," and "scopes trial." Equipping online systems with relevance feedback capabilities can help users find relevant headings to retrieve additional records. For example, most records retrieved in keyword searches for the query "environmental art" contain the heading "Environment (Art)," which could be used to find additional bibliographic records. Users entering "world war ii" would certainly benefit from relevance feedback because so many more bibliographic records can be retrieved through the subject heading used to express this topic, that is, "World War, 1939–1945," than through title keyword searches for the original query. Furthermore, subdivided forms of this subject heading could help users refine their searches because of the sheer amount of material available on this topic.

A few queries submitted to the search tree for keyword approaches fail to retrieve any bibliographic records, and fail to retrieve either relevant subject headings or bibliographic records. An example is the frequently entered query "summer olympics," which retrieves bibliographic records through the keyword-in-record approach that are not relevant to the query.

Chapter 12 described several techniques—stemming, automatic spelling correction, combinatorial retrieval—that may be helpful for producing relevant retrievals when the various keyword approaches fail. Although the final step in the search tree for keyword approaches (Figure 13.10) recommends stemming, additional research is needed to determine the most effective techniques to apply at this point in the search.

13.6 Search Trees for Personal-Name Queries

To elicit the different elements of personal-name queries, systems need to prompt users for them. Figure 12.11 shows one method to obtain the following

Table 13.5
Frequently Entered Personal-Name Queries

Direct order	Inverted order
woody allen	lowell, robert
bob dylan	roosevelt, theodore
louis kahn	
charles manson	
andy warhol	
Surnames	**Other**
carter	frank lloyd wright
dali	joan of arc
degas	malcolm x
freud	nostradamus
mies van der rohe	
shakespeare	
tolstoy	

elements: (1) last name, (2) first name, (3) middle name or initial, and (4) topic. The particular elements users provide and the system's ability to find these elements in personal-name headings determine the subject searching approach(es) used by the system. None of the three systems contributing queries to frequently occurring lists prompts users for the elements of personal-name queries; consequently, the personal-name queries users frequently enter into online catalogs contain elements for first and last names in any order and surnames only (Table 13.5).

None of the queries from frequently entered lists contains topics. Chapter 10 gives several examples of such queries. When interfaces for eliciting the elements of personal-name queries are being designed, they should be tested with users to ensure that users understand the information that is being requested and respond by entering the appropriate elements.

Figure 13.11 presents the search tree for personal-name queries. The first step is for systems to single out queries containing topics. These queries are submitted to the keyword-in-subdivided-heading search followed by the keyword-in-record search in order to find headings and bibliographic records that contain both name and topic elements. If systems fail to find both elements, they omit the topic element from the query and continue searching through the alphabetical approach. Personal-name queries consisting exclusively of name elements are submitted to the alphabetical approach only.

All queries in Table 13.5 would be submitted to the alphabetical approach because they contain no topic elements. Except for the surname "carter," surnames listed in this table are rather unique and would place users close to the desired name in an alphabetical index of subject headings. Figure 13.12 shows names in the alphabetical neighborhood of "carter." Users would have to browse forward in this list to find personal-name access points for Jimmy Carter and other members of his family.

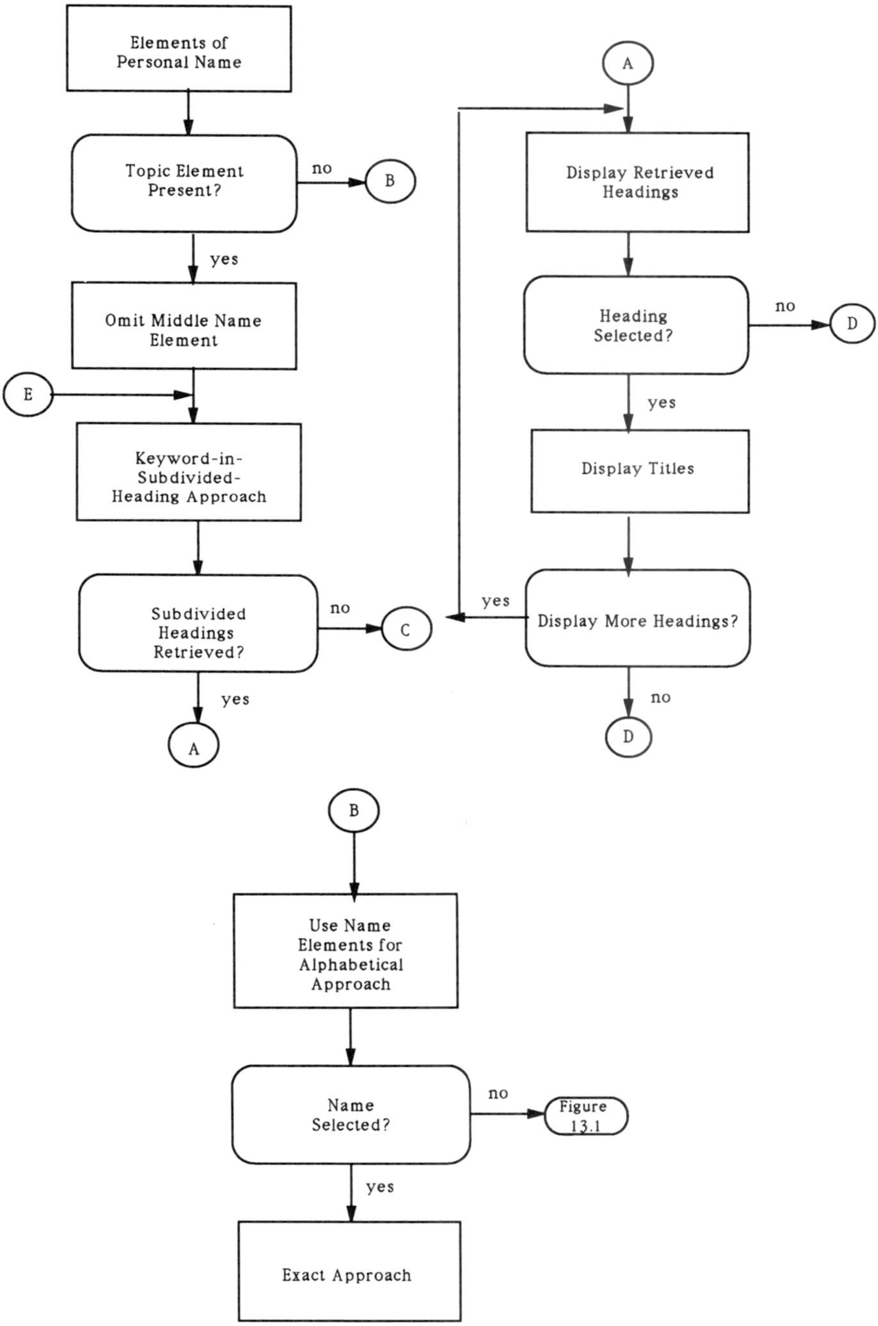

Figure 13.11
Search tree for personal-name queries.

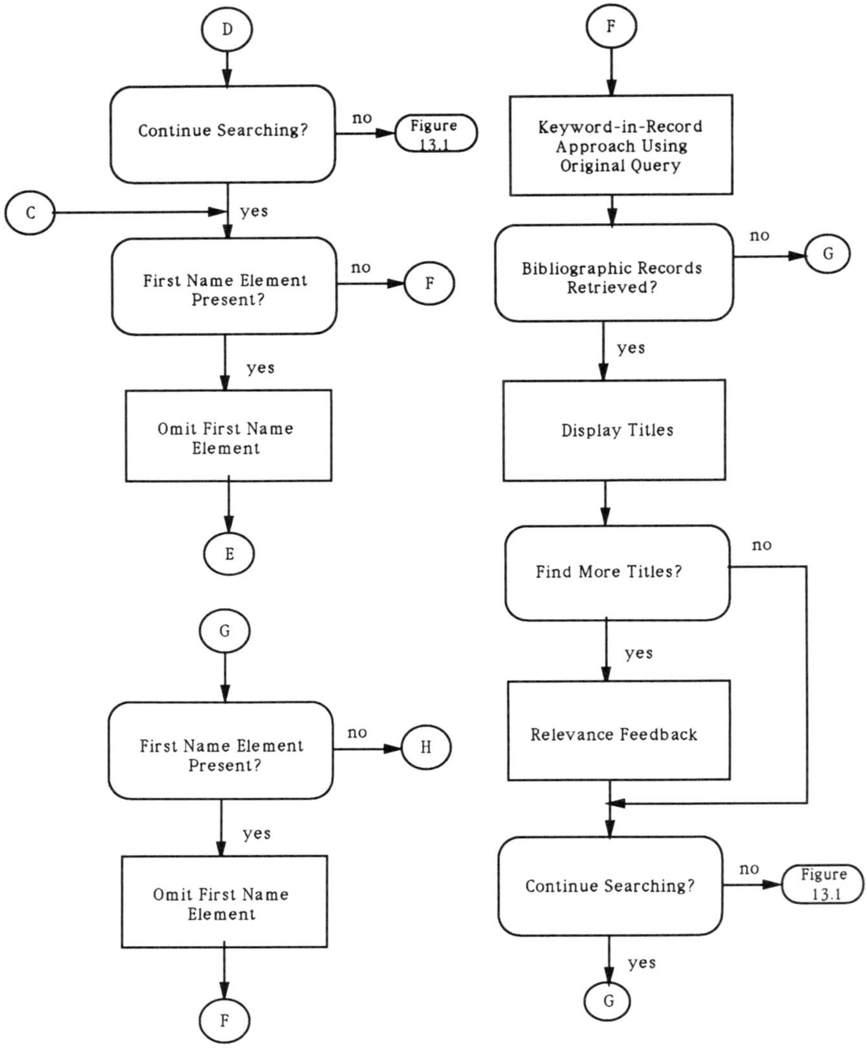

Figure 13.11 *(continued)*

13.7 Synthesis and Summary

Except for the exact approach, the subject searching approaches embedded in search trees are currently operational in several existing online systems. When systems offer users more than one approach to subject searching, users themselves must deter-

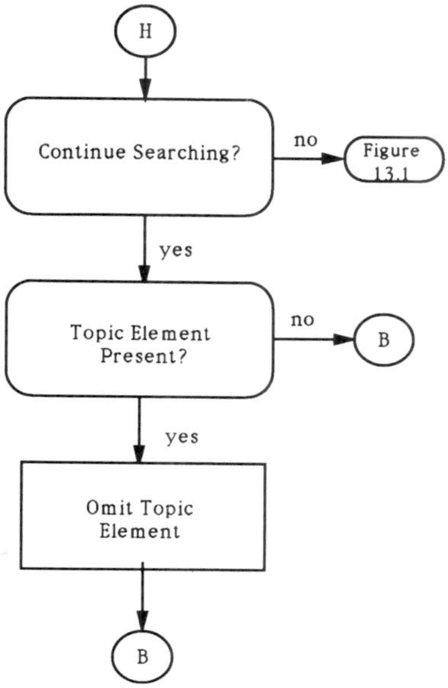

Figure 13.11 *(continued)*

mine which approach produces usable results. Users now do this on a trial-and-error basis by attempting every available approach until they retrieve satisfactory results.

The burden of determining which subject searching approach produces the best results can be placed on online systems. Users need not explicitly choose a particular approach. Rather, systems respond with a particular approach based on the extent to which user queries match the catalog's controlled vocabulary and produce retrievals. The search trees presented in this chapter control system responses and determine appropriate subject searching approaches to user queries.

Of the subject searching approaches available to users, systems prefer exact, alphabetical, and keyword-in-heading approaches because they are two-step subject searching approaches that enlist the catalog's controlled vocabulary to help users find appropriate controlled vocabulary terms for expressing their topics of interest. Users can refine their searches using related terms, subdivided forms of the matched or selected heading, or controlled vocabulary terms in close alphabetical proximity to the subject queries they originally entered into the system. Controlled vocabulary terms also ensure precision of search results because they are assigned to bibliographic records by catalogers to express the subject matter of original items.

Online systems always provide a response to the personal-name queries users enter through the alphabetical approach. In this way, systems serve as an automatic directory of personal names because they place users at a directory location where the personal name they entered would be listed. When users offer topic elements in

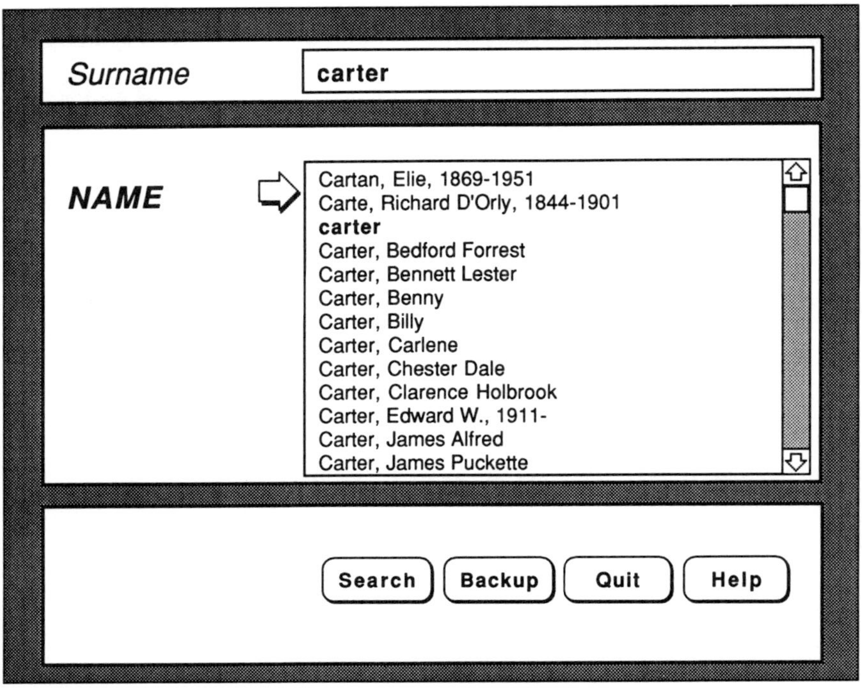

Figure 13.12
Alphabetical approach to "carter."

addition to name elements, systems may be able to satisfy the topic element through various keyword search approaches; however, their failure to produce retrievals for the combination of topic and name elements invokes the alphabetical approach.

Online systems may not be able to produce retrievals or relevant retrievals for some user queries for subjects generally. Several techniques such as stemming, automatic spelling correction, and the combinatorial retrieval method may be appropriate; however, additional research is needed to determine the most effective sequence for applying these techniques to such user queries.

Too many retrievals are a problem in subject searching. Unfortunately, high-posted queries are ones containing terms used in controlled vocabulary terms. Online systems should not penalize users who are successful matching their terms with those used in the catalog by overwhelming them with many retrievals. New browsing approaches must be made available to such users. These approaches should encourage users to explore catalog material available on topics and use related terms and subdivided forms of relevant subject headings to narrow their topics or to describe aspects of the topics they have in mind but have not made explicit in their queries.

The subject searching approaches presented in this book are not new. They are implemented in one or more operational online bibliographic systems. What is new are search trees. Search trees control system responses and determine appropriate subject searching approaches to user queries based on the extent to which queries match controlled vocabulary terms and produce retrievals. Search trees endow online systems with the responsibility of determining which subject searching approach is best.

References

Library of Congress. (1989). *Discussion paper #34: Recording indirect geographic subject subdivision form information*. Washington, DC: Library of Congress.

Library of Congress. (1992). *The future of subdivisions in the Library of Congress subject headings system: Report from the Subject Subdivisions Conference*. Martha O'Hara Conway (Ed.). Washington, DC: Library of Congress.

Miter, Nathalie Nadia, Venner, Gillian, & Walker, Stephen (1985). *Designing an online public access catalogue: Okapi, a catalogue on a local area network*. London: British Library. Library and Information Science Report No. 39.

O'Neill, Edward T., & Aluri, Rao. (1979). *Research report on subject heading patterns in OCLC monographic records*. Columbus, OH: OCLC. ERIC ED 183 167.

Walker, Stephen, & Jones, Richard M. (1987). *Improving subject retrieval in online catalogues; 1. Stemming, automatic spelling correction and cross-reference tables*. London: British Library. British Library Research Paper No. 24.

14

The Future of Subject Headings for Online Information Retrieval

14.1 Introduction

Search trees are a set of paths with branches or choices that enable systems to carry out the most sensible approach at each stage of the search. The search trees presented in this book are the result of an empirical study of the subject terms users enter into online catalogs (Chapters 5–10). This study places much emphasis on the closeness of user queries to subject headings based on the LCSH system and subject searching capabilities that would respond to user queries with appropriate subject headings. Because the vast majority of bibliographic records created by American libraries are based on the LCSH system, the search trees recommended in this book for subject searching of bibliographic records are based on this system.

Search trees are not a panacea for subject access in online catalogs, but they can solve problems connected with large retrievals by favoring subject searching capabilities that enlist the catalog's controlled vocabulary over those that include uncontrolled terms. They can solve problems connected with terminology by extending searches to uncontrolled fields, making multiple postings of controlled vocabulary terms, and enlisting automatic stemming techniques to effect matches of subject terms from controlled and uncontrolled fields of bibliographic records. Unfortunately, they cannot solve problems stemming from weaknesses or defects in the LCSH system such as specificity, inconsistent syndetic structure, or its mixed system of various grammatical forms.

This chapter speculates on the future of the LCSH system, emphasizing its strengths and the ability of computer systems to overcome certain weaknesses. It discusses how the availability of the machine-readable LCSH (LCSH-mr) has been responsible for both improving subject access in online systems and exposing weaknesses in the system. It advises on the support needed to undertake proposals for revamping the entire LCSH system. The book concludes with a summary of recommended improvements to online bibliographic systems that would make them more responsive to user needs and behavior.

14.2 Is LCSH Here to Stay?

LCSH will continue to be applied in libraries throughout North America for the following important reasons:

1. Public catalog users with varying levels of subject knowledge can find materials on the topics they seek using LCSH.
2. In terms of subject retrieval, a better system has not been devised, nor will be in the near future.
3. Online systems have capitalized on some desirable features of the LCSH system.
4. Online systems have overcome some limitations of the LCSH system.
5. Improvements can be made to LCSH.
6. Tens of millions of bibliographic records are available to the users of online bibliographic systems through LCSH.

These reasons are discussed below with reference to search trees because, if implemented in online bibliographic systems, they will carry even greater weight.

Supporting the first reason is the research finding that subject experts and nonexperts have about the same levels of success in terms of their ability to retrieve materials using the LCSH system (Bates 1977; Allen 1991). About the only difference between the two groups is the inclination of subject experts to enter more search statements in their subject searches than their nonexpert counterparts (Allen 1991, 202). There are two unencouraging explanations for this: (1) the inability of online systems to respond to queries so that subject experts are stimulated to explore the controlled vocabulary used in the catalog for a topic instead of entering another subject term, and (2) the failure of the LCSH system to enlist controlled vocabulary terms that address the specificity of subject experts' requests. Search trees could help users in both situations because they are partial to displays of controlled vocabulary terms. Selecting listed terms, users can display narrower terms or subdivided forms of selected terms that express the specific topic or aspect of a topic that users have in mind.

Increasing overall specificity could be accomplished only through an editorial review of the entire LCSH system. If the experience of the developers of *The Art & Architecture Thesaurus Project* (AAT) is used as a model, increasing the specificity of LCSH could be an enormous undertaking. For example, the AAT developers reviewed every term in LCSH to extract terms on architecture; however, only 30% of AAT terms in architecture can trace their roots to LCSH (Petersen 1983, 209). A quantitative solution to the problem of LCSH specificity would be difficult to apply. Should an editorial review of LCSH be undertaken with the intent of increasing its specificity, the expanded tool must serve subject and nonsubject specialists alike.

The one factor that has been found to have a significant beneficial effect on users' ability to enter queries that match controlled vocabulary terms is familiarity with the principles and forms of subject headings (Bates 1977, 164). Search trees will be a boon to catalog users because they do not require users to be familiar with LCSH principles and forms of headings. Search trees select a search approach based on the extent to which queries match controlled vocabulary terms. Furthermore, these approaches enlist techniques such as normalization, implicit right-hand truncation, and stemming or suffix removal that produce retrievals regardless of the form of subject headings.

Supporting the second reason that LCSH is here to stay are research efforts aimed at identifying a more effective system than LCSH (Keen 1977; Schabas 1982). Such efforts have led to inconclusive results. Retrieval tests have paired LCSH with other approaches including PRECIS, an indexing language that has many advantages in principle over LCSH (Dykstra 1987). Performance differences are minimal between these two systems. The one factor that significantly improves retrieval is the addition of title words to either LCSH or PRECIS (Schabas 1982, 35). The earliest online catalogs gave users access to title words, for example, MELVYL at the University of California (Hildreth 1982, 84), PALS at Mankato State University (Hildreth 1982, 92), and SULIRS at Syracuse University (Bullard 1982). Search trees incorporate title terms into subject searching approaches; however, they do so only after exhausting approaches that produce retrievals based on the presence of query words in single-subject headings.

Underlying the third reason why LCSH is here to stay is the ability of online catalogs to take advantage of the desirable features of the LCSH system and make them available to online catalog users. One such feature is the precoordination of phrase subject headings and subdivided subject headings. Precoordination is useful for helping users find topics they have in mind but have not made explicit in their queries (Mann 1991). The empirical study of user queries gives many examples of queries on broad topics, such as those that name fields of study, human activities, and places (see Chapters 7, 8, and 13). Subsequent access points demonstrate that users have more specific topics in mind, but do not make them explicit in their initial access points. To support such users, online systems should feature displays of controlled vocabulary terms to help users find appropriate terms or to narrow their topics when too many retrievals is a problem. The search tree for the exact approach features displays of controlled vocabulary terms to draw users into their topics using subdivided forms of matched subject headings. It also gives them the option to display narrower terms or browse terms in the alphabetical index that may be similar in meaning but not in form to terms in the matched subject heading.

Precoordination in phrase and subdivided subject headings often produces terms that refer to specific topics. User queries may match some but not all terms in such headings. To help users find them, subject searching capabilities have been suggested that rotate the subfields of subdivided subject headings so that subdivisions occur as the entry element and thus can be found by users browsing the alphabetical index (Mischo 1982, 120; Studwell 1990). Search trees feature alternatives to the rotation approach, such as keyword-in-heading approaches that retrieve main headings or subdivided subject headings bearing query words regardless of word order or the presence of additional words in the string.

Underlying the fourth reason that LCSH is here to stay is the ability of online systems to overcome some of the limitations of the LCSH system that are inherent in manual systems. One limitation of manual systems is linear access. "Each subject entry contains one access point—the initial word—only" (Chan 1986, 337). Multidirectional access to subject entries is possible through certain subject searching capabilities of online systems. This ease of access should place to rest criticisms of LCSH regarding the entry element in main headings, particularly the choice between direct and inverted forms of subject headings (Cochrane & Kirtland 1981, 20; Mischo 1982, 111).

Subject searching capabilities that give multidirectional access to subject headings are usually associated with keyword, Boolean-based searching approaches. Such approaches can make retrievals from all subject-rich fields of bibliographic records or restrict retrievals to certain sets of fields, or single fields or subfields. Retrievals coming from controlled vocabulary fields—especially from a single field or subfields—ensure the precision of search results because the subject terms that are responsible for producing retrievals are assigned to bibliographic records by catalogers to express the subject matter of original items. Search trees favor subject searching capabilities that produce retrievals for user queries using subject information in controlled vocabulary fields over capabilities that produce retrievals using information from uncontrolled fields. They also favor two-step subject searching approaches that enlist the catalog's controlled vocabulary. If users find controlled vocabulary terms for expressing their topics of interest, they can refine their searches using related terms, subdivided forms of relevant terms, or controlled vocabulary terms in close alphabetical proximity to relevant ones. By giving users the option to continue searching for their queries, search trees may eventually invoke subject searching capabilities that make retrievals from uncontrolled fields; however, search trees would invoke such capabilities long after exhausting subject searching capabilities connected with controlled vocabulary fields.

The fifth reason why LCSH is here to stay is the possibility for improving the existing LCSH system. On its own and in response to the interest of the library community, LC has undertaken numerous projects to improve the existing system, for example, instituting new rules for making cross-references, making *see* references from canceled to replacement headings, and adding scope notes (Pietris 1987). LC recently enlisted the library community's assistance in recommending changes to the existing subdivisions system (Library of Congress 1992). Recommended changes that the LC is likely to adopt are those that can be accomplished through computer programming, for example, transposing dates and names of periods in period subdivisions, and those that will simplify cataloging.

Search trees make an improvement on LCSH because they do not require users to know exactly which terms this controlled vocabulary uses to represent their topics of interest in response to their queries. Furthermore, they place the responsibility of determining which subject searching approach is likely to provide relevant information on online systems. Operational systems typically offer more than one subject searching approach. Few users will be patient enough to review the results of several subject searching approaches to determine the most appropriate one; therefore, online catalogs should make this assessment for users through system features such as search trees.

The sixth reason the LCSH system will continue to be applied in libraries throughout North America is that vast stores of bibliographic records bear subject headings based on it. Twenty-seven million bibliographic records are accessible to libraries through the OCLC Online Union Catalog. Research libraries such as The University of Michigan and The Ohio State University have databases numbering between five and six million bibliographic records. Thousands of library staff members are trained in LCSH practice and application, and library schools add to the number of professional librarians trained in the LCSH system by producing hundreds of graduates each year. The library community has an incalculable investment in the LCSH system. Search trees add to this investment because they are designed for subject searching of online bibliographic systems based on the LCSH system.

Of several good reasons that LCSH is here to stay, some are connected with online system functionality, that is, overcoming LCSH limitations, capitalizing on desirable features of the LCSH system, and offering users new subject searching capabilities that they never had in the card catalog environment. Others address libraries and library users, that is, users find materials on the topics they seek using LCSH, and libraries have millions of bibliographic records in which LCSH describes the subject matter of their collections. For the most part, there is no compelling evidence to warrant a change to a different system at this time.

14.3 Future of the LCSH System

14.3.1 Benefits of the Machine-Readable LCSH

Before LC made LCSH-mr available, a few approaches were employed by libraries to provide catalog users with access to LCSH entry vocabulary and syndetic structure. In one approach, library staff placed the printed *LCSH* volumes close to the library catalog and instructed catalog users to consult them during their subject searches. One problem with this approach was that LCSH was not a physical component of the library catalog; therefore, few catalog users knew to consult it in the course of the search (Pritchard 1981, 35; Steinberg and Metz 1984, 69; Markey 1984, 109; Frost 1987, 62). Another problem is that not all subject headings printed in *LCSH* are used in a library's catalog. Furthermore, the topics users seek might not be printed in *LCSH* because of the many categories of unprinted subject headings that do not appear there, but do exist in the LCSH system. In another approach, libraries maintained a local subject authority file containing subject headings and tracings used in the catalog. They also added *see also* references on guide cards suggesting other subject headings in addition to the one consulted. Unfortunately, this approach failed because libraries had neither the staff nor the financial resources to maintain the cross-reference system used in the local catalog (Palmer 1986, 88).

Since April 1986, the availability of an LCSH in the form of a cumulative master tape and weekly tape update subscription service has provided libraries with the opportunity to maintain currency in assigned subject headings and entry vocabulary and to build a cross-reference structure for subject headings used in their local catalogs. Libraries typically turn to library automation vendors such as OCLC and Blackwell North America to build the initial subject authority file from their bibliographic databases and to regularly update the file (Miller 1984). To optimize this arrangement, local systems must work in tandem with the updating approach offered by vendors or bibliographic utilities. This work includes local systems capabilities for integrating deleted, changed, and new records into the local bibliographic and authority databases (Drabenstott 1991, 5). In the absence of such capabilities, libraries will be in no better position than that in the days of manual catalogs because the cross-reference structure is not kept current and does not adequately represent the subject headings used in the local catalog.

Incorporated in online bibliographic systems, LCSH-mr can be a cataloger's tool for the selection and assignment of subject headings to bibliographic records. It can also provide online catalog users with entry vocabulary to direct users to authorized terms for the topics they seek and allow them to see a list of subject headings related to their topics of interest.

14.3.2 Drawbacks of the Machine-Readable LCSH

Now that the LCSH is in machine-readable form, researchers are scrutinizing this file assiduously, enlisting computer programs to analyze it. They are finding quite desirable aspects of LCSH-mr and are asking some difficult questions about enhancements to this file of subject authority records. They are also finding some shortcomings in LCSH-mr and are asking even more difficult questions about revamping the system.

First, consider some desirable aspects. The usefulness of entry vocabulary has been demonstrated by the many users whose queries match *see* references in LCSH-mr (Markey 1984, 66; Lester 1989, 239; Figure 6.3). Furthermore, many queries that fail to produce retrievals could have succeeded had *see* references been available (Cochrane 1986, 49–50; Chapters 9 and 10). Cochrane recognized the need for enhancing LCSH entry vocabulary and made it possible for libraries to formally submit *see* references to LC for inclusion in LCSH through the Vocabulary Improvement Project (Cochrane 1983). Today, nearly two dozen libraries participating in the Cooperative Subject Cataloging Projects regularly submit proposals for new subject headings and *see* references directly to LC. Bates's ideas about entry vocabulary are more ambitious. She calls for the development of a "Superthesaurus" containing "all the variety of terminology existing in searchers' natural, spontaneous expressions of subject need" (1989, 40/25).

Discussions on the usefulness of scope notes are accompanied by calls for additional ones (Greenberg 1982; Cochrane 1986, 36). The percentage (less than 2.5%) of LCSH-mr records bearing scope notes is extremely small; any enhancement of LCSH-mr in this area would be welcomed (see Tables 2.1 and 2.2). We give examples of the choice of subject headings that sometimes precede the exact approach because of unqualified and qualified forms of subject headings (Chapter 11). The availability of scope notes for these various forms would help users pinpoint the subject heading that interests them without having to display bibliographic records under one or more headings to determine which one is relevant.

Another desirable feature of LCSH-mr records are LC class numbers because they support the strategy of catalog users who identify a particularly fruitful location of the library bookshelves for browsing (Markey 1984, 92; Willard & Teece 1983; Hancock 1987). Unfortunately, more than half of LCSH-mr records have no suggested LC class numbers (see Tables 2.1 and 2.2). Furthermore, the class numbers in existing records may not be current because LC's Subject Cataloging Division has not maintained the integrity of this information (Cochrane & Markey 1985, 100). The Chief of LC's Subject Cataloging Policy recognized this shortcoming and embarked on a project to review and update class numbers (Pietris 1987, 16).

Now consider the shortcomings of LCSH-mr. Before LCSH was converted to machine-readable form, criticism was raised about its syndetic structure. Sinkankas followed *see also* references under "Hunting" and found many nonrelevant subject headings at the end of the chain, for example, "Clothing, Waterproof," "Panic," and "Pimps"; he concluded "The reader is led away from the subject very quickly, and is seldom led even partially through it" (1972, 49).

In 1985, LC revised its rules for creating *see also* references to increase their compatibility with rules used in modern thesaurus construction. At the same time, the library community urged LC to adopt standard thesaural codes for designating LCSH cross-reference structure but cautioned LC that "it would be a long and labor-intensive project for LC because they would want to do it accurately" (SAC 1985). LC's announcement regarding the adoption of these codes acknowledges that they are not accurate indicators of relationships between subject headings (Library of Congress 1986, 62).

Although LC embarked on projects to review existing references in view of their new policy on creating *see also* references (Pietris 1987, 17), this action did not stave off critics. Dykstra (1988a,b) explains how LCSH violates use of standard thesaural codes. The plan of action she gives to transform LCSH into a thesaurus is an attractive one because existing subject headings would remain viable in the new list. It would still require an editorial review of existing subject headings. Those contemplating a review can learn from the experiences of the creators of AAT, a hierarchically arranged thesaurus that conforms to modern rules on thesaurus construction. LCSH is one of the many sources of subject terms from which relevant terminology was gathered and transformed into subject terms for the AAT (Petersen 1983). Although the AAT creators were aided by the use of an automated system for thesaurus construction and maintenance, much of the work involving creation of hierarchies and relationships between terms was done manually with the extensive assistance of subject specialists (The Art and Architecture Thesaurus Project 1990, ix–xvii).

14.3.3 Making LCSH Revamping a Priority

Should a thorough revamping of the LCSH system be undertaken? What organizations would be involved? Would the revamping be limited to a review of existing subject headings in the cross-reference structure? Would it start with a subject heading code? Would it involve modernization of awkward, archaic, or unfamiliar subject headings? Would it include subject access to formats that are underrepresented in the LC collection but heavily represented in other libraries' collections? These questions are difficult. Surely many more questions can be raised in view of criticism leveled at the LCSH system throughout the years.

LC must not be solely responsible for giving answers to these questions. Every library that uses the LCSH system must answer for themselves. Consider the first question: Should a thorough revamping of the LCSH system be undertaken? If libraries agree that LCSH should be revamped, answers to all remaining questions will be given in time. *To undertake a comprehensive editorial review of LCSH, LC has to reorder its priorities and it must receive a groundswell of support for doing so from libraries.* This reordering of priorities will come at the expense of certain LC-provided products and services that libraries rely on.

The most obvious candidate for priority modification is original cataloging. There are already new models available for redressing cataloging backlogs and obtaining current cataloging that could take the burden of original cataloging off LC. First, LC could expand its use of the OCLC Online System to support its cataloging backlog and current cataloging (Smith 1990, 3; "Library of Congress" 1990, 4). Second, LC could expand the National Coordinated Cataloging Project for the production of quality records for current cataloging (Avram & Wiggins 1988). Third, it could adopt the notion of cataloging simplification and take a leading role in defining how cataloging could be simplified (Gregor & Mandel 1991).

LC need not act alone in an editorial review of LCSH. The many libraries that use its controlled vocabulary and have built large bibliographic databases based on it must be included by enlisting the latest computer technology to transmit data and communications between organizations and online systems. In this regard, the library community already has a successful model in the exchange of information (i.e., Linked Systems Project) (McCallum 1988). A comparable model is needed for a thorough revamping of LCSH to enable participation by many libraries, individuals, and professional organizations. Here is a list of some of the information that librarians, subject experts, and lexicographers can transmit to the principal editorial team charged with LCSH revamping:

- Identification of terms from existing phrase subject headings.
- Candidates for new subject terms resulting from the examination of phrase subject headings.
- Scope notes for submitted subject terms.
- Updated LC classification numbers based on searches of online catalogs available on the Internet.
- Entry vocabulary for submitted subject terms including references culled from user queries in online catalog transaction logs.
- Cross-reference structure for submitted terms with contributions from subject specialists.

The formal structure for revamping LCSH should not be disassembled at the end of the project. It should be transformed into an ongoing program to ensure that the new tool remains viable and current.

In the absence of the comprehensive review, what will happen to the LCSH system? Wellisch (1984) gave this answer in Cochrane's continuing education course on LCSH published in *American Libraries*: "We have the tools and the techniques, but 10 years from now we will still have LC headings and they will look pretty much the same as today." Wellisch made this remark ten years ago!

The most recent effort by LC to effect change in the LCSH system is recommendations issued by the LC Subject Subdivisions Conference held in May 1991 (Library of Congress 1992). Of the six recommendations, four have an impact on subdivided subject headings, albeit a marginal impact, that is, loosening restrictions on adding subdivisions to topical-subject headings (recommendations 1, 3, and 6), and reaffirming the use of indirect geographic subdivision (recommendation 5). Until LC addresses the main heading in topical-subject headings, the outlook for significant changes to the LCSH system is quite gloomy. Regardless of the extent to which LC follows up recommendations from the subdivisions conference, the LCSH system will remain "pretty much the same." How prophetic Wellisch was.

A thorough revamping of LCSH is possible; however, libraries must make a concerted effort to convince LC that they will support a reordering of priorities. This will curtail certain products and services that the library community currently depends on and the costs of these products and services may be passed onto libraries to enable LC to seek alternatives from the private sector.

At the annual meeting of the American Library Association in summer 1991, several speakers addressed the viability of the LCSH system and needed improvements. Miksa began his remarks with the comment, "I wonder if the audience is thinking 'I wish someone would do something about this'" (Is the revolution 1991). To get something done about this, the entire library community must support LC in the reordering of its priorities in order to undertake a comprehensive review of the LCSH system. Otherwise, ten years from now Wellisch's words may haunt us still.

Ten years from now, the problem of too many retrievals will still be with us. New subject headings will be added daily to the alphabetical index, and the index will continue to expand at an ever-increasing rate. Moderately used subject headings will become heavily used headings and heavily used headings will become still more heavily used. We could place our hopes on the possibility that future computer systems will have navigational techniques to facilitate browsing of textual material in ways that we have not yet dreamed of. Should these techniques fail to materialize, future library users may abandon the library catalog altogether in favor of searching bibliographic and full-text databases available through electronic sources that are more responsive to the subject searching needs and behavior of information seekers than is the library's online catalog.

14.4 Recommended Changes to Optimize the Use of Search Trees

This book has described subject analysis and subject searching in online catalogs, discussed their limitations on retrieval, and demonstrated how such limitations can be overcome through system design and programming to enable systems to respond to user queries with the subject searching approach most likely to succeed in providing relevant information. Of the many system design recommendations made in this book, the five most important ones are summarized below:

1. *Enhance subject indexes with normalized forms of controlled vocabulary terms and other equivalent terms.* Normalized forms are system-generated terms. They are added to searchable indexes of online bibliographic systems to enhance the catalog's entry vocabulary. Such forms enable system users to match their queries with the catalog's controlled vocabulary regardless of capitalization, punctuation, stopwords, word order, and parenthetical qualifiers. Systems staff can also write programs to record frequently entered queries that fail to produce retrievals for review as local *see* references.

2. *Make available to users the wide range of subject searching capabilities in operational online bibliographic systems.* Operational online catalogs now feature alphabetical, keyword-in-heading, and keyword-in-record searching approaches. The exact approach is merely a variation of the alphabetical approach that anticipates the user's selection of the exact match from an alphabetical index and thus begins with a report of the results of exact matches. These approaches have been discussed in this book along with the characteristics of queries suited to each approach.

3. *Implement system responses that effectively manage large retrievals.* Too many retrievals is a problem in subject searching. Unfortunately, high-posted queries are ones containing terms used in the controlled vocabulary. To ensure precision of retrievals, systems must be programmed to prefer subject searching approaches that enlist the catalog's controlled vocabulary. New browsing approaches must be available to users to encourage them to explore the controlled vocabulary. Such approaches may require more distinctive coding of subject subdivisions than is given at the present time.

4. *Elicit the topic and name elements of personal-name queries from users.* The unpredictable nature of personal-name queries makes it imperative that systems elicit the elements of personal-name queries from public catalog users. The particular subject searching approach that queries invoke in online systems depends on the type(s) of elements users offer and the ability of online systems to produce retrievals for these elements.

5. *Implement search trees in online systems to control system responses and determine appropriate subject searching approaches to user queries.* Search trees are a set of paths with branches or choices that enable systems to carry out the most sensible search approach at each stage. Future online systems will have a wide range of subject searching approaches available to system users. Search trees will govern online systems in their selection of a subject searching approach based on the extent to which user queries match the catalog's controlled vocabulary and produce retrievals. Since few users are patient enough to choose every search approach and review the results of each to determine the most appropriate system response for their queries, online catalogs will make such an assessment for users. Thus, search trees place the burden of determining which approach is likely to provide relevant information for user queries on the system.

System design recommendations made in this book stretch subject searching approaches in operational online catalogs to the limit. These approaches still may not produce retrievals or useful retrievals for some user queries. Combinatorial retrieval methods that use stemming and ranked output may be more appropriate because, unlike results produced by Boolean search capabilities, combinatorial methods do not require all query words to be present in retrieved records. Determining the most effective sequence for applying these techniques to such queries is a challenge to future researchers.

The machine cannot solve all the problems of subject retrieval, but we have tried to offer recommendations that do not require editorial review of LCSH. Several recommendations cannot be implemented in full until more distinctive coding than is presently available is given to subject subdivisions. Systems can enlist such coding to manage large retrievals that characterize system responses to user queries that contain controlled vocabulary terms. Editorial changes will be more difficult to implement than machine changes because they require a concerted effort by the library community to support LC in making LCSH revamping a top priority.

This book demonstrates how the limitations of subject analysis and subject searching can be overcome through system design and programming to enable systems to respond to user queries with the subject searching approach most likely to succeed. It furthers our general knowledge of library patron use of online catalogs. Discussions and recommendations address the interests of LC staff involved in the construction and maintenance of LCSH, library administrators who decide about enhancements to a library's online catalog, and technical systems staff who design and implement online catalogs in general and subject searching capabilities specifically. The new design for subject access presented in this book will ensure that future online bibliographic systems will be increasingly responsive to end user needs and behavior.

References

Allen, Bryce. (1991). Topic knowledge and online catalog search formulation. *Library Quarterly, 61*, 2, 188–213.

The Art and Architecture Thesaurus Project, 1980–1990. (1990). In *Art & Architecture Thesaurus*, ix–xvii. New York: Oxford University Press.

Avram, Henriette D., & Wiggins, Beacher. (1988). The National Coordinated Cataloging Program. *Library Resources & Technical Services, 32*, 2 (April), 111–115.

Bates, Marcia J. (1977). Factors affecting subject catalog search success. *Journal of the American Society for Information Science, 28*, 3 (May), 161–169.

Bates, Marcia J. (1989). Designing online catalog subject access to meet user needs. *55th IFLA Council and General Conference, Paris, France, 8/19–26, 1989* (pp. 40/24–40/26). IFLA, Division of Bibliographic Control/Section on Classification and Indexing.

Bullard, Gregory N. (1982). The Syracuse University Libraries Information Retrieval System. *Research Libraries in OCLC: A Quarterly*, 7 (July), 1–2.

Chan, Lois Mai. (1986). *Library of Congress Subject Headings: Principles and application*. Littleton, CO: Libraries Unlimited.

Cochrane, Pauline. A. (1983). *LCSH entry vocabulary project: Final report to the Council on Library Resources and to the Library of Congress*. ERIC ED 233746.

Cochrane, Pauline A. (1986). *Improving LCSH for use in online catalogs*. Littleton, CO: Libraries Unlimited.

Cochrane, Pauline A., & Kirtland, Monika. (1981). *Critical views of LCSH—the Library of Congress Subject Headings; a bibliographic and bibliometric essay*. Syracuse, NY: ERIC/Information Resources Clearinghouse.

Cochrane, Pauline A., & Markey, Karen. (1985). Preparing for the use of classification in online cataloging systems and in online catalogs. *Information Technology and Libraries, 4*, 2, 91–111.

Drabenstott, Karen M. (1991). Introduction. In Karen M. Drabenstott (Ed.), *Subject authorities in the online environment; Papers from a conference program held in San Francisco, June 29, 1987* (pp. 1–8). Chicago: American Library Association.

Dykstra, Mary. (1987). Subject indexing and retrieval: What more can technology do? *Canadian Library Journal, 44*, 3 (June), 187–189.

Dykstra, Mary. (1988a). Can subject headings be saved? *Library Journal, 113* (15), 55–58.

Dykstra, Mary. (1988b). LC Subject Headings disguised as a thesaurus. *Library Journal, 113* (4), 42–46.

Frost, Carolyn O. (1987). Subject searching in an online catalog. *Information Technology and Libraries, 6*, 1 (March), 60–63.

Greenberg, Alan M. (1982). Scope notes in Library of Congress Subject Headings. *Cataloging & Classification Quarterly, 1*, 95–104.

Gregor, Dorothy, & Mandel, Carol. (1991). Cataloging must change! *Library Journal*, (April 1), 42–47.

Hancock, Micheline. (1987). Subject searching behaviour at the library catalogue and at the shelves: Implications for online interactive catalogs. *Journal of Documentation, 43*, 303–321.

Hildreth, Charles R. (1982). *Online public access catalogs: The user interface*. Dublin, OH: OCLC.

Is the revolution now for subject cataloging? (1991). *American Libraries, 22*, 8 (September), 719–720.

Keen, E. Michael. (1977). Review of *PRECIS, LCSH, and KWOC: Report of a research project designed to examine the applicability of PRECIS to the subject catalogue of an academic library* by Roslyn Hunt and others. *Journal of Documentation, 34*, 4 (December), 356–357.

Lester, Marilyn Ann. (1989). *Coincidence of user vocabulary and Library of Congress Subject Headings: Experiments to improve subject access in academic library online catalogs*. Ph.D. dissertation, University of Illinois at Urbana-Champaign.

Library of Congress. (1986). Cross-reference structure in the LC automated subject authority file. *Cataloging Service Bulletin, 33*, 62.

Library of Congress. (1992). *The future of subdivisions in the Library of Congress Subject Headings System: Report from the Subject Subdivisions Conference*. Martha O'Hara Conway (Ed.). Washington, DC: Library of Congress.

"Library of Congress to use OCLC System in two-year pilot project." (1990). *OCLC Newsletter* #187 (September/October), 4.

McCallum, Sally H. (1988). Overview of the Linked Systems Project, in Judith G. Fenly & Beacher Wiggins (Eds.). *The Linked Systems Project: A networking tool for Libraries* (pp. 7–18). OCLC Library, Information, and Computer Science series, No. 6.

Mann, Thomas. (1991). A reference librarian's response to the papers of the Library of Congress Subject Subdivisions Conference. General Reading Rooms Division, Library of Congress (photocopy).

Markey, Karen. (1984). *Subject searching in library catalogs: Before and after the introduction of online catalogs*. Dublin, OH: OCLC.

Miller, Dan. (1984). Authority control in the retrospective conversion process. *Information Technology and Libraries, 3*(3), 286–292.

Mischo, William H. (1982). Library of Congress Subject Headings: A review of the problems, and prospects for improved subject access. *Cataloging & Classification Quarterly, 1* (2/3), 105–124.

Palmer, Joseph W. (1986). Subject authority control and syndetic structure—myth and realities. *Cataloging & Classification Quarterly*, 7, 2 (Winter), 71–95.

Petersen, Toni. (1983). The AAT: A model for the restructuring of LCSH. *Journal of Academic Librarianship, 9*, 4 (September), 207–210.

Pietris, Mary K. D. (1987). Library of Congress Subject Headings: Past imperfect, future indicative. *Cataloguing Australia, 13*, 3 (September), 8–19.

Pritchard, Sarah M. (1981). *SCORPIO: A study of public users of the Library of Congress Information System*. Washington, DC: Library of Congress.

SAC (Subject Analysis Committee). (1985). Format of LCSH: Report of survey. January (photocopy of original).

Schabas, Ann H. (1982). Postcoordinate retrieval: A comparison of two indexing languages. *Journal of the American Society for Information Science, 33*, 1 (January), 32–37.

Sinkankas, George M. (1972). *A study in the syndetic structure of the Library of Congress Subject Headings*. Pittsburgh: University of Pittsburgh. Pittsburgh Studies in Library and Information Sciences.

Smith, K. Wayne (1990). A good beginning for LC and OCLC. *OCLC Newsletter* #185 (May/June), 3.

Steinberg, David, & Metz, Paul. (1984). User response to and knowledge about an online catalog. *College & Research Libraries, 45*, 1 (January), 66–70.

Studwell, William E. (1990). Subject access theory no 7: The role of universal unlimited machine manipulation in online subject access. *Technicalities, 10*, 7 (July), 5–6.

Wellisch, Hans H. (1984). Subject access mess is a political problem. *American Libraries, 15* (April), 254.

Willard, Patricia, & Teece, Viva. (1983). The browser and the library. *Public Library Quarterly, 4*, 1, 55–63.

Appendix A
SULIRS Subject Search

```
ENTER SEARCH: SB;RENE MARGRITE

SEARCHING "SB; RENE "
SEARCHING "SB; MARGRITE "

NO ITEMS FOUND FOR THE SEARCH: SB;RENE      SB;MARGRITE
TYPE    HELP    FOR FURTHER GUIDANCE

ENTER SEARCH: SB;SURREALIST ARTIST

SEARCHING "SB; SURREALIST "
SEARCHING "SB; ARTIST "

NO ITEMS FOUND FOR THE SEARCH: SB; SURREALIST    SB; ARTIST
TYPE    HELP    FOR FURTHER GUIDANCE

ENTER SEARCH: WD;SURREALISM

SEARCHING "WD; SURREALISM "

 204 ITEMS. PRESS RETURN FOR DISPLAY, OR S AND RETURN FOR NEW SEARCH:


    1. READ, HERBERT EDWARD, SIR, 1893-1968 *
    SURREALISM ;  LONDON, FABER AND FABER LIMITED, 1936
      N6490.R45 1936 ; 2ND FLOOR-BIRD ; IN CIRCULATION - DUE 5/15/89

    2. NEW YORK (CITY). MUSEUM OF MODERN ART *
    AMERICAN REALISTS AND MAGIC REALISTS
   NEW YORK, PUBLISHED FOR THE MUSEUM OF MODERN ART BY ARNO
   PRESS, 1969 C1943
      N6512.N4 1969 ; 2ND FLOOR-BIRD

    3. EXETER CITY GALLERY, EXETER, ENGLAND *
    THE ENCHANTED DOMAIN : SURREALIST ART AT EXETER CITY GALLERY
   1967 ;  ILFORD, ESSEX, LITHOFAST CO, 1967
      ND196.S8E8 '  2ND FLOOR-BIRD ; IN CIRCULATION - DUE 5/23/89

    4. ALQUIE, FERDINAND
    THE PHILOSOPHY OF SURREALISM *
   ANN ARBOR, UNIVERSITY OF MICHIGAN PRESS, 1965
      BH301.S75A43 C.3 ; 3RD FLOOR-BIRD


 204 ITEMS. PRESS RETURN FOR DISPLAY, OR S AND RETURN FOR NEW SEARCH:
```

Appendix B
ORION Subject Search

```
COMMAND-> b su cuba revolution

Current Search: b su cuba revolution
   Type R1 (or R2, R3 ... ) to retrieve the record(s) in a group.
               Type HELP or press PF1 for options.
 -- Headings List Screen --------------------------------------

    22 RESULTS
     <-> NUMBER OF ONLINE ORION RECORDS CONTAINED IN EACH GROUP.
R1  70  Cuba--History--Revolution, 1895-1898.
R2   2  Cuba--History--Revolution, 1895-1898--Campaigns and battles.
R3   4  Cuba--History--Revolution, 1895-1898--Fiction.
R4   1  Cuba--History--Revolution, 1895-1898--Periodicals.
R5   3  Cuba--History--Revolution, 1895-1898--Personal narratives.
R6   3  Cuba--History--Revolution, 1895-1898--Sources.
R7  11  Cuba--History--Revolution, 1933.
R8   1  Cuba--History--Revolution, 1933--Causes.
R9  29  Cuba--History--Revolution, 1959.
R10  1  Cuba--History--Revolution, 1959--Anniversaries, etc.
R11  4  Cuba--History--Revolution, 1959--Campaigns.

 Current Search: b su cuba revolution
 COMMAND->
   Type R1 (or R2, R3 ... ) to retrieve the record(s) in a group.
               Type HELP or press PF1 for options.
 -- Headings List Screen --------------------------------------

    22 RESULTS
     <-> NUMBER OF ONLINE ORION RECORDS CONTAINED IN EACH GROUP.
R12  4  Cuba--History--Revolution, 1959--Causes.
R13  1  Cuba--History--Revolution, 1959--Chronology.
R14  4  Cuba--History--Revolution, 1959--Influence.
R15  1  Cuba--History--Revolution, 1959--Journalists--Congresses.
R16  1  Cuba--History--Revolution, 1959--Juvenile literature.
R17  1  Cuba--History--Revolution, 1959--Literary collections.
R18  1  Cuba--History--Revolution, 1959--Literature and the
        revolution.
R19  6  Cuba--History--Revolution, 1959--Personal narratives.
R20  1  Cuba--History--Revolution, 1959--Public opinion.
R21  1  Cuba--History--Revolution, 1959--Refugees.
R22  2  Cuba--Politics and government--Revolution, 1959.
```

```
Current Search: b su cuba revolution
COMMAND-> b su fulgencio batista
              Type HELP or press PF1 for options.
-- Zero Results Screen ------------------------------------

-----------------------------------------------------------
|    ***There are no results in ORION which match your search |
|    request.  Please verify your subject terms in the        |
|    LIBRARY OF CONGRESS SUBJECT HEADINGS LIST (LCSH) or      |
|    the MEDICAL SUBJECT HEADINGS LIST (MeSH) or try your     |
|    search a different way.                                  |
|    For information on the 'BROWSE SUBJECT' search,          |
|    type: HELP BSU                                           |
-----------------------------------------------------------

COMMAND->
```

Appendix C
LS/2000 Subject Search

```
                ** WELCOME TO THE LS/2000 SYSTEM **
         ** YOU ARE IN THE UNIVERSITY OF KENTUCKY SYSTEM **

           Enter the NUMBER of search you wish to perform
                          1 - By AUTHOR
                          2 - By TITLE
                          3 - By SUBJECT
                          4 - By SUBJECT - MEDICAL
                          5 - For OTHER Searches
                               OR
           Enter a KEY WORD to see possible matches

CHOICE: THERAPY

KEY WORD:  ** THERAPY **

REF  TITLES    KEY WORD
---  ------    --------
R1     5916    THERAPY
R2        2    THERAPY/HOSPITAL
(END)

CHOICE: R1

TERM: ** THERAPY **

REF     TERM APPEARS IN
---     ---------------
R1      496 SUBJECTS
R2     2384 SUBJECT SUBDIVISIONS
R3      100 AUTHORS
R4     1394 SUBJECTS - MEDICAL
R5     1542 TITLES
(END)

CHOICE: R2

Your search has identified many citations. What would you like to
do next?
               1. Narrow search
               2. View citations sequentially
               3. Start new search
```

```
CHOICE: 1

          Enter the NUMBER of the limitation search you wish to
          perform
                    1 - Limit by PUBLICATION YEAR
                    2 - Limit by LANGUAGE
                    3 - Limit by MATERIAL TYPE IDENTIFIER
                    4 - Limit by SUBJECT
                    5 - Limit by SUBJECT SUBDIVISION
                    6 - Limit by SUBJECT - MEDICAL
                    7 - Limit by Other Searches
                          OR
          Enter a KEY WORD to see possible limiting matches

CHOICE: FAMILY

KEY WORD:  ** FAMILY **

REF  TITLES    KEY WORD
---  ------    --------
R1     8537    FAMILY
R2       23    FAMILY'S
R3        1    FAMILY-BOOK
R4        1    FAMILY-CAN
R5        1    FAMILY-CARE
R6        1    FAMILY-CAREER
R7        1    FAMILY-CENTERED
R8        1    FAMILY-FARM
R9        1    FAMILY-FAVORITE
R10       1    FAMILY-FOCUSED
(MORE)

CHOICE: [carriage return to produce the next list of ten words]

R11       1    FAMILY-LETTERS
R12       1    FAMILY-PLANNING
R13       1    FAMILY-REARED
R14       1    FAMILY-RELIGION
R15       1    FAMILY-RENT
R16       1    FAMILY-SCHOOL
R17       1    FAMILY-SIZE
R18       1    FAMILY-SUPPORTIVE
R19       1    FAMILY-WORSHIP
R20       1    FAMILY/WORK
(MORE)
```

```
CHOICE: ^ [symbol to go backwards one screen]

          Enter the NUMBER of the limitation search you wish to
          perform
                    1 - Limit by PUBLICATION YEAR
                    2 - Limit by LANGUAGE
                    3 - Limit by MATERIAL TYPE IDENTIFIER
                    4 - Limit by SUBJECT
                    5 - Limit by SUBJECT SUBDIVISION
                    6 - Limit by SUBJECT - MEDICAL
                    7 - Limit by Other Searches
                         OR
          Enter a KEY WORD to see possible limiting matches

CHOICE: FAMILY THERAPY

SUBJECT: ** FAMILY THERAPY **

REF  TITLES    TERM
---  ------    ----
R1        4    FAMILY THERAPY
(END)

CHOICE: R1

** SEARCHING... **

Your last search has no titles in common with your previous
searches.  Try narrowing with a different search.

CHOICE: ^ [symbol to go backwards one screen]

SUBJECT: ** FAMILY THERAPY **

REF  TITLES    TERM
---  ------    ----
R1        4    FAMILY THERAPY
(END)

CHOICE: ^ [symbol to go backwards one screen]

          Enter the NUMBER of the limitation search you wish to
          perform
                    1 - Limit by PUBLICATION YEAR
                    2 - Limit by LANGUAGE
                    3 - Limit by MATERIAL TYPE IDENTIFIER
                    4 - Limit by SUBJECT
                    5 - Limit by SUBJECT SUBDIVISION
                    6 - Limit by SUBJECT - MEDICAL
                    7 - Limit by Other Searches
                         OR
```

```
          Enter a KEY WORD to see possible limiting matches

CHOICE: ^ [symbol to go backwards one screen]

Your search has identified many citations. What would you like to
do next?
                 1. Narrow search
                 2. View citations sequentially
                 3. Start new search

CHOICE: ^ [symbol to go backwards one screen]

TERM: ** THERAPY **

REF     TERM APPEARS IN
---     ---------------
R1       496 SUBJECTS
R2      2384 SUBJECT SUBDIVISIONS
R3       100 AUTHORS
R4      1394 SUBJECTS - MEDICAL
R5      1542 TITLES
(END)

CHOICE: ^ [symbol to go backwards one screen]

KEY WORD: ** THERAPY **

REF  TITLES    KEYWORD
---  ------    -------
R1     5916    THERAPY
R2        2    THERAPY/HOSPITAL
(END)

CHOICE: ^ [symbol to go backwards one screen]

         Enter the NUMBER of search you wish to perform
                    1 - By AUTHOR
                    2 - By TITLE
                    3 - By SUBJECT
                    4 - By SUBJECT - MEDICAL
                    5 - For OTHER Searches
                         OR
          Enter a KEY WORD to see possible matches

CHOICE: FAMILY THERAPY

KEY WORD: ** FAMILY THERAPY **

REF  TITLES    KEY WORD
---  ------    --------
R1     8537    FAMILY
R2       23    FAMILY'S
```

```
R3        1     FAMILY-BOOK
R4        1     FAMILY-CAN
R5        1     FAMILY-CARE
R6        1     FAMILY-CAREER
R7        1     FAMILY-CENTERED
R8        1     FAMILY-FARM
R9        1     FAMILY-FAVORITE
R10       1     FAMILY-FOCUSED
(MORE)

CHOICE: R1

TERM: ** FAMILY **

REF     TERM APPEARS IN
---     ---------------
R1    3530 SUBJECTS
R2     262 SUBJECT SUBDIVISIONS
R3     400 AUTHORS
R4     662 SUBJECTS - MEDICAL
R5       5 SP COLL ACQ NOTES
R6    3683 TITLES
(END)

CHOICE: R1

KEY WORD: FAMILY

Your search has identified many citations. What would you like to
do next?
               1. Narrow search
               2. View citations sequentially
               3. Start new search

CHOICE: 1

          Enter the NUMBER of the limitation search you wish to
          perform
                   1 - Limit by PUBLICATION YEAR
                   2 - Limit by LANGUAGE
                   3 - Limit by MATERIAL TYPE IDENTIFIER
                   4 - Limit by SUBJECT
                   5 - Limit by SUBJECT SUBDIVISION
                   6 - Limit by SUBJECT - MEDICAL
                   7 - Limit by Other Searches
                        OR
          Enter a KEY WORD to see possible limiting matches

CHOICE: 5

ENTER A KEY WORD: THERAPY
```

```
KEY WORD: ** THERAPY **

REF  TITLES    KEYWORD
---  ------    -------
R1     5916    THERAPY
R2        2    THERAPY/HOSPITAL
(END)

CHOICE: R1

TERM: ** THERAPY **

REF      TERM APPEARS IN
---      ---------------
R1       496 SUBJECTS
R2      2384 SUBJECT SUBDIVISIONS
R3       100 AUTHORS
R4      1394 SUBJECTS - MEDICAL
R5      1542 TITLES
(END)

CHOICE: R5

** SEARCHING... **
KEY WORD: THERAPY

Your search has identified many citations. What would you like to
do next?
               1. Narrow search
               2. View citations sequentially
               3. Start new search

CHOICE: ^

TERM: ** THERAPY **

REF      TERM APPEARS IN
---      ---------------
R1       496 SUBJECTS
R2      2384 SUBJECT SUBDIVISIONS
R3       100 AUTHORS
R4      1394 SUBJECTS - MEDICAL
R5      1542 TITLES
(END)

CHOICE: /EXIT
```

Appendix D
Multiple-Heading Match Categories

1. Exact Multiple-Heading Match*

User query consists of the same substantive words that are in two or more LCSH and/or assigned subject headings.

Example: User "erosion sand"
LCSH "Erosion"
"Sand"

2. Spelling Variation*

One or more LCSH and/or assigned subject headings include a spelling variant or variants of a word or words in the user query. This general category is split into five more specific categories (2a–2e).

2a. Multiple-Heading Match with Correct Spelling Variant Variation

One or more LCSH and/or assigned subject headings contains a correct but variant spelling of one word.

Example: User "watercolour brush"
LCSH "Watercolor"
"Brush"

2b. Multiple-Heading Match with One-Word/Two-Word Variation

One or more LCSH and/or assigned subject headings contains one word that the user enters as two words or contains two words that the user enters as one word.

Example: User "water color brush"
LCSH "Watercolor"
"Brush"

2c. Multiple-Heading Match with Substitution/Transposition

User query differs from one or more LCSH and/or assigned subject headings with regard to one character being incorrectly substituted for another or two letters being incorrectly transposed.

Example: User "crystallograhpy geometry"
LCSH "Crystallography"
"Geometry"

2d. Multiple-Heading Match with Addition/Omission

User query differs from one or more LCSH and/or assigned subject headings with regard to one character being incorrectly added to the query or one letter being incorrectly omitted from the query.

Example: User "crystalography geometry"
LCSH "Crystallography"
"Geometry"

2e. Multiple-Heading Match with Incorrect Spelling

User query differs from one or more LCSH and/or assigned subject headings with regard to more than one spelling variation.

Example: User "books typesetting comuterised"
LCSH "Books"
"Computerized typesetting"

3. Multiple-Heading Match with Singular/Plural Variation*

Multiple LCSH and/or assigned subject headings differ from user query in that one or more contains a word or words that is plural (ending in "s" or "es") and the other contains a word or words that is singular.

Example: User "joint prosthesis"
LCSH "Joints"
"Prosthesis"

4. Multiple-Heading Match with Abbreviation Variation*

User query contains an abbreviation of a word or phrase in an LCSH or assigned subject headings or vice versa.

Example: User "engineering and mba"
LCSH "Engineering"
"Master of Business Administration"

5. Multiple-Heading Match with Date or Numerical Variation*

LCSH and/or assigned subject headings contain a date that differs from a date in user expression, or LCSH and/or assigned subject headings do not include a date that a user requests; or a difference such as "20"/"twenty" occurs.

Example:	User	"computers and privacy 1980s"
	LCSH	"Computers"
		"Privacy"

6. Partial Multiple-Heading Match

LCSH and/or assigned subject headings consist of the same substantive words that are in the user expression, but the former contain more words.

Example:	User	"notions of buddha"
	LCSH	"Notions (Philosophy)"
		"Buddha and Buddhism"

Index

E

F

G

H

M

Library and Information Science

(Continued from page ii)

Nancy Jones Pruett
Scientific and Technical Libraries: Functions and Management
Volume 1 and Volume 2

Peter Judge and Brenda Gerrie
Small Bibliographic Databases

Dorothy B. Lilley and Ronald W. Trice
A History of Information Sciences 1945-1985

Elaine Svenonius
The Conceptual Foundations of Descriptive Cataloging

Robert M. Losee, Jr.
The Science of Information: Measurement and Applications

Irene P. Godden
Library Technical Services: Operations and Management,
Second Edition

Donald H. Kraft and Bert R. Boyce
Operations Research for Libraries and Information Agencies:
Techniques for the Evaluation of Management Decision Alternatives

James Cabeceiras
The Multimedia Library: Matertials Selection and Use, Second Edition

Charles T. Meadow
Text Information Retrieval Systems

Robert M. Losee, Jr. and Karen A. Worley
Research and Evaluation for Information Professionals

Carmel Maguire, Edward J. Kazlauskas, and Anthony D. Weir
Information Services for Innovative Organizations

Karen Markey Drabenstott and Diane Vizine-Goetz
Using Subject Headings for Online Retrieval